CONTENTS

Articles and Ordering Information

Home Plans

Welcome Home 750 Inviting Home Plans is published by Home Design Alternatives, Inc. (HDA, Inc.) 4390 Green Ash Drive, St. Louis, MO 63045. All rights reserved. Reproduction in whole or in part without written permission of the publisher is prohibited. Printed in U.S.A © 2004. Artist drawings and photos shown in this publication may vary slightly from the actual working drawings. Some photos are shown in mirror reverse. Please refer to the floor plan for accurate layout.

Current Printing 5 4 3 2 1

Welcome Home - 750 Inviting Home Plans is a collection of our best-selling homes in a variety styles and sizes. These plans cover a wide range of architectural styles including Small and Narrow Lot, Country/Victorian, Vacation, Multi-Family, Multi-Story, Elegant Homes, Apartment Garages and our overall Best-Selling designs. A broad assortment is presented to match a wide variety of lifestyles and budgets. Each design page features floor plans, a front view of the house, interior square footage of the home, number of bedrooms, baths, garage size and foundation types. All floor plans show room and exterior dimensions.

House shown on front cover is Plan #577-0836 and is featured on page 212. Photo Credit: Michael Marxer, St. Louis, Missouri.

Technical Specifications - At the time the construction drawings were prepared, every effort was made to ensure that these plans and specifications meet nationally recognized building codes (BOCA, Southern Building Code Congress and others). Because national building codes change or vary from area to area some drawing modifications and/or the assistance of a professional designer or architect may be necessary to comply with your local codes or to accommodate specific building site conditions. We advise you consult with your local building official for information regarding codes governing your area.

Blueprint Ordering - Fast and Easy - Your ordering is made simple by following the instructions on page 608. See page 607 for more information on which types of blueprint packages are available and how many plan sets to order.

Your Home, Your Way - The blueprints you receive are a master plan for building your new home. T... start you on your way to what may well be the ... rewarding experience of your life.

Welcome Home

Constructed by Dublen Homes in St. Louis, Missouri, this home is plan #577-0836 and is also featured on page 212. Photos shown may vary slightly from the actual working drawings. Please refer to the floor plan for accurate layout.
Photos courtesy of Michael Marxer, St. Louis, Missouri.

Stylish and sophisticated, this spacious home located in St. Louis, Missouri has a timeless exterior. Detailed brickwork surrounds palladian windows and the quoined corners are not only decorative, but create a considerable amount of curb appeal.

The interior, on the other hand, is dramatic and animated with the use of bright primary colors allowing the design elements of this home to come alive with personality. The two-story entry (photo, above) is just as striking as the artwork above the door that greets guests.

The use of hardwood floors and richly stained cabinetry creates an elegant, yet inviting feel to the kitchen, breakfast area and hearth room (photo, above left). These gathering areas flow together effortlessly making it a natural place for entertaining.

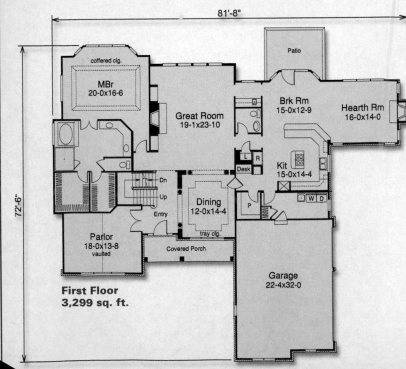

81'-8"

72'-6"

coffered clg.
MBr 20-0x16-6
Great Room 19-1x23-10
Patio
Brk Rm 15-0x12-9
Hearth Rm 16-0x14-0
Desk
Kit 15-0x14-4
Dn
Up
Entry
Dining 12-0x14-4
tray clg.
P
W D
Parlor 18-0x13-8 vaulted
Covered Porch
Garage 22-4x32-0

First Floor 3,299 sq. ft.

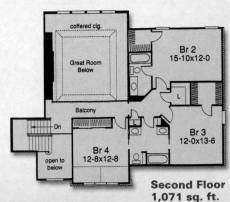

coffered clg.
Great Room Below
Br 2 15-10x12-0
Balcony
Dn
Br 4 12-8x12-8
open to below
Br 3 12-0x13-6

Second Floor 1,071 sq. ft.

ABOUT THE COVER HOME

This stunning home is filled with luxurious surprises around every corner. Come take a look inside our cover home.

Equally eye-catching is the high-style of the hearth room. (photo, above) The vaulted ceiling creates an open, airy feel while the fireplace becomes a pleasant focal point. Because of its proximity to the kitchen and breakfast area, this is the ideal place for relaxing casually with friends and family .

Decorative columns create the illusion of an open, formal dining room (photo, above right). They allow the feeling of openness while still maintaining a separate space for enjoying more formal meals. With the addition of a tray ceiling, intricate carpentry details, inlaid hardwood floors and views into the exceptional great room, this dining room is not only inviting but exquisite.

This parlor is highly distinctive and anything but ordinary (photo, below). The bright blue walls highlight the beautiful palladian window while enhancing the contrasting carpentry of the bookshelves and chair rail. Just steps away from the formal dining room; when entering these double-doors you'll find a private place that is delightfully different and sure to become a favorite place to retreat.

Exciting is the perfect word to describe this spectacular great room (photo, above). A substantial two-story wall of windows floods this room with sunlight while an impressive fireplace magically warms the surroundings. Built-in bookshelves have a custom feel covering an entire wall of this room. They are the perfect place for displaying artwork, collectibles or a variety of books. In addition, the second floor is lucky enough to take in views of below from the lovely balcony.

ABOUT THE COVER HOME

QUICK AND EASY CUSTOMIZING
MAKE CHANGES TO YOUR HOME PLAN IN 4 STEPS

HERE'S AN **AFFORDABLE** AND **EFFICIENT** WAY TO MAKE CHANGES TO YOUR PLAN.

1 **Select the house plan that most closely meets your needs.** Purchase of a reproducible master is necessary in order to make changes to a plan.

2 **Call 1-800-373-2646 to place your order.** Tell the sales representative you're interested in customizing a plan. A $50 refundable consultation fee will be charged. You will then be instructed to complete a customization checklist indicating all the changes you wish to make to your plan. You may attach sketches if necessary. <u>If you proceed with the custom changes the $50 will be credited to the total amount charged.</u>

3 **FAX the completed customization checklist** to our design consultant at 1-866-477-5173 or e-mail **custom@drummonddesigns.com**. Within *24-48 business hours you will be provided with a written cost estimate to modify your plan. Our design consultant will contact you by phone if you wish to discuss any of your changes in greater detail.

4 **Once you approve the estimate,** a 75% retainer fee is collected and customization work gets underway. Preliminary drawings can usually be completed within *5-10 business days. Following approval of the preliminary drawings your design changes are completed within *5-10 business days. Your remaining 25% balance due is collected prior to shipment of your completed drawings. You will be shipped five sets of revised blueprints or a reproducible master, plus a customized materials list if required.

*Terms are subject to change without notice.

BEFORE

Plan 2829

Customized Version of Plan 2829

AFTER

MODIFICATION PRICING GUIDE

CATEGORIES	Average Cost from...	to
Adding or removing living space (square footage)	Quote required	
Adding or removing a garage	$400	$680
Garage: Front entry to side load or vice versa	Starting at $300	
Adding a screened porch	$280	$600
Adding a bonus room in the attic	$450	$780
Changing full basement to crawl space or vice versa	Starting at $220	
Changing full basement to slab or vice versa	Starting at $260	
Changing exterior building material	Starting at $200	
Changing roof lines	$360	$630
Adjusting ceiling height	$280	$500
Adding, moving or removing an exterior opening	$55 per opening	
Adding or removing a fireplace	$90	$200
Modifying a non-bearing wall or room	$55 per room	
Changing exterior walls from 2"x4" to 2"x6"	Starting at $200	
Redesigning a bathroom or a kitchen	$120	$280
Reverse plan right reading	Quote required	
Adapting plans for local building code requirements	Quote required	
Engineering stamping only	Quote required	
Any other engineering services	Quote required	
Adjust plan for handicapped accessibility	Quote required	
Interactive illustrations (choices of exterior materials)	Quote required	
Metric conversion of home plan	$400	

Note: Any home plan can be customized to accommodate your desired changes. The average prices specified above are provided only as examples for the most commonly requested changes, and are subject to change without notice. Prices for changes will vary according to the number of modifications requested, plan size, style, and method of design used by the original designer. To obtain a detailed cost estimate, please contact us.

Atrium's Dramatic Ambiance

Total Living Area: 1,721

- Roof dormers add great curb appeal
- Vaulted dining and great rooms immersed in light from atrium window wall
- Breakfast room opens onto covered porch
- Functionally designed kitchen
- 3 bedrooms, 2 baths, 3-car garage
- Walk-out basement foundation, drawings also include crawl space and slab foundations

Rear View

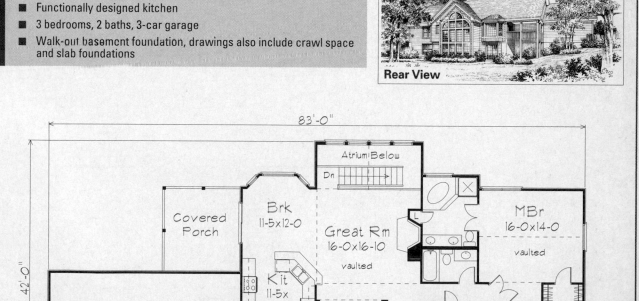

BEST-SELLING

TO ORDER SEE **PAGE 608** OR CALL TOLL-FREE 1-800-DREAM HOME (373-2646)

Classic Ranch Has Grand Appeal

Total Living Area: 1,400

- Master bedroom is secluded for privacy
- Large utility room with additional cabinet space
- Covered porch provides an outdoor seating area
- Roof dormers add great curb appeal
- Vaulted ceilings in living room and master bedroom
- Oversized two-car garage with storage
- 3 bedrooms, 2 baths, 2-car garage
- Basement foundation, drawings also include crawl space foundation

BEST-SELLING

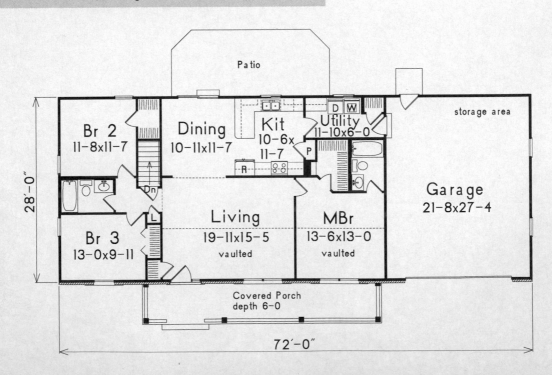

TO ORDER SEE **PAGE 608** OR CALL TOLL-FREE **1-800-DREAM HOME** (373-2646)

Functional Layout For Comfort

Total Living Area: 1,360

- Kitchen/dining room features island work space and plenty of dining area
- Master bedroom with large walk-in closet and private bath
- Laundry room adjacent to the kitchen for easy access
- Convenient workshop in garage
- Large closets in secondary bedrooms
- 3 bedrooms, 2 baths, 2-car side entry garage
- Basement foundation, drawings also include crawl space and slab foundations

BEST-SELLING

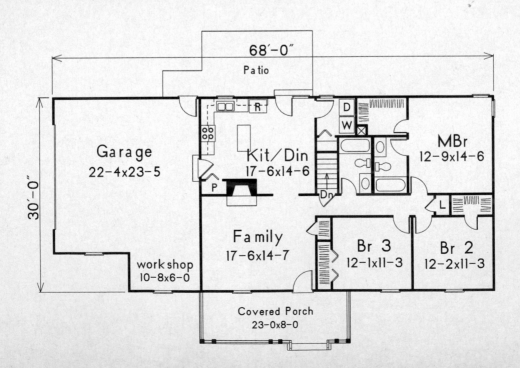

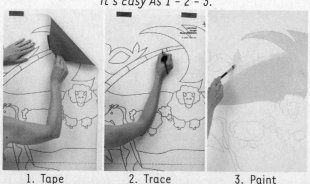

Prestige Abounds In A Classic Ranch

Total Living Area: 2,723

- Large porch invites you into an elegant foyer which accesses a vaulted study with private hall and coat closet

- Great room is second to none, comprised of fireplace, built-in shelves, vaulted ceiling and a 1 1/2 story window wall

- A spectacular hearth room with vaulted ceiling and masonry fireplace opens to an elaborate kitchen featuring two snack bars, cooking island and walk-in pantry

- 3 bedrooms, 2 1/2 baths, 3-car side entry garage

- Basement foundation

BEST-SELLING

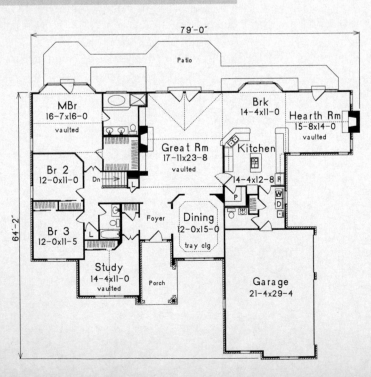

Bay Window Adds To Master Bedroom

Total Living Area: 1,668

- Large bay windows in breakfast area, master bedroom and dining room
- Extensive walk-in closets and storage spaces throughout the home
- Handy covered entry porch
- Large living room has fireplace, built-in bookshelves and sloped ceiling
- 3 bedrooms, 2 baths, 2-car drive under garage
- Basement foundation

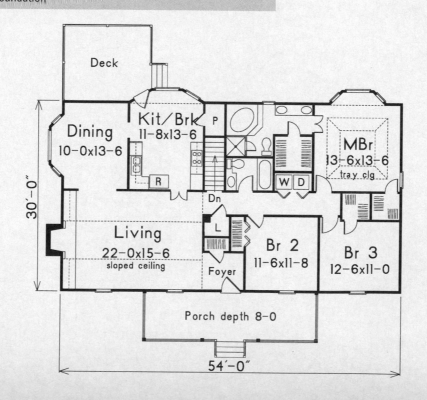

Deck

Dining
10-0x13-6

Kit/Brk
11-8x13-6

P

MBr
13-6x13-6
tray clg

W D

Dn

Living
22-0x15-6
sloped ceiling

L

Foyer

Br 2
11-6x11-8

Br 3
12-6x11-0

30'-0"

Porch depth 8-0

54'-0"

Rambling Country Bungalow

Total Living Area: 1,475

- Family room features a high ceiling and prominent corner fireplace
- Kitchen with island counter and garden window makes a convenient connection between the family and dining rooms
- Hallway leads to three bedrooms all with large walk-in closets
- Covered breezeway joins main house and garage
- Full-width covered porch entry lends a country touch
- 3 bedrooms, 2 baths, 2-car side entry garage
- Slab foundation, drawings also include crawl space foundation

BEST-SELLING

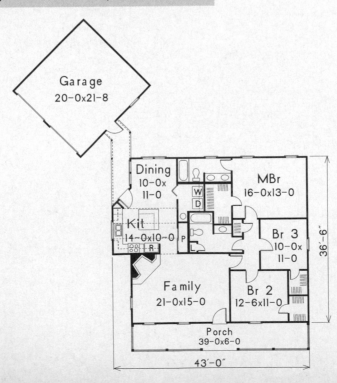

Garage
20-0x21-8

Dining
10-0x
11-0

MBr
16-0x13-0

W
D

Kit
14-0x10-0

P

Br 3
10-0x
11-0

Family
21-0x15-0

Br 2
12-6x11-0

Porch
39-0x6-0

36'-6"

43'-0"

TO ORDER SEE **PAGE 608** OR CALL TOLL-FREE 1-800-DREAM HOME (373-2646)

Stylish Living For A Narrow Lot

Total Living Area: 1,575

- Inviting porch leads to spacious living and dining rooms
- Kitchen with corner windows features an island snack bar, attractive breakfast room bay, convenient laundry and built-in pantry
- A luxury bath and walk-in closet adorn master bedroom suite
- 3 bedrooms, 2 1/2 baths, 2-car garage
- Basement foundation

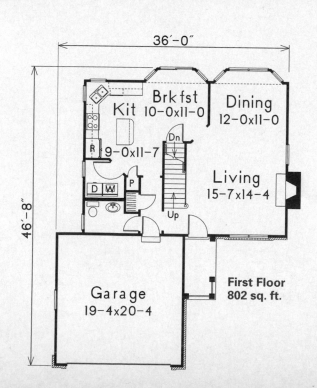

36'-0"

46'-8"

Kit
9-0x11-7

Brkfst

Dining
12-0x11-0

Living
15-7x14-4

Dn

Up

D W P

Garage
19-4x20-4

First Floor
802 sq. ft.

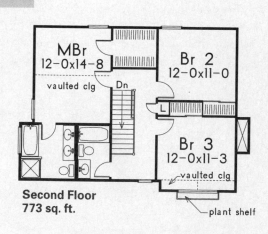

MBr
12-0x14-8

vaulted clg

Dn

Br 2
12-0x11-0

Br 3
12-0x11-3

vaulted clg

Second Floor
773 sq. ft.

plant shelf

Charming Country Styling In This Ranch

Total Living Area: 1,600

- Energy efficient home with 2" x 6" exterior walls
- Impressive sunken living room has massive stone fireplace and 16' vaulted ceilings
- Dining room conveniently located next to kitchen and divided for privacy
- Special amenities include sewing room, glass shelves in kitchen and master bath and a large utility area
- Sunken master bedroom features a distinctive sitting room
- 3 bedrooms, 2 baths, 2-car side entry garage
- Slab foundation, drawings also include crawl space and basement foundations

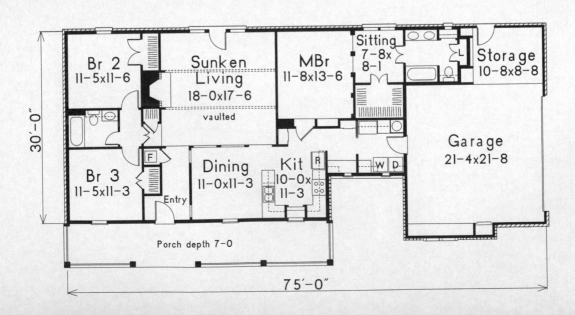

TO ORDER SEE **PAGE 608** OR CALL TOLL-FREE **1-800-DREAM HOME** (373-2646)

Wrap-Around Porch Adds Charm

Total Living Area: 1,619

- Private second floor bedroom and bath
- Kitchen features a snack bar and adjacent dining area
- Master bedroom has a private bath
- Centrally located washer and dryer
- 3 bedrooms, 3 baths
- Basement foundation, drawings also include crawl space and slab foundations

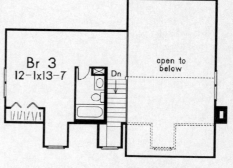

Second Floor
360 sq. ft.

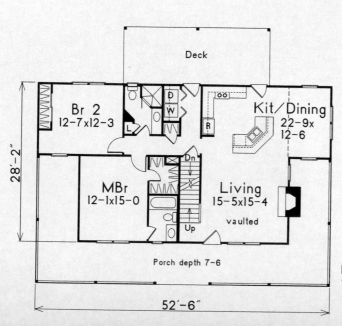

First Floor
1,259 sq. ft.

BEST-SELLING

15

TO ORDER SEE **PAGE 608** OR CALL TOLL-FREE 1-800-DREAM HOME (373-2646)

Ultimate Atrium For A Sloping Lot

Total Living Area: 3,814

- Massive sunken great room with vaulted ceiling includes exciting balcony overlook of towering atrium window wall
- Breakfast bar adjoins open "California" kitchen
- Seven vaulted rooms for drama and four fireplaces for warmth
- Master bath complemented by colonnade and fireplace surrounding sunken tub and deck
- 3 bedrooms, 2 1/2 baths, 3-car side entry garage
- Walk-out basement foundation
- 3,566 square feet on the first floor and 248 square feet on the lower level atrium

Rear View

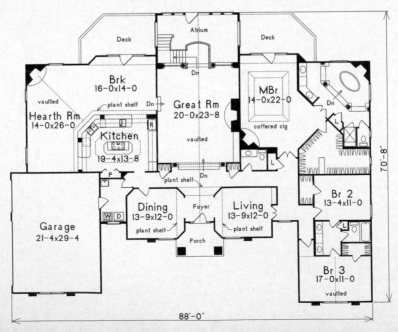

Compact Home For Functional Living

Total Living Area: 1,220

- Vaulted ceilings add luxury to living room and master suite
- Spacious living room accented with a large fireplace and hearth
- Gracious dining area is adjacent to the convenient wrap-around kitchen
- Washer and dryer handy to the bedrooms
- Covered porch entry adds appeal
- Rear sun deck adjoins dining area
- 3 bedrooms, 2 baths, 2-car drive under garage
- Basement foundation

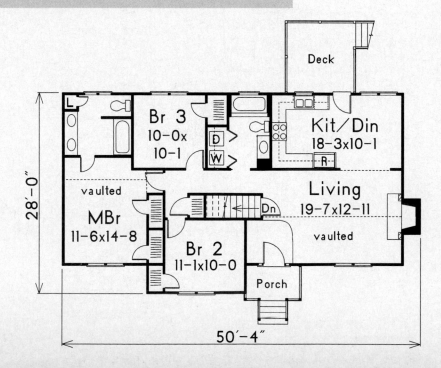

BEST-SELLING

17

Impressive Master Suite

Total Living Area: 2,287

- Double-doors lead into an impressive master suite which accesses covered porch and features deluxe bath with double closets and step-up tub
- Kitchen easily serves formal and informal areas of home
- The spacious foyer opens into formal dining and living rooms
- 4 bedrooms, 2 1/2 baths, 2-car side entry garage
- Slab foundation

BEST-SELLING

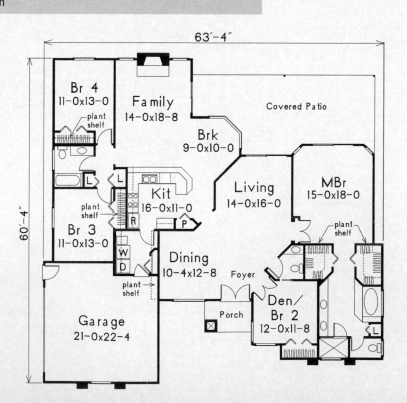

63'-4"

60'-4"

Br 4
11-0x13-0

plant shelf

Family
14-0x18-8

Covered Patio

Brk
9-0x10-0

Kit
16-0x11-0

Living
14-0x16-0

MBr
15-0x18-0

plant shelf

plant shelf

Br 3
11-0x13-0

R

P

plant shelf

Dining
10-4x12-8

Foyer

W
D

Garage
21-0x22-4

Porch

Den/
Br 2
12-0x11-8

plant shelf

Small Home Is Remarkably Spacious

Total Living Area: 914

- Large porch for leisure evenings
- Dining area with bay window, open stair and pass-through kitchen creates openness
- Basement includes generous garage space, storage area, finished laundry and mechanical room
- 2 bedrooms, 1 bath, 2-car drive under garage
- Basement foundation

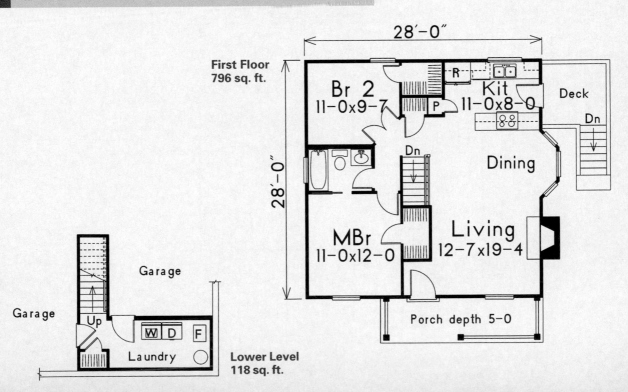

First Floor
796 sq. ft.

28'-0"

28'-0"

Br 2
11-0x9-7

Kit
11-0x8-0

Deck

Dn

P

R

Dn

Dining

MBr
11-0x12-0

Living
12-7x19-4

Porch depth 5-0

Garage

Garage

Up

W D F

Laundry

Lower Level
118 sq. ft.

BEST-SELLING

19

Small Ranch Is A Perfect Country Haven

Total Living Area: 1,761

- Exterior window dressing, roof dormers and planter boxes provide visual warmth and charm
- Great room boasts a vaulted ceiling, fireplace and opens to a pass-through kitchen
- Master bedroom is vaulted with luxury bath and walk-in closet
- Home features eight separate closets with an abundance of storage
- 4 bedrooms, 2 baths, 2-car side entry garage
- Basement foundation

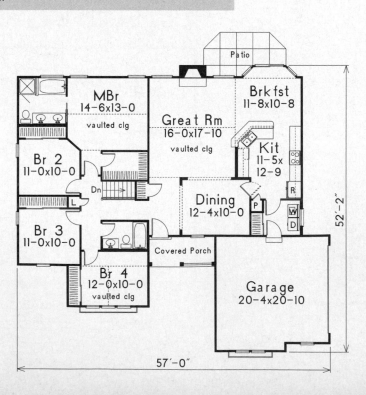

Patio

MBr
14-6x13-0
vaulted clg

Great Rm
16-0x17-10
vaulted clg

Brk fst
11-8x10-8

Kit
11-5x
12-9

Br 2
11-0x10-0

Dn

Dining
12-4x10-0

P

R

W D

Br 3
11-0x10-0

Covered Porch

Br 4
12-0x10-0
vaulted clg

Garage
20-4x20-10

52'-2"

57'-0"

TO ORDER SEE **PAGE 608** OR CALL TOLL-FREE 1-800-DREAM HOME (373-2646)

Classic Exterior
Total Living Area: 1,791

- Vaulted great room and octagon-shaped dining area enjoy views of covered patio
- Kitchen features a pass-through to dining area, center island, large walk-in pantry and breakfast room with large bay window
- Master bedroom is vaulted with sitting area
- 4 bedrooms, 2 baths, 2-car garage with storage
- Basement foundation

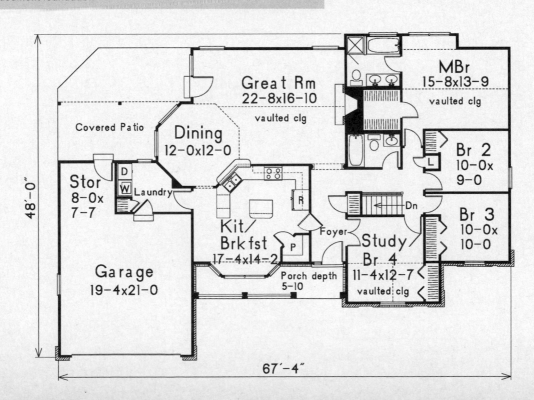

Best-Selling

21

Attractive Entry With Full-Length Porch

Total Living Area: 2,357

- 9' ceilings on first floor
- Secluded master bedroom includes private bath with double walk-in closets and vanity
- Balcony overlooks living room with large fireplace
- Second floor has three bedrooms and an expansive game room
- 4 bedrooms, 3 1/2 baths, 2-car side entry garage
- Slab foundation, drawings also include crawl space foundation

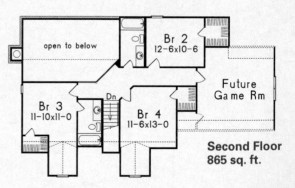

Second Floor
865 sq. ft.

Br 2
12-6x10-6

open to below

Br 3
11-10x11-0

Br 4
11-6x13-0

Future
Game Rm

Dn

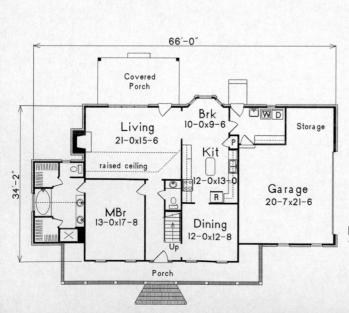

66'-0"

34'-2"

Covered
Porch

Living
21-0x15-6

raised ceiling

Brk
10-0x9-6

W D

Storage

Kit
12-0x13-0

MBr
13-0x17-8

Dining
12-0x12-8

Garage
20-7x21-6

Up

Porch

First Floor
1,492 sq. ft.

Plan# 577-0449

TO ORDER SEE PAGE 608 OR CALL TOLL-FREE 1

Spacious And Functional House

Total Living Area: 2,505

- The garage features extra storage area and ample work space
- Laundry room accessible from the garage and the outdoors
- Deluxe raised tub and immense walk-in closet grace master bath
- 3 bedrooms, 2 1/2 baths, 2-car side entry garage
- Basement foundation, drawings also include crawl space foundation

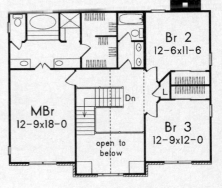

Second Floor
1,069 sq. ft.

MBr
12-9x18-0

Br 2
12-6x11-6

Br 3
12-9x12-0

open to below

Dn

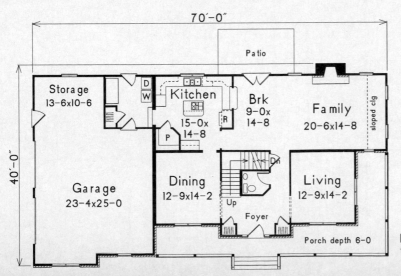

70'-0"

40'-0"

Patio

Storage
13-6x10-6

Kitchen
15-0x
14-8

Brk
9-0x
14-8

Family
20-6x14-8

sloped clg

Garage
23-4x25-0

Dining
12-9x14-2

Living
12-9x14-2

Up

Dn

Foyer

Porch depth 6-0

First Floor
1,436 sq. ft.

Distinguished Styling For A Small Lot

Total Living Area: 1,268

- Multiple gables, large porch and arched windows create classy exterior
- Innovative design provides openness in great room, kitchen and breakfast room
- Secondary bedrooms have private hall with bath
- 3 bedrooms, 2 baths, 2-car garage
- Basement foundation

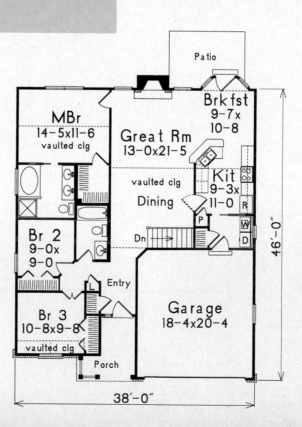

Massive Ranch With Classy Features
Total Living Area: 2,874

- Large family room with sloped ceiling and wood beams adjoins the kitchen and breakfast area with windows on two walls
- Large foyer opens to family room with massive stone fireplace and open stairs to the basement
- Private master bedroom with raised tub under the bay window, dramatic dressing area and a huge walk-in closet
- 4 bedrooms, 2 1/2 baths, 2-car side entry garage
- Basement foundation

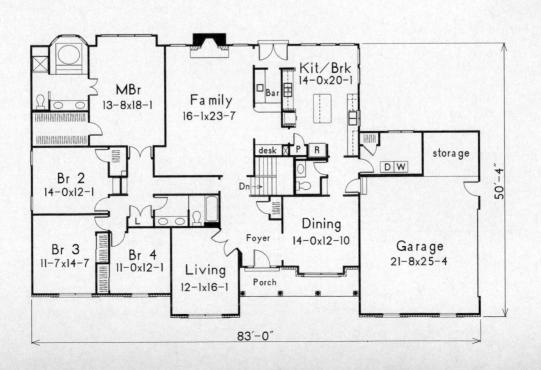

Irresistible Grandeur

Total Living Area: 2,624

- Dramatic two-story entry opens to bayed dining room through classic colonnade
- Magnificent great room with 18' ceiling brightly lit with three palladian windows
- Master suite includes bay window, walk-in closets, plant shelves and sunken bath
- 4 bedrooms, 2 1/2 baths, 2-car side entry garage
- Basement foundation

Interior View - Master Bath

First Floor
1,774 sq. ft.

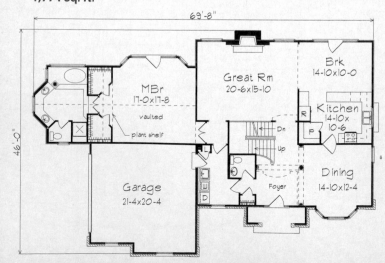

69'-8"
46'-0"

MBr
17-0x17-8
vaulted
plant shelf

Great Rm
20-6x15-10

Brk
14-10x10-0

Kitchen
14-10x
10-6

Dining
14-10x12-4

Foyer

Garage
21-4x20-4

Dn
Up

Second Floor
850 sq. ft.

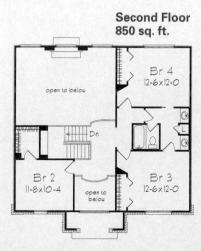

Br 4
12-6x12-0

open to below

Br 2
11-8x10-4

Br 3
12-6x12-0

open to below

Dn

BEST-SELLING

TO ORDER SEE **PAGE 608** OR CALL TOLL-FREE **1-800-DREAM HOME** (373-2646)

Country Home With Front Orientation
Total Living Area: 2,029

- Stonework, gables, roof dormer and double porches create a country flavor
- Kitchen enjoys extravagant cabinetry and counterspace in a bay, island snack bar, built-in pantry and cheery dining area with multiple tall windows
- Angled stair descends from large entry with wood columns and io open to vaulted great room with corner fireplace
- Master bedroom boasts his and hers walk-in closets, double-doors leading to an opulent master bath and private porch
- 4 bedrooms, 2 baths, 2-car side entry garage
- Basement foundation

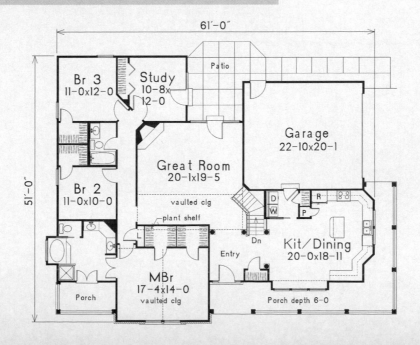

BEST-SELLING

Traditional Exterior

Total Living Area: 1,882

- Wide, handsome entrance opens to the vaulted great room with fireplace
- Living and dining areas are conveniently joined but still allow privacy
- Private covered porch extends breakfast area
- Practical passageway runs through laundry and mud room from garage to kitchen
- Vaulted ceiling in master bedroom
- 3 bedrooms, 2 baths, 2-car garage
- Basement foundation

BEST-SELLING

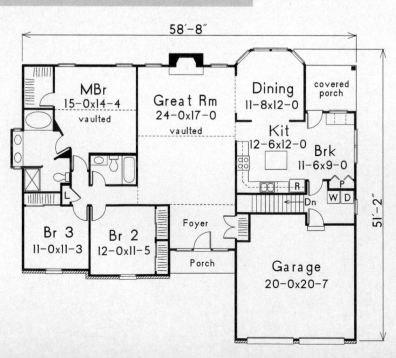

Picture Perfect For A Country Setting

Total Living Area: 2,967

- An exterior with charm graced with country porch and multiple arched projected box windows
- Dining area is oversized and adjoins a fully equipped kitchen with walk-in pantry
- Two bay windows light up the enormous informal living area to the rear
- 4 bedrooms, 3 1/2 baths, 3-car side entry garage
- Basement foundation

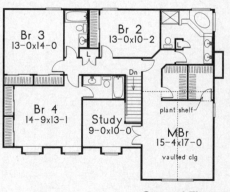

Second Floor
1,517 sq. ft.

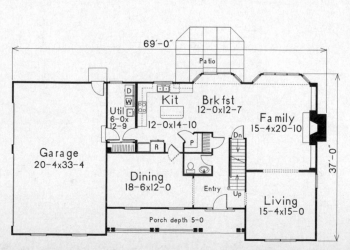

First Floor
1,450 sq. ft.

Tranquility Of An Atrium Cottage

Total Living Area: 1,384

- Wrap-around country porch for peaceful evenings
- Vaulted great room enjoys a large bay window, stone fireplace, pass-through kitchen and awesome rear views through atrium window wall
- Master suite features double entry doors, walk-in closet and a fabulous bath
- Atrium open to 611 square feet of optional living area below
- 2 bedrooms, 2 baths, 1-car side entry garage
- Walk-out basement foundation

BEST-SELLING

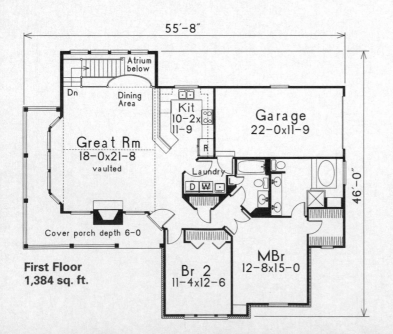

First Floor
1,384 sq. ft.

55'–8"

46'–0"

Atrium below

Dn

Dining Area

Kit
10-2x
11-9

Garage
22-0x11-9

Great Rm
18-0x21-8
vaulted

Laundry

D W

R

Cover porch depth 6-0

Br 2
11-4x12-6

MBr
12-8x15-0

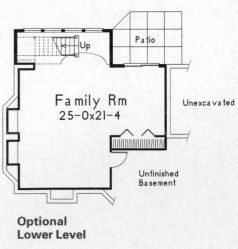

Up

Patio

Family Rm
25-0x21-4

Unexcavated

Unfinished Basement

Optional
Lower Level

TO ORDER SEE PAGE 608 OR CALL TOLL-FREE 1-800-DREAM HOME (373-2646)

Impressive Home For Country Living

Total Living Area: 1,991

■ A large porch with roof dormers and flanking stonework create a distinctive country appeal

■ The highly functional U-shaped kitchen is open to dining and living rooms defined by a colonade

■ Large bay windows are enjoyed by both the living room and master bedroom

■ Every bedroom features spacious walk-in closets and its own private bath

■ 3 bedrooms, 3 1/2 baths, 2-car side entry garage

■ Basement foundation

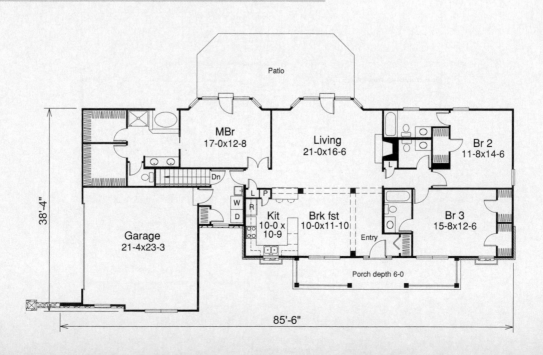

BEST-SELLING

Enchanting Country Cottage

Total Living Area: 1,140

- Open and spacious living and dining areas for family gatherings
- Well-organized kitchen with an abundance of cabinetry and a built-in pantry
- Roomy master bath features double-bowl vanity
- 3 bedrooms, 2 baths, 2-car drive under garage
- Basement foundation

BEST-SELLING

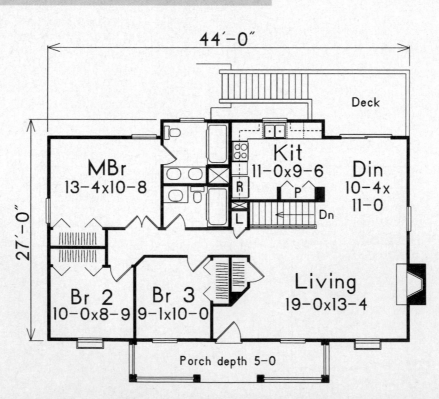

44'-0"

27'-0"

Deck

MBr
13-4x10-8

Kit
11-0x9-6

Din
10-4x
11-0

R

P

Dn

L

Br 2
10-0x8-9

Br 3
9-1x10-0

Living
19-0x13-4

Porch depth 5-0

TO ORDER SEE **PAGE 608** OR CALL TOLL-FREE 1-800-DREAM HOME (373-2646)

Classic Atrium Ranch

Total Living Area: 1,977

- Classic traditional exterior always in style
- Spacious great room boasts a vaulted ceiling, dining area, atrium with elegant staircase and feature windows
- Atrium open to 1,416 square feet of optional living area below which consists of an optional family room, two bedrooms, two baths and a study
- 4 bedrooms, 2 1/2 baths, 3-car side entry garage
- Walk-out basement foundation

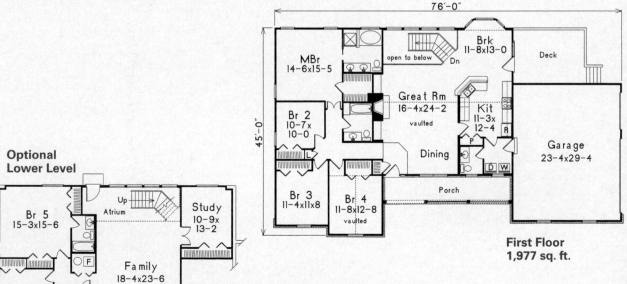

Optional Lower Level

Br 5 15-3x15-6
Br 6 11-5x12-7
Up Atrium
Study 10-9x 13-2
Family 18-4x23-6
storage

76'-0"
45'-0"

MBr 14-6x15-5
Br 2 10-7x 10-0
Br 3 11-4x11x8
Br 4 11-8x12-8 vaulted
open to below Dn
Brk 11-8x13-0
Deck
Great Rm 16-4x24-2 vaulted
Kit 11-3x 12-4
Dining
Porch
Garage 23-4x29-4

First Floor
1,977 sq. ft.

BEST-SELLING

33

Vaulted Ceilings Enhance Home

Total Living Area: 2,073

- Family room provides ideal gathering area with a fireplace, large windows and vaulted ceiling
- Private first floor master bedroom suite with a vaulted ceiling and luxury bath
- Kitchen features angled bar connecting kitchen and breakfast area
- 4 bedrooms, 2 1/2 baths, 2-car side entry garage
- Basement foundation

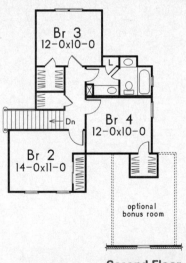

Br 3
12-0x10-0

Br 4
12-0x10-0

Br 2
14-0x11-0

optional bonus room

Second Floor
632 sq. ft.

First Floor
1,441 sq. ft.

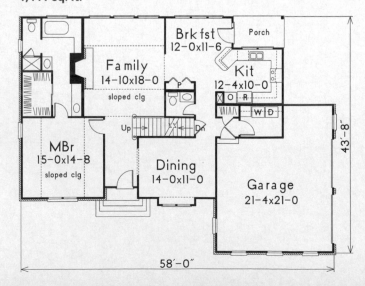

Brk fst
12-0x11-6

Porch

Family
14-10x18-0
sloped clg

Kit
12-4x10-0

P

Up

Dn

MBr
15-0x14-8
sloped clg

Dining
14-0x11-0

Garage
21-4x21-0

43'-8"

58'-0"

Plan# 577-0754

Price Code F

Prestigious And Family Oriented

Total Living Area: 3,420

- Hip roofs, elliptical windows and brick facade with quoins emphasize stylish sophisticated living

- Grand foyer has flared staircase in addition to secondary stair from kitchen

- Enormous kitchen features a cooktop island, walk-in pantry, angled breakfast bar and computer desk

- Splendid gallery connects family room and wet bar with vaulted hearth room

- Master bedroom has a coffered ceiling, his and hers walk-in closets and a lavish bath

- 4 bedrooms, 3 1/2 baths, 3-car rear entry garage

- Walk-out basement foundation

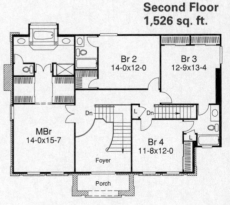

**Second Floor
1,526 sq. ft.**

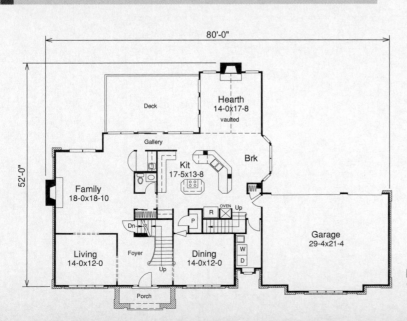

**First Floor
1,894 sq. ft.**

Ranch Offers Country Elegance

Total Living Area: 1,787

- Large great room with fireplace and vaulted ceiling features three large skylights and windows galore
- Cooking is sure to be a pleasure in this L-shaped well-appointed kitchen which includes bayed breakfast area with access to rear deck
- Every bedroom offers a spacious walk-in closet with a convenient laundry room just steps away
- 415 square feet of optional living area on the lower level
- 3 bedrooms, 2 baths, 2-car drive under garage
- Walk-out basement foundation

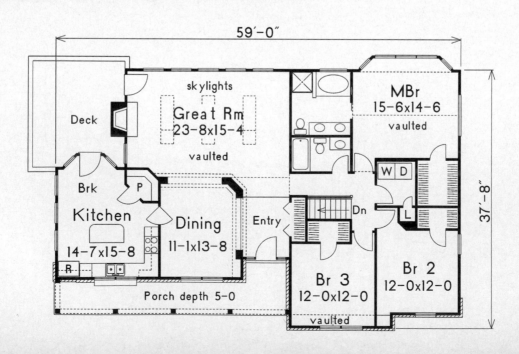

Deck

sky lights

Great Rm
23-8x15-4

vaulted

MBr
15-6x14-6

vaulted

Brk

P

Kitchen
14-7x15-8

Dining
11-1x13-8

Entry

W D

Dn

L

Br 3
12-0x12-0

Br 2
12-0x12-0

R

Porch depth 5-0

vaulted

59'-0"

37'-8"

TO ORDER SEE PAGE 608 OR CALL TOLL-FREE 1-800-DREAM HOME (373-2646)

Casual Dining In Breakfast Room

Total Living Area: 1,708

- Massive family room enhanced with several windows, fireplace and access to porch
- Deluxe master bath accented by step-up corner tub flanked by double vanities
- Closets throughout maintain organized living
- Bedrooms isolated from living areas
- 3 bedrooms, 2 baths, 2 car garage
- Basement foundation, drawings also include crawl space foundation

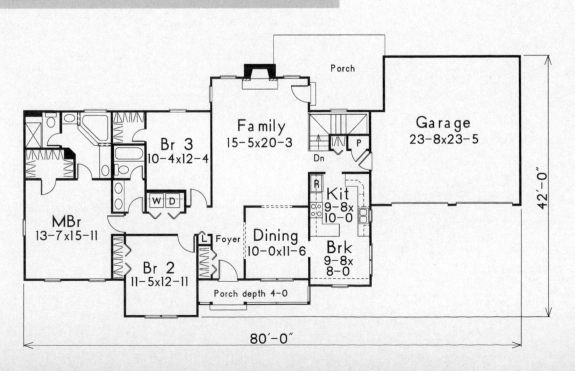

BEST-SELLING

37

Country-Style With Wrap-Around Porch

Total Living Area: 1,597

- Spacious family room includes fireplace and coat closet
- Open kitchen and dining room provide breakfast bar and access to the outdoors
- Convenient laundry area located near kitchen
- Secluded master suite with walk-in closet and private bath
- 4 bedrooms, 2 1/2 baths, 2-car detached garage
- Basement foundation

Br 3
14-0x10-0

Br 4
12-0x12-4

Dn

Br 2
14-0x10-10

Second Floor
615 sq. ft.

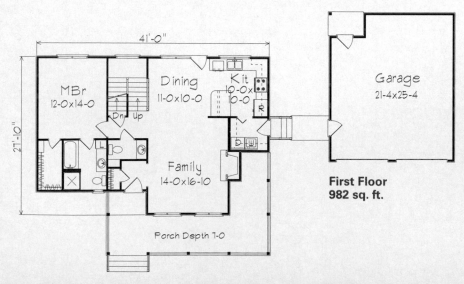

41'-0"

27'-10"

MBr
12-0x14-0

Dn Up

Dining
11-0x10-0

Kit
10-0x
10-0

Garage
21-4x25-4

Family
14-0x16-10

First Floor
982 sq. ft.

Porch Depth 7-0

Plan# 577-0739

Price Code B

TO ORDER SEE PAGE 608 OR CALL TOLL-FREE 1-800-DREAM HOME (373-2646)

A Special Home For Views

Total Living Area: 1,684

- Delightful wrap-around porch anchored by full masonry fireplace
- The vaulted great room includes a large bay window, fireplace, dining balcony and atrium window wall
- His and hers walk-in closets, large luxury bath and sliding doors to exterior balcony are a few fantastic features of the master bedroom
- Atrium open to 611 square feet of optional living area on the lower level
- 3 bedrooms, 2 baths, 2-car drive under garage
- Walk-out basement foundation

Rear View

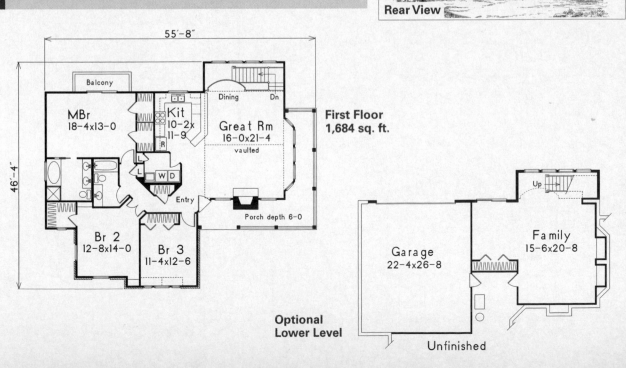

55'-8"

46'-4"

Balcony

MBr
18-4x13-0

Kit
10-2x
11-9

Dining   Dn

Great Rm
16-0x21-4
vaulted

First Floor
1,684 sq. ft.

Entry

Porch depth 6-0

Br 2
12-8x14-0

Br 3
11-4x12-6

Garage
22-4x26-8

Up

Family
15-6x20-8

Optional Lower Level

Unfinished

BEST-SELLING

39

Impressive Two-Story Entry

Total Living Area: 2,336

- Stately sunken living room with partially vaulted ceiling and classic arched transom windows
- Family room features plenty of windows and a fireplace with flanking bookshelves
- 4 bedrooms, 2 1/2 baths, 2-car garage
- Basement foundation

First Floor
1,291 sq. ft.

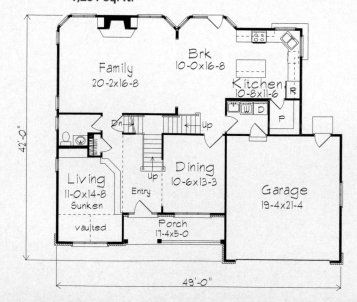

Second Floor
1,045 sq. ft.

TO ORDER SEE **PAGE 608** OR CALL TOLL-FREE **1-800-DREAM HOME** (373-2646)

Country-Style Home With Front Porch

Total Living Area: 1,501

- Spacious kitchen with dining area is open to the outdoors
- Convenient utility room is adjacent to garage
- Master suite with private bath, dressing area and access to large covered porch
- Large family room creates openness
- 3 bedrooms, 2 baths, 2-car side entry garage
- Basement foundation, drawings also include crawl space and slab foundations

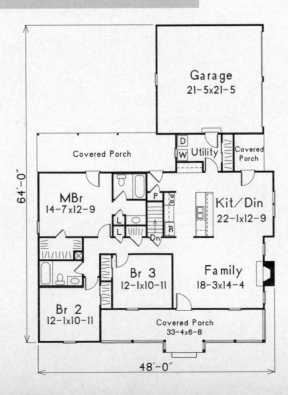

Garage
21-5x21-5

Covered Porch

D
W   Utility   Covered Porch

64-0"

MBr
14-7x12-9

P

Kit/Din
22-1x12-9

L
L   Dn
R

Br 3
12-1x10-11

Family
18-3x14-4

Br 2
12-1x10-11

Covered Porch
33-4x6-8

48-0"

Dining With A View

Total Living Area: 1,524

- Delightful balcony overlooks two-story entry illuminated by oval window
- Roomy first floor master suite offers quiet privacy
- All bedrooms feature one or more walk-in closets
- 3 bedrooms, 2 1/2 baths, 2-car garage
- Basement foundation

BEST-SELLING

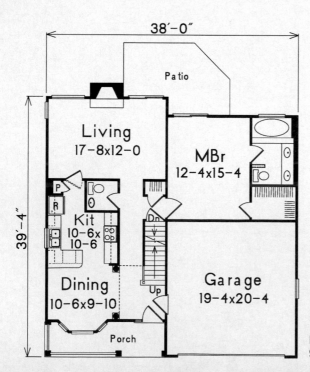

38'-0"

Patio

Living
17-8x12-0

MBr
12-4x15-4

39'-4"

P
R

Kit
10-6x
10-6

Dn

Dining
10-6x9-10

Up

Garage
19-4x20-4

Porch

First Floor
951 sq. ft.

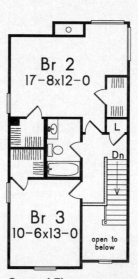

Br 2
17-8x12-0

L

Dn

Br 3
10-6x13-0

open to
below

Second Floor
573 sq. ft.

42

TO ORDER SEE **PAGE 608** OR CALL TOLL-FREE **1-800-DREAM HOME** (373-2646)

Ideal Large Family Five Bedroom Home
Total Living Area: 2,828

- Popular wrap-around porch gives home country charm
- Secluded, oversized family room with vaulted ceiling and wet bar features many windows
- Any chef would be delighted to cook in this smartly designed kitchen with island and corner windows
- Spectacular master suite
- 5 bedrooms, 3 1/2 baths, 2 car side entry garage
- Basement foundation, drawings also include crawl space and slab foundations

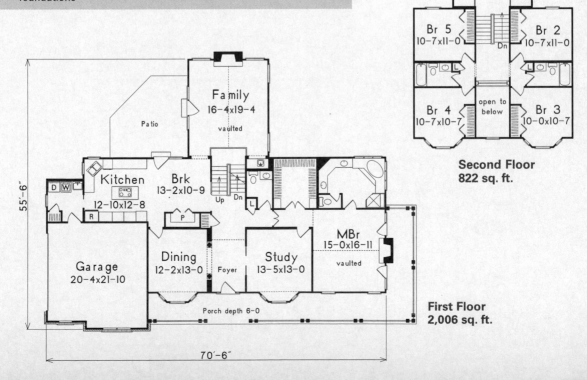

Second Floor
822 sq. ft.

First Floor
2,006 sq. ft.

BEST-SELLING

Organized Kitchen, Center Of Activity

Total Living Area: 1,882

- Handsome brick facade
- Spacious great room and dining room combination brightened by unique corner windows and patio access
- Well-designed kitchen incorporates breakfast bar peninsula, sweeping casement window above sink and walk-in pantry island
- Master suite features large walk-in closet and private bath with bay window
- 4 bedrooms, 2 baths, 2-car side entry garage
- Basement foundation

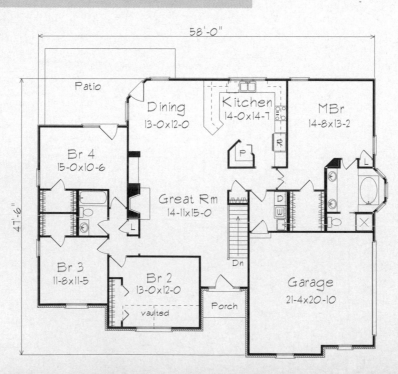

Fireplaces Add Warm Cozy Feeling

Total Living Area: 2,932

- 9' ceilings throughout home
- Rear stairs create convenient access to second floor from living area
- Spacious kitchen has pass-through to the family room, a convenient island and pantry
- Cozy built-in table in breakfast area
- Secluded master suite with luxurious bath and patio access
- 4 bedrooms, 3 1/2 baths, 2-car side entry garage
- Slab foundation

First Floor
1,999 sq. ft.

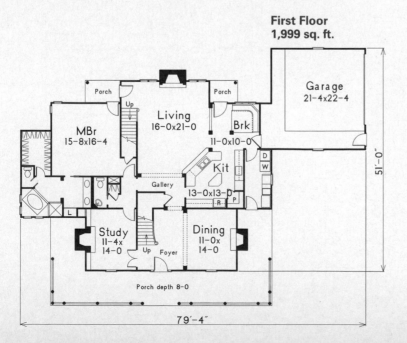

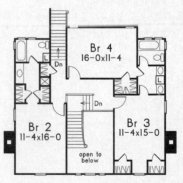

Second Floor
933 sq. ft.

BEST-SELLING

45

Stylish Exterior
Total Living Area: 3,216

- All bedrooms include private full baths
- Hearth room and combination kitchen/breakfast area create a large informal gathering area
- Oversized family room boasts fireplace, wet bar and bay window
- Master bath has double walk-in closets and a luxurious bath
- 4 bedrooms, 4 1/2 baths, 3-car side entry garage
- Basement foundation

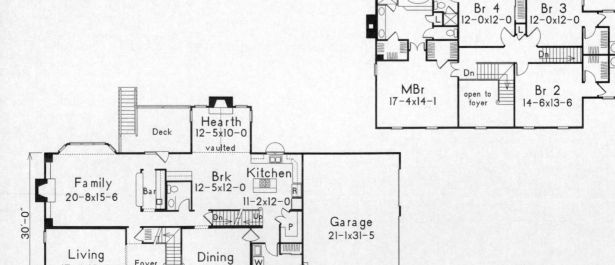

Second Floor
1,382 sq. ft.

Br 4
12-0x12-0

Br 3
12-0x12-0

MBr
17-4x14-1

open to foyer

Br 2
14-6x13-6

First Floor
1,834 sq. ft.

Deck

Hearth
12-5x10-0
vaulted

Family
20-8x15-6

Bar

Brk
12-5x12-0

Kitchen
11-2x12-0

Garage
21-1x31-5

Living
17-4x13-3

Foyer

Dining
14-6x13-3

Porch
45-0x6-0

30'-0"

77'-6"

TO ORDER SEE PAGE 608 OR CALL TOLL-FREE 1-800-DREAM HOME (373-2646)

Ranch Of Enchantment

Total Living Area: 1,559

- A cozy country appeal is provided by a spacious porch, masonry fireplace, roof dormers and a perfect balance of stonework and siding
- Large living room enjoys a fireplace, bayed dining area and separate entry
- A U-shaped kitchen is adjoined by a breakfast room with bay window and large pantry
- 3 bedrooms, 2 1/2 baths, 2-car side entry drive under garage
- Basement foundation

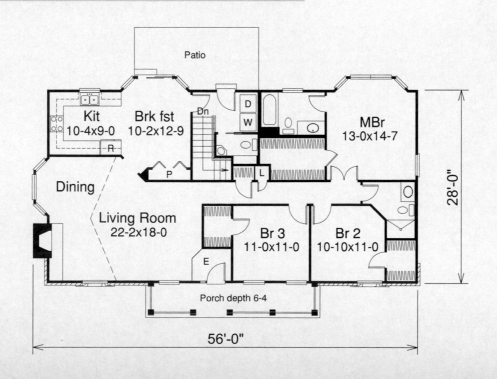

Patio

Kit
10-4x9-0

Brk fst
10-2x12-9

Dn

D

W

MBr
13-0x14-7

Dining

R

P

L

Living Room
22-2x18-0

Br 3
11-0x11-0

Br 2
10-10x11-0

E

Porch depth 6-4

28'-0"

56'-0"

BEST-SELLING

47

Classic Elegance

Total Living Area: 2,483

- A large entry porch with open brick arches and palladian door welcomes guests
- The vaulted great room features an entertainment center alcove and ideal layout for furniture placement
- Dining room is extra large with a stylish tray ceiling
- Study can easily be converted to a fourth bedroom
- 3 bedrooms, 2 baths, 2-car side entry garage
- Basement foundation

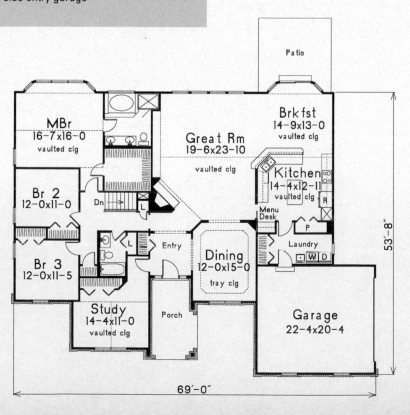

Patio

MBr
16-7x16-0
vaulted clg

Br 2
12-0x11-0

Dn

Br 3
12-0x11-5

Great Rm
19-6x23-10
vaulted clg

Brkfst
14-9x13-0
vaulted clg

Kitchen
14-4x12-11
vaulted clg

Menu Desk

Laundry
W D

Entry

Dining
12-0x15-0
tray clg

Study
14-4x11-0
vaulted clg

Porch

Garage
22-4x20-4

53'-8"

69'-0"

TO ORDER SEE PAGE 608 OR CALL TOLL-FREE 1-800-DREAM HOME (373-2646)

Charming Design Features Home Office

Total Living Area: 2,452

- Cheery and spacious home office room with private entrance and bath, two closets, vaulted ceiling and transomed window perfect shown as a home office or a fourth bedroom

- Delightful great room with vaulted ceiling, fireplace, extra storage closets and patio doors to sundeck

- Extra-large kitchen features walk-in pantry, cooktop island and bay window

- Vaulted master suite includes transomed windows, walk-in closet and luxurious bath

- 4 bedrooms, 2 1/2 baths, 3-car garage

- Basement foundation

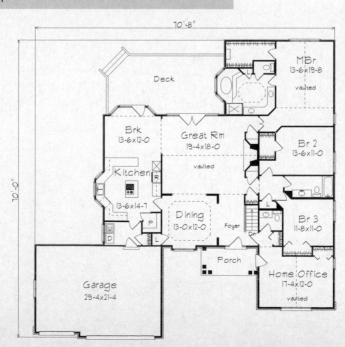

BEST-SELLING

TO ORDER SEE **PAGE 608** OR CALL TOLL-FREE **1-800-DREAM HOME** (373-2646)

Impressive Front Entry

Total Living Area: 1,800

- Energy efficient home with 2" x 6" exterior walls
- Covered front and rear porches add outdoor living area
- 12' ceilings in kitchen, eating area, dining and living rooms
- Private master suite features expansive bath
- Side entry garage with two storage areas
- Pillared styling with brick and stucco exterior finish
- 3 bedrooms, 2 baths, 2-car side entry garage
- Crawl space foundation, drawings also include slab foundation

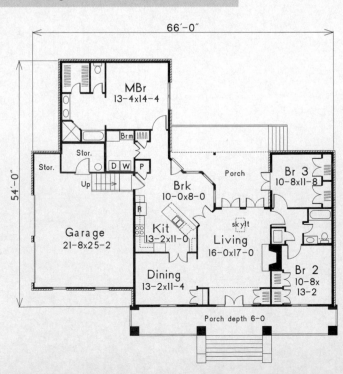

Plan# 577-0138

Price Code E

TO ORDER SEE **PAGE 608** OR CALL TOLL-FREE **1-800-DREAM HOME** (373-2646)

Impressive Victorian

Total Living Area: 2,286

- Fine architectural detail makes this home a showplace with its large windows, intricate brickwork and fine woodwork and trim
- Stunning two-story entry with attractive wood railing and balustrades in foyer
- Convenient wrap-around kitchen with window view, planning center and pantry
- Oversized master suite with walk-in closet and master bath
- 4 bedrooms, 2 1/2 baths, 2-car garage
- Basement foundation, drawings also include crawl space and slab foundations

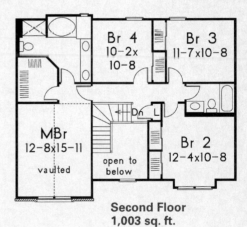

Second Floor
1,003 sq. ft.

Br 4
10-2x 10-8

Br 3
11-7x10-8

MBr
12-8x15-11
vaulted

open to below

Br 2
12-4x10-8

Dn

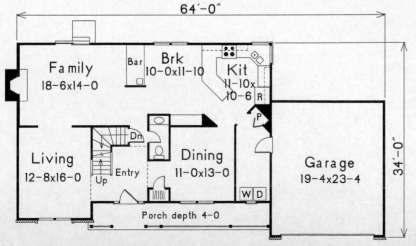

64'-0"

Family
18-6x14-0

Bar

Brk
10-0x11-10

Kit
11-10x 10-6

Living
12-8x16-0

Dn

Entry

Up

Dining
11-0x13-0

Garage
19-4x23-4

P

W D

34'-0"

Porch depth 4-0

First Floor
1,283 sq. ft.

BEST-SELLING

51

Practical Two-Story, Full Of Features
Total Living Area: 2,058

- Handsome two-story foyer with balcony creates a spacious entrance area
- Vaulted ceiling in the master bedroom with private dressing area and large walk-in closet
- Skylights furnish natural lighting in the hall and master bath
- Conveniently located second floor laundry near bedrooms
- 3 bedrooms, 2 1/2 baths, 2-car garage
- Basement foundation, drawings also include slab and crawl space foundations

First Floor
1,098 sq. ft.

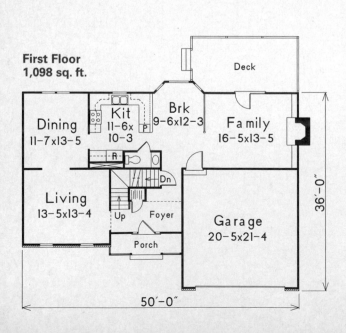

Deck

Dining
11-7x13-5

Kit
11-6x
10-3

Brk
9-6x12-3

Family
16-5x13-5

Living
13-5x13-4

Dn

Up

Foyer

Porch

Garage
20-5x21-4

36'-0"

50'-0"

Second Floor
960 sq. ft.

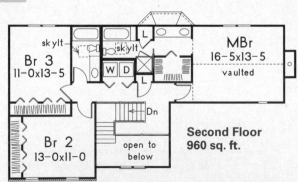

Br 3
11-0x13-5

skylt

skylt

W D

L

L

MBr
16-5x13-5
vaulted

Br 2
13-0x11-0

Dn

open to
below

52

Sophisticated Ranch

Total Living Area: 2,808

- An impressive front exterior showcases three porches for quiet times
- Large living and dining rooms flank an elegant entry
- Bedroom #3 shares a porch with the living room and a spacious bath with bedroom #2
- Vaulted master suite enjoys a secluded screened porch and sumptuous bath with corner tub, double vanities and huge walk-in closet
- Living room can easily convert to an optional fourth bedroom
- 3 bedrooms, 2 1/2 baths, 3-car side entry garage
- Basement foundation

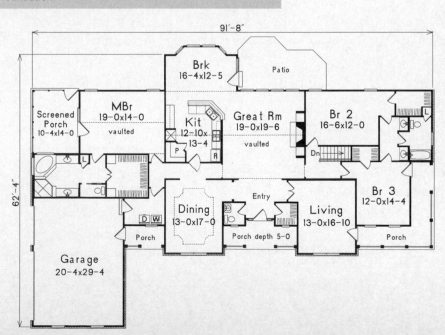

BEST-SELLING

TO ORDER SEE **PAGE 608** OR CALL TOLL-FREE **1-800-DREAM HOME** (373-2646)

Smaller Home Offers Stylish Exterior

Total Living Area: 1,700

- Two-story entry with T-stair is illuminated with decorative oval window
- Skillfully designed U-shaped kitchen has a built-in pantry
- All bedrooms have generous closet storage and are common to spacious hall with walk-in cedar closet
- 4 bedrooms, 2 1/2 baths, 2-car side entry garage
- Basement foundation

BEST-SELLING

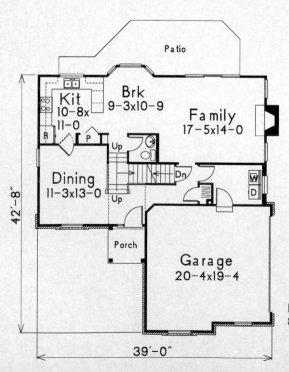

First Floor
896 sq. ft.

Patio

Kit
10-8x
11-0

Brk
9-3x10-9

Family
17-5x14-0

Dining
11-3x13-0

Up

Dn

W D

Porch

Garage
20-4x19-4

42'-8"

39'-0"

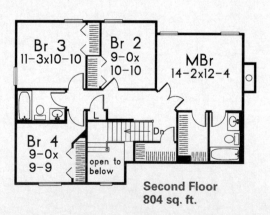

Second Floor
804 sq. ft.

Br 3
11-3x10-10

Br 2
9-0x
10-10

MBr
14-2x12-4

Br 4
9-0x
9-9

open to
below

TO ORDER SEE **PAGE 608** OR CALL TOLL-FREE **1-800-DREAM HOME** (373-2646)

Innovative Ranch Has Cozy Corner Patio

Total Living Area: 1,092

- Box window and inviting porch with dormers create a charming facade
- Eat-in kitchen offers a pass-through breakfast bar, corner window wall to patio, pantry and convenient laundry with half bath
- Master bedroom features double entry doors and walk-in closet
- 3 bedrooms, 1 1/2 baths, 1-car garage
- Basement foundation

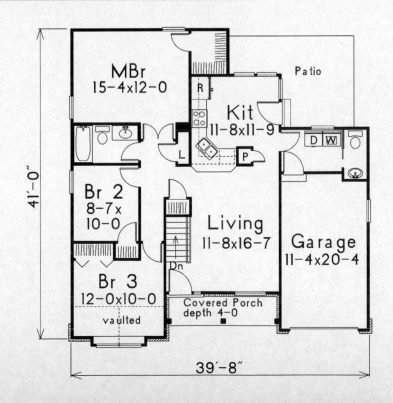

MBr
15-4x12-0

Kit
11-8x11-9

Patio

Br 2
8-7x
10-0

Living
11-8x16-7

Garage
11-4x20-4

Br 3
12-0x10-0

vaulted

Covered Porch
depth 4-0

41'-0"

39'-8"

TO ORDER SEE PAGE 608 OR CALL TOLL-FREE 1-800-DREAM HOME (373-2646)

A Spectacular Showplace

Total Living Area: 4,826

- Brightly lit entry connects to great room with balcony and massive bay-shaped atrium
- Kitchen has island/snack bar, walk-in pantry, computer area and atrium overlook
- Master suite has sitting area, walk-in closets, atrium overlook and luxury bath with private courtyard
- Family room/atrium, home theater area with wet bar, game room and guest bedroom comprise the lower level
- 4 bedrooms, 3 1/2 baths, 3-car side entry garage
- Walk-out basement foundation with lawn and garden workroom

Great Room/Atrium Interior View

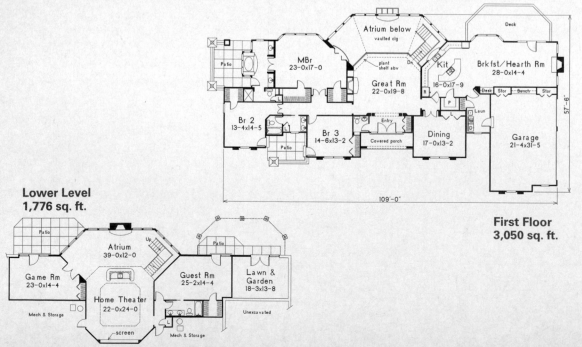

Lower Level 1,776 sq. ft.

First Floor 3,050 sq. ft.

Plan# 577-0224

Price Code D

TO ORDER SEE PAGE 608 OR CALL TOLL-FREE 1-800-DREAM HOME (373-2646)

Great Traffic Flow On Both Floors

Total Living Area: 2,461

- Unique corner tub, double vanities and walk-in closet enhance the large master bedroom
- Fireplace provides focus in the spacious family room
- Centrally located half bath for guests
- 4 bedrooms, 2 1/2 baths, 2-car garage
- Basement foundation, drawings also include slab and crawl space foundations

Second Floor
1,209 sq. ft.

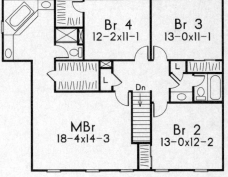

Br 4
12-2x11-1

Br 3
13-0x11-1

MBr
18-4x14-3

Br 2
13-0x12-2

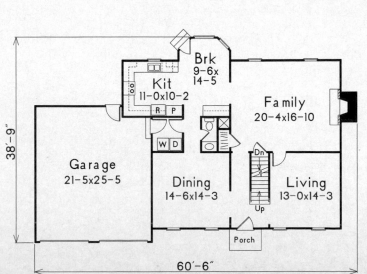

Brk
9-6x
14-5

Kit
11-0x10-2

Family
20-4x16-10

Garage
21-5x25-5

Dining
14-6x14-3

Living
13-0x14-3

Porch

38'-9"

60'-6"

First Floor
1,252 sq. ft.

BEST-SELLING

57

Vaulted Ceilings Add Dimension
Total Living Area: 1,676

- The living area skylights and large breakfast room with bay window provide plenty of sunlight
- The master bedroom has a walk-in closet and both the secondary bedrooms have large closets
- Vaulted ceilings, plant shelving and a fireplace provide a quality living area
- 3 bedrooms, 2 baths, 2-car garage
- Basement foundation, drawings also include crawl space and slab foundations

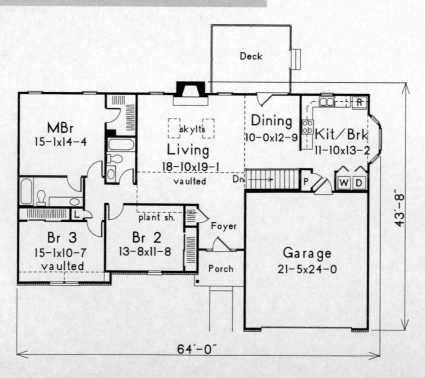

TO ORDER SEE **PAGE 608** OR CALL TOLL-FREE **1-800-DREAM HOME** (373-2646)

Traditional Exterior

Total Living Area: 2,531

- Charming porch with dormers leads into vaulted great room with atrium
- Well-designed kitchen and breakfast bar adjoins extra large laundry/mud room
- Double sinks, tub with window above and plant shelf complete vaulted master suite bath
- 4 bedrooms, 2 1/2 baths, 2-car side entry garage
- Walk-out basement foundation

Rear View

**First Floor
1,297 sq. ft.**

**Lower Level
1,234 sq. ft.**

Stately Country Home

Total Living Area: 2,727

- Wrap-around porch and large foyer create impressive entrance
- A state-of-the-art vaulted kitchen has walk-in pantry and is open to the breakfast room and adjoining screened porch
- A walk-in wet bar, fireplace bay window and deck access are features of the family room
- Vaulted master bedroom suite enjoys a luxurious bath with skylight and an enormous 13' deep walk-in closet
- 4 bedrooms, 2 1/2 baths, 2-car side entry garage
- Walk-out basement foundation

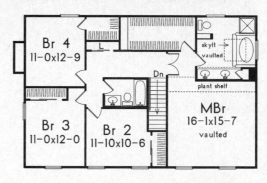

Second Floor
1,204 sq. ft.

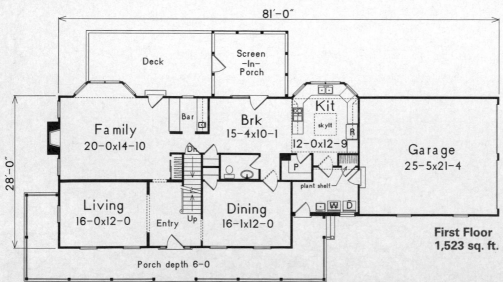

First Floor
1,523 sq. ft.

BEST-SELLING

Arched Elegance

Total Living Area: 3,222

- Two-story foyer features central staircase and views to second floor, dining and living rooms
- Built-in breakfast booth surrounded by windows
- Gourmet kitchen with view to the great room
- Two-story great room features large fireplace and arched openings to the second floor
- Elegant master suite has separate reading room with bookshelves and fireplace
- 4 bedrooms, 3 1/2 baths, 2-car side entry garage
- Basement foundation, drawings also include crawl space and slab foundations

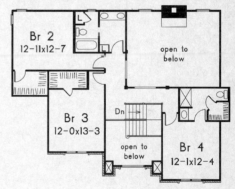

Second Floor
946 sq. ft.

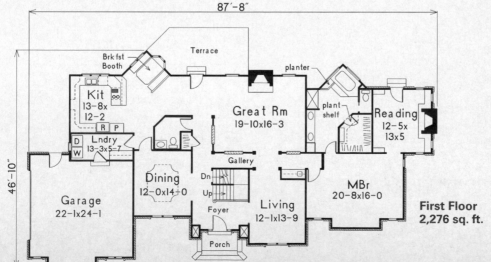

First Floor
2,276 sq. ft.

TO ORDER SEE PAGE 608 OR CALL TOLL-FREE 1-800-DREAM HOME (373-2646)

Two-Story Foyer With Curved Stairway

Total Living Area: 3,144

- 9' ceilings on first floor
- Kitchen offers large pantry, island cooktop and close proximity to laundry and dining rooms
- Expansive family room includes wet bar, fireplace and attractive bay window
- 4 bedrooms, 4 1/2 baths, 3-car side entry garage
- Basement foundation

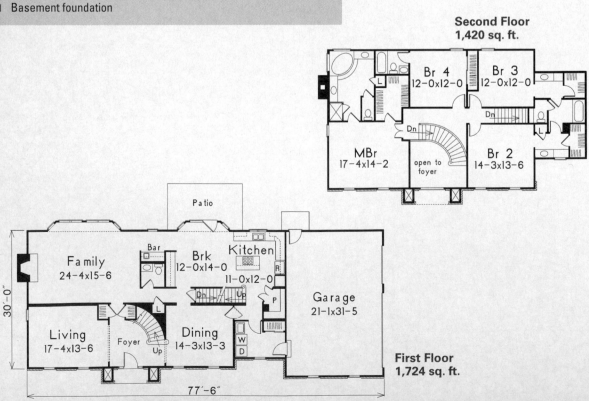

Second Floor
1,420 sq. ft.

Br 4
12-0x12-0

Br 3
12-0x12-0

MBr
17-4x14-2

open to foyer

Br 2
14-3x13-6

Patio

Family
24-4x15-6

Bar

Brk
12-0x14-0

Kitchen

11-0x12-0

Garage
21-1x31-5

30'-0"

Living
17-4x13-6

Foyer

Dining
14-3x13-3

W
D

First Floor
1,724 sq. ft.

77'-6"

BEST-SELLING

Plan# 577-0322

Price Code D

TO ORDER SEE **PAGE 608** OR CALL TOLL-FREE 1-800-DREAM HOME (373-2646)

Open Breakfast/Family Room

Total Living Area: 2,135

- Family room features extra space, impressive fireplace and full wall of windows that joins breakfast room creating spacious entertainment area
- Washer and dryer conveniently located on the second floor
- Kitchen features island counter and pantry
- 4 bedrooms, 2 1/2 baths, 2-car garage
- Basement foundation

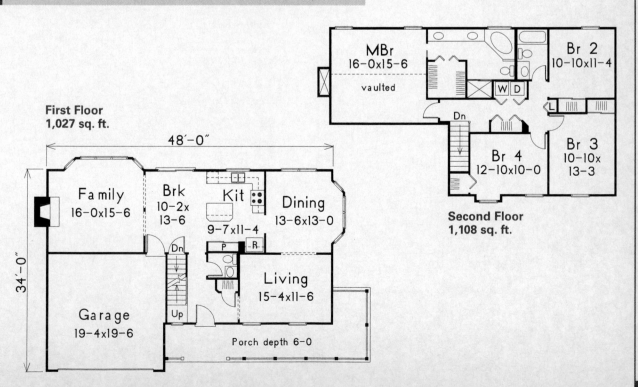

First Floor
1,027 sq. ft.

48'-0"

Family
16-0x15-6

Brk
10-2x
13-6

Kit
9-7x11-4

Dining
13-6x13-0

34'-0"

Dn

Living
15-4x11-6

Up

Garage
19-4x19-6

Porch depth 6-0

MBr
16-0x15-6
vaulted

Br 2
10-10x11-4

W D

Dn

Br 4
12-10x10-0

Br 3
10-10x
13-3

Second Floor
1,108 sq. ft.

BEST-SELLING

63

Quaint Exterior, Full Front Porch

Total Living Area: 1,657

- Stylish pass-through between living and dining areas
- Master bedroom is secluded from living area for privacy
- Large windows in breakfast and dining areas
- 3 bedrooms, 2 1/2 baths, 2-car drive under garage
- Basement foundation

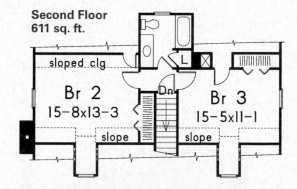

Second Floor
611 sq. ft.

sloped clg

Br 2
15-8x13-3

Dn

Br 3
15-5x11-1

slope   slope

Deck

vaulted

Kit

Brk
9-0x
17-5

R

Dining
9-10x
11-6

W
D

Living
18-1x13-7

Up

Dn

MBr
15-5x13-6

32'-0"

Porch
38-0x6-0

40'-0"

First Floor
1,046 sq. ft.

TO ORDER SEE **PAGE 608** OR CALL TOLL-FREE 1-800-DREAM HOME (373-2646)

Layout Creates Large Open Living Area

Total Living Area: 1,285

- Accommodating home with ranch-style porch
- Large storage area on back of home
- Master bedroom includes dressing area, private bath and built-in bookcase
- Kitchen features pantry, breakfast bar and complete view to dining room
- 3 bedrooms, 2 baths
- Crawl space foundation, drawings also include basement and slab foundations

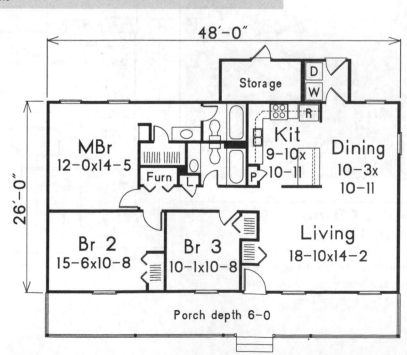

48'-0"

26'-0"

Storage

D
W

MBr
12-0x14-5

Kit
9-10x
10-11

Dining
10-3x
10-11

Furn   L

R

P

Living
18-10x14-2

Br 2
15-6x10-8

Br 3
10-1x10-8

Porch depth 6-0

RANCH

Plan# **577-FB1119**

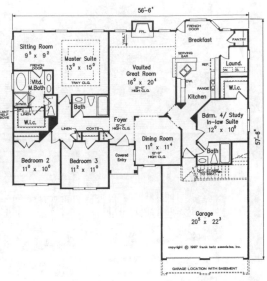

56'-6"

Sitting Room 9⁵ x 9²

Master Suite 13⁰ x 15⁰ TRAY CLG.

Vaulted Great Room 16⁰ x 20⁴ 12'-0" HIGH CLG.

Breakfast

PANTRY

SERVING BAR

REF.

Laund. tw. | b.

Vltd. M.Bath

FRENCH DOOR

Bath

Kitchen RANGE DW

W.i.c.

PLANT SHELF ABOVE

W.i.c.

LINEN

Foyer 12'-0" HIGH CLG.

COATS

LINEN

Bdrm. 4/ Study In-law Suite 12⁰ x 10⁰

57'-6"

Bedroom 2 11⁰ x 10⁰

Bedroom 3 11² x 11⁰

Covered Entry

Dining Room 11⁰ x 11⁴ 12'-0" HIGH CLG.

Bath

Garage 20⁵ x 22³

copyright © 1997 frank betz associates, inc.

GARAGE LOCATION WITH BASEMENT

Bayed Breakfast Room

Total Living Area: 1,915

- Large breakfast area overlooks vaulted great room
- Master suite has cheerful sitting room and a private bath
- Plan features unique in-law suite with private bath and walk-in closet
- 4 bedrooms, 3 baths, 2-car garage
- Walk-out basement, slab or crawl space foundation, please specify when ordering

Plan# **577-GSD-1748**

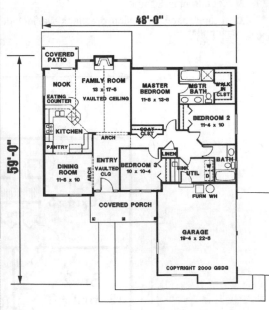

48'-0"

COVERED PATIO

NOOK

FAMILY ROOM 13 x 17-6 VAULTED CEILING

MASTER BEDROOM 11-8 x 13-8

MSTR BATH

WALK IN CLST

EATING COUNTER

KITCHEN

PANTRY

ARCH

COAT CLST

BEDROOM 2 11-4 x 10

59'-0"

DINING ROOM 11-6 x 10

ENTRY VAULTED CLG

ARCH

BEDROOM 3 10 x 10-4

LINEN

SINK

UTIL

W D

BATH

COVERED PORCH

FURN WH

GARAGE 19-4 x 22-8

COPYRIGHT 2000 GSDG

Cottage-Style Adds Charm

Total Living Area: 1,496

- Large utility room with sink and extra counterspace
- Covered patio off breakfast nook extends dining to the outdoors
- Eating counter in kitchen overlooks vaulted family room
- 3 bedrooms, 2 baths, 2-car side entry garage
- Crawl space foundation

RANCH

Dramatic Cathedral Ceilings

Total Living Area: 1,436

- Covered entry is inviting
- Kitchen has handy breakfast bar which overlooks great room and dining room
- Private master suite with bath and walk-in closet is separate from other bedrooms
- 3 bedrooms, 2 baths, 2-car garage
- Basement foundation

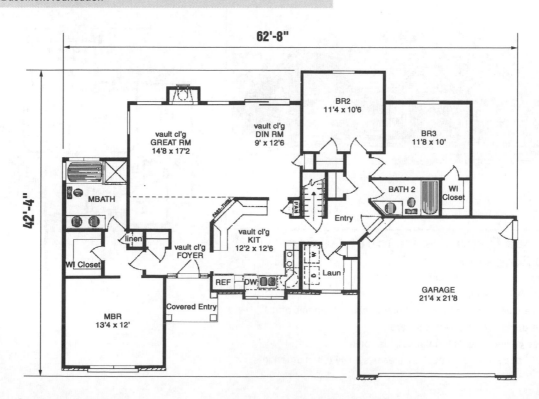

62'-8"

42'-4"

vault cl'g
GREAT RM
14'8 x 17'2

vault cl'g
DIN RM
9' x 12'6

BR2
11'4 x 10'6

BR3
11'8 x 10'

MBATH

Entry

BATH 2

WI Closet

linen

vault cl'g
KIT
12'2 x 12'6

vault cl'g
FOYER

WI Closet

REF DW

Laun

MBR
13'4 x 12'

Covered Entry

GARAGE
21'4 x 21'8

RANCH

67

Plan# 577-DBI-1748-19

Price Code C

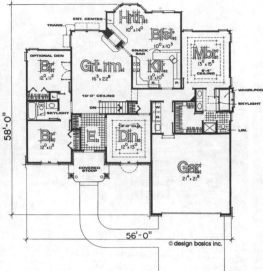

Whirlpool With Skylight Above

Total Living Area: 1,911

- Large entry opens into beautiful great room with angled see-through fireplace
- Terrific design includes kitchen and breakfast area with adjacent sunny bayed hearth room
- Private master suite with bath features skylight and walk-in closet
- 3 bedrooms, 2 baths, 2-car garage
- Basement foundation

Plan# 577-FD8166-L

Price Code C

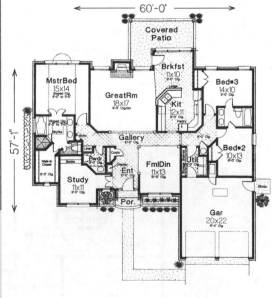

Covered Patio For Outdoor Dining

Total Living Area: 2,061

- Charming stone facade entry
- Centrally located great room
- Private study in the front of the home is ideal as a home office
- 3 bedrooms, 2 1/2 baths, 2-car garage
- Varied ceiling heights throughout this home
- Crawl space or slab foundation, please specify when ordering

© Michael E. Nelson
NELSON DESIGN GROUP,

Dining Area Ideal For Entertaining
Total Living Area: 1,381

- Plenty of closet space in all bedrooms
- Kitchen has large eating bar for extra dining
- Great room has a sunny wall of windows creating a cheerful atmosphere
- 3 bedrooms, 2 baths, 2-car garage
- Slab, crawl space, walk-out basement or basement foundation, please specify when ordering

TO ORDER SEE **PAGE 608** OR CALL TOLL-FREE 1-800-DREAM

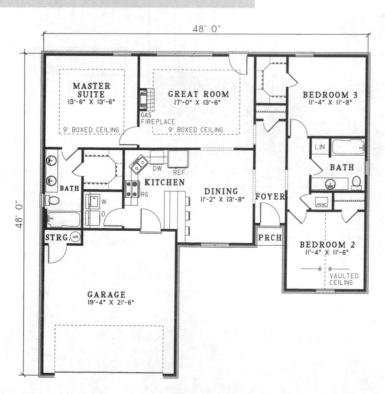

RANCH

69

Optional Second Floor

FUTURE GAMER'M 12'-8" X 24'-11"

First Floor 1,677 sq. ft.

Distinctive Stone And Stucco Facade

Total Living Area: 1,677

- Master suite has a secluded feel with a private and remote location from other bedrooms
- Great room is complete with fireplace and beautiful windows
- Bonus room on the second floor has an addtional 350 square feet of living area
- 3 bedrooms, 2 baths, 2-car side entry garage
- Slab foundation

Plan# 577-HDS-1558-2

Price Code C

Width: 52'-0"
Depth: 61'-6"

Rustic Styling With All The Comforts

Total Living Area: 1,885

- Enormous covered patio
- Dining and great rooms combine to create one large and versatile living area
- Utility room directly off kitchen for convenience
- 3 bedrooms, 2 baths, 2-car side entry garage
- Basement foundation

Traditional Elegance

Total Living Area: 1,945

- Large gathering room with corner fireplace and 12' high ceiling
- Master suite has a coffered ceiling and French door leading to the patio/deck
- Master bath has a cultured marble seat, separate shower and tub
- All bedrooms have walk-in closets
- 3 bedrooms, 2 baths, 2-car side entry garage
- Slab or crawl space foundation, please specify when ordering

TO ORDER SEE **PAGE 608** OR CALL TOLL-FREE 1-800-DREAM HOME (373-2646)

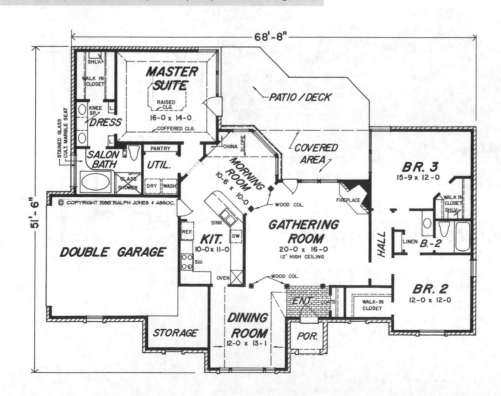

RANCH

71

Plan# **577-AP-1717**

Price Code B

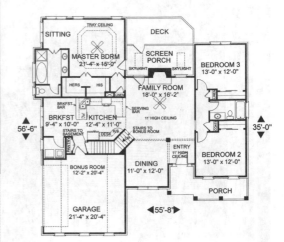

Uncommon Style With This Ranch

Total Living Area: 1,787

- Skylights brighten screened porch which connects to family room and deck outdoors
- Master bedroom features a comfortable sitting area, large private bath and direct access to screened porch
- Kitchen has serving bar which extends dining into family room
- 3 bedrooms, 2 baths, 2-car side entry garage
- Basement, crawl space or slab foundation, please specify when ordering

Plan# **577-JA-51394**

Price Code B

Lots Of Windows In Great Room

Total Living Area: 1,508

- A spacious kitchen layout makes food preparation easy
- A vaulted entry is inviting
- Varied ceiling heights throughout
- 3 bedrooms, 2 baths, 2-car garage
- Basement foundation

RANCH

TO ORDER SEE **PAGE 608** OR CALL TOLL-FREE 1-800-DREAM HOME (373-2646)

Great Room Forms Core Of This Home

Total Living Area: 2,076

- Vaulted great room has fireplace flanked by windows and skylights that welcome the sun
- Kitchen leads to vaulted breakfast room and rear deck
- Study located off foyer provides great location for home office
- Large bay windows grace master bedroom and bath
- 3 bedrooms, 2 baths, 2-car garage
- Basement foundation

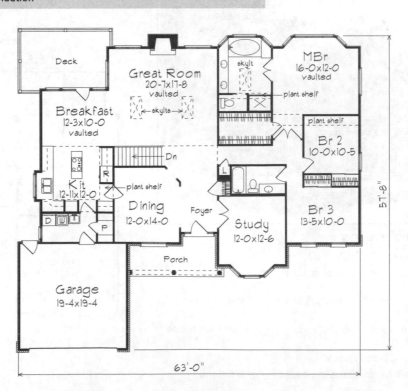

RANCH

Ranch-Style Home With Many Extras

Total Living Area: 1,295

- Wrap-around porch is a lovely place for dining
- A fireplace gives a stunning focal point to the great room that is heightened with a sloped ceiling
- The master suite is full of luxurious touches such as a walk-in closet and a lush private bath
- 2 bedrooms, 2 baths, 2-car garage
- Basement foundation

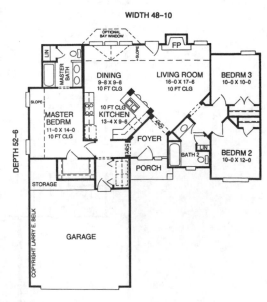

High Impact Angles

Total Living Area: 1,282

- Angled entry creates the illusion of space making home appear larger
- Dining room located off kitchen serves both formal and informal occasions
- Master bedroom has walk-in closet and private bath with whirlpool/ shower combination
- 3 bedrooms, 2 baths, 2-car garage
- Crawl space or slab foundation, please specify when ordering

RANCH

© 2003, Garrell Associates, Inc.

Open And Airy Grand Room

Total Living Area: 2,111

- 9' ceilings throughout first floor
- Formal dining room has columns separating it from other areas while allowing it to maintain an open feel
- Master bedroom has privacy from other bedrooms
- Bonus room on the second floor has an additional 345 square feet of living area
- 3 bedrooms, 2 baths, 2-car side entry garage
- Basement foundation

TO ORDER SEE PAGE 608 OR CALL TOLL-FREE 1-800-DREAM HOME (373-2646)

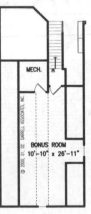

Optional Second Floor

BONUS ROOM
10'-10" x 26'-11"

MECH.

© 2000, 01, 02 GARRELL ASSOCIATES, INC.

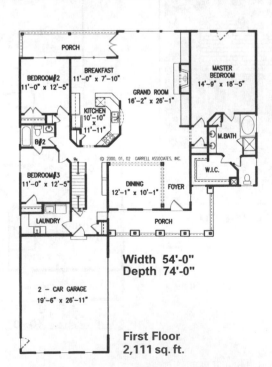

PORCH

BEDROOM#2
11'-0" x 12'-5"

BREAKFAST
11'-0" x 7'-10"

GRAND ROOM
16'-2" x 26'-1"

MASTER BEDROOM
14'-9" x 18'-5"

KITCHEN
10'-10" x 11'-11"

B#2

M.BATH

BEDROOM#3
11'-0" x 12'-5"

© 2000, 01, 02 GARRELL ASSOCIATES, INC.

DINING
12'-1" x 10'-1"

FOYER

W.I.C.

LAUNDRY

PORCH

Width 54'-0"
Depth 74'-0"

2 – CAR GARAGE
19'-6" x 26'-11"

First Floor
2,111 sq. ft.

RANCH

75

Formal Country Charm

Total Living Area: 1,325

- Sloped ceiling and a fireplace in living area creates a cozy feeling
- Formal dining and breakfast areas have an efficiently designed kitchen between them
- Master bedroom has walk-in closet with luxurious private bath
- 3 bedrooms, 2 baths, 2-car drive under garage
- Basement foundation

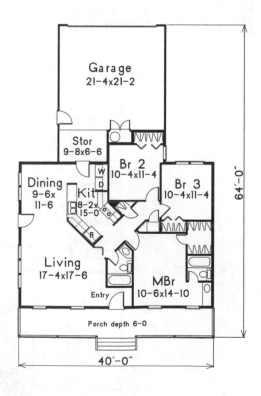

Compact, Convenient And Charming

Total Living Area: 1,266

- Narrow frontage is perfect for small lots
- Energy efficient home with 2" x 6" exterior walls
- A central hall provides a convenient connection for all main rooms
- Design incorporates full-size master bedroom complete with dressing room, bath and walk-in closet
- Kitchen has handy laundry facilities
- 3 bedrooms, 2 baths, 2-car rear entry garage
- Crawl space foundation, drawings also include slab foundation

RANCH

TO ORDER SEE **PAGE 608** OR CALL TOLL-FREE 1-800-DREAM HOME (373-2646)

Full Windows Grace Family Room

Total Living Area: 2,558

- 9' ceilings throughout home
- Angled counter in kitchen serves breakfast and family rooms
- Entry foyer flanked by formal living and dining rooms
- Garage includes storage space
- 4 bedrooms, 3 baths, 2-car side entry garage
- Slab foundation, drawings also include crawl space foundation

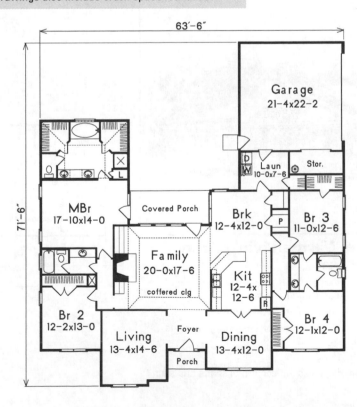

RANCH

Plan# 577-0400

Price Code C

Inviting And Cozy Covered Arched Entry

Total Living Area: 1,923

- Foyer opens into large living room with fireplace and view of covered porch
- Kitchen has a walk-in pantry next to laundry area and breakfast room
- All bedrooms feature walk-in closets
- Master bedroom includes unique angled bath with walk-in closet
- 3 bedrooms, 2 baths, 2-car garage
- Slab foundation

Plan# 577-0225

Price Code A

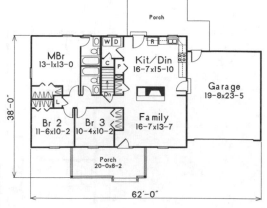

Central Fireplace Warms Living Area

Total Living Area: 1,260

- Spacious kitchen and dining area features large pantry, storage area, easy access to garage and laundry room
- Pleasant covered front porch adds a practical touch
- Master bedroom with a private bath adjoins two other bedrooms, all with plenty of closet space
- 3 bedrooms, 2 baths, 2-car garage
- Basement foundation, drawings also include crawl space and slab foundations

Attractive Styling
Total Living Area: 1,791

- Dining area has 10' high sloped ceiling
- Kitchen opens to large living room with fireplace and access onto a covered porch
- Master suite features private bath, double walk-in closets and whirlpool tub
- 3 bedrooms, 2 baths, 2-car garage
- Slab or crawl space foundation, please specify when ordering

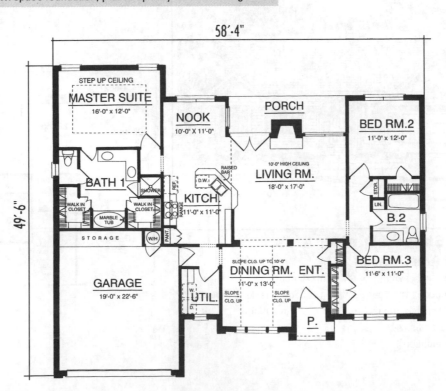

TO ORDER SEE **PAGE 608** OR CALL TOLL-FREE 1-800-DREAM HOME (373-2646)

RANCH

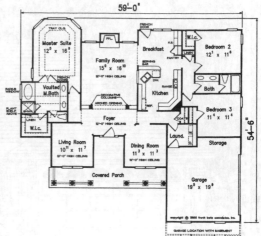

Impressive Foyer

Total Living Area: 1,856

- Beautiful covered porch creates a Southern accent
- Kitchen has an organized feel with lots of cabinetry
- Large foyer has a grand entrance and leads into family room through columns and arched opening
- 3 bedrooms, 2 baths, 2-car side entry garage
- Walk-out basement, crawl space or slab foundation, please specify when ordering

© Urban Design Group, Inc.

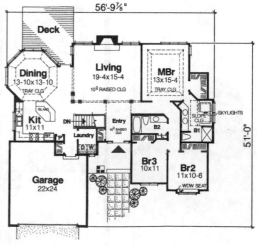

Octagon-Shaped Dining Area

Total Living Area: 1,753

- Sloped ceiling and skylights brighten master bath
- Living room flooded with sunlight from windows flanking fireplace
- Kitchen has large island ideal for workspace or dining
- 3 bedrooms, 2 baths, 2-car garage
- Basement foundation

RANCH

Central Living Area
Total Living Area: 1,546

- Spacious, open rooms create a casual atmosphere
- Master suite secluded for privacy
- Dining room features large bay window
- Kitchen and dinette combine for added space and include access to the outdoors
- Large laundry room includes convenient sink
- 3 bedrooms, 2 baths, 2-car garage
- Basement foundation

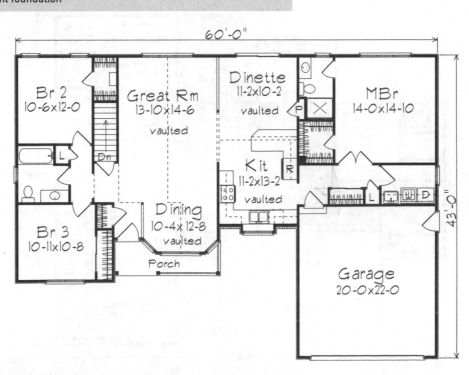

60'-0"

Br 2
10-6x12-0

Great Rm
13-10x14-6
vaulted

Dinette
11-2x10-2
vaulted

MBr
14-0x14-10

Kit
11-2x13-2
vaulted

Dining
10-4x12-8
vaulted

Br 3
10-11x10-8

Porch

43'-0"

Garage
20-0x22-0

RANCH

81

Inviting Vaulted Entry

Total Living Area: 2,097

- Angled kitchen, family room and eating area adds interest to this home
- Family room includes a T.V. niche making this a cozy place to relax
- Sumptuous master suite includes sitting area, walk-in closet and a full bath with double vanities
- 3 bedrooms, 3 baths, 3-car side entry garage
- Crawl space or slab foundation, please specify when ordering

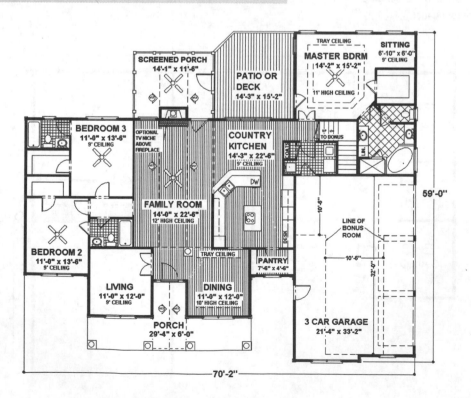

RANCH

Open And Spacious Feel To This Home

Total Living Area: 1,611

- Sliding doors lead to a delightful screened porch creating a wonderful summer retreat
- Master bedroom has a lavishly appointed dressing room and large walk-in closet
- The kitchen offers an abundance of cabinets and counter space with convenient access to the laundry room and garage
- 3 bedrooms, 2 baths, 2-car side entry garage
- Basement foundation

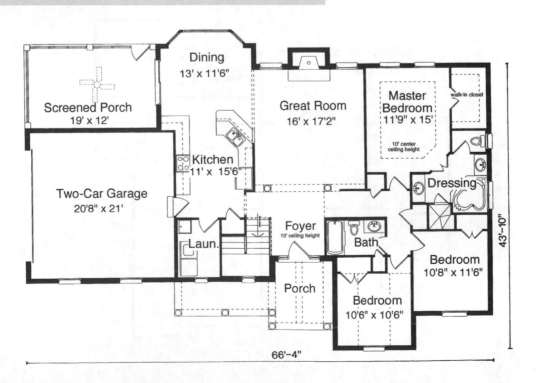

RANCH

Vaulted Rear Porch

Total Living Area: 1,849

- Open floor plan creates an airy feeling
- Kitchen and breakfast area include center island, pantry and built-in desk
- Master bedroom has private entrance off breakfast area and a view of vaulted porch
- 3 bedrooms, 2 baths, 2-car garage
- Crawl space or slab foundation, please specify when ordering

Width: 66'-5"
Depth: 60'-0"

RANCH

Modest Farmhouse Ranch

Total Living Area: 1,480

- Split bedroom floor plan has private master bedroom with large bath and walk-in closet
- Fabulous great room features 11' high step ceiling, fireplace and media center
- Floor plan designed to be fully accessible for handicapped
- 3 bedrooms, 2 baths, 2-car side entry garage
- Basement, crawl space or slab foundation, please specify when ordering

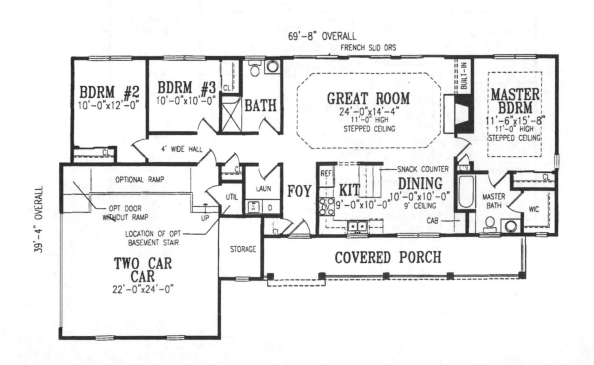

RANCH

Unique Three-Way Fireplace

Total Living Area: 2,126

- Elegant bay windows in master bedroom welcome the sun
- Double vanities in master bath separated by large whirlpool tub
- 3 bedrooms, 2 baths, 2-car side entry garage
- Slab foundation

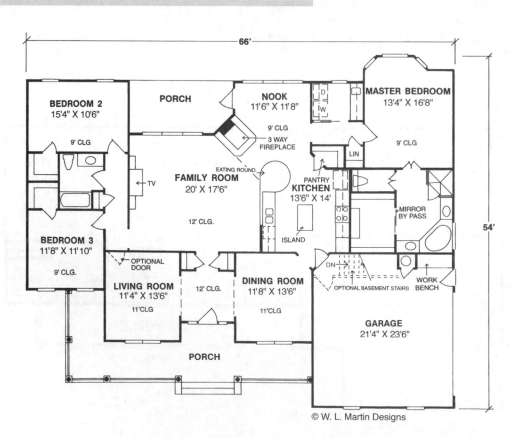

66'

54'

BEDROOM 2
15'4" X 10'6"
9' CLG

PORCH

NOOK
11'6" X 11'8"

9' CLG

3 WAY FIREPLACE

D
W

MASTER BEDROOM
13'4" X 16'8"
9' CLG

LIN

EATING ROUND

FAMILY ROOM
20' X 17'6"

12' CLG.

TV

PANTRY

KITCHEN
13'6" X 14'

ISLAND

MIRROR BY PASS

BEDROOM 3
11'8" X 11'10"
9' CLG.

OPTIONAL DOOR

LIVING ROOM
11'4" X 13'6"
11'CLG

12' CLG.

DINING ROOM
11'8" X 13'6"
11'CLG

DN

OPTIONAL BASEMENT STAIRS

WORK BENCH

GARAGE
21'4" X 23'6"

PORCH

© W. L. Martin Designs

TO ORDER SEE PAGE 608 OR CALL TOLL-FREE 1-800-

HOME (373-2646)

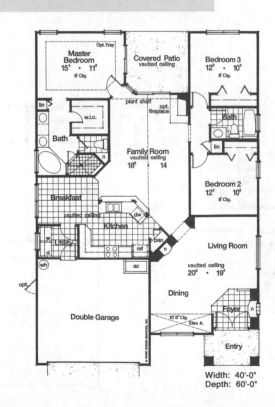

Decorative Accents Highlight Facade

Total Living Area: 1,768

- Uniquely designed living/dining room combination with vaulted ceiling makes great use of space
- Informal family room has vaulted ceiling plant shelf accents and kitchen overlook
- Sunny breakfast area conveniently accesses kitchen
- 3 bedrooms, 2 baths, 2-car garage
- Slab foundation

Master Bedroom
15⁴ · 11⁰
8' Clg.

Opt. Tray

Covered Patio
vaulted ceiling

Bedroom 3
12⁰ · 10⁰
8' Clg.

lin

w.i.c.

plant shelf

opt. fireplace

Bath

Bath

lin

Family Room
vaulted ceiling
18⁸   14

Breakfast

Bedroom 2
12⁰ · 10⁰
8' Clg.

vaulted ceiling

Kitchen

dw

pan

w
Utility
d

ref

Living Room

pan

wh

ac

vaulted ceiling
20⁸ · 19⁴

opt

Dining

Double Garage

10' 8" Clg.

Foyer

Elev. A.

Entry

Width: 40'-0"
Depth: 60'-0"

RANCH

87

Fabulous Curb Appeal

Total Living Area: 1,588

- ■ Workshop in garage ideal for storage and projects
- ■ 12' vaulted master suite has his and hers closets as well as a lovely bath with bayed soaking tub and compartmentalized shower and toilet area
- ■ Lovely arched entry to 14' vaulted great room that flows open to the dining room and sky-lit kitchen
- ■ 3 bedrooms, 2 baths, 2-car garage
- ■ Basement foundation

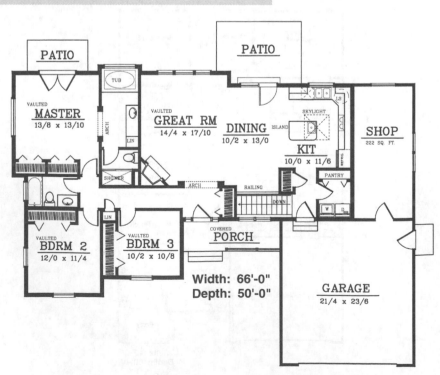

PATIO

PATIO

VAULTED
MASTER
13/8 x 13/10

TUB

VAULTED
GREAT RM
14/4 x 17/10

DINING
10/2 x 13/0

ISLAND

SKYLIGHT

SHOP
222 SQ. FT.

ARCH

LIN

KIT
10/0 x 11/6

REFRIG.

PANTRY

SHOWER

ARCH

RAILING

DOWN

LIN

VAULTED
BDRM 2
12/0 x 11/4

VAULTED
BDRM 3
10/2 x 10/8

COVERED
PORCH

W   D

Width: 66'-0"
Depth: 50'-0"

GARAGE
21/4 x 23/6

RANCH

TO ORDER SEE **PAGE 608** OR CALL TOLL-FREE 1-800-DRE...

Open Ranch Gives Expansive Look

Total Living Area: 1,630

- Crisp facade and full windows front and back offer open viewing
- Wrap-around rear deck is accessible from breakfast room, dining room and master bedroom
- Vaulted ceiling in living room and master bedroom
- Sitting area and large walk-in closet complement master bedroom
- 3 bedrooms, 2 baths, 2-car garage
- Basement foundation

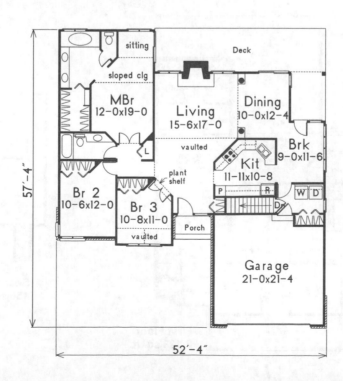

RANCH

Expansive Counter Space

Total Living Area: 2,123

- Energy efficient home with 2" x 6" exterior walls
- Living room has wood burning fireplace, built-in bookshelves and a wet bar
- Skylights make the sunporch bright and comfortable
- 3 bedrooms, 2 1/2 baths, 2-car side entry garage
- Crawl space, slab or basement foundation, please specify when ordering

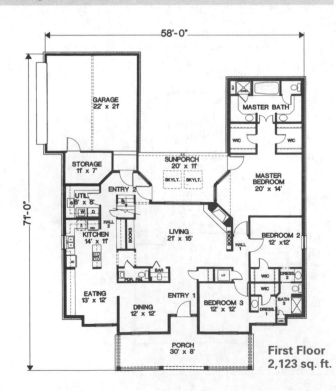

First Floor
2,123 sq. ft.

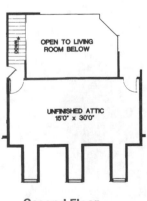

Second Floor
450 sq. ft.

Ranch Style Combines Brick And Siding

Total Living Area: 1,802

- Massive storage area at rear of garage could easily be converted to a workshop
- Classic foyer leads to large great room with cathedral ceiling and centered fireplace
- Master bath features double vanity and separate shower and tub
- 3 bedrooms, 2 baths, 2-car garage
- Basement foundation

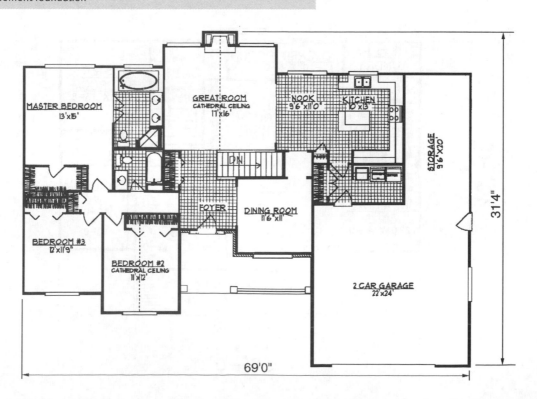

RANCH

Traditional Southern Style Home
Total Living Area: 1,785

- 9' ceilings throughout home
- Luxurious master bath includes whirlpool tub and separate shower
- Cozy breakfast area is convenient to kitchen
- 3 bedrooms, 3 baths, 2-car detached garage
- Basement, crawl space or slab foundation, please specify when ordering

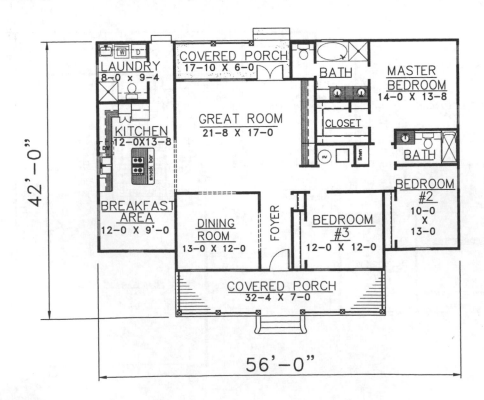

RANCH

Formal Facade

Total Living Area: 1,890

- 10' ceilings give this home a spacious feel
- Efficient kitchen has breakfast bar which overlooks living room
- Master bedroom has a private bath with walk-in closet
- 3 bedrooms, 2 baths, 2-car side entry garage
- Crawl space or slab foundation, please specify when ordering

WIDTH 65–10

MASTER BATH

PORCH

BRKFST RM
10-8 X 11-8
10 FT CLG

UTIL
8-0 X 5-8

STORAGE

STORAGE

DEPTH 53–5

MASTER BEDRM
14-4 X 15-6
10 FT CLG

FP

LIVING ROOM
17-4 X 15-8
10 FT CLG

KITCHEN
10-8 X 13-6
10 FT CLG

GARAGE

BUILT INS

BATH 2

LIN

BEDROOM 2
12-6 X 11-6

FOYER
10 FT CLG

BEDROOM 3
12-0 X 13-4
10 FT CLG

DINING ROOM
11-0 X 13-0
10 FT COFFERED CLG

PAN

COPYRIGHT LARRY E. BELK

PORCH

RANCH

93

Country Living At Its Finest

Total Living Area: 1,993

- Kitchen and nook share open view onto the covered porch
- Ample-sized secondary bedrooms
- Well-designed master bath
- 3 bedrooms, 2 baths, 2-car side entry garage
- Slab foundation

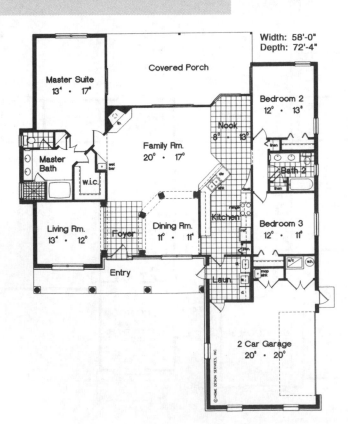

Width: 58'-0"
Depth: 72'-4"

RANCH

TO ORDER SEE **PAGE 608** OR CALL TOLL-FREE 1-800-DREAM HOME (373-2646)

Country Ranch With Wrap-Around Porch

Total Living Area: 1,541

- Dining area offers access to a screened porch for outdoor dining and entertaining
- Country kitchen features a center island and a breakfast bay for casual meals
- Great room is warmed by a woodstove
- 3 bedrooms, 2 baths, 2 car garage
- Basement or crawl space foundation, please specify when ordering

Width: 87'-0"
Depth: 39'-0"

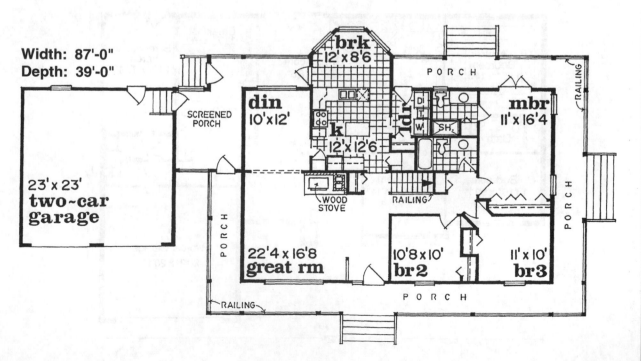

RANCH

Sloped Ceilings Throughout

Total Living Area: 1,782

- Outstanding breakfast area accesses the outdoors through French doors
- Generous counter space and cabinets combine to create an ideal kitchen
- The master bedroom is enhanced with a beautiful bath featuring a whirlpool tub and double-bowl vanity
- 3 bedrooms, 2 baths, 2-car garage
- Basement foundation

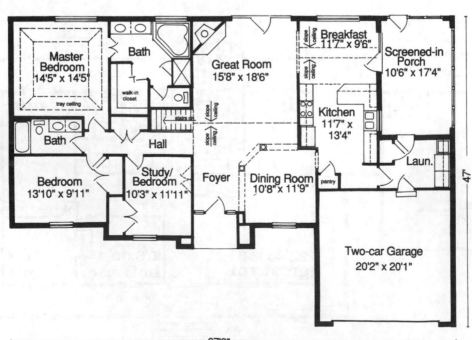

Master Bedroom 14'5" x 14'5"
tray ceiling

Bath

walk-in closet

Bath

Bedroom 13'10" x 9'11"

Study/ Bedroom 10'3" x 11'11"

Hall

stairs dn.

Great Room 15'8" x 18'6"

slope ceiling

Breakfast 11'7" x 9'6"
slope ceiling

Screened-in Porch 10'6" x 17'4"

Kitchen 11'7" x 13'4"

Laun.

Foyer

Dining Room 10'8" x 11'9"

pantry

Two-car Garage 20'2" x 20'1"

47'

67'2"

RANCH

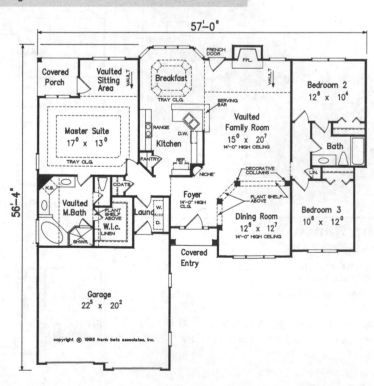

Elaborate Dining Room

Total Living Area: 1,779

- Well-designed floor plan has vaulted family room with fireplace and access to the outdoors
- Decorative columns separate dining area from foyer
- Vaulted ceiling adds spaciousness in master bath with walk-in closet
- 3 bedrooms, 2 baths, 2-car garage
- Walk-out basement, slab or crawl space foundation, please specify when ordering

RANCH

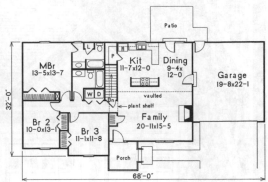

Spacious And Open Family Living Area

Total Living Area: 1,416

- Family room includes fireplace, elevated plant shelf and vaulted ceiling
- Patio is accessible from dining area and garage
- Centrally located laundry area
- Oversized walk-in pantry
- 3 bedrooms, 2 baths, 2-car garage
- Basement foundation, drawings also include crawl space and slab foundations

---

Plan# 577-0729

Price Code D

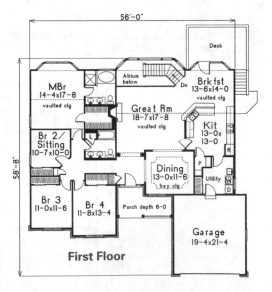

First Floor

Gracious Atrium Ranch

Total Living Area: 2,218

- Vaulted great room has an arched colonade entry, bay windowed atrium with staircase and a fireplace
- Vaulted kitchen enjoys bay doors to deck, pass-through breakfast bar and walk-in pantry
- Breakfast room offers bay window and snack bar open to kitchen
- Atrium open to 1,217 square feet of optional living area below
- 4 bedrooms, 2 baths, 2-car garage
- Walk-out basement foundation

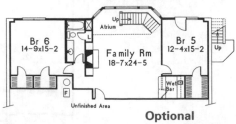

Optional Lower Level

Country Flair

Total Living Area: 1,675

- Country flair gives this home curb appeal
- Spacious laundry room is located off master bedroom
- Cathedral ceiling in living area
- Alternate floor plan design includes handicap accessibility that is 100% ADA compliant
- 3 bedrooms, 2 baths, 2-car side entry garage
- Crawl space or slab foundation, please specify when ordering

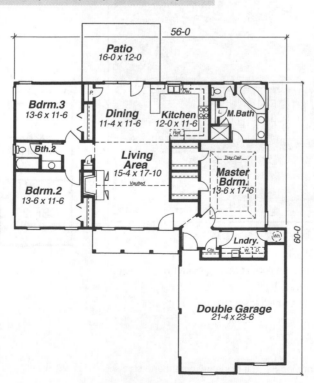

RANCH

Plan# 577-VL1267

Price Code A

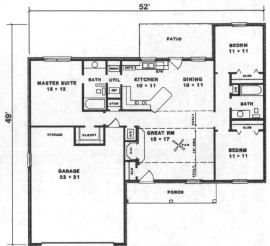

Stylish Ranch

Total Living Area: 1,267

- 10' vaulted ceiling in great room
- Open floor plan creates spacious feeling
- Master bedroom separated from other bedrooms for privacy
- 3 bedrooms, 2 baths, 2-car garage
- Slab or crawl space foundation, please specify when ordering

Plan# 577-0534

Price Code A

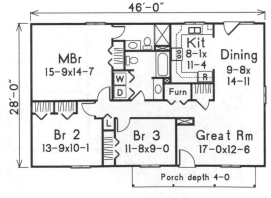

Peaceful Shaded Front Porch

Total Living Area: 1,288

- Kitchen, dining area and great room join creating open living
- Master bedroom includes private bath
- Secondary bedrooms include ample closet space
- Hall bath features convenient laundry closet
- Dining room accesses the outdoors
- 3 bedrooms, 2 baths
- Crawl space foundation, drawings also include basement and slab foundations

TO ORDER SEE **PAGE 608** OR CALL TOLL-FREE 1-800-DREAM HOME (373-2646)

Old-Fashioned Comfort And Privacy

Total Living Area: 1,772

- Extended porches in front and rear provide a charming touch
- Large bay windows lend distinction to dining room and bedroom #3
- Efficient U-shaped kitchen
- Master bedroom includes two walk-in closets
- Full corner fireplace in family room
- 3 bedrooms, 2 baths, 2-car detached garage
- Slab foundation, drawings also include crawl space foundation

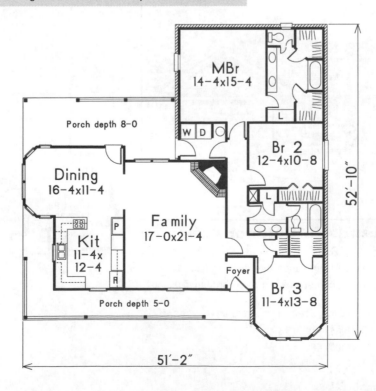

Porch depth 8-0

MBr
14-4x15-4

W D

Dining
16-4x11-4

Br 2
12-4x10-8

L

Family
17-0x21-4

P

Kit
11-4x
12-4

R

Foyer

Br 3
11-4x13-8

Porch depth 5-0

52'-10"

51'-2"

RANCH

Plan# 577-CHD-20-50

Price Code C

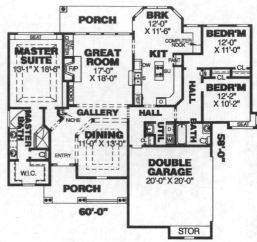

Lattice Is An Uncommon Touch

Total Living Area: 2,080

- Gallery hall creates a grand entrance into the great room
- Computer nook located in breakfast room is a functional living area
- A window seat in one of the secondary bedrooms adds enjoyment
- Built-in entertainment center and bookshelves make relaxing a breeze in the great room
- 3 bedrooms, 2 baths, 2-car side entry garage
- Basement, crawl space or slab foundation, please specify when ordering

Plan# 577-0272

Price Code A

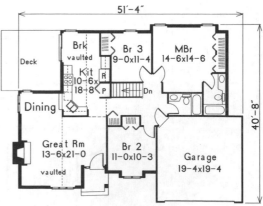

Corner Deck Lends To Outdoor Area

Total Living Area: 1,283

- Vaulted breakfast room with sliding doors that open onto deck
- Kitchen features convenient corner sink and pass-through to dining room
- Open living atmosphere in dining area and great room
- Vaulted great room features a fireplace
- 3 bedrooms, 2 baths, 2-car garage
- Basement foundation

RANCH

TO ORDER SEE **PAGE 608** OR CALL TOLL-FREE 1-800-DREAM HOME (373-2646)

Excellent Ranch For Country Setting
Total Living Area: 2,758

- Vaulted great room excels with fireplace, wet bar, plant shelves and skylights
- Fabulous master suite enjoys a fireplace, large bath, walk-in closet and vaulted ceiling
- Trendsetting kitchen and breakfast room adjoin spacious screened porch
- Convenient office near kitchen is perfect for computer room, hobby enthusiast or fifth bedroom
- 4 bedrooms, 2 1/2 baths, 3-car side entry garage
- Basement foundation

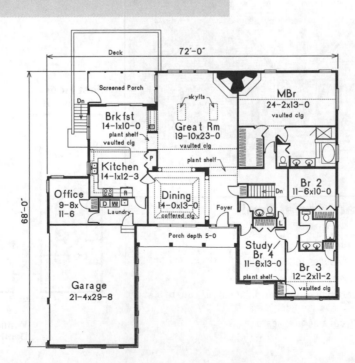

RANCH

Plan# 577-HDS-1806

Price Code C

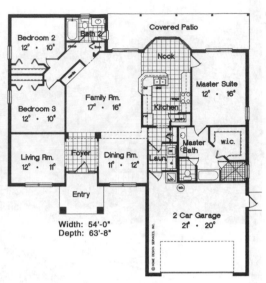

Width: 54'-0"
Depth: 63'-8"

Trio Of Dormers Adds Curb Appeal

Total Living Area: 1,806

- Covered porch in the rear of the home adds an outdoor living area
- Private and formal living room
- Kitchen has snack counter that extends into family room
- 3 bedrooms, 2 baths, 2-car garage
- Slab foundation

Plan# 577-MG-02236

Price Code G

© 2003, Garrell Associates, Inc.

Optional Second Floor

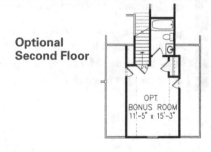

OPT. BONUS ROOM
11'-5" x 15'-3"

First Floor
1,985 sq. ft.

Width 54'-0"
Depth 54'-0"
© 2003 GARRELL ASSOCIATES, INC.

Ranch With Traditional Feel

Total Living Area: 1,985

- 9' ceilings throughout home
- Master suite has direct access into sunroom
- Sunny breakfast room features bay window
- Bonus room on the second floor has an additional 191 square feet of living area
- 3 bedrooms, 3 baths, 2-car side entry garage
- Slab foundation

RANCH

TO ORDER SEE **PAGE 608** OR CALL TOLL-FREE 1-800-DREAM HOME (373-2646)

Traditional Ranch With Extras

Total Living Area: 1,771

- Den has sloped ceiling and charming window seat
- Private master bedroom has access outdoors
- Central kitchen allows for convenient access when entertaining
- 2 bedrooms, 2 baths, 2-car garage
- Basement, crawl space or slab foundation, please specify when ordering

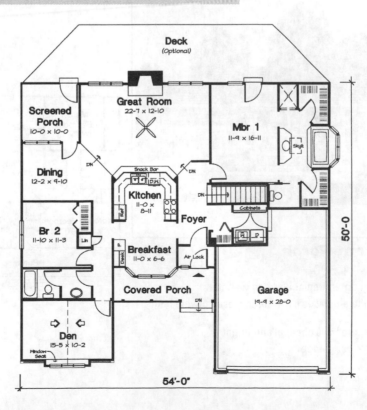

Deck
(Optional)

Great Room
22-7 x 12-10

Screened Porch
10-0 x 10-0

Mbr 1
11-9 x 16-11

Skylt

Dining
12-2 x 9-10

DN

DN

Snack Bar

Kitchen
11-0 x 8-11

DN

Cabinets

Br 2
11-10 x 11-3

Foyer

Lin

Desk P.

Breakfast
11-0 x 6-6

Air Lock

Covered Porch

Garage
19-9 x 28-0

50'-0"

Den
15-5 x 10-2

Window Seat

DN

54'-0"

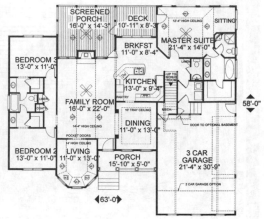

Arches Add Drama To Facade

Total Living Area: 1,982

- Large screened porch creates a great casual living area and connects to a covered deck leading into the master suite
- Dramatic formal living room has a sunny bay window and high ceilings
- Master suite has a private sitting area as well as a private luxury-filled bath
- 3 bedrooms, 2 1/2 baths, 3-car side entry garage
- Basement, crawl space or slab foundation, please specify when ordering

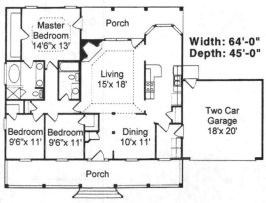

Full-Length Front Porch

Total Living Area: 1,500

- Living room features corner fireplace adding warmth
- Master suite has all the amenities like walk-in closet, private bath and porch access
- Sunny bayed breakfast room is cheerful and bright
- 3 bedrooms, 2 baths, 2-car garage
- Slab foundation

RANCH

TO ORDER SEE **PAGE 608** OR CALL TOLL-FREE 1-800-DREAM HOME (373-2646)

Terrific Master Suite Provides Escape

Total Living Area: 2,517

- Energy efficient home with 2" x 6" exterior walls
- Central living room with large windows and attractive transoms
- Varied ceiling heights throughout home
- Secluded master suite features double-door entry, luxurious bath with separate shower, step-up whirlpool tub, double vanities and walk-in closets
- Kitchen with walk-in pantry overlooks large family room with fireplace and unique octagon-shaped breakfast room
- 4 bedrooms, 2 1/2 baths, 2-car garage
- Slab foundation, drawings also include crawl space foundation

RANCH

Plan# 577-CHP-1732-A-101

Price Code B

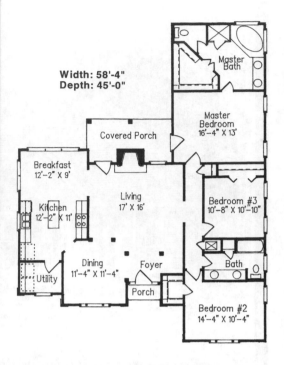

Width: 58'-4"
Depth: 45'-0"

Open Ranch Living

Total Living Area: 1,704

- ■ Open floor plan combines foyer, dining and living rooms together for an open airy feeling
- ■ Kitchen has island that adds workspace and storage
- ■ Bedrooms are situated together and secluded from the rest of the home
- ■ 3 bedrooms, 2 baths
- ■ Slab foundation

Plan# 577-DL-16653L1

Price Code B

Width: 50'-0"
Depth: 55'-0"

Quaint Box Window Seat

Total Living Area: 1,665

- ■ Oversized family room has corner fireplace and double-doors leading to patio
- ■ Bedroom locations give privacy from gathering areas
- ■ 3 bedrooms, 2 baths, 2-car garage
- ■ Slab foundation

RANCH

Plan# 577-FB-1132

Price Code A

Ranch Style With Many Extras

Total Living Area: 1,342

- 9' ceilings throughout this home
- Master suite has tray ceiling and wall of windows that overlook backyard
- Dining room includes serving bar connecting it to the kitchen and sliding glass doors that lead outdoors
- 3 bedrooms, 2 baths, 2-car garage
- Optional second floor has an additional 350 square feet of living area
- Slab, walk-out basement or crawl space foundation, please specify when ordering

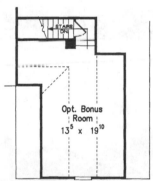

**Optional
Second Floor**

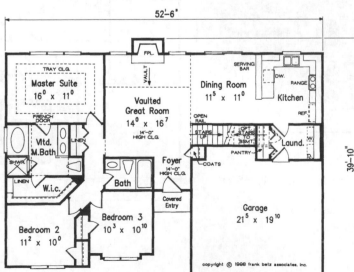

**First Floor
1,342 sq. ft.**

RANCH

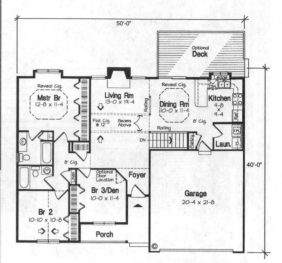

Lots Of Details In This Modest Ranch

Total Living Area: 1,312

- A beamed ceiling and fireplace create an exciting feel to the living room
- Box window behind double sink in kitchen is a nice added feature
- Private bath and generous closet space in the master bedroom
- 3 bedrooms, 2 baths, 2-car garage
- Basement or crawl space foundation, please specify when ordering

Plan# **577-JA-59195**   **Price Code B**

Superb Ranch Style

Total Living Area: 1,739

- Cheerful and bright living room has an open, airy feel with lots of windows and a cathedral ceiling
- Two secondary bedrooms have direct access to a jack and jill bath
- U-shaped kitchen has an adjacent dining room
- 3 bedrooms, 2 1/2 baths, 2-car garage
- Basement foundation

RANCH

TO ORDER SEE **PAGE 608** OR CALL TOLL-FREE 1-800-DREAM HOME (373-2646)

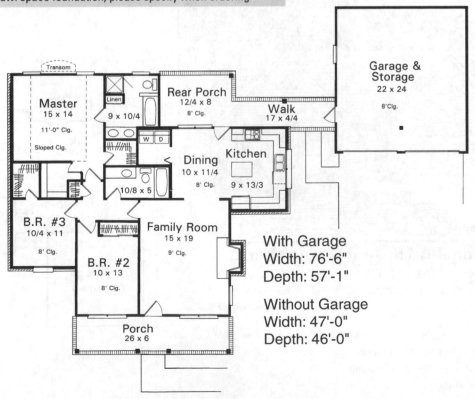

Covered Breezeway To Garage

Total Living Area: 1,406

- Master bedroom has a sloped ceiling
- Kitchen and dining area merge becoming a gathering place
- Enter family room from charming covered front porch and find fireplace and lots of windows
- 3 bedrooms, 2 baths, 2-car detached garage
- Slab or crawl space foundation, please specify when ordering

Transom

Master
15 x 14
11'-0" Clg.
Sloped Clg.

Linen
9 x 10/4

Rear Porch
12/4 x 8
8' Clg.

Walk
17 x 4/4

Garage &
Storage
22 x 24
8' Clg.

W D

Dining
10 x 11/4
8' Clg.

Kitchen
9 x 13/3

10/8 x 5

B.R. #3
10/4 x 11
8' Clg.

Family Room
15 x 19
9' Clg.

B.R. #2
10 x 13
8' Clg.

Porch
26 x 6

With Garage
Width: 76'-6"
Depth: 57'-1"

Without Garage
Width: 47'-0"
Depth: 46'-0"

RANCH

111

Plan # 577-AX-97359

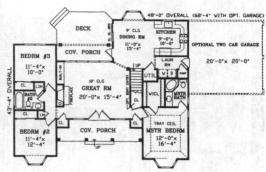

Symmetrical Design Pleasing To The Eye

Total Living Area: 1,380

- Built-in bookshelves flank fireplace in great room
- Lots of storage space near laundry room and kitchen
- Covered porch has views of the backyard
- 3 bedrooms, 2 baths, optional 2-car side entry garage
- Basement, crawl space or slab foundation, please specify when ordering

Plan # 577-0670

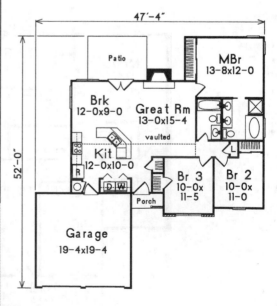

Traditional Brick And Siding Home

Total Living Area: 1,170

- Master bedroom enjoys privacy at the rear of this home
- Kitchen has angled bar that overlooks great room and breakfast area
- Living areas combine to create a greater sense of spaciousness
- Great room has a cozy fireplace
- 3 bedrooms, 2 baths, 2-car garage
- Slab foundation

RANCH

TO ORDER SEE **PAGE 608** OR CALL TOLL-FREE 1-800-DREAM HOME (373-2646)

© HOME DESIGN SERVICES, INC.

J.N. HANSEN FEL.

Stately And Functional Family Room

Total Living Area: 1,783

- Formal living and dining rooms in the front of the home
- Kitchen overlooks breakfast area
- Convenient laundry area near kitchen and master bedroom
- 3 bedrooms, 2 baths, 2-car garage
- Slab foundation

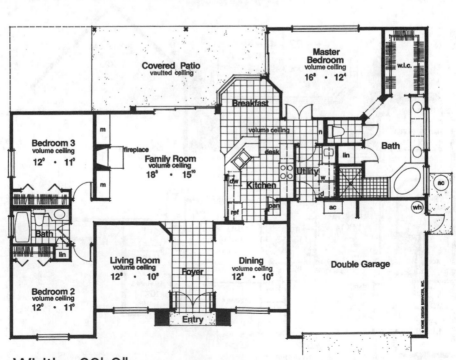

Width: 60'-0"
Depth: 45'-0"

RANCH

113

Double Bays Accent Front

Total Living Area: 2,529

- Kitchen and breakfast area are located between the family and living rooms for easy access
- Master bedroom includes sitting area, private bath and access to covered patio
- 4 bedrooms, 3 baths, 3-car side entry garage
- Slab foundation

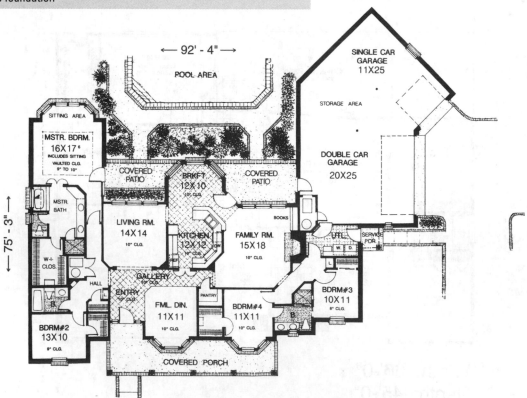

RANCH

© Michael E. Nelson
NELSON DESIGN GROUP, LLC

Attractive Exterior

Total Living Area: 2,107

■ Master bedroom is separate from other bedrooms for privacy

■ Spacious breakfast room and kitchen include center island with eating space

■ Centralized great room has fireplace and easy access to any area in the home

■ 4 bedrooms, 2 1/2 baths, 2-car garage

■ Crawl space, basement, walk-out basement or slab foundation, please specify when ordering

RANCH

Corner Fireplace In Great Room

Total Living Area: 1,642

- Built-in cabinet in dining room adds a custom feel
- Secondary bedrooms share an oversized bath
- Master bedroom includes private bath with dressing table
- 3 bedrooms, 2 baths, 2-car garage
- Basement, crawl space or slab foundation, please specify when ordering

Optional Basement Stairs

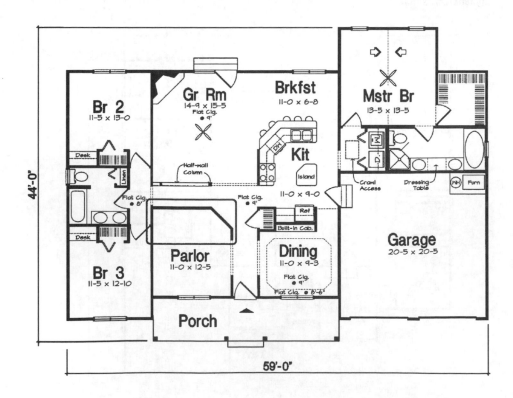

RANCH

TO ORDER SEE **PAGE 608** OR CALL TOLL-FREE 1-800-DREAM HOME (373-2646)

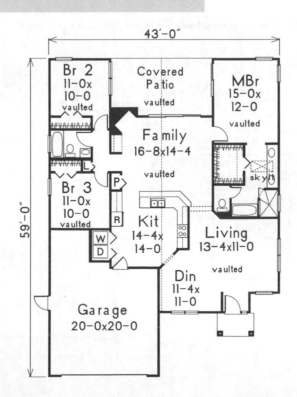

Vaulted Ceilings Add Dimension

Total Living Area: 1,550

- Cozy corner fireplace provides focal point in family room
- Master bedroom features large walk-in closet, skylight and separate tub and shower
- Convenient laundry closet
- Kitchen with pantry and breakfast bar connects to family room
- Family room and master bedroom access covered patio
- 3 bedrooms, 2 baths, 2 car garage
- Slab foundation

43'-0"

59'-0"

Br 2
11-0x
10-0
vaulted

Covered
Patio
vaulted

MBr
15-0x
12-0
vaulted

Family
16-8x14-4
vaulted

sky lt

Br 3
11-0x
10-0
vaulted

P

R

Kit
14-4x
14-0

Living
13-4x11-0
vaulted

W
D

Din
11-4x
11-0

Garage
20-0x20-0

RANCH

117

Terrific Ranch

Total Living Area: 1,540

- Spacious master bedroom has a large walk-in closet and sweeping windows overlooking yard
- First floor laundry conveniently located between the garage and kitchen
- Living room features a cathedral ceiling and corner fireplace
- 3 bedrooms, 2 baths, 2-car garage
- Basement foundation

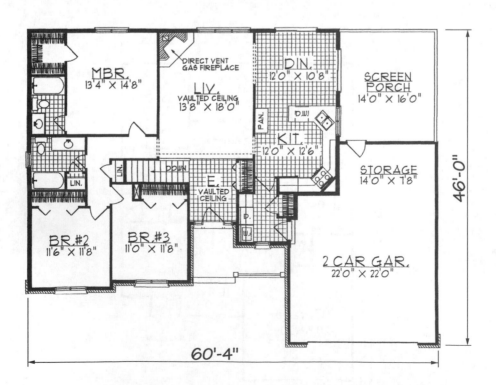

TO ORDER SEE **PAGE 608** OR CALL TOLL-FREE 1-800-DREAM HOME (373-2646)

Vaulted Ceilings Add Spaciousness

Total Living Area: 1,408

- A bright country kitchen boasts an abundance of counterspace and cupboards
- The front entry is sheltered by a broad verandah
- A spa tub is brightened by a box bay window in the master bath
- 3 bedrooms, 2 baths, 2-car side entry garage
- Basement or crawl space foundation, please specify when ordering

Width: 70'-0"
Depth: 28'-0"

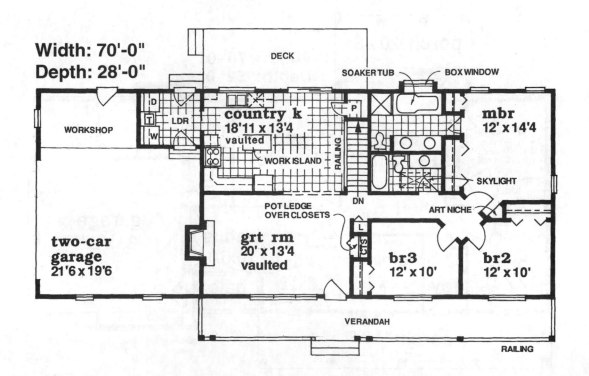

RANCH

Sunny Eating Area
Total Living Area: 1,925

- Energy efficient home with 2" x 6" exterior walls
- Balcony off eating area adds character
- Master suite has dressing room, bath, walk-in closet and access to utility room
- 3 bedrooms, 2 baths, 2-car side entry garage
- Crawl space or slab foundation, please specify when ordering

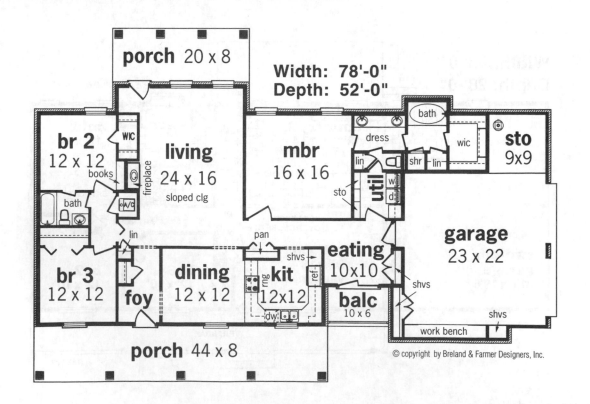

Width: 78'-0"
Depth: 52'-0"

porch 20 x 8

br 2 12 x 12 — WIC — living 24 x 16 sloped clg — mbr 16 x 16 — bath — dress — wic — sto 9x9

br 3 12 x 12 — foy — dining 12 x 12 — kit 12x12 — eating 10x10 — balc 10 x 6 — garage 23 x 22

porch 44 x 8

work bench

© copyright by Breland & Farmer Designers, Inc.

RANCH

120

Plan# 577-RJ-A1491

Price Code A

TO ORDER SEE **PAGE 608** OR CALL TOLL-FREE 1-800-**DREAM HOME** (373-2646)

Cozy Country Appeal

Total Living Area: 1,482

- Coffered ceiling in master suite adds a dramatic feel
- Half-wall in breakfast room helps maintain an open flowing floor plan
- Covered front porch creates a place for a quiet retreat
- 3 bedrooms, 2 baths, 2-car garage
- Slab or crawl space foundation, please specify when ordering

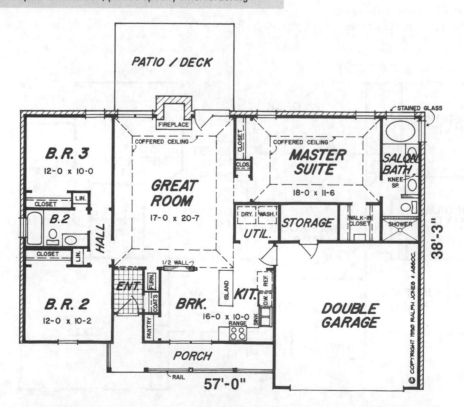

RANCH

TO ORDER SEE **PAGE 608** OR CALL TOLL-FREE 1-800-DREAM HOME (373-2646)

Brick And Stucco Exterior
Total Living Area: 2,187

- Lots of windows create a sunny atmosphere in the breakfast room
- Exceptional master suite with an enormous bath and unique morning porch
- Vaulted and raised ceilings adorn many rooms throughout this home
- The roomy deck may be accessed from the family room and master suite
- 4 bedrooms, 2 1/2 baths, 2-car garage
- Basement, crawl space or slab foundation, please specify when ordering

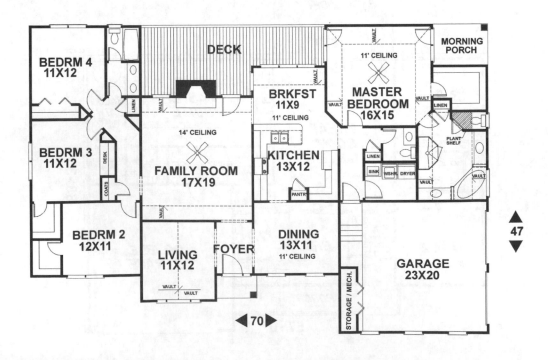

RANCH

TO ORDER SEE **PAGE 608** OR CALL TOLL-FREE 1-800-DREAM HOME (373-2646)

© Michael E. Nelson
NELSON DESIGN GROU

Built-In Computer Desk
Total Living Area: 1,525

- Corner fireplace highlighted in great room
- Unique glass block window over whirlpool tub in master bath
- Open bar overlooks both the kitchen and great room
- Breakfast room leads to an outdoor grilling and covered porch
- 3 bedrooms, 2 baths, 2-car garage
- Basement, walk-out basement, crawl space or slab foundation, please specify when ordering

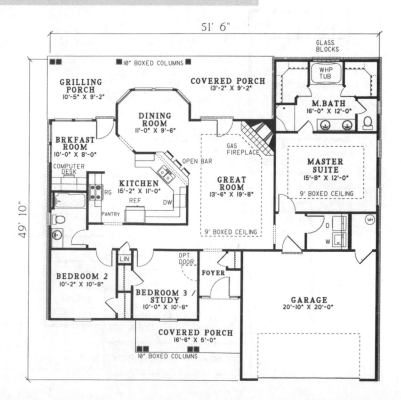

RANCH

Traditional Home Has Modern Floor Plan

Total Living Area: 2,214

■ Great room has built-in cabinets for entertainment system, fireplace and French doors leading to private rear covered porch

■ Dining room has an arched opening from foyer

■ Breakfast room has lots of windows for a sunny open feel

■ 3 bedrooms, 2 baths, 2-car side entry garage

■ Crawl space or slab foundation, please specify when ordering

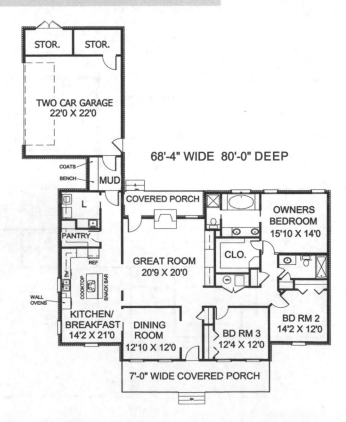

RANCH

TO ORDER SEE PAGE 608 OR CALL TOLL-FREE 1-800-DREAM HOME (373-2646)

Formal Facade

Total Living Area: 1,606

- Kitchen has snack bar which overlooks dining area for convenience
- Master bedroom has lots of windows with a private bath and large walk-in closet
- Cathedral vault in great room adds spaciousness
- 3 bedrooms, 2 baths, 2-car garage
- Slab foundation

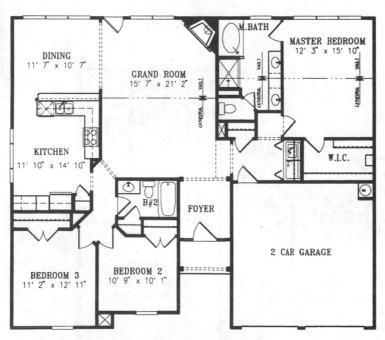

Width: 50'-0"
Depth: 42'-0"

RANCH

Vaulted Ceilings Throughout Home
Total Living Area: 1,634

- Enter foyer to find a nice-sized dining room to the right and a cozy great room with fireplace straight ahead
- Secluded master suite offers privacy from other bedrooms and living areas
- Plenty of storage throughout this home
- Future playroom on the second floor has an additional 256 square feet of living area
- 3 bedrooms, 2 baths, 2-car garage
- Slab foundation

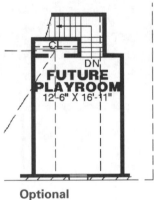

FUTURE PLAYROOM
12'-6" X 16'-11"

DN
CL

**Optional
Second Floor**

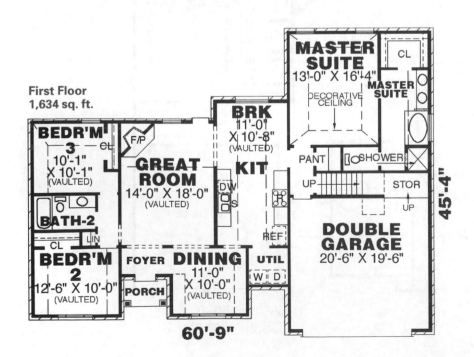

First Floor
1,634 sq. ft.

MASTER SUITE
13'-0" X 16'-4"

CL

MASTER SUITE

DECORATIVE CEILING

PANT

SHOWER

UP

STOR

UP

DOUBLE GARAGE
20'-6" X 19'-6"

45'-4"

BRK
11'-0" X 10'-8"
(VAULTED)

KIT

GREAT ROOM
14'-0" X 18'-0"
(VAULTED)

DW

REF

BEDR'M 3
10'-1" X 10'-1"
(VAULTED)

F/P

CL

BATH-2

CL   LIN

BEDR'M 2
12'-6" X 10'-0"
(VAULTED)

FOYER

DINING
11'-0" X 10'-0"
(VAULTED)

UTIL

W D

PORCH

60'-9"

Kitchen Is A Chef's Dream

Total Living Area: 2,193

- Master suite includes a sitting room
- Dining room has decorative columns and overlooks family room
- Kitchen has lots of storage
- Optional bonus room with bath on second floor has an additional 400 square feet of living area
- 3 bedrooms, 3 baths, 2 car side entry garage
- Walk-out basement, crawl space or slab foundation, please specify when ordering

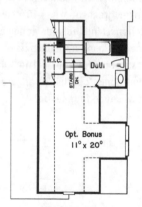

**Optional
Second Floor**

Opt. Bonus
11⁰ x 20⁰

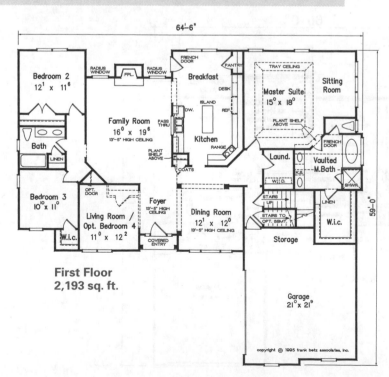

**First Floor
2,193 sq. ft.**

copyright © 1995 frank betz associates, inc.

RANCH

127

Bedrooms Separated From Living Areas
Total Living Area: 1,734

- Large entry with coffered ceiling and display niches
- Sunken great room has 10' ceiling
- Kitchen island includes eating counter
- 9' ceiling in master bedroom
- Master bath features corner tub and double sinks
- 3 bedrooms, 2 baths, 2-car garage
- Crawl space foundation

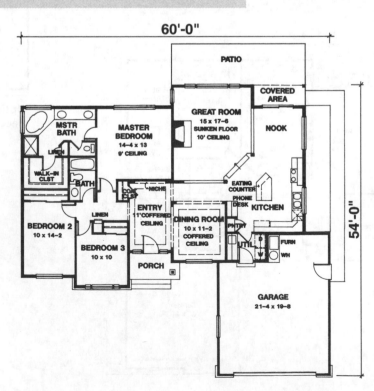

RANCH

TO ORDER SEE **PAGE 608** OR CALL TOLL-FREE 1-800-DREAM-HOME (373-2646)

Office Room With Separate Entrance

Total Living Area: 2,361

- Enormous breakfast area and kitchen create a perfect gathering place
- Family room enhanced with wall of windows and a large fireplace
- Office/gameroom easily accessible through separate side entrance
- 4 bedrooms, 3 baths, 2-car side entry garage
- Basement foundation

Width: 66'-10"
Depth: 69'-5"

RANCH

Plan# 577-BF-1711

Price Code B

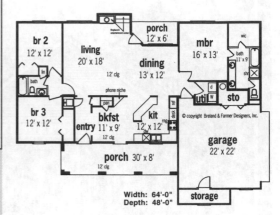

Open Living

Total Living Area: 1,770

- Open floor plan makes this home feel spacious
- 12' ceilings in kitchen, living, breakfast and dining areas
- Kitchen is the center of activity with views into all gathering places
- 3 bedrooms, 2 baths, 2-car side entry garage
- Slab or crawl space foundation, please specify when ordering

Floor plan labels: br 2 12' x 12', living 20' x 18' 12' clg, porch 12' x 6', dining 13' x 12', mbr 16' x 13', wic, bath 11' x 9', phone niche, br 3 12' x 12', bkfst 11' x 9' 12' clg, entry, kit 12' x 12', uti, sto, © copyright Breland & Farmer Designers, Inc., garage 22' x 22', porch 30' x 8' 12' clg, storage

Width: 64'-0"
Depth: 48'-0"

Plan# 577-CHD-13-61

Price Code A

Comfortable Living In This Ranch

Total Living Area: 1,379

- Vaulted great room makes a lasting impression with corner fireplace and windows
- Formal dining room easily connects to kitchen making entertaining easy
- Master bath includes all the luxuries such as a spacious walk-in closet, oversized tub and separate shower
- 3 bedrooms, 2 baths, 2-car garage
- Slab foundation

Floor plan labels: W.I.C., MASTER BATH, F/P, GREAT ROOM 13'-0" X 17'-0" (VAULTED), BRK (VAULTED), BEDR'M 10'-0" X 10'-0", CL, PANT, LIN, BATH, 7' HIGH WALL WITH PLANT LEDGE, KIT, MASTER SUITE 12'-0" X 13'-0", 40'-4", FOYER, DINING 11'-0" X 10'-0", BEDR'M 10'-0" X 10'-0", CL, 48'-10", DOUBLE GARAGE 19'-0" X 20'-0"

RANCH

Secluded Master Suite

Total Living Area: 1,937

- Upscale great room offers a sloped ceiling, fireplace with extended hearth and built-in shelves for an entertainment center
- Gourmet kitchen includes a cooktop island counter and a quaint morning room
- Master suite features a sloped ceiling, cozy sitting room, walk-in closet and a private bath with whirlpool tub
- 3 bedrooms, 2 baths, 2 car side entry garage
- Crawl space foundation

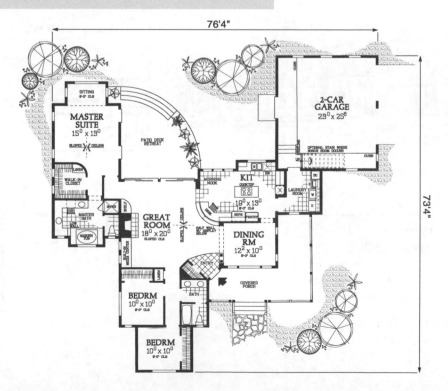

RANCH

131

Plan# 577-FB-543

Price Code C

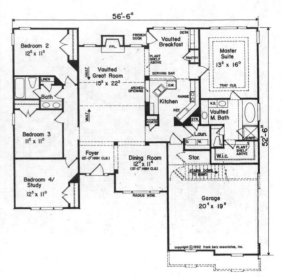

Plenty Of Detail

Total Living Area: 1,945

- Master suite separated from other bedrooms for privacy
- Vaulted breakfast room is directly off great room
- Kitchen includes a built-in desk area
- Elegant dining room has an arched window
- 4 bedrooms, 2 baths, 2-car side entry garage
- Walk-out basement, crawl space or slab foundation, please specify when ordering

Plan# 577-GSD-1085

Price Code C

GSDG 1085

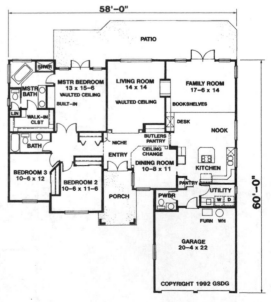

Modern Style

Total Living Area: 2,086

- Family room has desk and built-in bookshelves
- Master bath has corner tub and spacious walk-in closet
- Master bedroom has double-door entry, vaulted ceiling and access to patio outdoors
- 3 bedrooms, 2 1/2 baths, 2-car garage with 3-car garage option
- Crawl space foundation

TO ORDER SEE **PAGE 608** OR CALL TOLL-FREE 1-800-DREAM HOME (373-2646)

Master Suite With Media Center
Total Living Area: 1,429

- Master suite with sitting area and private bath includes double walk-in closets
- Kitchen and dining area overlook living room
- Living room has fireplace, media center and access to covered porch
- 3 bedrooms, 2 baths, 2-car garage
- Slab or crawl space foundation, please specify when ordering

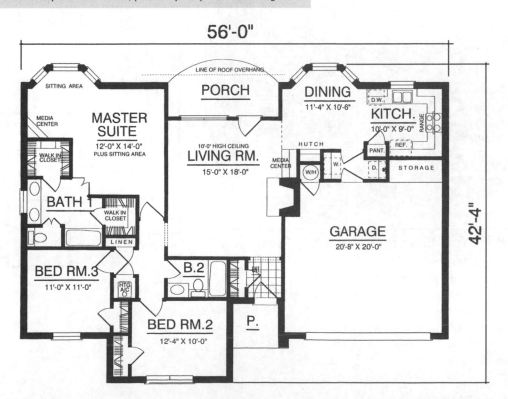

RANCH

Price Code B

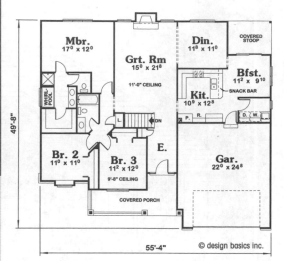

© design basics inc.

All The Amenities

Total Living Area: 1,758

- Secluded covered porch off breakfast area is a charming touch
- Great room and dining room combine for terrific entertaining possibilities
- Master bedroom with all the amenities
- Spacious foyer area opens into large great room with 11' ceiling
- 3 bedrooms, 2 baths, 2-car garage
- Basement foundation

Price Code A

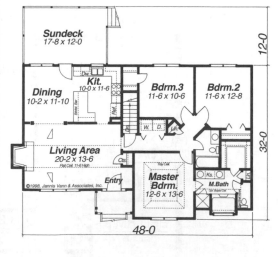

Gabled Porch Gives A Country Flair

Total Living Area: 1,379

- Living area has spacious feel with 11'-6" ceiling
- Kitchen has eat-in breakfast bar open to dining area
- Laundry located near bedrooms
- Large cased opening with columns opens the living and dining areas
- 3 bedroom, 2 baths, 2-car drive under garage
- Basement foundation

RANCH

TO ORDER SEE PAGE 608 OR CALL TOLL-FREE 1-800-DREAM HOME (373-2646)

Covered Porch Adds Charm

Total Living Area: 2,069

- 9' ceilings throughout this home
- Kitchen has many amenities including a snack bar
- Large front and rear porches
- 3 bedrooms, 2 1/2 baths, 2-car garage
- Slab or crawl space foundation, please specify when ordering

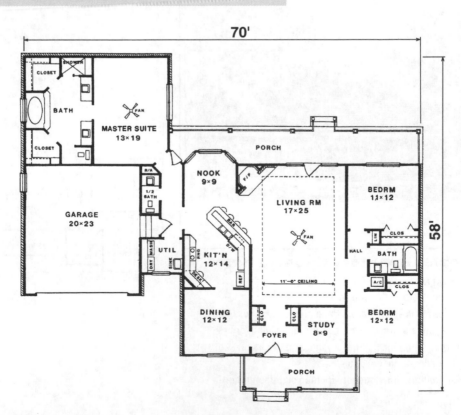

RANCH

TO ORDER SEE **PAGE 608** OR CALL TOLL-FREE 1-800-DREAM HOME (373-2646)

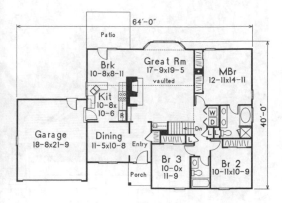

Vaulted Ceilings Create Spacious Feeling

Total Living Area: 1,605

- Spacious great room features large bay window, fireplace, built-in bookshelves, vaulted ceiling and a convenient wet bar
- Dine in formal dining room or breakfast area with vaulted ceiling overlooking rear yard, perfect for entertaining or everyday living
- Master bedroom has a spacious master bath with oval tub and separate shower
- 3 bedrooms, 2 baths, 2-car garage
- Basement foundation, drawings also include slab and crawl space foundations

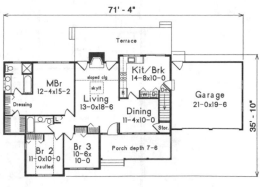

Comfortable One-Story Country Home

Total Living Area: 1,367

- Neat front porch shelters the entrance
- Dining room has full wall of windows and convenient storage area
- Breakfast area leads to the rear terrace through sliding doors
- Large living room with high ceiling, skylight and fireplace
- 3 bedrooms, 2 baths, 2-car garage
- Basement foundation, drawings also include slab foundation

RANCH

TO ORDER SEE **PAGE 608** OR CALL TOLL-FREE 1-800-DREAM HOME (373-2646)

Dormers Create Terrific Curb Appeal

Total Living Area: 1,992

- Interesting angled walls add drama to many of the living areas including family room, master bedroom and breakfast area
- Covered porch includes spa and an outdoor kitchen with sink, refridgerator and cooktop
- Enter majestic master bath to find a dramatic corner oversized tub
- 4 bedrooms, 3 baths, 2-car side entry garage
- Basement, crawl space or slab foundation, please specify when ordering

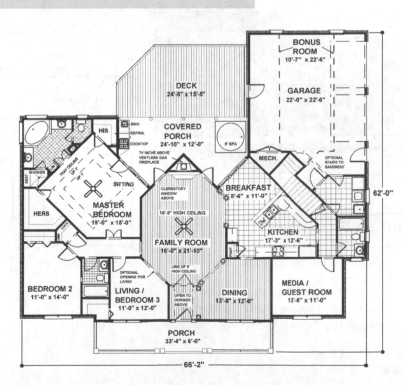

RANCH

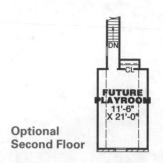

Optional Second Floor

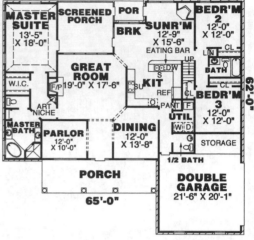

First Floor 2,414 sq. ft.

Sunroom Warmed By Fireplace

Total Living Area: 2,414

■ 9' ceilings throughout this home

■ Versatile screened porch connects to master suite, outdoor porch and breakfast room for convenience

■ Quiet parlor makes an ideal place for reading a cozy home office

■ Future playroom on the second floor has an additional 305 square feet of living area

■ 3 bedrooms, 2 1/2 baths, 2-car side entry garage

■ Slab foundation

Plan# **577-0702** **Price Code B**

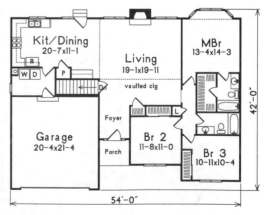

Lovely, Spacious Floor Plan

Total Living Area: 1,558

■ Spacious utility room located conveniently between garage and kitchen/dining area

■ Private bedrooms separated off main living area by hallway

■ Vaulted living area with fireplace opens to kitchen and dining area

■ Master suite enhanced with large bay window, walk-in closet and private bath

■ 3 bedrooms, 2 baths, 2-car garage

■ Basement foundation

RANCH

Perfect Family-Sized Ranch

Total Living Area: 1,869

- Kitchen counter overlooks breakfast and living rooms creating a feeling of openness
- Dining room features columns separating it from the other spaces in a unique and formal way
- A sunny spa tub is featured in the master bath
- 3 bedrooms, 2 baths, 2-car side entry garage
- Basement, crawl space or slab foundation, please specify when ordering

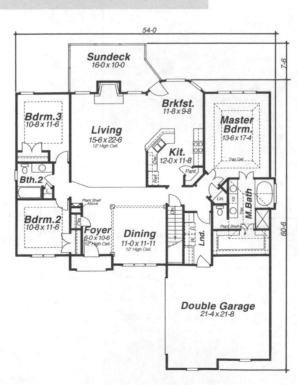

RANCH

Plan# **577-0585**

Price Code A

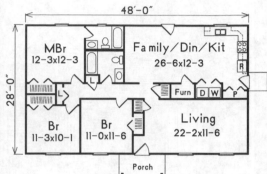

All The Essentials For Comfortable Living

Total Living Area: 1,344

- Kitchen has side entry, laundry area, pantry and joins family/dining area
- Master bedroom includes private bath
- Linen and storage closets in hall
- Covered porch opens to spacious living room with handy coat closet
- 3 bedrooms, 2 baths
- Crawl space foundation, drawings also include basement and slab foundations

Plan# **577-0186**

Price Code A

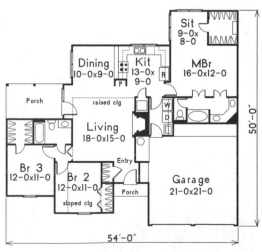

Fireplace Warms This Cozy Contemporary

Total Living Area: 1,442

- Centrally located living room with recessed fireplace and 10' ceiling
- Large U-shaped kitchen offers an eating bar and pantry
- Expanded garage provides extra storage and work area
- Spacious master bedroom with sitting area and large walk-in closet
- 3 bedrooms, 2 baths, 2-car garage
- Slab foundation, drawings also include crawl space foundation

RANCH

Luxurious Ranch

Total Living Area: 2,196

- Covered front porch leads to the vaulted foyer which invites guests into the great room
- Master bedroom features walk-in closet, private bath with double vanity, spa tub and linen closet
- Large open kitchen
- 3 bedrooms, 2 1/2 baths, 3-car garage
- Basement foundation

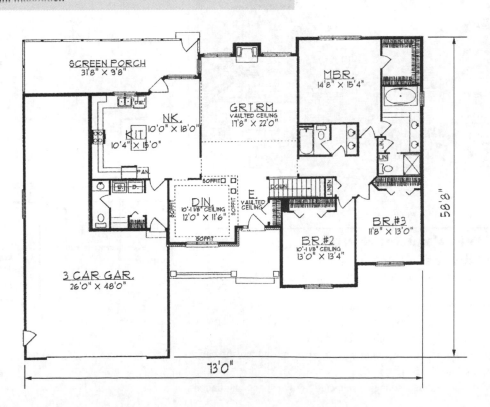

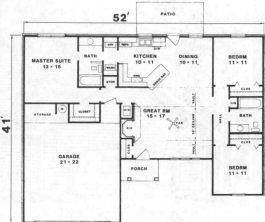

52'

41'

MASTER SUITE 12 × 15 | BATH | DRY | REFG | KITCHEN 10 × 11 | DINING 10 × 11, | BEDRM 11 × 11

GREAT RM 15 × 17

STORAGE | CLOSET | BATH

GARAGE 21 × 22 | PORCH | BEDRM 11 × 11

Simple Elegance With This Design
Total Living Area: 1,243

- Large great room is vaulted for extra openness
- Private master suite has direct access to bath and connects to laundry area as well
- Angled snack bar counter extends into great room
- 3 bedrooms, 2 baths, 2-car garage
- Slab or crawl space foundation, please specify when ordering

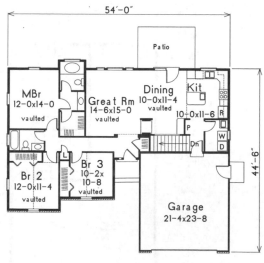

54'-0"

44'-6"

Patio

MBr 12-0x14-0 vaulted | Great Rm 14-6x15-0 vaulted | Dining 10-0x11-4 vaulted | Kit 10-0x11-6

Br 2 12-0x11-4 vaulted | Br 3 10-2x 10-8 vaulted | Garage 21-4x23-8

High-Style Vaulted Ranch
Total Living Area: 1,453

- Decorative vents, window trim, shutters and brick blend to create dramatic curb appeal
- Energy efficient home with 2" x 6" exterior walls
- Kitchen opens to living area and includes a salad sink in the island
- Exquisite master bedroom highlighted by vaulted ceiling
- Dressing area with walk-in closet, private bath and spa tub/shower
- 3 bedrooms, 2 baths, 2-car garage
- Basement foundation, drawings also include crawl space foundation

TO ORDER SEE **PAGE 608** OR CALL TOLL-FREE 1-800-DREAM HOME (373-2646)

COPYRIGHT LARRY E. BELK

Circle-Top Details
Total Living Area: 1,932

- Double arches form entrance to this elegantly styled home
- Two palladian windows add distinction to facade
- Kitchen has angled eating bar opening to the breakfast and living rooms
- 3 bedrooms, 2 baths, 2-car side entry garage
- Crawl space or slab foundation, please specify when ordering

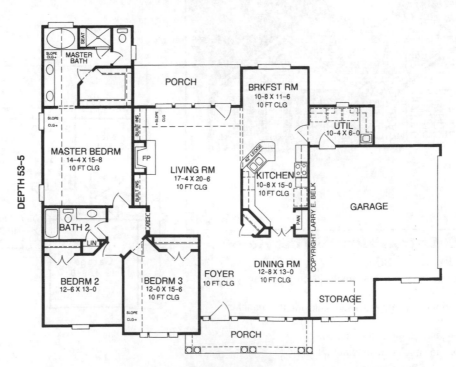

RANCH

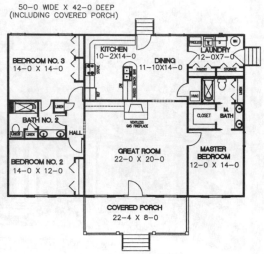

50-0 WIDE X 42-0 DEEP
(INCLUDING COVERED PORCH)

Perfect Home For Family Living

Total Living Area: 1,700

- Oversized laundry room has large pantry and storage area as well as access to the outdoors
- Master bedroom separated from other bedrooms for privacy
- Raised snack bar in kitchen allows extra seating for dining
- 3 bedrooms, 2 baths
- Crawl space foundation

Plan# **577-0669**

Price Code A

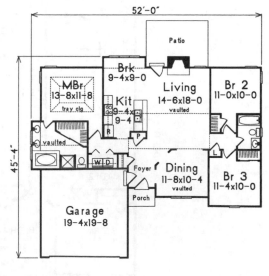

Stonework Entry Adds To This Home

Total Living Area: 1,358

- Vaulted master bath has walk-in closet, double-bowl vanity, large tub, shower and toilet area
- Galley kitchen opens to both the living room and the breakfast area
- Vaulted ceiling joins dining and living rooms
- Breakfast room has a full wall of windows
- 3 bedrooms, 2 baths, 2-car garage
- Slab foundation

TO ORDER SEE **PAGE 608** OR CALL TOLL-FREE 1-800-DREAM HOME (373-2646)

Fireplace Warms Large Great Room

Total Living Area: 2,578

- Enormous entry has an airy feel with gallery area nearby
- Living room with bay window is tucked away from traffic areas
- Large kitchen and breakfast area access covered patio
- Great room has entertainment center, fireplace and cathedral ceiling
- 4 bedrooms, 3 1/2 baths, 3-car side entry garage
- Slab foundation

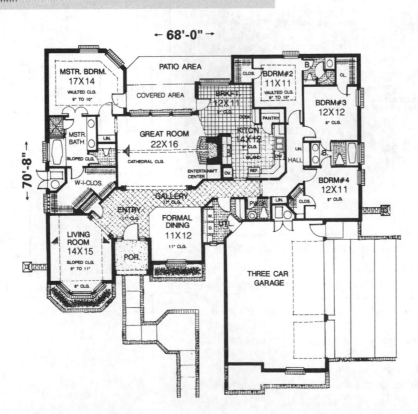

RANCH

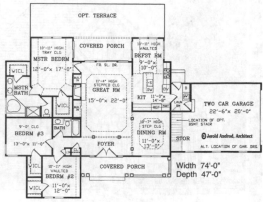

Country Ranch With Open Interior

Total Living Area: 1,783

- The front to rear flow of the great room, with built-ins on one side is a furnishing delight
- Bedrooms are all quietly zoned on one side
- The master bedroom is separated for privacy
- Every bedroom features walk-in closets
- 3 bedrooms, 2 baths, 2-car side entry garage
- Basement, crawl space or slab foundation, please specify when ordering

Covered Rear Porch Is A Nice Dining Place

Total Living Area: 1,593

- Large sitting area is enjoyed by the master bedroom which also features a walk-in closet and bath
- Centrally located kitchen acceses the family dining and breakast rooms with ease
- Storage/mechanical area is ideal for seasonal storage or hobby supplies
- 3 bedrooms, 2 baths, 2-car garage
- Basement, crawl space or slab foundation, please specify when ordering

RANCH

Bounty Of Bay Windows

Total Living Area: 2,322

- ■ Vaulted family room has fireplace and access to kitchen
- ■ Decorative columns and arched openings surround dining area
- ■ Master suite has a sitting room and grand scale bath
- ■ Kitchen includes island with serving bar
- ■ 3 bedrooms, 2 1/2 baths, 2-car side entry garage
- ■ Walk-out basement, crawl space or slab foundation, please specify when ordering

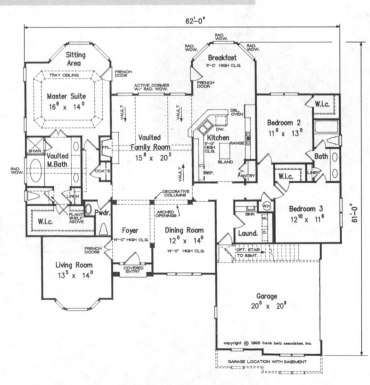

Plan# 577-GM-1333

Price Code A

Width: 55'-6"
Depth: 64'-3"

Storage 20 x 6 — 8' Clg.
Carport 20 x 20 — 8' Clg.
Master 15 x 13 — 9' Recessed Clg.
10/6 x 8
Rear Porch 22 x 4
Dining 10 x 13 — 8' Clg.
Kitchen 9/9 x 13
B.R. #3 10 x 12 — 8' Clg.
B.R. #2 10 x 11 — 8' Clg.
Family Room 17 x 14/7 — 9' Clg.
Porch 40/6 x 6 — 8' Clg.

Carport With Storage

Total Living Area: 1,333

- Country charm with covered front porch
- Dining area looks into family room with fireplace
- Master suite has walk-in closet and private bath
- 3 bedrooms, 2 baths, 2-car attached carport
- Slab or crawl space foundation, please specify when ordering

Plan# 577-UDG-99003

Price Code A

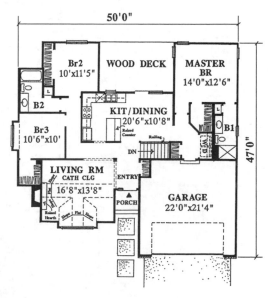

50'0"

Br2 10'x11'5"
WOOD DECK
MASTER BR 14'0"x12'6"
B2
KIT/DINING 20'6"x10'8" — Raised Counter
Br3 10'6"x10"
B1
LIVING RM CATH CLG 16'8"x13'8" — Raised Hearth
Railing
DN
ENTRY
PORCH
GARAGE 22'0"x21'4"
47'0"

Traditional Style With Extras

Total Living Area: 1,425

- Living room has very interesting cathedral ceiling
- Secondary bedrooms have plenty of closet space
- Raised eating counter separates kitchen and dining area
- Bedroom #3 has window seat overlooking landscape
- 3 bedrooms, 2 baths, 2-car garage
- Basement foundation

RANCH

Trio Of Dormers Add Appeal

Total Living Area: 2,164

- Country-styled front porch adds charm
- Plenty of counterspace in kitchen
- Large utility area meets big families laundry needs
- Double-doors lead to covered rear porch
- 4 bedrooms, 2 1/2 baths, 2-car side entry garage
- Slab foundation

Width: 70'-6"
Depth: 57'-0"

© David C. Lutz

RANCH

149

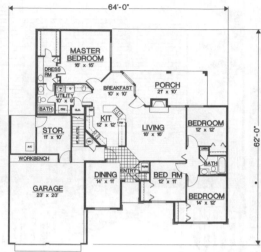

Rooflines Add Interest

Total Living Area: 1,828

- Energy efficient home with 2" x 6" exterior walls
- Master bath features a giant walk-in closet, built-in linen storage with convenient access to utility room
- Kitchen has a unique design that is elegant and practical
- 4 bedrooms, 2 baths, 2-car garage
- Slab, crawl space or basement foundation, please specify when ordering

Study Off Main Entrance

Total Living Area: 1,760

- Stone and brick exterior has old world charm
- Master bedroom includes a sitting area and is situated away from other bedrooms for privacy
- Kitchen and dinette access the outdoors
- Great room includes fireplace, built-in bookshelves and entertainment center
- 3 bedrooms, 2 baths, 2-car side entry garage
- Slab foundation

RANCH

Plan# 577-JA-53594

Price Code B

TO ORDER SEE **PAGE 608** OR CALL TOLL-FREE 1-800-DREAM HOME (373-2646)

Great Dining Room For Entertaining

Total Living Area: 1,730

- Energy efficient home with 2" x 6" exterior walls
- All bedrooms are large and open with plenty of closet space
- Great room is cheerful and bright and includes a cozy fireplace
- 3 bedrooms, 2 baths, 2-car garage
- Basement foundation

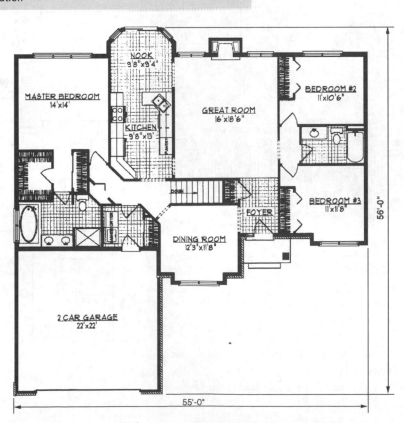

RANCH

Plan# 577-DBI-2461

Price Code C

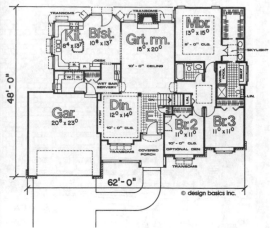

© design basics inc.

48' - 0"

62' - 0"

Convenient Wet Bar

Total Living Area: 1,850

- Oversized rooms throughout
- Great room spotlights fireplace with sunny windows on both sides
- Master bedroom has private skylighted bath
- Interesting wet bar between kitchen and dining area is an added bonus when entertaining
- 3 bedrooms, 2 baths, 2-car garage
- Basement foundation

Plan# 577-FB-960

Price Code D

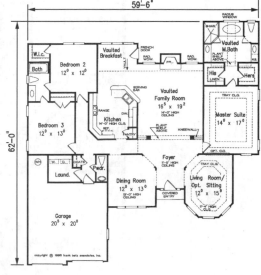

59'-6"

62'-0"

copyright © 1996 frank betz associates, inc.

Angles Add Interest

Total Living Area: 2,201

- Open floor plan makes home feel airy and bright
- Beautiful living room has cheerful bay window
- Master suite has his/her walk-in closets
- Family room, kitchen and breakfast area combine for added space
- 3 bedrooms, 2 1/2 baths, 2-car garage
- Walk-out basement, slab or crawl space foundation, please specify when ordering

RANCH

© COPYRIGHT 1990
RALPH JONES

Modest Ranch Style
Total Living Area: 1,192

■ Kitchen eating bar overlooks well-designed great room

■ Private bath in master suite

■ Extra storage space in garage

■ 3 bedrooms, 2 baths, 2-car garage

■ Slab or crawl space foundation, please specify when ordering

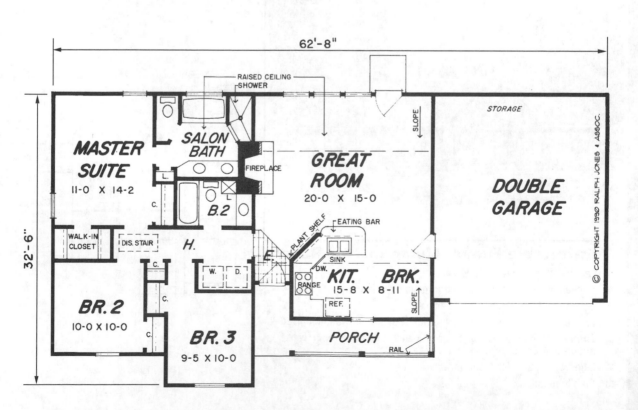

RANCH

153

Plan # 577-JA-77798

Price Code A

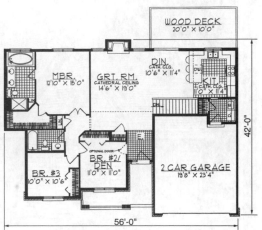

WOOD DECK
20'0" X 10'0"

DIN.
CATH. CLG.
10'6" X 11'4"

KIT.

MBR.
12'0" X 15'0"

GRT. RM.
CATHEDRAL CEILING
14'6" X 19'0"

BR. #2/
DEN
11'0" X 11'0"

OPTIONAL DOOR

BR. #3
10'0" X 10'6"

2 CAR GARAGE
19'8" X 23'4"

42'-0"

56'-0"

Country Flair In A Flexible Ranch

Total Living Area: 1,461

- Casual dining room
- Cathedral ceilings in great room and dining room give home a spacious feel
- Two bedroom home has option to become three bedroom
- 3 bedrooms, 2 baths, 2-car garage
- Basement foundation

Plan # 577-0244

Price Code D

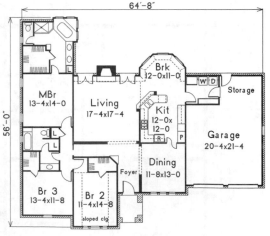

64'-8"

56'-0"

MBr
13-4x14-0

Living
17-4x17-4

Brk
12-0x11-0

W D

Storage

Kit
12-0x
12-0

Garage
20-4x21-4

Dining
11-8x13-0

Foyer

Br 3
13-4x11-8

Br 2
11-4x14-8

sloped clg

Comfortable Family Living In This Ranch

Total Living Area: 1,994

- Convenient entrance from the garage into the laundry room
- Bedroom #2 has a 12' vaulted ceiling
- Master has an oversized tub, separate shower and walk-in closet
- Entry leads to formal dining room and attractive living room with double French doors and fireplace
- 3 bedrooms, 2 baths, 2-car garage
- Slab foundation

RANCH

TO ORDER SEE **PAGE 608** OR CALL TOLL-FREE 1-800-DREAM HOME (373-2646)

Handsome Front Porch

Total Living Area: 1,769

- Stylish transom and bay windows as well as columns on front porch give distinguished appearance
- Enter living area from foyer and view vaulted ceiling leading to fireplace and built-in shelving
- Breakfast area with bayed door leads to rear sun deck
- 3 bedrooms, **2** baths, 2-car drive under garage
- Basement foundation

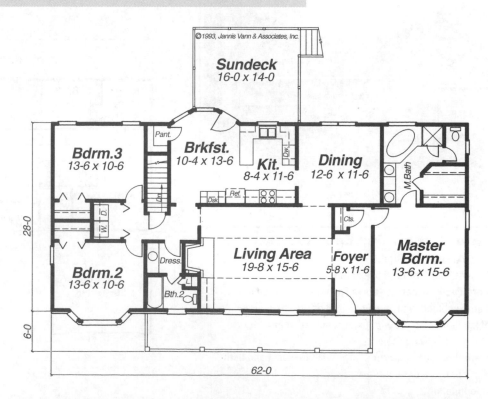

© 1993, Jannis Vann & Associates, Inc.

Sundeck
16-0 x 14-0

Bdrm.3
13-6 x 10-6

Pant.

Brkfst.
10-4 x 13-6

Kit.
8-4 x 11-6

Dw.

Dining
12-6 x 11-6

M.Bath

Ref.

Dsk.

W. D.

28-0

Dress.

Bdrm.2
13-6 x 10-6

Bth.2

Cts.

Living Area
19-8 x 15-6

Foyer
5-8 x 11-6

Master Bdrm.
13-6 x 15-6

6-0

62-0

RANCH

Plan# 577-0284

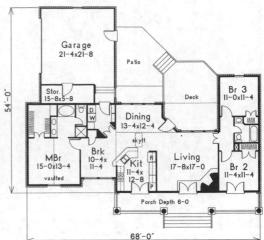

Circle-Top Windows Grace The Facade

Total Living Area: 1,672

- Vaulted master suite features walk-in closet and adjoining bath with separate tub and shower
- Energy efficient home with 2" x 6" exterior walls
- 12' ceilings in living room, kitchen and bedroom #2
- Kitchen complete with pantry, angled bar and adjacent eating area
- 3 bedrooms, 2 baths, 2-car side entry garage
- Crawl space foundation, drawings also include basement and slab foundations

Plan# 577-0265

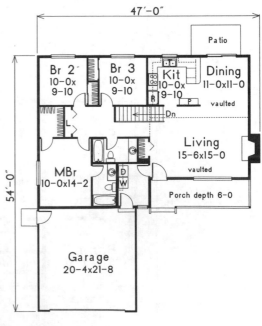

Economical Ranch For Easy Living

Total Living Area: 1,314

- Energy efficient home with 2" x 6" exterior walls
- Covered porch adds immediate appeal and welcoming charm
- Open design combined with vaulted ceiling offers spacious living
- Functional kitchen complete with pantry and eating bar
- Cozy fireplace in the living room
- Private master bedroom features a large walk-in closet and bath
- 3 bedrooms, 2 baths, 2-car garage
- Basement foundation

RANCH

Kitchen Designed For Efficiency

Total Living Area: 2,140

- Living and dining areas traditionally separated by foyer
- Media wall and fireplace are located in cozy family room
- Generous master bedroom has sliding glass doors onto patio, walk-in closet and a private bath
- 4 bedrooms, 3 baths, 2-car side entry garage
- Slab foundation

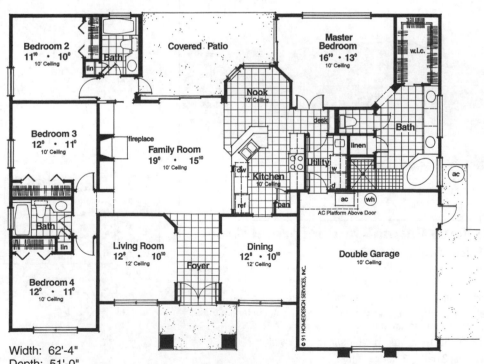

Width: 62'-4"
Depth: 51'-0"

RANCH

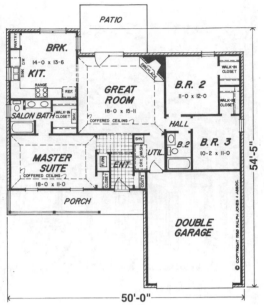

Terrific Use Of Space

Total Living Area: 1,436

- Corner fireplace in great room warms home
- Kitchen and breakfast room combine for convenience
- Centrally located utility room
- 3 bedrooms, 2 baths, 2-car garage
- Slab foundation

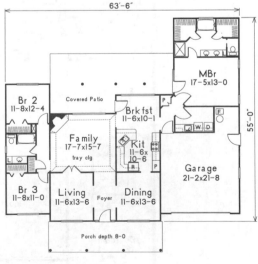

Ranch With Formal And Informal Areas

Total Living Area: 1,969

- Master bedroom boasts luxurious bath with double sinks, two walk-in closets and an oversized tub
- Corner fireplace warms a conveniently located family area
- Formal living and dining areas in the front of the home lend a touch of privacy when entertaining
- Spacious utility room has counter space and a sink
- 3 bedrooms, 2 baths, 2-car garage
- Crawl space foundation, drawings also include slab foundation

RANCH

TO ORDER SEE **PAGE 608** OR CALL TOLL-FREE 1-800-DREAM HOME (373-2646)

Award Winning Style With This Design
Total Living Area: 2,156

- Secluded master bedroom has spa-style bath with corner whirlpool tub, large shower, double sinks and a walk-in closet
- Kitchen overlooks rear patio
- Plenty of windows add an open, airy feel to the great room
- 3 bedrooms, 3 baths, 2-car side entry garage
- Basement, crawl space or slab foundation, please specify when ordering

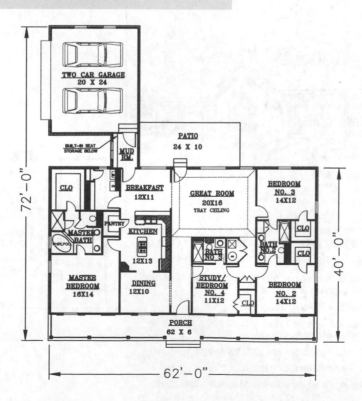

RANCH

Plan# 577-UD-C142 — Price Code B

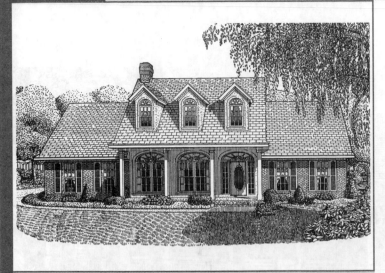

GARAGE 21'-0"x22'-0" (CARPORT OR NO GARAGE OPTIONAL)

PATIO 20'-0"x12'-0"

WALK-IN CLOSET

MSTR BATH

PWDR

KITCHEN 13'-0"x10'-0"

DINING 11'-0"x10'-0"

BEDROOM #3 13'-0"x11'-10"

GREAT ROOM 24'-0"x20'-0" (10' CLG)

MASTER BEDROOM 15'-5"x16'-0" (VAULTED CLG)

SITTING AREA

BATH

BEDROOM #2 13'-0"x11'-10"

COVERED PORCH 25'-0"x8'-0" (10' CLG)

Width 59'-0"
Depth 61'-0"

Stunning Triple Dormers And Arches
Total Living Area: 1,698

- Vaulted master bedroom has a private bath and a walk-in closet
- Decorative columns flank the entrance to the dining room
- Open great room is perfect for gathering family together
- 3 bedrooms, 2 1/2 baths, 2-car side entry garage with storage
- Basement, crawl space or slab foundation, please specify when ordering

Plan# 577-0191 — Price Code D

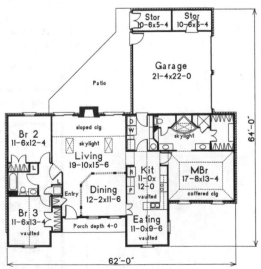

Stor 10-6x5-4

Stor 10-6x5-4

Garage 21-4x22-0

Patio

Br 2 11-6x12-4

Living 19-10x15-6

Kit 11-0x12-0

MBr 17-8x13-4

Dining 12-2x11-6

Br 3 11-6x13-4

Eating 11-0x9-6

Porch depth 4-0

62'-0"

64'-0"

Open Areas Separate Remote Bedrooms
Total Living Area: 1,868

- Luxurious master bath is impressive with angled quarter-circle tub, separate vanities and large walk-in closet
- Energy efficient home with 2" x 6" exterior walls
- Dining room is surrounded by a series of arched openings which complement the open feeling of this design
- Living room has a 12' ceiling accented by skylights and a fireplace
- 3 bedrooms, 2 baths, 2-car side entry garage
- Slab foundation, drawings also include crawl space foundation

RANCH

160

TO ORDER SEE **PAGE 608** OR CALL TOLL-FREE 1-800-DREAM HOME (373-2646)

Master Suite With Sitting Area

Total Living Area: 2,188

- Master bedroom includes private covered porch, sitting area and two large walk-in closets
- Spacious kitchen has center island, snack bar and laundry access
- Great room has 10' ceiling and dramatic corner fireplace
- 3 bedrooms, 2 baths, 3-car side entry garage
- Basement foundation

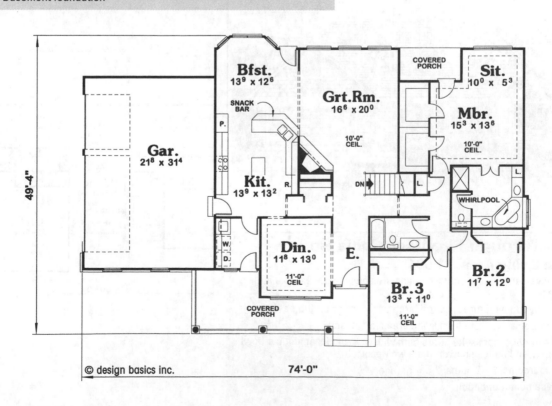

© design basics inc.   74'-0"

RANCH

Plan# 577-CHD-14-18

Price Code A

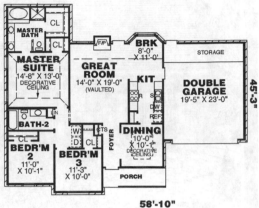

58'-10"

Perfect Ranch With All The Amenities

Total Living Area: 1,429

- Master bedroom features a spacious private bath and double walk-in closets
- Formal dining room has convenient access to kitchen perfect when entertaining
- Additional storage can be found in the garage
- 3 bedrooms, 2 baths, 2-car garage
- Slab foundation

Plan# 577-0393

Price Code B

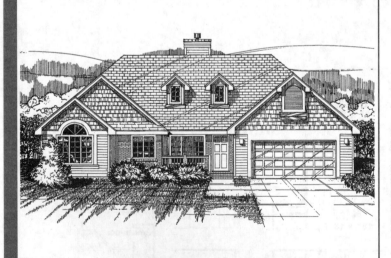

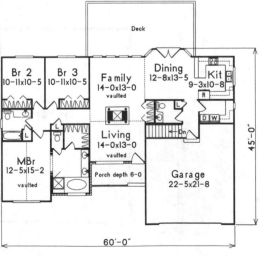

See-Through Fireplace Joins Rooms

Total Living Area: 1,684

- Convenient double-doors in dining area provide access to a large deck
- Family room features several large windows for brightness
- Bedrooms separate from living areas for privacy
- Master bedroom suite offers bath with walk-in closet, double-bowl vanity and both a shower and a whirlpool tub
- 3 bedrooms, 2 1/2 baths, 2-car garage
- Basement foundation

RANCH

Comfortable Dinette

Total Living Area: 1,434

- Isolated master suite for privacy includes walk-in closet and bath
- Elegant formal dining room
- Efficient kitchen has an adjacent dinette which includes shelves and access to laundry facilities
- Extra storage in garage
- 3 bedrooms, 2 baths, 2-car side entry garage
- Crawl space or slab foundation, please specify when ordering

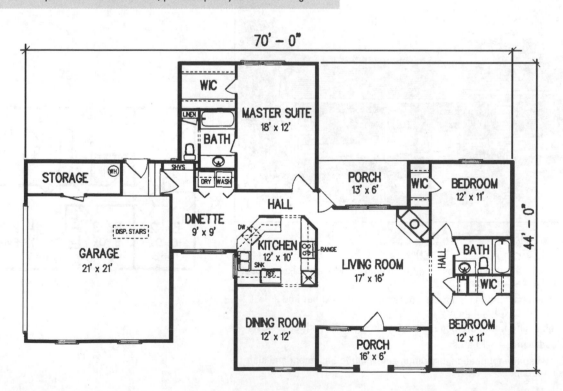

RANCH

163

Plan# **577-JV-1772-A-SJ**

Price Code B

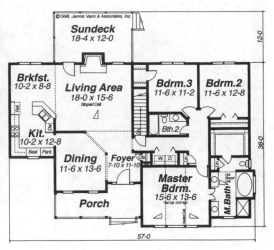

- Sundeck 18-4 x 12-0
- Brkfst. 10-2 x 8-8
- Living Area 18-0 x 15-6 Sloped Ceil.
- Bdrm.3 11-6 x 11-2
- Bdrm.2 11-6 x 12-8
- Bth.2
- Kit. 10-2 x 12-8
- Dining 11-6 x 13-6
- Foyer 7-10 x 11-10
- Master Bdrm. 15-6 x 13-6
- M.Bath
- Porch

©1998, Jannis Vann & Associates, Inc.

Scalloped Porch Cornice Adds Flair

Total Living Area: 1,772

- Dramatic palladian window and scalloped porch are attention grabbers
- Island kitchen sink allows for easy access and views into the living/breakfast areas
- Washer and dryer closet easily accessible from all bedrooms
- 3 bedrooms, 2 baths, 3-car drive under garage
- Basement foundation

Plan# **577-0587**

Price Code AA

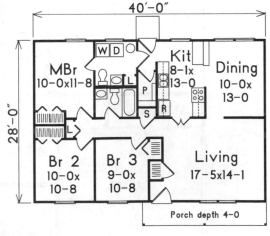

- 40'-0"
- 28'-0"
- MBr 10-0x11-8
- W D
- Kit 8-1x 13-0
- Dining 10-0x 13-0
- Br 2 10-0x 10-8
- Br 3 9-0x 10-8
- Living 17-5x14-1
- Porch depth 4-0

Convenient Ranch

Total Living Area: 1,120

- Master bedroom includes a half bath with laundry area, linen closet and kitchen access
- Kitchen has charming double-door entry, breakfast bar and a convenient walk-in pantry
- Welcoming front porch opens to large living room with coat closet
- 3 bedrooms, 1 1/2 baths
- Crawl space foundation, drawings also include basement and slab foundations

RANCH

Porches Bring Outdoor Living In

Total Living Area: 2,500

- Master bedroom has its own separate wing with front porch, double walk-in closets, private bath and access to back porch and patio
- Large unfinished gameroom on second floor has an additional 359 square feet of living area
- Living area is oversized and has a fireplace
- 3 bedrooms, 2 1/2 baths
- Basement, slab or crawl space foundation, please specify when ordering

TO ORDER SEE **PAGE 608** OR CALL TOLL-FREE 1-800-DREAM HOME (373-2646)

MULTI-STORY

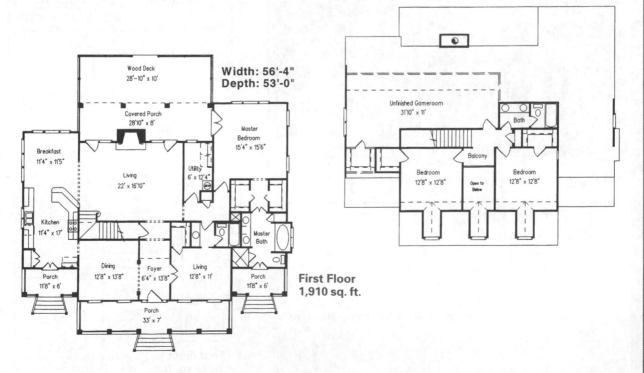

Second Floor
590 sq. ft.

Width: 56'-4"
Depth: 53'-0"

First Floor
1,910 sq. ft.

165

Plan# 577-DBI-2408

Price Code D

Second Floor
1,120 sq. ft.

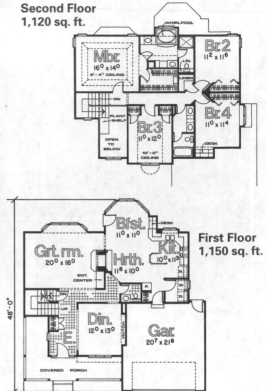

First Floor
1,150 sq. ft.

© design basics inc.

Cozy Family Home
Total Living Area: 2,270

- Great room and hearth room share a see-through fireplace
- Oversized rooms throughout
- First floor has terrific floor plan for entertaining with large kitchen/breakfast area and adjacent great room
- 4 bedrooms, 2 1/2 baths, 2-car garage
- Basement foundation

Plan# 577-FB-1085

Price Code C

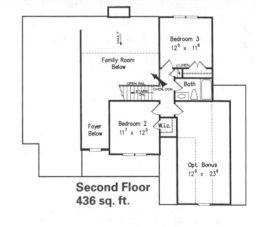

Second Floor
436 sq. ft.

Open Family Living
Total Living Area: 1,818

- Spacious breakfast area extends into family room and kitchen
- Master suite has tray ceiling and a vaulted bath with walk-in closet
- Optional bonus room has an additional 298 square feet of living area
- 3 bedrooms, 2 1/2 baths, 2-car garage
- Walk-out basement, slab or crawl space foundation, please specify when ordering

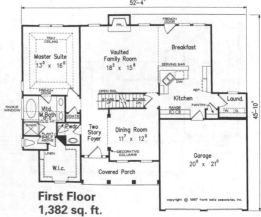

copyright © 1997 frank betz associates, inc.

First Floor
1,382 sq. ft.

MULTI-STORY

Vaulted Great Room With Open Entrance

Total Living Area: 1,851

- High-impact entrance to great room also leads directly to the second floor
- First floor master bedroom suite with corner window and walk-in closet
- Kitchen/breakfast room has center work island and pass-through to the dining room
- Second floor bedrooms share a bath
- 4 bedrooms, 2 1/2 baths, 2-car garage
- Basement foundation

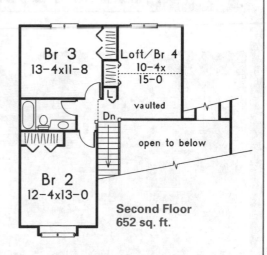

Br 3
13-4x11-8

Loft/Br 4
10-4x
15-0
vaulted

Dn

open to below

Br 2
12-4x13-0

Second Floor
652 sq. ft.

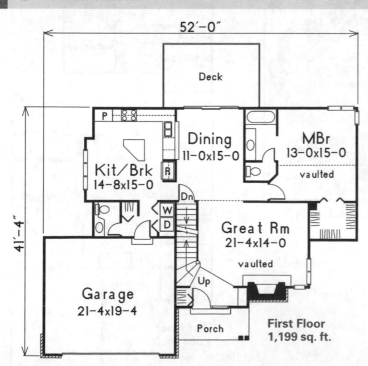

52'-0"

Deck

41'-4"

P

Kit/Brk
14-8x15-0

R

Dining
11-0x15-0

MBr
13-0x15-0

vaulted

Dn

W
D

Great Rm
21-4x14-0

vaulted

Up

Garage
21-4x19-4

Porch

First Floor
1,199 sq. ft.

MULTI-STORY

167

Plan# 577-DDI-100213

Price Code D

Second Floor 1,028 sq. ft.

Width: 34'-0"   Depth: 46'-0"

First Floor 1,174 sq. ft.

Warm And Cozy Feeling

Total Living Area: 2,202

- 9' ceilings on first floor
- Guest bedroom located on the first floor for convenience could easily be converted to an office area
- Large kitchen with oversized island overlooks dining area
- 5 bedrooms, 4 full baths, 2 half baths, 2-car drive under garage
- Basement or walk-out basement foundation, please specify when ordering

Plan# 577-GH-20230

Price Code C

Second Floor 630 sq. ft.

First Floor 1,365 sq. ft.

Large Window Seat In Master Bedroom

Total Living Area: 1,995

- 9' ceilings throughout the first floor
- Pass-through from kitchen into formal dining room is a quick and easy access
- Two-story great room has a wonderful corner fireplace
- 4 bedrooms, 2 1/2 baths, 2-car garage
- Basement, crawl space or slab foundation, please specify when ordering

MULTI-STORY

Plan # 577-0426

Price Code D

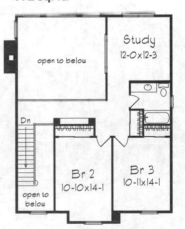

TO ORDER SEE PAGE 608 OR CALL TOLL-FREE 1-800-DREAM HOME (373-2646)

Balcony Offers Sweeping Views

Total Living Area: 2,444

- Laundry room with work space, pantry and coat closet adjacent to kitchen
- Two bedrooms, study, full bath and plenty of closets on second floor
- Large walk-in closet and private bath make this master suite one you're sure to enjoy
- Kitchen with cooktop island and easy access to living area
- 3 bedrooms, 2 1/2 baths, 2-car side entry garage
- Basement foundation

Second Floor
772 sq. ft.

Study
12-0x12-3

open to below

Dn

Br 2
10-10x14-1

Br 3
10-11x14-1

open to below

First Floor
1,672 sq. ft.

64'-0"

48'-0"

Great Rm
17-0x15-9

skylt

Brk
11-8x11-6

Patio

Kitchen
11-8x11-0

MBr
13-8x 20-0

Dn

up

Dining
14-1x11-11

P

Garage
19-8x19-5

Porch

MULTI-STORY

Plan# 577-DDI-95-234

Price Code B

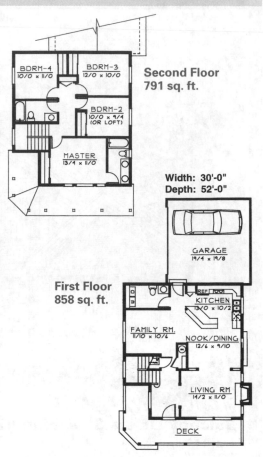

Second Floor
791 sq. ft.

BDRM-4 10/0 x 11/0
BDRM-3 12/0 x 10/0
BDRM-2 10/0 x 9/4 (OR LOFT)
MASTER 13/4 x 11/0

Width: 30'-0"
Depth: 52'-0"

First Floor
858 sq. ft.

GARAGE 19/4 x 19/8
KITCHEN 13/0 x 10/2
FAMILY RM. 11/10 x 10/6
NOOK/DINING 12/6 x 9/10
LIVING RM 14/2 x 11/0
DECK

Craftsman Cottage

Total Living Area: 1,649

- Energy efficient home with 2" x 6" exterior walls
- Ideal design for a narrow lot
- Country kitchen includes an island and eating bar
- Master bedroom has 12' vaulted ceiling and a charming arched window
- 4 bedrooms, 2 1/2 baths, 2-car side entry garage
- Basement or crawl space foundation, please specify when ordering

Plan# 577-GSD-2107

Price Code D

WIDTH 40'-0"
DEPTH 66'-6"

First Floor
1,495 sq. ft.

GARAGE 19-6 x 29-10
COVERED PORCH
FURN WH
UTIL
FAMILY ROOM VAULTED CEILING 13-6x14-6
PLANT LEDGE ABOVE
MASTER BATH
WALK-IN CLST
NOOK
EATING COUNTER
PHONE DESK
MASTER BEDROOM 13-8x14
ENTRY OPEN TO ABOVE
BUTLER'S PANTRY
KITCHEN
COVERED PORCH
DINING ROOM 13-4x12-2 VAULTED
TRELLIS
COPYRIGHT 1999 GSDG, INC.

Second Floor
927 sq. ft.

VAULTED CEILING LINE
ATTIC STOR.
OPEN TO BELOW
PLANT LEDGE
BEDROOM 2 11-6 x 11-2
STOR
OPEN RAILING
PLAYROOM 13-2 x 19-2
BATH
OPEN RAILING
STOR LINEN
SLOPED CLG
BEDROOM 3 11-6 x 12
OPEN TO BELOW

Vaulted Dining Room With Pantry

Total Living Area: 2,422

- Covered porches invite guests into home
- Convenient and private first floor master suite
- Family room has vaulted ceiling
- 10' ceiling in dining room has a formal feel
- Kitchen has walk-in pantry and eating bar
- 3 bedrooms, 2 1/2 baths, 3-car side entry garage
- Crawl space foundation

MULTI-STORY

TO ORDER SEE **PAGE 608** OR CALL TOLL-FREE **1-800-DREAM HOME (373-2646)**

Striking, Covered Arched Entry

Total Living Area: 1,859

- Fireplace highlights vaulted great room
- Master suite includes large closet and private bath
- Kitchen adjoins breakfast room providing easy access to the outdoors
- 3 bedrooms, 2 1/2 baths, 2-car garage
- Basement foundation

Br 2
10-8x11-3

MBr
11-10x17-2

Dn

open to below

Br 3
11-8x10-2

Second Floor
789 sq. ft.

63'-4"

Brk
9-8x
11-6

Kit
10-0x13-8

Great Rm
15-2x19-0

P

Dn

R

vaulted

Up   Foyer

Dining
11-8x11-2

36'-0"

Garage
21-8x21-8

First Floor
1,070 sq. ft.

MULTI-STORY

171

Plan # 577-JA-83899

Price Code A

Attractive Gables

Total Living Area: 1,342

- Kitchen/dining area includes a handy desk area
- High ceiling in living room adds a spacious feel
- First floor master bedroom has a private bath and large walk-in closet
- 3 bedrooms, 2 1/2 baths, 2-car garage
- Basement foundation

Second Floor
415 sq. ft.

BR. #2
10'0" x 12'0"

BR. #3
11'0" x 11'0"

First Floor
927 sq. ft.

MBR.
14'0" x 12'0"

KIT.
9'0" x 12'0"

DIN.
10'0" x 12'0"

LIV.
10'-1 1/8" CEILING HGT.
15'0" x 15'0"

2 CAR GARAGE
20'0" x 22'0"

44' 0"

42' 0"

Plan # 577-MG-01240

Price Code G

© 2003, Garrell Associates, Inc.

A Cozy Ranch With Rustic Touches

Total Living Area: 2,272

- 10' ceilings throughout first floor and 9' ceilings on the second floor
- Lots of storage area on the second floor
- First floor master bedroom has a lovely sitting area with arched entry
- Second floor bedrooms share a jack and jill bath
- 3 bedrooms, 2 1/2 baths, 2-car rear entry garage
- Slab foundation

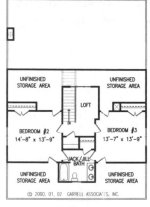

UNFINISHED STORAGE AREA

UNFINISHED STORAGE AREA

LOFT

BEDROOM #2
14'-8" x 13'-9"

BEDROOM #3
13'-7" x 13'-9"

JACK/JILL BATH

UNFINISHED STORAGE AREA

UNFINISHED STORAGE AREA

© 2000, 01, 02 GARRELL ASSOCIATES, INC.

Second Floor
685 sq. ft.

Width 38'-0"
Depth 55'-0"

© 2000, 01, 02 GARRELL ASSOCIATES, INC.

FAMILY ROOM
18'-2" x 18'-7"

TWO CAR GARAGE
18'-11" x 18'-11"

KITCHEN
14'-9" x 13'-9"

MSTR. BATH

W.I.C.

PDR. RM.

DINING ROOM
10'-3" x 12'-11"

MSTR. BD. RM.
12'-10" x 16'-4"

LAUN.

STUDY
10'-11" x 11'-0"

COVERED PORCH

SITTING RM.
9'-0" x 8'-2"

First Floor
1,587 sq. ft.

MULTI-STORY

172

Circular Stairway Adds To Front Entry

Total Living Area: 2,360

- Master suite includes sitting area and large bath
- Sloped family room ceiling provides view from second floor balcony
- Kitchen features island bar and walk-in butler's pantry
- 3 bedrooms, 2 1/2 baths, 2-car side entry garage
- Crawl space foundation, drawings also include slab and basement foundations

Second Floor
595 sq. ft.

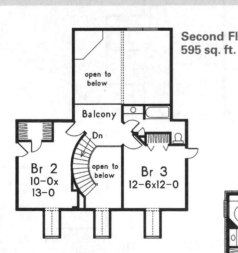

First Floor
1,766 sq. ft.

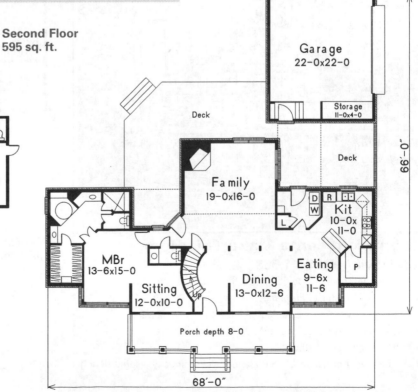

MULTI-STORY

173

Second Floor 886 sq. ft.

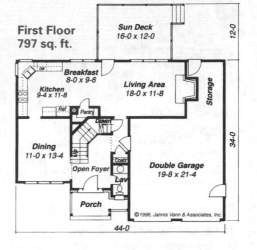

First Floor 797 sq. ft.

©1996, Jannis Vann & Associates, Inc.

Stucco With Brick Accents

Total Living Area: 1,683

- Open foyer and angled stairs add drama to entry
- Rear living area is open and spacious
- Master bath features garden tub, double vanities and a private toilet area
- 3 bedrooms, 2 1/2 baths, 2-car garage
- Walk-out basement foundation

Plan# **577-SH-SEA-400**

Price Code B

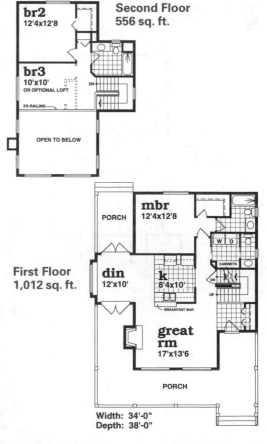

Second Floor 556 sq. ft.

First Floor 1,012 sq. ft.

Width: 34'-0"
Depth: 38'-0"

Country Accents Make This Home

Total Living Area: 1,568

- Master bedroom is located on first floor for convenience
- Cozy great room has fireplace
- Dining room has access to both the front and rear porches
- Two secondary bedrooms and a bath complete the second floor
- 3 bedrooms, 2 1/2 baths
- Basement or crawl space foundation, please specify when ordering

MULTI-STORY

Breezeway Joins Home With Garage

Total Living Area: 1,874

- 9' ceilings throughout first floor
- Two-story foyer opens into large family room with fireplace
- First floor master bedroom includes private bath with tub and shower
- 4 bedrooms, 2 1/2 baths, 2-car garage
- Basement foundation, drawings also include slab foundation

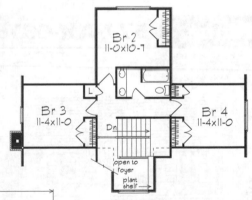

Second Floor
633 sq. ft.

Br 2
11-0x10-7

Br 3
11-4x11-0

Br 4
11-4x11-0

Dn

open to foyer

plant shelf

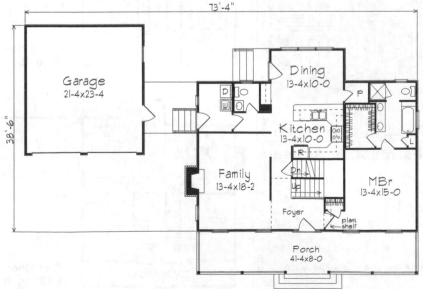

73'-4"

38'-6"

Garage
21-4x23-4

Dining
13-4x10-0

Kitchen
13-4x10-0

Family
13-4x18-2

MBr
13-4x15-0

Foyer

plant shelf

Porch
41-4x8-0

First Floor
1,241 sq. ft.

MULTI-STORY

175

Plan # 577-AMD-2189

Price Code D

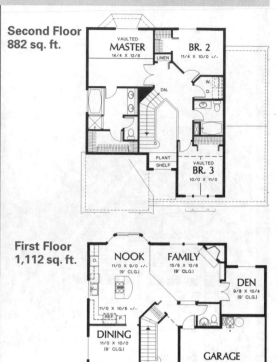

Second Floor 882 sq. ft.

First Floor 1,112 sq. ft.

43'

◀ 40' ▶

Cozy Corner Fireplace

Total Living Area: 1,994

- Breakfast nook overlooks kitchen and great room creating an airy feeling
- Enter double-doors to find a cozy den ideal as a home office
- Master suite has walk-in closet and private bath
- 3 bedrooms, 2 1/2 baths, 2-car garage
- Crawl space foundation

Plan # 577-AX-5376

Price Code D

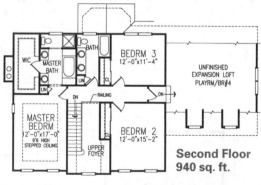

Second Floor 940 sq. ft.

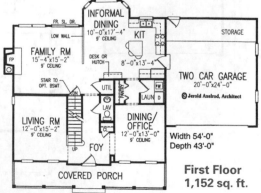

First Floor 1,152 sq. ft.

Width 54'-0"
Depth 43'-0"

MULTI-STORY

Affordable Home Has Farmhouse Appeal

Total Living Area: 2,092

- Dining room can used as an office or den
- Living room can be converted to a guest room
- Expansion loft is ideal for a playroom or a fourth bedroom and includes an additional 300 square feet of living area
- 3 bedrooms, 2 1/2 baths, 2-car garage
- Basement, crawl space or slab foundation, please specify when ordering

Great Media Room

Total Living Area: 2,750

- Oversized rooms throughout
- 9' ceilings on first floor
- Unique utility bay workshop off garage
- Spacious master suite with luxurious bath
- Optional sixth bedroom plan also included
- 5 bedrooms, 3 1/2 baths, 2-car side entry garage
- Basement foundation, drawings also include crawl space and slab foundations

TO ORDER SEE **PAGE 608** OR CALL TOLL-FREE 1-800-DREAM HOME (373-2646)

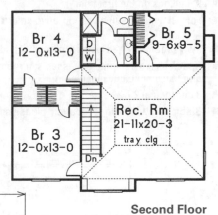

Br 4 12-0x13-0

Br 5 9-6x9-5

Br 3 12-0x13-0

Rec. Rm 21-11x20-3 tray clg

Second Floor
1,050 sq. ft.

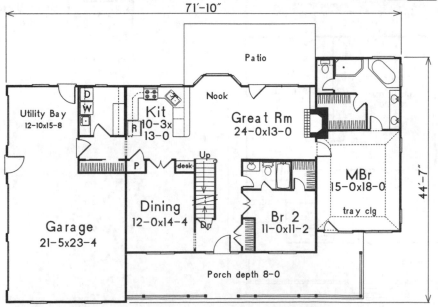

71'-10"

Patio

Nook

Utility Bay 12-10x15-8

Kit 10-3x 13-0

Great Rm 24-0x13-0

MBr 15-0x18-0 tray clg

Dining 12-0x14-4

Br 2 11-0x11-2

desk

Up

P

Dn

Garage 21-5x23-4

Porch depth 8-0

44'-7"

First Floor
1,700 sq. ft.

MULTI-STORY

177

Trio Of Dormers Add Appeal

Total Living Area: 3,011

- 9' ceilings on the first floor
- Formal dining room has decorative columns separating it from foyer and great room
- Two secondary bedrooms share a full bath on the second floor
- Spacious master suite accesses sun room through double-doors and has a spacious master bath
- 3 bedrooms, 2 1/2 baths
- Slab or crawl space foundation, please specify when ordering

Second Floor 650 sq. ft.

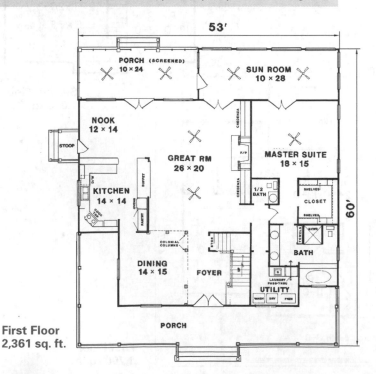

First Floor 2,361 sq. ft.

Traditional With Gabled Entrance

Total Living Area: 2,529

- Distinguished appearance enhances this home's classic interior arrangement
- Bonus room over the garage with direct access from the attic and the second floor hall
- Garden tub, walk-in closet and coffered ceiling enhance the master bedroom suite
- 4 bedrooms, 2 1/2 baths, 2-car garage
- Basement foundation

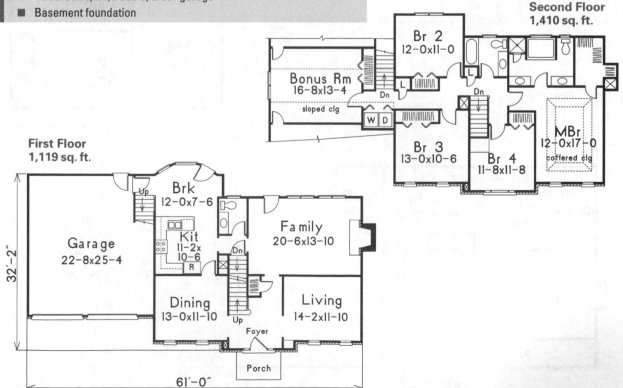

Second Floor
1,410 sq. ft.

Br 2
12-0x11-0

Bonus Rm
16-8x13-4

sloped clg

W D

Br 3
13-0x10-6

Dn

Br 4
11-8x11-8

MBr
12-0x17-0
coffered clg

First Floor
1,119 sq. ft.

Garage
22-8x25-4

Brk
12-0x7-6

Up

Kit
11-2x
10-6

R

Family
20-6x13-10

Dn

Dining
13-0x11-10

Living
14-2x11-10

Foyer

Up

Porch

32'-2"

61'-0"

MULTI-STORY

Two-Story Features Large Living Areas

Total Living Area: 1,998

- Large family room features fireplace and access to kitchen and dining area
- Skylights add daylight to second floor baths
- Utility room conveniently located near garage and kitchen
- Kitchen/breakfast area includes pantry, island work space and easy access to the patio
- 3 bedrooms, 2 1/2 baths, 2-car side entry garage
- Basement foundation, drawings also include crawl space and slab foundations

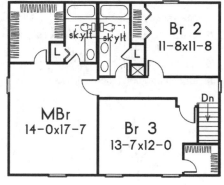

Second Floor
938 sq. ft.

Br 2
11-8x11-8

MBr
14-0x17-7

Br 3
13-7x12-0

Dn

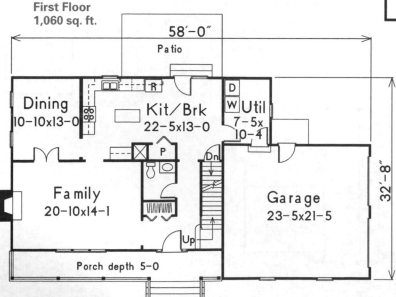

First Floor
1,060 sq. ft.

58'-0"

Patio

Dining
10-10x13-0

Kit/Brk
22-5x13-0

Util
7-5x
10-4

Family
20-10x14-1

Garage
23-5x21-5

32'-8"

Porch depth 5-0

TO ORDER SEE **PAGE 608** OR CALL TOLL-FREE 1-800-DREAM HOME (373-2646)

Covered Porch Highlights This Home

Total Living Area: 1,808

- Master bedroom has a walk-in closet, double vanities and separate tub and shower
- Two second floor bedrooms share a study area and full bath
- Partially covered patio is complete with a skylight
- Side entrance opens to utility room with convenient counterspace and laundry sink
- 3 bedrooms, 2 1/2 baths, 2-car side entry garage
- Basement foundation

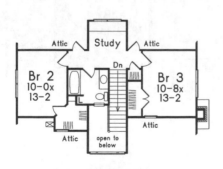

Second Floor
537 sq. ft.

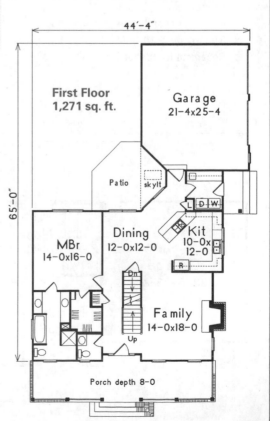

MULTI-STORY

181

TO ORDER SEE **PAGE 608** OR CALL TOLL-FREE 1-800-DREAM HOME (373-2646)

Country Classic With Modern Floor Plan

Total Living Area: 1,921

- Energy efficient home with 2" x 6" exterior walls
- Sunken family room includes a built-in entertainment center and coffered ceiling
- Sunken formal living room features a coffered ceiling
- Dressing area has double sinks, spa tub, shower and French door to private deck
- Large front porch adds to home's appeal
- 3 bedrooms, 2 1/2 baths, 2-car garage
- Basement foundation

MULTI-STORY

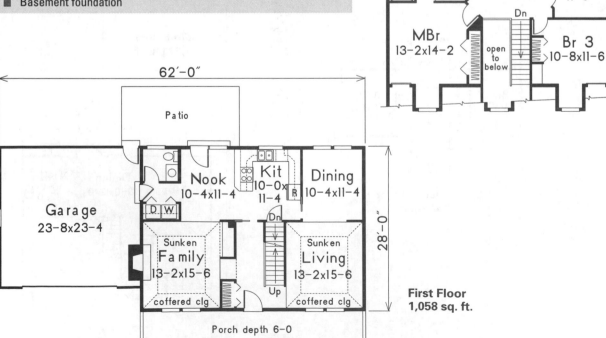

Second Floor
863 sq. ft.

First Floor
1,058 sq. ft.

Stairway Highlights Two-Story Foyer

Total Living Area: 2,511

- Screened porch is accessible from three different living areas
- Feeling of spaciousness created by vaulted kitchen and family area
- Unfinished area on the second floor has an additional 533 square feet of living area
- 3 bedrooms, 2 1/2 baths, 2-car side entry garage
- Basement foundation, drawings also include crawl space and slab foundations

Second Floor
659 sq. ft.

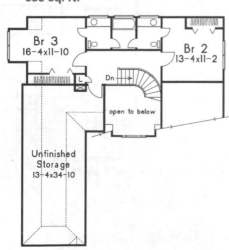

Br 3
16-4x11-10

Br 2
13-4x11-2

Dn

open to below

Unfinished Storage
13-4x34-10

First Floor
1,852 sq. ft.

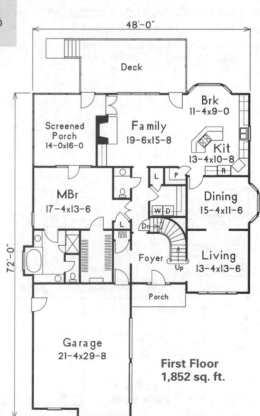

48'-0"

Deck

Brk
11-4x9-0

Screened Porch
14-0x16-0

Family
19-6x15-8

Kit
13-4x10-8

MBr
17-4x13-6

Dining
15-4x11-6

W D

Dn

72'-0"

Foyer

Up

Living
13-4x13-6

Porch

Garage
21-4x29-8

MULTI-STORY

183

TO ORDER SEE **PAGE 608** OR CALL TOLL-FREE 1-800-DREAM HOME (373-2646)

Striking Turret Created By Sitting Area

Total Living Area: 2,246

- Two-story foyer
- Master suite has sitting area with bay window
- Breakfast area near kitchen
- Bedroom #4 easily converts to an office
- Optional bonus room has an additional 269 square feet of living area
- 4 bedrooms, 3 baths, 2-car side entry garage
- Walk-out basement, slab or crawl space foundation, please specify when ordering

MULTI-STORY

First Floor
1,688 sq. ft.

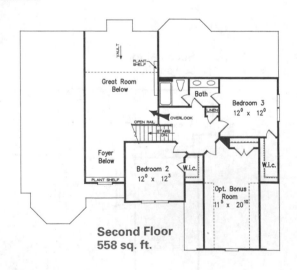

Second Floor
558 sq. ft.

Blends Open And Private Living Areas

Total Living Area: 1,996

- Dining area features octagon-shaped coffered ceiling and built-in china cabinet
- Both the master bath and second floor bath have cheerful skylights
- Family room includes wet bar and fireplace flanked by attractive quarter round windows
- 9' ceilings throughout first floor with plant shelving in foyer and dining area
- 3 bedrooms, 2 1/2 baths, 2-car side entry garage
- Basement foundation, drawings also include crawl space and slab foundations

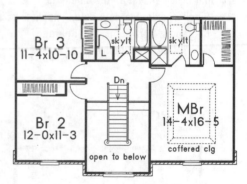

Second Floor
859 sq. ft.

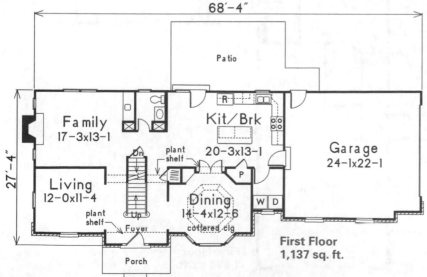

First Floor
1,137 sq. ft.

MULTI-STORY

185

Nice-Sized Porch Is A Stylish Shelter

Total Living Area: 2,120

- First floor vaulted master bedroom has a spacious and open feel
- Built-in shelves adorn the dining room
- Office has a double-door entry helping to maintain privacy
- 3 bedrooms, 2 1/2 baths, 3-car garage
- Crawl space foundation

Second Floor
517 sq. ft.

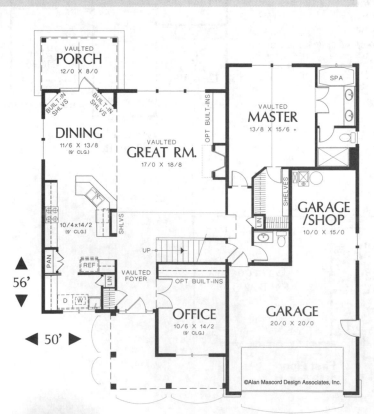

©Alan Mascord Design Associates, Inc.

First Floor
1,603 sq. ft.

MULTI-STORY

Plan# 577-0430

Price Code E

TO ORDER SEE **PAGE 608** OR CALL TOLL-FREE 1-800-DREAM HOME (373-2646)

Entry Collonade, Circle-Top Windows

Total Living Area: 2,869

- Foyer, flanked by columned living and dining rooms, leads to vaulted family room with fireplace and twin sets of French doors
- 10' ceilings on first floor and 9' ceilings on second floor
- 4 bedrooms, 3 baths, 2-car rear entry garage
- Slab foundation, drawings also include crawl space foundation

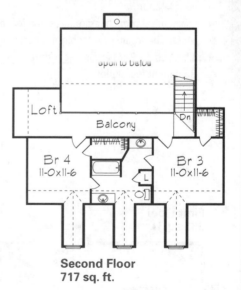

Second Floor
717 sq. ft.

First Floor
2,152 sq. ft.

MULTI-STORY

187

Traditional Styling

Total Living Area: 1,873

- Formal dining area in the front of the house is conveniently located near kitchen
- Large great room has fireplace and lots of windows
- Master bedroom has double-door entry with a private bath
- 3 bedrooms, 2 1/2 baths, 2-car garage
- Basement foundation

MULTI-STORY

188

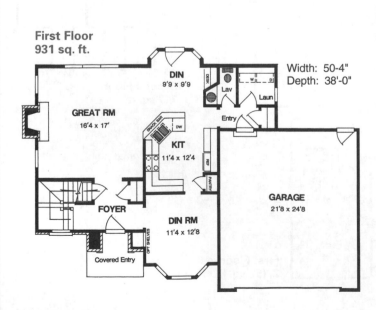

First Floor
931 sq. ft.

Width: 50-4"
Depth: 38'-0"

DIN 9'9 x 9'9
Lav
Laun
GREAT RM 16'4 x 17'
Entry
KIT 11'4 x 12'4
DW
FOYER
DIN RM 11'4 x 12'8
GARAGE 21'8 x 24'8
Covered Entry

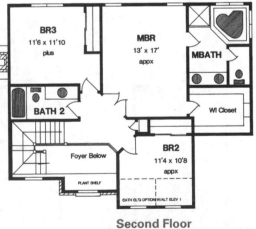

Second Floor
942 sq. ft.

BR3 11'6 x 11'10 plus
MBR 13' x 17' appx
MBATH
BATH 2
WI Closet
Foyer Below
BR2 11'4 x 10'8 appx
PLANT SHELF
CATH CL'G OPTIONEW/ALT ELEV 1

Plan# 577-SRD-142

Price Code C

TO ORDER SEE **PAGE 608** OR CALL TOLL-FREE 1-800-DREAM HOME (373-2646)

Computer Area Is A Handy Feature

Total Living Area: 2,082

- Master bedroom boasts a deluxe bath and a large walk-in closet
- Natural light floods the breakfast room through numerous windows
- Great room features 12' ceiling, a cozy fireplace and stylish French doors
- Bonus room on the second floor has an additional 267 square feet of living area
- 3 bedrooms, 2 1/2 baths, 2-car garage
- Basement foundation

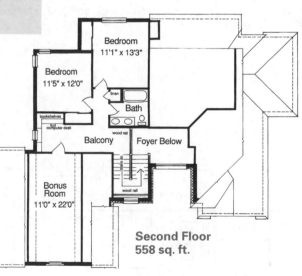

Second Floor
558 sq. ft.

First Floor
1,524 sq. ft.

MULTI-STORY

189

TO ORDER SEE **PAGE 608** OR CALL TOLL-FREE 1-800-DREAM HOME (373-2646)

Two-Story Offers Attractive Exterior
Total Living Area: 2,262

- Charming exterior features include large front porch, two patios, front balcony and double bay windows
- Den provides impressive entry to sunken family room
- Conveniently located first floor laundry
- Large master bedroom with walk-in closet, dressing area and bath
- 3 bedrooms, 2 1/2 baths, 2-car rear entry garage
- Crawl space foundation, drawings also include basement and slab foundations

Second Floor
1,135 sq. ft.

Br 2
15-2x11-3

Dn

MBr
13-7x22-9

Br 3
15-5x10-10

Balcony

70'-10 1/2"

25'-4"

Patio

Patio

Kit
11-4x10-3

W
D

Sunken
Family
13-7x17-8

Garage
23-5x23-5

Dining
9-8x13-5

P

Furn

Living
15-5x11-6

Up

Den
13-7x12-3

First Floor
1,127 sq. ft.

Porch depth 8-0

MULTI-STORY

Plan# 577-BF-2108

Price Code C

Two-Story Living Room

Total Living Area: 2,194

- Energy efficient home with 2" x 6" exterior walls
- Utility room has laundry drop conveniently located next to kitchen
- Both second floor bedrooms have large closets and their own bath
- 3 bedrooms, 3 1/2 baths, 2-car side entry garage
- Crawl space, slab or basement foundation, please specify when ordering

Width: 52'-0"
Depth: 74' 0"

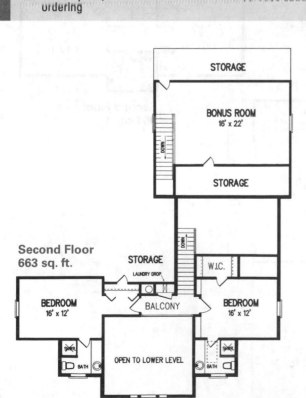

Second Floor
663 sq. ft.

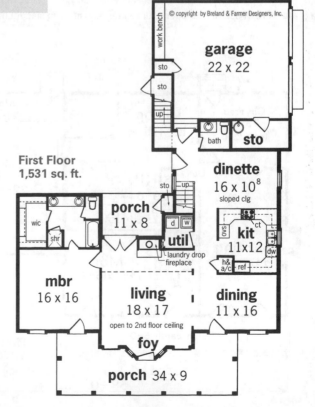

First Floor
1,531 sq. ft.

MULTI-STORY

TO ORDER SEE **PAGE 608** OR CALL TOLL-FREE 1-800-DREAM HOME (373-2646)

Two-Story Has Screened-In Rear Porch

Total Living Area: 1,600

- Energy efficient home with 2" x 6" exterior walls
- First floor master suite accessible from two points of entry
- Master suite dressing area includes separate vanities and a mirrored make-up counter
- Second floor bedrooms with generous storage, share a full bath
- 3 bedrooms, 2 baths, 2-car side entry garage
- Crawl space foundation, drawings also include slab foundation

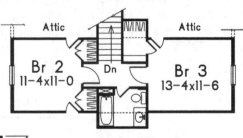

Br 2
11-4x11-0

Br 3
13-4x11-6

Second Floor
464 sq. ft.

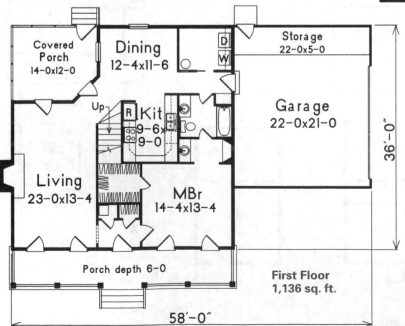

Covered Porch
14-0x12-0

Dining
12-4x11-6

Storage
22-0x5-0

Garage
22-0x21-0

Up

Kit
9-6x9-0

Living
23-0x13-4

MBr
14-4x13-4

36'-0"

Porch depth 6-0

First Floor
1,136 sq. ft.

58'-0"

MULTI-STORY

Terrific Traditional Brick Two-Story

Total Living Area: 2,900

- Master bedroom includes small sitting nook and spacious walk-in closet
- Formal living and dining rooms in the front of the home
- 9' ceilings on first floor
- 4 bedrooms, 3 1/2 baths, 2-car garage
- Basement foundation

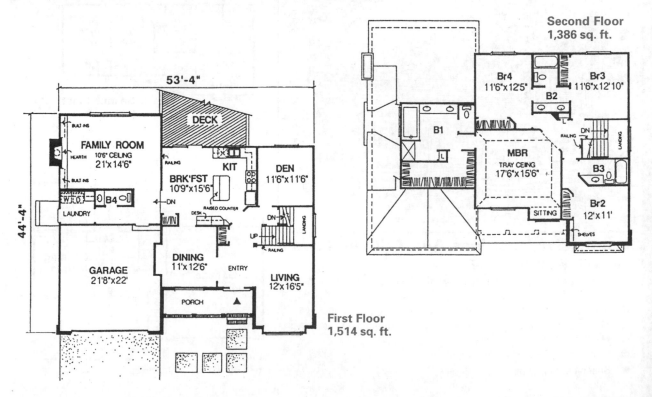

Second Floor
1,386 sq. ft.

Br4 11'6"x12'5"

Br3 11'6"x12'10"

B2

B1

MBR
TRAY CEING
17'6"x15'6"

B3

Br2 12'x11'

SITTING

SHELVES

RAILING

LANDING

DN

53'-4"

DECK

FAMILY ROOM
10'6" CEILING
21'x14'6"

BUILT-INS

HEARTH

BUILT-INS

KIT

BRK'FST
10'9"x15'6"

DEN
11'6"x11'6"

W.I.C.

B4

LAUNDRY

RAISED COUNTER

DESK

DN

RAILING

DN

UP

LANDING

44'-4"

GARAGE
21'8"x22'

DINING
11'x12'6"

ENTRY

LIVING
12'x16'5"

PORCH

First Floor
1,514 sq. ft.

MULTI-STORY

Plan# 577-GSD-2004

Price Code B

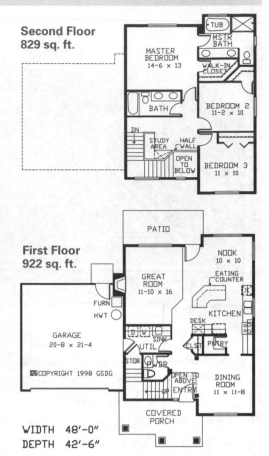

Second Floor
829 sq. ft.

MASTER BEDROOM 14-6 x 13

TUB

MSTR BATH

WALK-IN CLOSET

BATH

BEDROOM 2 11-2 x 10

DN

STUDY AREA

HALF WALL

OPEN TO BELOW

BEDROOM 3 11 x 10

First Floor
922 sq. ft.

PATIO

NOOK 10 x 10

GREAT ROOM 11-10 x 16

EATING COUNTER

FURN

HWT

KITCHEN

GARAGE 20-8 x 21-4

DW

SINK

UTIL

STOR

PWDR

DESK

CLST

PANTRY

OPEN TO ABOVE

UP

ENTRY

DINING ROOM 11 x 11-8

COPYRIGHT 1998 GSDG

COVERED PORCH

WIDTH 48'-0"
DEPTH 42'-6"

Second Floor Study Area

Total Living Area: 1,751

- Charming covered front porch
- Elegant two-story entry
- Beautifully designed great room with fireplace opens to kitchen
- Large eating counter and walk-in pantry
- Second floor study area perfect for a growing family
- 3 bedrooms, 2 1/2 baths, 2-car garage
- Crawl space foundation

Plan# 577-0103

Price Code A

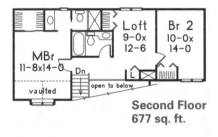

MBr 11-8x14-0

Loft 9-0x 12-6

Br 2 10-0x 14-0

Dn

vaulted

open to below

L

Second Floor
677 sq. ft.

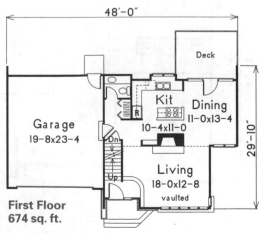

48'-0"

Deck

Garage 19-8x23-4

Kit 10-4x11-0

R

Dining 11-0x13-4

Dn

Up

Living 18-0x12-8
vaulted

29'-10"

First Floor
674 sq. ft.

Impressive Rooflines And Tall Windows

Total Living Area: 1,351

- Roof lines and vaulted ceilings make this home appear larger than its true size
- Central fireplace provides a focal point for dining and living areas
- Master bedroom suite is highlighted by a roomy window seat and a walk-in closet
- 3 bedrooms, 2 1/2 baths, 2-car garage
- Basement foundation

TO ORDER SEE **PAGE 608** OR CALL TOLL-FREE 1-800-DREAM HOME (373-2646)

Smart Floor Plan Makes Efficient Design

Total Living Area: 2,179

- Open floor plan and minimal halls eliminate wasted space and create efficiency
- First floor master suite is conveniently located near large kitchen
- Three bedrooms on the second floor share large bath with nearby linen closet
- 4 bedrooms, 2 1/2 baths, 2-car garage
- Basement foundation

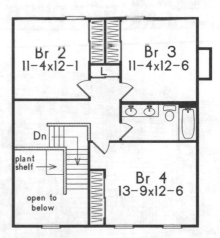

Second Floor
770 sq. ft.

Br 2
11-4x12-1

Br 3
11-4x12-6

L

Dn

plant shelf

open to below

Br 4
13-9x12-6

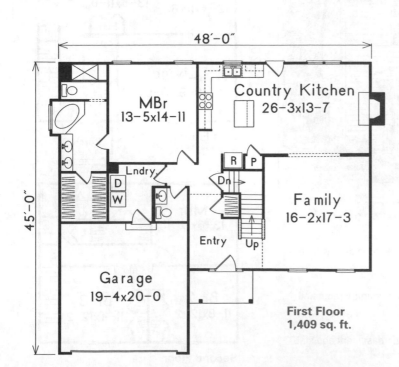

48'-0"

45'-0"

MBr
13-5x14-11

Country Kitchen
26-3x13-7

Lndry

D W

R P

Dn

Family
16-2x17-3

Entry

Up

Garage
19-4x20-0

First Floor
1,409 sq. ft.

MULTI-STORY

195

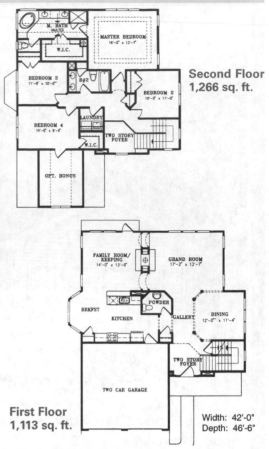

Second Floor
1,266 sq. ft.

First Floor Creates Open Living

Total Living Area: 2,379

- Second floor laundry room is convenient to all bedrooms
- See-through fireplace enhances the family room and grand room
- Dining room accented with columns is open to grand room
- 4 bedrooms, 2 1/2 baths, 2-car garage
- Basement foundation

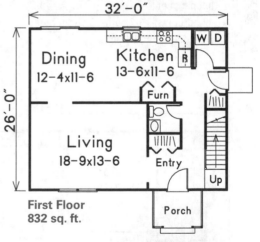

First Floor
1,113 sq. ft.

Width: 42'-0"
Depth: 46'-6"

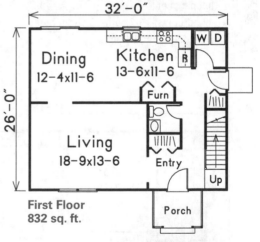

First Floor
832 sq. ft.

Two-Story With All The Conveniences

Total Living Area: 1,664

- Master bedroom includes private bath, dressing area and walk-in closet
- Spacious rooms throughout
- Kitchen features handy side entrance, adjacent laundry room and coat closet
- 3 bedrooms, 2 1/2 baths
- Crawl space foundation, drawings also include basement and slab foundations

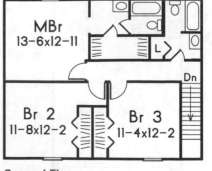

Second Floor
832 sq. ft.

Two-Story Atrium For Great Views

Total Living Area: 2,900

- Elegant entry foyer leads to balcony overlook of vaulted two-story atrium
- Spacious kitchen features an island breakfast bar, walk-in pantry, bayed breakfast room and adjoining screened porch
- Two large second floor bedrooms and stair balconies overlook a sun drenched two-story vaulted atrium
- 4 bedrooms, 3 1/2 baths, 2-car side entry garage
- Basement foundation

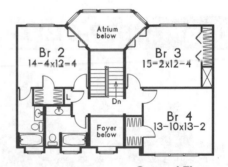

**Second Floor
1,065 sq. ft.**

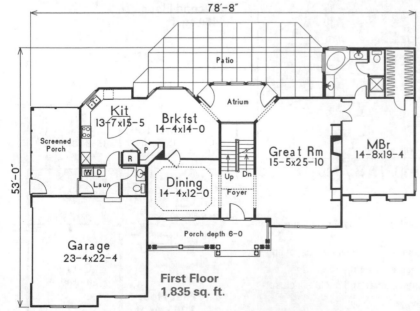

**First Floor
1,835 sq. ft.**

MULTI-STORY

Plan# 577-SRD-214

Price Code C

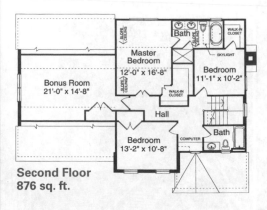

**Second Floor
876 sq. ft.**

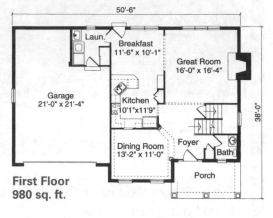

**First Floor
980 sq. ft.**

A Floor Plan For Family Living

Total Living Area: 1,856

- The roomy kitchen offers an abundance of cabinets and counter space as well as a convenient pantry
- Master bedroom includes a sloped ceiling and a deluxe bath
- Bonus room on the second floor has an additional 325 square feet of living area
- 3 bedrooms, 2 1/2 baths, 2-car garage
- Walk-out basement or basement foundation, please specify when ordering

Plan# 577-0109

Price Code B

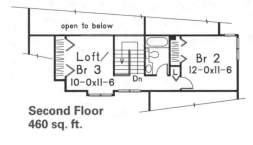

**Second Floor
460 sq. ft.**

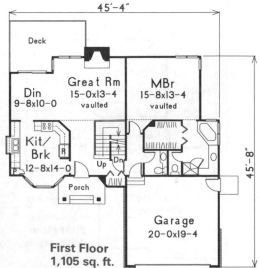

**First Floor
1,105 sq. ft.**

Stylish Master Bedroom Off By Itself

Total Living Area: 1,565

- Highly-detailed exterior adds value
- Large vaulted great room with a full wall of glass opens onto the corner deck
- Loft balcony opens to rooms below and adds to the spacious feeling
- Bay-windowed kitchen with a cozy morning room
- Master bath has platform tub, separate shower and a walk-in closet
- 3 bedrooms, 2 1/2 baths, 2-car garage
- Basement foundation

MULTI-STORY

Great Looks Accentuated By Brick Arches

Total Living Area: 2,521

- Large living and dining rooms are a plus for formal entertaining or large family gatherings
- Informal kitchen, breakfast and family rooms feature a 37' vista and double bay windows
- Generous-sized master bedroom and three secondary bedrooms grace the second floor
- 4 bedrooms, 2 1/2 baths, 2-car garage
- Basement foundation

Second Floor
1,146 sq. ft.

Br 3
12-0x13-0

Br 2
11-0x10-4

Br 4
12-0x13-0

Dn

plant shelf

open to below

MBr
13-4x17-5

vaulted clg

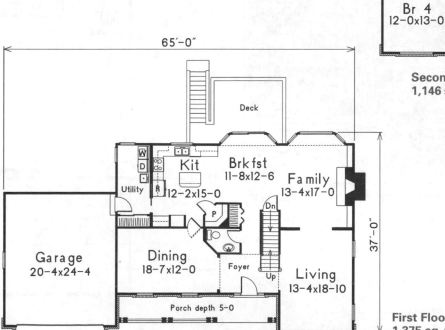

65'-0"

Deck

Kit
12-2x15-0

Brkfst
11-8x12-6

Family
13-4x17-0

Utility

W
D

P

Dn

37'-0"

Garage
20-4x24-4

Dining
18-7x12-0

Foyer

Up

Living
13-4x18-10

Porch depth 5-0

First Floor
1,375 sq. ft.

TO ORDER SEE **PAGE 608** OR CALL TOLL-FREE 1-800-DREAM HOME (373-2646)

MULTI-STORY

Plan# 577-SRD-106

Price Code C

Second Floor
475 sq. ft.

First Floor
1,626 sq. ft.

Exciting Roof Lines

Total Living Area: 2,101

- Sunken great room has balcony above
- Octagon-shaped master bedroom is private
- Luxurious amenities in a modest size
- 3 bedrooms, 2 1/2 baths, 2-car garage
- Basement foundation

Plan# 577-0384

Price Code D

Second Floor
988 sq. ft.

First Floor
1,025 sq. ft.

Charming Two-Story With Covered Entry

Total Living Area: 2,013

- Sliding doors in dinette allow convenient access outdoors
- Family room includes cozy fireplace for informal gathering
- All bedrooms located on second floor for privacy
- Master bath includes dressing area, walk-in closet and separate tub and shower
- 4 bedrooms, 2 1/2 baths, 2-car garage
- Basement foundation

MULTI-STORY

TO ORDER SEE **PAGE 608** OR CALL TOLL-FREE 1-800-DREAM HOME (373-2646)

Varied Exterior Finishes Enrich Facade

Total Living Area: 2,696

- Magnificent master suite with private covered porch and luxurious bath
- Second floor game room with balcony access and adjacent loft
- Well-planned kitchen includes walk-in pantry, island cooktop and nearby spacious breakfast room
- 4 bedrooms, 3 baths, 2-car side entry garage
- Slab foundation, drawings also include crawl space foundation

**First Floor
1,904 sq. ft.**

Garage
21-0x21-0

Kit
12-4x13-2

Great Rm
17-4x17-4
12-0 ceiling

Covered
Porch

Brk
12-4x12-6

Dining
15-4x11-4

Foyer

Up

MBr
16-8x14-8

Porch

Br 2
11-4x11-8

64'-0"

66'-10"

Br 3
12-4x12-5

Balcony

Game Rm
17-4x13-8

open to
below

Dn

plant
shelf

Loft

Br 4
12-0x12-4

**Second Floor
792 sq. ft.**

MULTI-STORY

201

Plan# 577-AMD-22138A

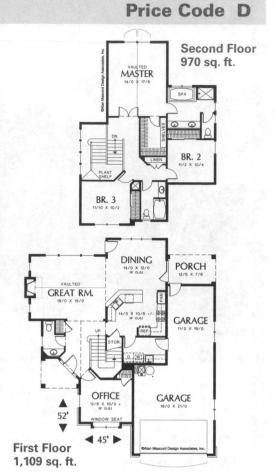

Second Floor 970 sq. ft.

First Floor 1,109 sq. ft.

Wood Shingles Create A Custom Feel

Total Living Area: 2,079

- A home office is convenient to the front entry making it very accessible for visitors
- Vaulted great room enjoys views of the dining room and kitchen
- The vaulted master bedroom has all the luxuries with an amenity full bath
- 3 bedrooms, 2 1/2 baths, 3-car garage
- Crawl space foundation

Plan# 577-0486

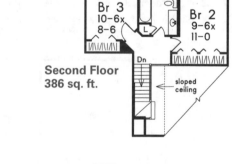

Second Floor 386 sq. ft.

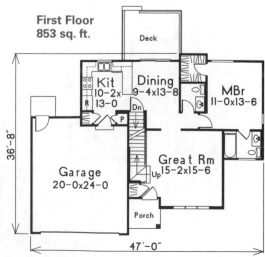

First Floor 853 sq. ft.

Gables Accent This Home

Total Living Area: 1,239

- Master suite has private bath and walk-in closet
- Convenient coat closet and pantry located near the garage entrance
- Kitchen and dining area open onto deck
- Open stairway with sloped ceiling creates an open atmosphere in the great room
- 3 bedrooms, 2 1/2 baths, 2-car garage
- Basement foundation

J.N. HANSEN S.P.G.

Spectacular Views In Atrium Home
Total Living Area: 2,806

- Harmonious charm throughout
- Sweeping balcony and vaulted ceiling soar above spacious great room and walk-in bar
- 4 bedrooms, 2 1/2 baths, 2-car garage
- Walk-out basement foundation

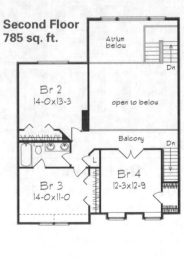

Rear View

54'-8"

Atrium below

Deck

Dining
10-2x13-3

Kit
11-0x
13-3

Great Rm
18-0x19-10

vaulted

vaulted

Bar

51'-0"

MBr
14-0x16-9

Foyer

Up

Garage
21-4x21-4

Porch

First Floor
1,473 sq. ft.

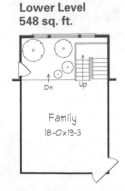

Lower Level
548 sq. ft.

Dn   Up

Family
18-0x19-3

Second Floor
785 sq. ft.

Atrium below

Br 2
14-0x13-3

open to below

Balcony

Br 3
14-0x11-0

Br 4
12-3x12-9

MULTI-STORY

203

Plan# 577-FB-963

Price Code C

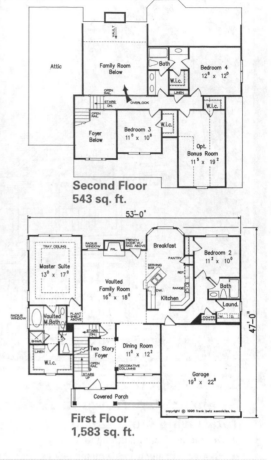

Second Floor
543 sq. ft.

First Floor
1,583 sq. ft.

Second Floor Overlook

Total Living Area: 2,126

- Kitchen overlooks vaulted family room with a handy serving bar
- Two-story foyer creates an airy feeling
- Second floor includes an optional bonus room with an additional 251 square feet of living area
- 4 bedrooms, 3 baths, 2-car side entry garage
- Walk-out basement, crawl space or slab foundation, please specify when ordering

Plan# 577-MG-01158

Price Code H

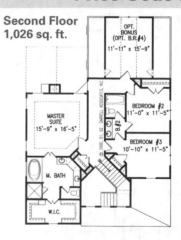

Second Floor
1,026 sq. ft.

First Floor
1,109 sq. ft.

Terrific Facade

Total Living Area: 2,135

- 10' ceilings throughout first floor and 9' ceilings on the second floor
- Angled entry leads through columns into a cozy social room
- Spacious kitchen has center island with a place for dining as well as food preparation
- Bonus room on the second floor has an additional 247 square feet of living area
- 3 bedrooms, 2 1/2 baths, 2-car rear entry garage
- Slab foundation

MULTI-STORY

TO ORDER SEE **PAGE 608** OR CALL TOLL-FREE 1-800-DREAM HOME (373-2646)

Appealing Two-Story For Family Living
Total Living Area: 2,316

- Raised hearth and built-in media center create an impressive feel to the family room
- Expansive kitchen has center island with cooktop range and is open to dining area featuring a trio of skylights
- 9' ceilings throughout first floor
- 3 bedrooms, 2 1/2 baths, 3-car garage
- Walk-out basement or basement foundation, please specify when ordering

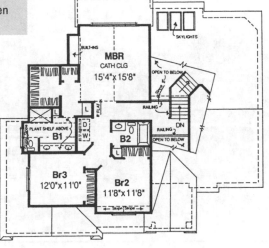

Second Floor
1,029 sq. ft.

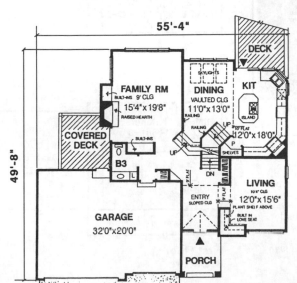

First Floor
1,287 sq. ft.

MULTI-STORY

Price Code B

Second Floor
780 sq. ft.

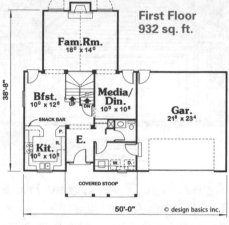

First Floor
932 sq. ft.

38'-8"

50'-0" © design basics inc.

Appealing Touches Abound

Total Living Area: 1,712

- Cathedral ceiling in family room adds drama and spaciousness
- Roomy utility area
- Master bedroom has a private bath, walk-in closet and whirlpool tub
- Efficient kitchen with snack bar
- 3 bedrooms, 2 1/2 baths, 2-car garage
- Basement foundation

Plan# **577-0536**

Price Code B

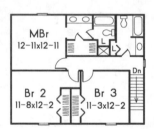

Second Floor
832 sq. ft.

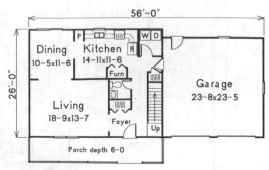

56'-0"

26'-0"

Porch depth 6-0

First Floor
832 sq. ft.

Old-Fashioned Porch Adds Appeal

Total Living Area: 1,664

- L-shaped country kitchen includes pantry and cozy breakfast area
- Bedrooms located on second floor for privacy
- Master bedroom includes walk-in closet, dressing area and bath
- 3 bedrooms, 2 1/2 baths, 2-car garage
- Crawl space foundation, drawings also include basement and slab foundations

MULTI-STORY

TO ORDER SEE **PAGE 608** OR CALL TOLL-FREE 1-800-DREAM HOME (373-2646)

Unique, Traditional Style, Farmhouse

Total Living Area: 1,763

- Dining room has a large box bay window and a recessed ceiling
- Living room includes a large fireplace
- Kitchen has plenty of workspace, a pantry and a double sink overlooking the deck
- Master bedroom features a large bath with walk-in closet
- 3 bedrooms, 2 1/2 baths, 2-car garage
- Basement foundation, drawings also include crawl space and slab foundations

Second Floor
854 sq. ft.

Master Br
14-3 x 17-5

Br 3
12-2 x 10-1

Br 2
13-11 x 11-9

Railing

Line of Floor Below

Flue

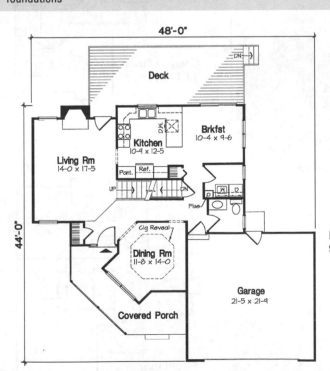

48'-0"

44'-0"

Deck

DN

Kitchen
10-4 x 12-5

Brkfst
10-4 x 9-6

Living Rm
14-0 x 17-5

Pant. Ref.

UP   DN

Flue

Clg Reveal

Dining Rm
11-8 x 14-0

Garage
21-5 x 21-4

Covered Porch

First Floor
909 sq. ft.

MULTI-STORY

207

Plan# 577-AP-2911

Price Code D

Second Floor
861 sq. ft.

First Floor
2,093 sq. ft.

Brick Makes Lasting Impression

Total Living Area: 2,954

- Master bedroom has a double-door entry into the luxurious bath
- Private study has direct access into the master bedroom
- Vaulted ceiling and bay window add light and dimension to the breakfast room
- 4 bedrooms, 3 1/2 baths, 2-car side entry garage
- Basement foundation

Plan# 577-GSD-2242

Price Code D

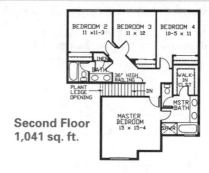

Second Floor
1,041 sq. ft.

Secluded Den/Office

Total Living Area: 2,450

- Oversized rooms throughout
- 12' ceiling in entry adds drama
- Coffered ceiling in dining room is a unique touch
- Kitchen includes island, walk-in pantry and a nook ideal as a breakfast area
- 4 bedrooms, 2 1/2 baths, 2-car garage
- Crawl space foundation

First Floor
1,409 sq. ft.

Outstanding For Year-Round Entertaining

Total Living Area: 2,597

- Large U-shaped kitchen features island cooktop and breakfast bar
- Entry and great room enhanced by sweeping balcony
- Bedrooms #2 and #3 share a bath, while the fourth bedroom has a private bath
- Vaulted great room with transomed arch windows
- 4 bedrooms, 3 1/2 baths, 2-car side entry garage
- Walk-out basement foundation, drawings also include crawl space and slab foundations

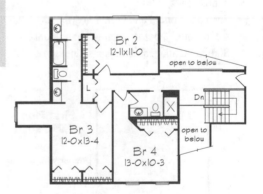

Second Floor
855 sq. ft.

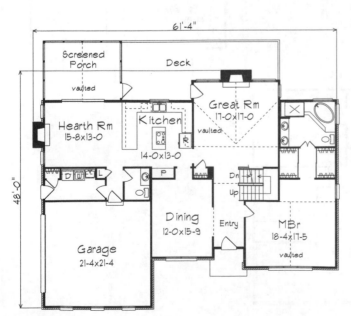

First Floor
1,742 sq. ft.

MULTI-STORY

Wrap-Around Front Country Porch

Total Living Area: 2,665

- 9' ceilings on first floor
- Spacious kitchen features many cabinets, center island cooktop and breakfast room with bay window, adjacent to laundry room
- Second floor bedrooms boast walk-in closets, dressing areas and share a bath
- Twin patio doors and fireplace grace living room
- 4 bedrooms, 3 baths, 2-car rear entry garage
- Slab foundation, drawings also include crawl space foundation

Second Floor
749 sq. ft.

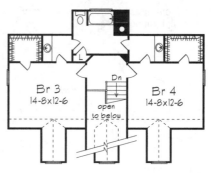

Br 3
14-8x12-6

Br 4
14-8x12-6

Dn

open to below

First Floor
1,916 sq. ft.

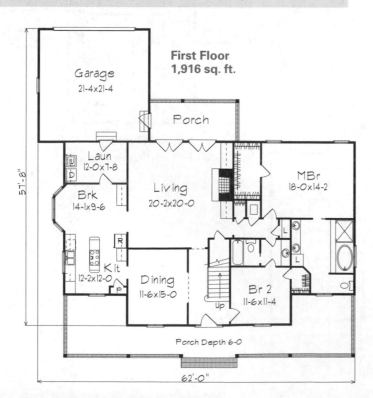

Garage
21-4x21-4

Porch

Laun
12-0x7-8

Brk
14-1x9-6

Living
20-2x20-0

MBr
18-0x14-2

Kit
12-2x12-0

Dining
11-6x15-0

Br 2
11-6x11-4

up

Porch Depth 6-0

51'-8"

62'-0"

Optimum Style For Family Living

Total Living Area: 2,431

- Second floor includes a wonderful casual family room with corner fireplace and reading nook
- The great room, living and dining areas all combine to create one large living area ideal for entertaining or family gatherings
- Built-in pantry in breakfast area
- 4 bedrooms, 2 1/2 baths, 2-car garage with shop/storage area
- Basement, crawl space or slab foundation, please specify when ordering

Second Floor
1,037 sq. ft.

First Floor
1,394 sq. ft.

Width 56'-8"
Depth 53'-0"

MULTI-STORY

TO ORDER SEE PAGE 608 OR CALL TOLL-FREE 1-800-DREAM HOME (373-2646)

Elegant, Stylish And Sophisticated

Total Living Area: 4,370

- Detailed brickwork surrounding the arched windows and quoined corners create a timeless exterior
- Two-story great room has a large fireplace, flanking bookshelves, massive window wall and balcony overlook
- State-of-the-art kitchen has an island cooktop, built-in oven/microwave, large pantry and menu desk
- A bay window and two walk-in closets adorn the master bedroom
- 4 bedrooms, 3 1/2 baths, 3-car side entry garage
- Basement foundation

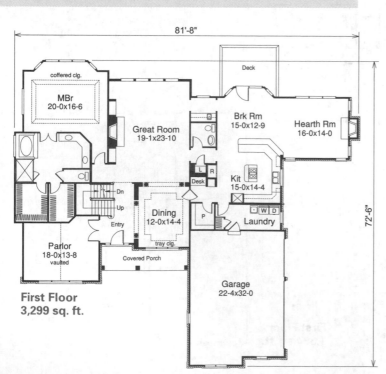

First Floor
3,299 sq. ft.

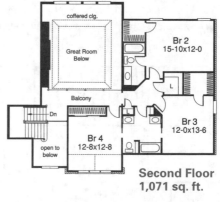

Second Floor
1,071 sq. ft.

MULTI-STORY

Plan# 577-GM-1966

Price Code C

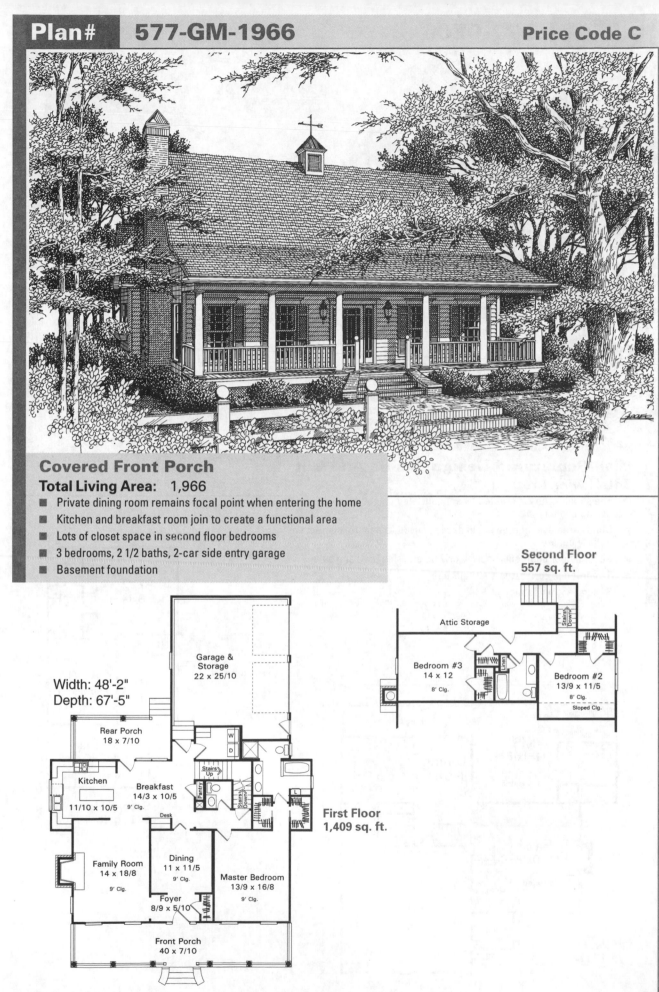

Covered Front Porch

Total Living Area: 1,966

- Private dining room remains focal point when entering the home
- Kitchen and breakfast room join to create a functional area
- Lots of closet space in second floor bedrooms
- 3 bedrooms, 2 1/2 baths, 2-car side entry garage
- Basement foundation

Second Floor
557 sq. ft.

Attic Storage

Stairs Down

Bedroom #3
14 x 12
8' Clg.

Linen

Bedroom #2
13/9 x 11/5
8' Clg.
Sloped Clg.

Width: 48'-2"
Depth: 67'-5"

Garage & Storage
22 x 25/10

Rear Porch
18 x 7/10

W
D

Kitchen
11/10 x 10/5

Breakfast
14/3 x 10/5
9' Clg.

Pantry

Stairs Up

Stairs Down

Desk

First Floor
1,409 sq. ft.

Family Room
14 x 18/8
9' Clg.

Dining
11 x 11/5
9' Clg.

Master Bedroom
13/9 x 16/8
9' Clg.

Foyer
8/9 x 5/10

Front Porch
40 x 7/10

MULTI-STORY

213

Well-Sculptured Design, Inside And Out

Total Living Area: 1,889

- The striking entry is created by a unique stair layout, an open high ceiling and a fireplace
- Bonus area over garage could easily convert to a fourth bedroom or activity center
- Second floor bedrooms share a private dressing area and bath
- 3 bedrooms, 2 1/2 baths, 2-car garage
- Basement foundation

MULTI-STORY

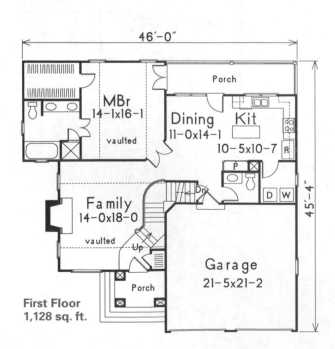

First Floor
1,128 sq. ft.

46'-0"

MBr
14-1x16-1
vaulted

Dining
11-0x14-1

Kit
10-5x10-7

Porch

Family
14-0x18-0
vaulted

Up

Dn

P

D   W

R

Garage
21-5x21-2

Porch

45'-4"

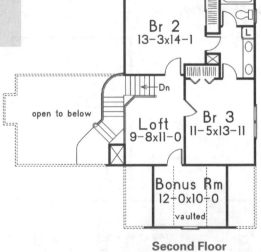

Second Floor
631 sq. ft.

Br 2
13-3x14-1

open to below

Dn

Loft
9-8x11-0

Br 3
11-5x13-11

Bonus Rm
12-0x10-0
vaulted

TO ORDER SEE **PAGE 608** OR CALL TOLL-FREE 1-800-DREAM HOME (373-2646)

Open Floor Plan With Extra Amenities

Total Living Area: 1,680

- Compact and efficient layout in an affordable package
- Second floor has three bedrooms all with oversized closets
- All bedrooms on second floor for privacy
- 3 bedrooms, 2 1/2 baths, 2 car garage
- Basement foundation

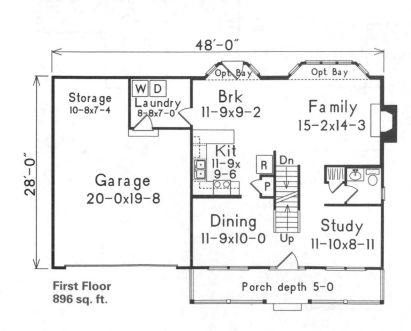

First Floor
896 sq. ft.

48'-0"

28'-0"

Storage
10-8x7-4

W D
Laundry
8-8x7-0

Opt. Bay

Brk
11-9x9-2

Opt. Bay

Family
15-2x14-3

Garage
20-0x19-8

Kit
11-9x
9-6

R

Dn

P

Dining
11-9x10-0

Up

Study
11-10x8-11

Porch depth 5-0

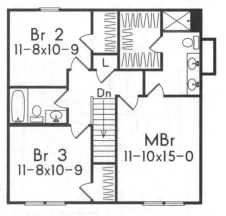

Second Floor
784 sq. ft.

Br 2
11-8x10-9

L

Dn

MBr
11-10x15-0

Br 3
11-8x10-9

MULTI-STORY

Stone Entry Accents This Stately Home

Total Living Area: 1,776

- Master bedroom has double-door entry into formal living room
- Large foyer has plenty of room for greeting guests
- Great room is open to second floor and features fireplace flanked by windows
- 3 bedrooms, 2 1/2 baths, 2-car side entry garage
- Basement foundation

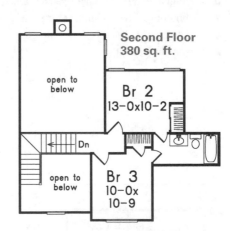

Second Floor
380 sq. ft.

open to below

Br 2
13-0x10-2

Dn

open to below

Br 3
10-0x
10-9

First Floor
1,396 sq. ft.

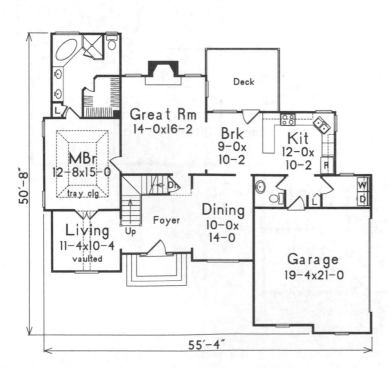

Deck

Great Rm
14-0x16-2

Brk
9-0x
10-2

Kit
12-0x
10-2

MBr
12-8x15-0
tray clg.

Up

Foyer

Dining
10-0x
14-0

Living
11-4x10-4
vaulted

Garage
19-4x21-0

50'-8"

55'-4"

MULTI-STORY

Plan# 577-0386

Price Code C

Centralized Living Area Is Appealing

Total Living Area: 2,186

- See-through fireplace is a focal point in family and living areas
- Columns grace the entrance into the living room
- Large laundry room with adjoining half bath
- Ideal ooooond floor bath includes separate vanity with double sinks
- 3 bedrooms, 2 1/2 baths, 2-car garage
- Basement foundation

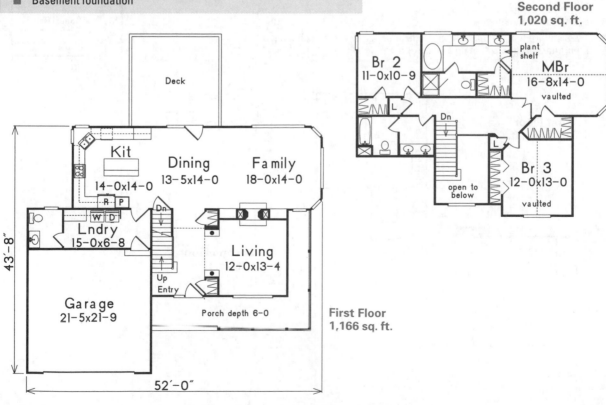

Second Floor
1,020 sq. ft.

Br 2
11-0x10-9

plant shelf

MBr
16-8x14-0
vaulted

Dn

L

open to below

Br 3
12-0x13-0
vaulted

L

First Floor
1,166 sq. ft.

Deck

Kit
14-0x14-0

Dining
13-5x14-0

Family
18-0x14-0

R P

W D

Lndry
15-0x6-8

Dn

Living
12-0x13-4

Up
Entry

Garage
21-5x21-9

Porch depth 6-0

43'-8"

52'-0"

MULTI-STORY

217

TO ORDER SEE PAGE 608 OR CALL TOLL-FREE 1-800-DREAM HOME (373-2646)

Country Comfort

Total Living Area: 3,025

- Master suite has generous walk-in closet, luxurious bath and a vaulted sitting area
- Spacious kitchen has an island cooktop and vaulted breakfast nook
- Bonus room above garage has its own private entrance and would make a great home office, hobby or exercise room
- 4 bedrooms, 3 1/2 baths, 2-car side entry garage, 1-car drive under garage
- Basement foundation
- 1,798 square feet on the first floor, 838 square feet on the second floor and 389 square feet on the lower level

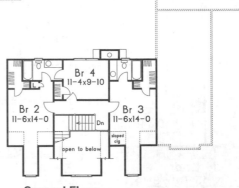

MULTI-STORY

First Floor
1,798 sq. ft.

Second Floor
838 sq. ft.

Bright And Cheery Sun Room

Total Living Area: 2,211

- Spacious sun room has three walls of windows and access outdoors
- Family room has open view into kitchen and dining area
- Large master bedroom has private luxurious bath with step-up tub
- Bonus room has an additional 241 square feet of living area
- 4 bedrooms, 2 1/2 baths, 2-car garage
- Basement foundation

Second Floor
1,022 sq. ft.

BR4
11' x 10'

BR2
11' x 12'

BATH2

MBATH

LIN

WI Closet

SLOPED CL'G

Balcony

Hall

BONUS RM 241 SF
18'8 X 13'

PLANT SHELF

tray cl'g
MBR
12'2 x 15'8

FLAT CL'G

BR3
11'4 x 11'2

SLOPED CL'G

Foyer Below

Width: 56'-8"
Depth: 44'-4"

SUN RM
177 SF
16'8 x 9'8

OPT. COUNTER

Laun

KIT
8'2 x 13'4

DW

DIN
8'6 x 11'4

FAMILY RM
15'6 x 15'4

OPT.

STORAGE AREA
11'4 x 12'4

Lav

Entry

FLOORING BREAK

OPT.

PANTRY

REF

PLANT SHELF ABOVE

GARAGE
21'4 x 21'8

DIN RM
11'2 x 11'2

Two-Story
FOYER

LIV RM
11' x 11'2

OPT.

First Floor
1,189 sq. ft.

Covered Entry

MULTI-STORY

Wrap-Around Porch Adds Outdoor Style
Total Living Area: 2,198

- Great room features a warm fireplace flanked by bookshelves for storage
- Double French doors connect the formal dining room to the kitchen
- An oversized laundry room has extra counterspace
- 4 bedrooms, 2 1/2 baths, 2-car side entry garage with shop/storage
- Basement, crawl space or slab foundation, please specify when ordering

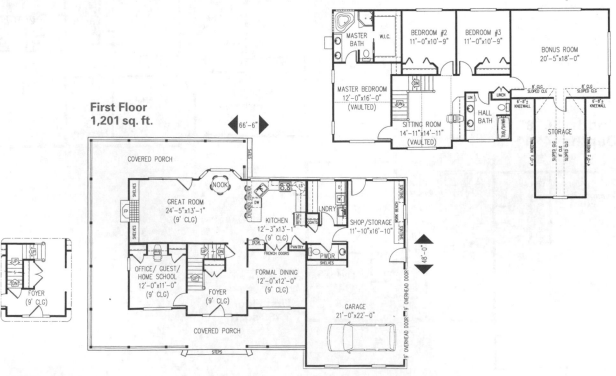

Second Floor
997 sq. ft.

First Floor
1,201 sq. ft.

MULTI-STORY

TO ORDER SEE **PAGE 608** OR CALL TOLL-FREE 1-800-DREAM HOME (373-2646)

Generous Closets In All The Bedrooms

Total Living Area: 2,240

- Floor plan makes good use of space above garage allowing for four bedrooms and a bonus room on the second floor
- Formal dining room easily accessible to kitchen
- Cozy family room with fireplace and sunny bay window
- 4 bedrooms, 2 1/2 baths, 2-car garage
- Basement foundation

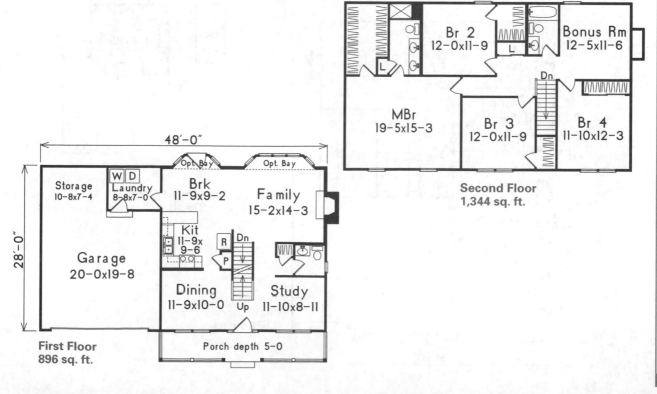

Second Floor
1,344 sq. ft.

First Floor
896 sq. ft.

MULTI-STORY

221

Circle-Top Details Grace This Facade

Total Living Area: 2,500

- Varied floor levels create dramatic interior
- Master bedroom includes a distinctive bath with large double walk-in closets
- U-shaped kitchen features walk-in pantry and corner sink
- 4 bedrooms, 3 baths, 3-car garage
- Partial slab/crawl space foundation

MULTI-STORY

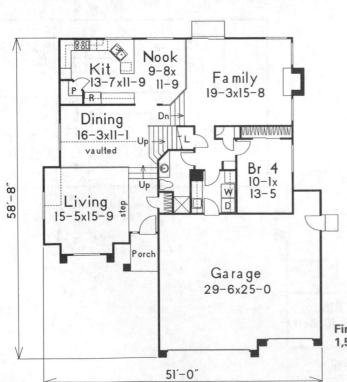

First Floor
1,525 sq. ft.

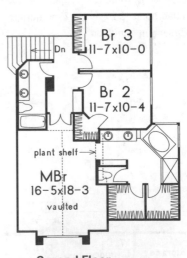

Second Floor
975 sq. ft.

Large Porches Bring In The Outdoors

Total Living Area: 3,153

- Energy efficient home with 2" x 6" exterior walls
- Master suite with full amenities
- Covered breezeway and front and rear porches
- Full-sized workshop and storage with garage below is a unique combination
- 4 bedrooms, 2 full baths, 2 half baths, 2-car drive under garage
- Basement foundation, drawings also include crawl space and slab foundations

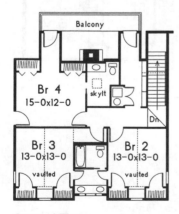

Second Floor
1,113 sq. ft.

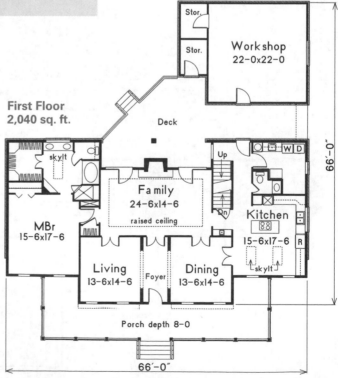

First Floor
2,040 sq. ft.

MULTI-STORY

TO ORDER SEE PAGE 608 OR CALL TOLL-FREE 1-800-DREAM HOME (373-2646)

Bright, Vaulted Spaces

Total Living Area: 2,459

- Kitchen has an open feel with angled counter to enjoy views through family and breakfast rooms
- Secluded master bedroom includes dressing area, access to the outdoors and private bath with tub and shower
- Stylish, open stairway overlooks two-story foyer
- Energy efficient home with 2" x 6" exterior walls
- 4 bedrooms, 2 1/2 baths, 2-car garage
- Basement foundation

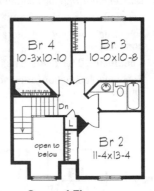

Second Floor
598 sq. ft.

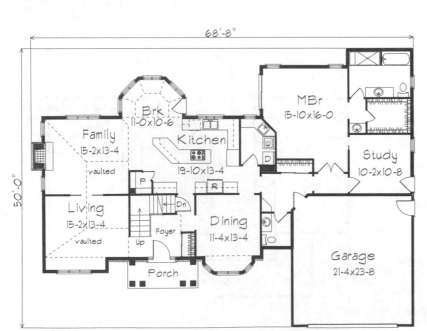

First Floor
1,861 sq. ft.

MULTI-STORY

TO ORDER SEE **PAGE 608** OR CALL TOLL-FREE 1-800-DREAM HOME (373-2646)

Private Master Bedroom

Total Living Area: 2,018

- Family room situated near dining area and kitchen create a convenient layout
- First floor master bedroom features private bath with step-up tub and bay window
- Laundry area located on the first floor
- 4 bedrooms, 2 1/2 baths, 2-car garage
- Basement foundation

First Floor
1,448 sq. ft.

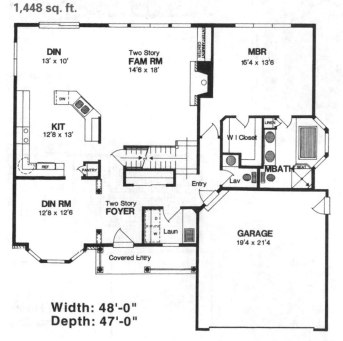

Width: 48'-0"
Depth: 47'-0"

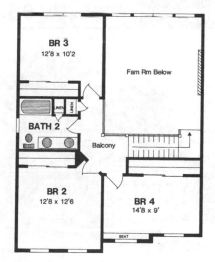

Second Floor
570 sq. ft.

MULTI-STORY

225

Second Floor
905 sq. ft.

Large Utility Room

Total Living Area: 1,998

- Lovely designed family room offers double-door entrance into living area
- Roomy kitchen with breakfast area is a natural gathering place
- 10' ceiling in master bedroom
- 3 bedrooms, 2 1/2 baths, 2-car garage
- Basement foundation

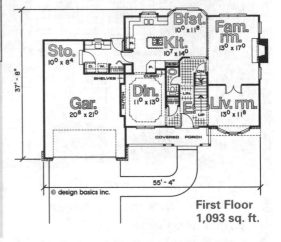

First Floor
1,093 sq. ft.

Plan# **577-JA-65396**

Price Code B

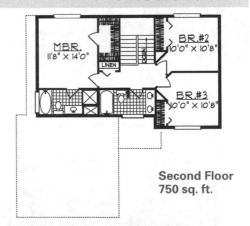

Second Floor
750 sq. ft.

A Two-Story With Modern Appeal

Total Living Area: 1,536

- 9' ceilings throughout this home
- All bedrooms located on second floor for privacy from living areas
- Spacious great room has corner fireplace and a cheerful wall of windows
- 3 bedrooms, 2 1/2 baths, 2-car garage
- Basement foundation

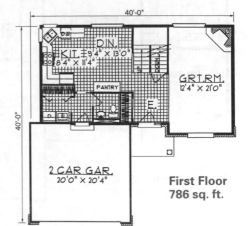

First Floor
786 sq. ft.

MULTI-STORY

TO ORDER SEE **PAGE 608** OR CALL TOLL-FREE 1-800-DREAM HOME (373-2646)

Perfect Home For A Small Family

Total Living Area: 864

- L-shaped kitchen with convenient pantry is adjacent to dining area
- Easy access to laundry area, linen closet and storage closet
- Both bedrooms include ample closet space
- 2 bedrooms, 1 bath
- Crawl space foundation, drawings also include basement and slab foundations

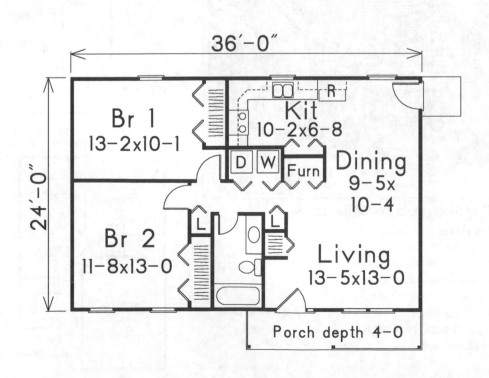

36'-0"

24'-0"

Br 1
13-2x10-1

Kit
10-2x6-8

D W Furn

Dining
9-5x
10-4

Br 2
11-8x13-0

Living
13-5x13-0

Porch depth 4-0

SMALL AND NARROW LOT

Plan# **577-AMD-1135**

Price Code C

43'

◀ 49' ▶

Striking Plant Shelf

Total Living Area: 1,467

- Vaulted ceilings, an open floor plan and a wealth of windows create an inviting atmosphere
- Efficiently arranged kitchen has an island with built-in cooktop and a snack counter
- Plentiful storage and closet space throughout this home
- 3 bedrooms, 2 baths, 2-car garage
- Crawl space foundation

Plan# **577-GSD-2073**

Price Code C

Second Floor
1,104 sq. ft.

WIDTH 34'-0"
DEPTH 50'-0"

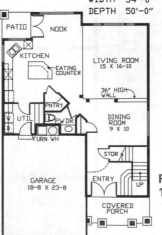

First Floor
1,058 sq. ft.

Sunny Garden Tub In Master Bath

Total Living Area: 2,162

- Lovely covered porch
- Appealing double-door two-story entry
- Kitchen has eat-in island bar
- French doors lead to patio from nook
- Master suite has double-door entry, private bath and walk-in closet
- 3 bedrooms, 2 1/2 baths, 2-car garage
- Crawl space foundation

Plan# 577-1197   Price Code B

Energy Efficient Home
Total Living Area: 1,536

- Formal living room area featured in the front of the home
- Combined living areas create the back of the home with great room, dining and kitchen all in one
- Second floor master bedroom includes private bath
- 3 bedrooms, 2 1/2 baths, 1-car garage
- Basement foundation, drawings also include crawl space and slab foundations

Second Floor
768 sq. ft.

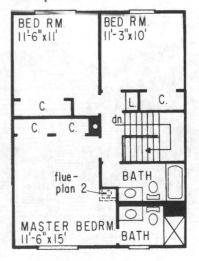

BED RM. 11'-6"x11'   BED RM. 11'-3"x10'
C.   C. C.   dn.
flue-plan 2   BATH
MASTER BEDRM. 11'-6"x15'   BATH

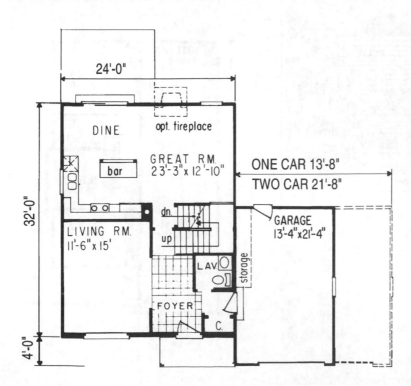

24'-0"
DINE.   opt. fireplace
GREAT RM. 23'-3" x 12'-10"   bar
ONE CAR 13'-8"   TWO CAR 21'-8"
32'-0"
LIVING RM. 11'-6" x 15'   dn. up
GARAGE 13'-4"x21'-4"   storage
LAV
FOYER   C.
4'-0"

First Floor
768 sq. ft.

SMALL AND NARROW LOT

Plan# 577-DBI-8545

Price Code A

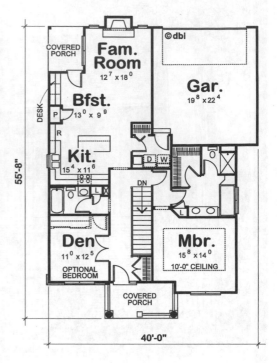

Craftsman Cottage

Total Living Area: 1,375

- Den can easily convert to a second bedroom
- A center island in the kitchen allows extra space for organizing and food preparation
- Centrally located laundry room
- 1 bedrooms, 2 baths, 2-car garage
- Basement foundation

Plan# 577-HDG-97006

Price Code AA

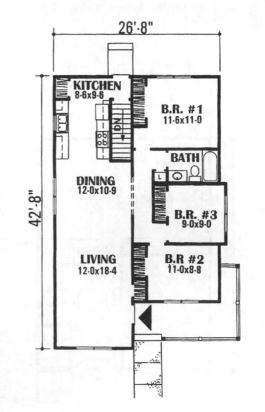

Perfect For A Narrow Lot

Total Living Area: 1,042

- Dining and living areas combine for added space
- Cozy covered front porch
- Plenty of closet space throughout
- 3 bedrooms, 1 bath
- Basement foundation

Pillared Front Porch Generates Charm

Total Living Area: 1,567

- Living room flows into dining room shaped by an angled pass-through into the kitchen
- Cheerful, windowed dining area
- Future area available on the second floor has an additional 338 square feet of living area
- Master bedroom separated from other bedrooms for privacy
- 3 bedrooms, 2 baths, 2-car side entry garage
- Basement foundation, drawings also include slab foundation

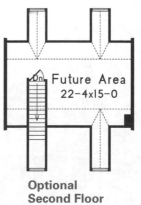

**Optional
Second Floor**

Future Area
22-4x15-0

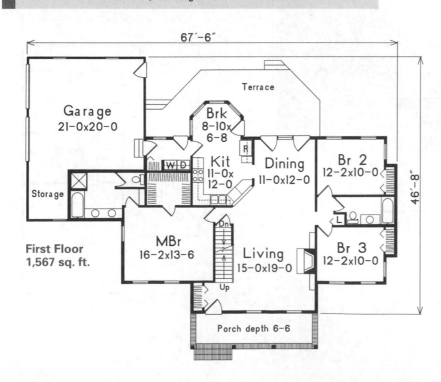

**First Floor
1,567 sq. ft.**

67'-6"

46'-8"

Garage
21-0x20-0

Storage

Terrace

Brk
8-10x
6-8

Kit
11-0x
12-0

Dining
11-0x12-0

Br 2
12-2x10-0

W D

MBr
16-2x13-6

Living
15-0x19-0

Br 3
12-2x10-0

Dn

Up

Porch depth 6-6

SMALL AND NARROW LOT

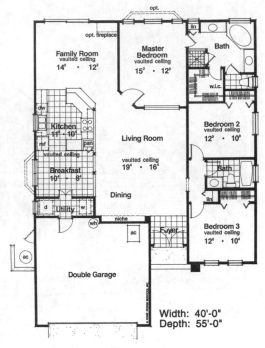

Width: 40'-0"
Depth: 55'-0"

Beautiful Entry Graces This Home

Total Living Area: 1,565

- Master bedroom has enormous luxury bath with corner step up tub and double sinks
- Majestic living and dining rooms are open and airy
- Vaulted ceilings are highlighted throughout this home
- 3 bedrooms, 2 baths, 2-car garage
- Slab foundation

SMALL AND NARROW LOT

Inviting Porch Enhances Design

Total Living Area: 1,389

- Formal living room has warming fireplace and a delightful bay window
- U-shaped kitchen shares a snack bar with the bayed family room
- Lovely master suite has its own private bath
- 3 bedrooms, 2 baths, 2-car garage
- Slab foundation

Graciously Designed Traditional Ranch

Total Living Area: 1,477

- Oversized porch provides protection from the elements
- Innovative kitchen employs step-saving design
- Breakfast room offers bay window and snack bar open to kitchen with convenient laundry nearby
- 3 bedrooms, 2 baths, 2-car side entry garage with storage area
- Basement foundation

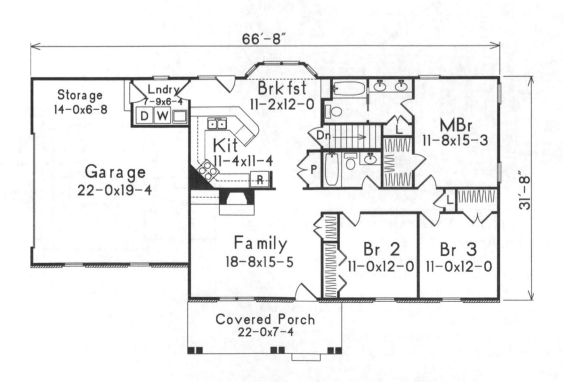

66'-8"

Storage
14-0x6-8

Lndry
7-9x6-4

Brkfst
11-2x12-0

MBr
11-8x15-3

Kit
11-4x11-4

Garage
22-0x19-4

31'-8"

Family
18-8x15-5

Br 2
11-0x12-0

Br 3
11-0x12-0

Covered Porch
22-0x7-4

SMALL AND NARROW LOT

Width: 65'-0"
Depth: 54'-6"

Spacious Foyer Is A Grand Entrance

Total Living Area: 2,148

- 9' ceilings throughout this home
- 11' ceilings in great room, kitchen, nook and foyer
- Eating bar in kitchen extends the dining space for extra guests or casual seating
- 3 bedrooms, 2 baths, 2-car side entry garage
- Basement foundation

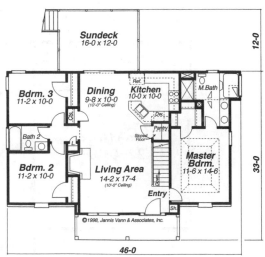

Split Bedroom, Drive Under Garage Design

Total Living Area: 1,268

- Raised gable porch is focal point creating a dramatic look
- 10' ceilings throughout living and dining areas
- Open kitchen is well-designed
- Master bedroom offers tray ceiling and private bath with both a garden tub and a 4' shower
- 3 bedrooms, 2 baths, 2-car drive under garage
- Basement foundation

SMALL AND NARROW LOT

Plan# 577-0335

Price Code D

TO ORDER SEE **PAGE 608** OR CALL TOLL-FREE 1-800-DREAM HOME (373-2646)

Wonderful Great Room

Total Living Area: 1,865

- Large foyer opens into expansive dining area and great room
- Home features vaulted ceilings throughout
- Master suite features bath with double-bowl vanity, shower, tub and toilet in separate room for privacy
- 4 bedrooms, 2 baths, 2-car garage
- Slab foundation, drawings also include crawl space foundation

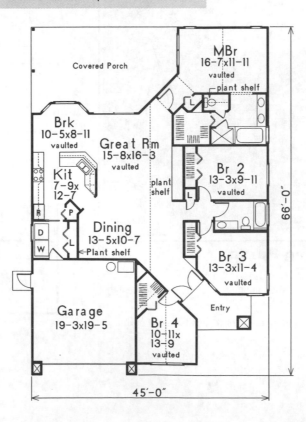

SMALL AND NARROW LOT

Plan# **577-JFD-15-14931**　　Price Code A

Second Floor
520 sq. ft.

First Floor
973 sq. ft.

Width: 40'-0"
Depth: 41'-0"

Surprisingly Spacious

Total Living Area: 1,493

- First floor master bedroom maintains privacy
- Dining and great rooms have a feeling of spaciousness with two-story high ceilings
- Utilities are conveniently located near garage entrance
- 3 bedrooms, 2 1/2 baths, 2-car garage
- Basement foundation

Plan# **577-NDG-106**　　Price Code AA

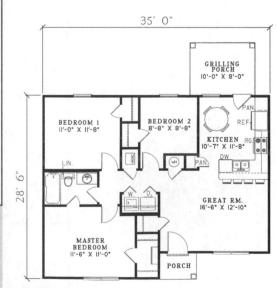

Convenient Grilling Porch

Total Living Area: 930

- Kitchen overlooks great room and includes space for counter dining
- Convenient laundry closet
- Master bedrom has walk-in closet and direct access to hall bath
- 3 bedrooms, 1 bath
- Slab or crawl space foundation, please specify when ordering

TO ORDER SEE **PAGE 608** OR CALL TOLL-FREE 1-800-DREAM HOME (373-2646)

Spacious Living In This Ranch

Total Living Area: 1,433

- Vaulted living room includes cozy fireplace and an oversized entertainment center
- Bedrooms #2 and #3 share a full bath
- Master bedroom has a full bath and large walk-in closet
- 3 bedrooms, 2 baths, 2-car garage
- Basement foundation, drawings also include crawl space and slab foundations

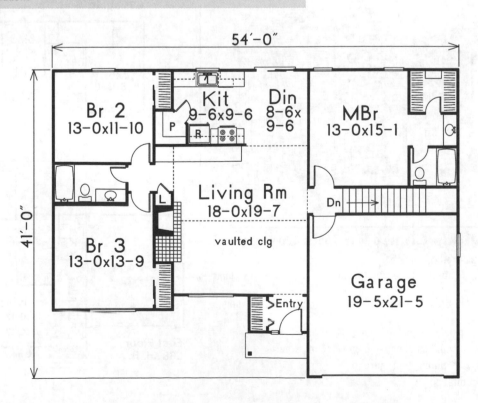

SMALL AND NARROW LOT

COPYRIGHT LARRY E. BELK

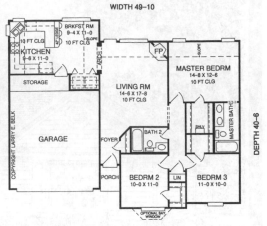

WIDTH 49-10

Cozy Traditional

Total Living Area: 1,310

- Family room features corner fireplace adding warmth
- Efficiently designed kitchen has a corner sink with windows
- Master bedroom includes large walk-in closet and private bath
- 3 bedrooms, 2 baths, 2-car garage
- Crawl space or slab foundation, please specify when ordering

SMALL AND NARROW LOT

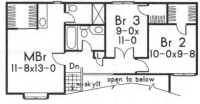

Second Floor
691 sq. ft.

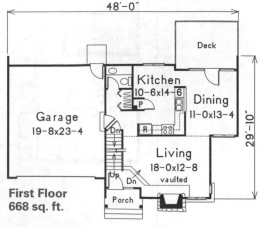

First Floor
668 sq. ft.

Exterior Adds Charm To This Cottage

Total Living Area: 1,359

- Lattice-trimmed porch, stone chimney and abundant windows lend outdoor appeal
- Spacious, bright breakfast area with pass-through to formal dining room
- Large walk-in closets in all bedrooms
- Extensive deck expands dining and entertaining areas
- 3 bedrooms, 2 1/2 baths, 2-car garage
- Basement foundation

TO ORDER SEE **PAGE 608** OR CALL TOLL-FREE 1-800-DREAM HOME (373-2646)

Compact, Charming And Functional

Total Living Area: 1,404

- Split foyer entrance
- Bayed living area features unique vaulted ceiling and fireplace
- Wrap-around kitchen has corner windows for added sunlight and a bar that overlooks dining area
- Master bath features a garden tub with separate shower
- Rear deck provides handy access to dining room and kitchen
- 3 bedrooms, 2 baths, 2-car drive under garage
- Basement foundation, drawings also include partial crawl space foundation

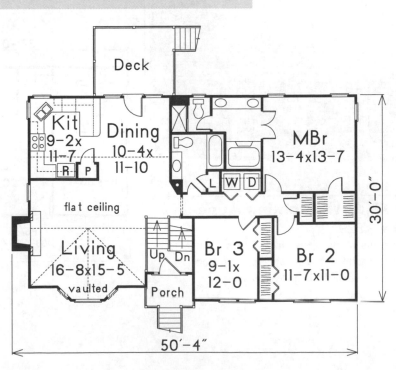

SMALL AND NARROW LOT

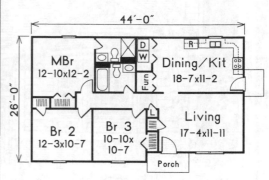

Spacious Dining And Living Areas

Total Living Area: 1,104

- Master bedroom includes private bath
- Convenient side entrance to dining area/kitchen
- Laundry area located near kitchen
- Large living area creates comfortable atmosphere
- 3 bedrooms, 2 baths
- Crawl space foundation, drawings also include basement and slab foundations

SMALL AND NARROW LOT

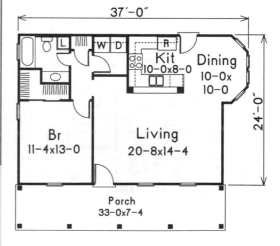

Front Porch Adds Welcoming Appeal

Total Living Area: 829

- U-shaped kitchen opens into living area by a 42" high counter
- Oversized bay window and French door accent dining room
- Gathering space is created by the large living room
- Convenient utility room and linen closet
- 1 bedroom, 1 bath
- Slab foundation

Design Revolves Around Central Space

Total Living Area: 1,364

- Master bedroom includes full bath
- Pass-through kitchen opens into breakfast room with laundry closet and access to deck
- Adjoining dining and living rooms with vaulted ceilings and a fireplace create an open living area
- Dining room features large bay window
- 3 bedrooms, 2 baths, 2-car drive under garage
- Basement foundation

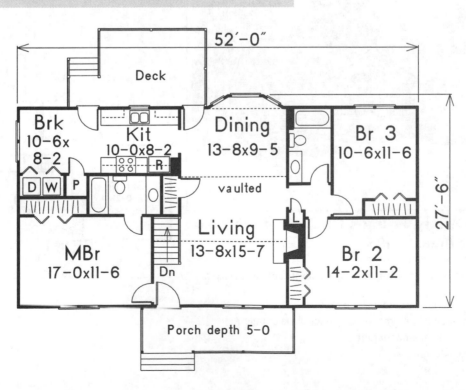

TO ORDER SEE **PAGE 608** OR CALL TOLL-FREE 1-800-DREAM HOME (373-2646)

SMALL AND NARROW LOT

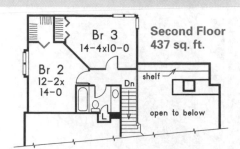

Second Floor
437 sq. ft.

Br 3
14-4x10-0

Br 2
12-2x
14-0

shelf

Dn

open to below

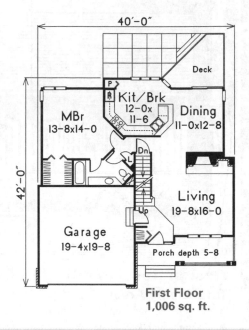

First Floor
1,006 sq. ft.

40'-0"

42'-0"

Deck

Kit/Brk
12-0x
11-6

Dining
11-0x12-8

MBr
13-8x14-0

Living
19-8x16-0

Dn

Up

Garage
19-4x19-8

Porch depth 5-8

Front Porch Adds Charm And Value

Total Living Area: 1,443

- Raised foyer and cathedral ceiling in living room
- Impressive tall-wall fireplace between living and dining rooms
- Open U-shaped kitchen with breakfast bay
- Angular side deck accentuates patio and garden
- First floor master bedroom suite has a walk-in closet and a corner window
- 3 bedrooms, 2 baths, 2-car garage
- Basement foundation

SMALL AND NARROW LOT

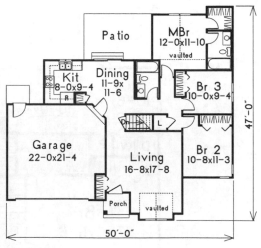

Patio

MBr
12-0x11-10
vaulted

Kit
8-0x9-4

Dining
11-9x
11-6

Br 3
10-0x9-4

Garage
22-0x21-4

Living
16-8x17-8

Br 2
10-8x11-3

Porch

vaulted

47'-0"

50'-0"

Vaulted Ceiling Frames Circle-Top Window

Total Living Area: 1,195

- Dining room opens onto the patio
- Master bedroom features vaulted ceiling, private bath and walk-in closet
- Coat closets located by both the entrances
- Convenient secondary entrance at the back of the garage
- 3 bedrooms, 2 baths, 2-car garage
- Basement foundation

TO ORDER SEE **PAGE 608** OR CALL TOLL-FREE 1-800-DREAM HOME (373-2646)

Appealing Charming Porch

Total Living Area: 1,643

- First floor master bedroom has private bath, walk-in closet and easy access to laundry closet
- Comfortable family room features a vaulted ceiling and a cozy fireplace
- Two bedrooms on the second floor share a bath
- 3 bedrooms, 2 1/2 baths, 2-car drive under garage
- Basement or crawl space foundation, please specify when ordering

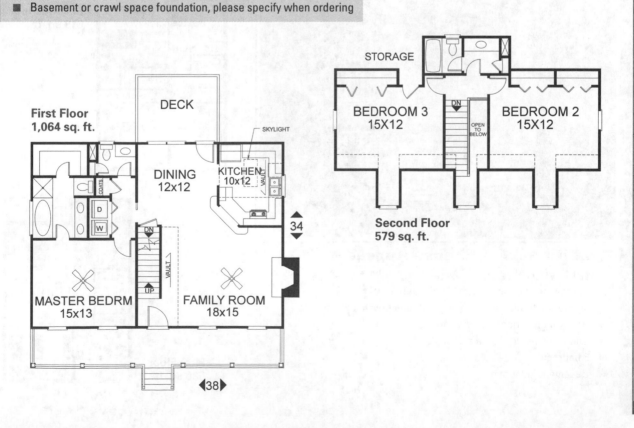

First Floor
1,064 sq. ft.

DECK

SKYLIGHT

DINING
12x12

KITCHEN
10x12

34

MASTER BEDRM
15x13

FAMILY ROOM
18x15

38

STORAGE

BEDROOM 3
15X12

BEDROOM 2
15X12

OPEN TO BELOW

Second Floor
579 sq. ft.

SMALL AND NARROW LOT

Plan# 577-AX-94341

Price Code B

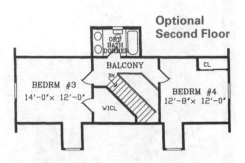

Optional Second Floor

First Floor
1,040 sq. ft.

Width 40'-0"
Depth 32'-0"

Nostalgic Porch And Charming Interior

Total Living Area: 1,040

- Home has the ability to accommodate a small or large family
- The kitchen island greatly simplifies your food preparation efforts
- A wide archway joins the formal living room to the dramatic angled kitchen and dining room
- Optional second floor has an additional 597 square feet of living area
- 4 bedrooms, 2 baths
- Basement, crawl space or slab foundation, please specify when ordering

---

Plan# 577-DR-1738

Price Code A

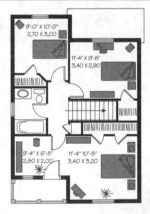

Second Floor
619 sq. ft.

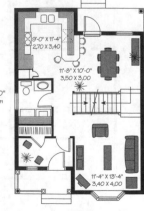

First Floor
626 sq. ft.

32'-0"
9,6 m

◄ 22'-0" ►
6,6 m

Traditional Farmhouse Appeal

Total Living Area: 1,245

- Energy efficient home with 2" x 6" exterior walls
- Master bedroom has a reading area and private balcony
- Bay window brightens living area
- Combined laundry area and half bath
- 3 bedrooms, 1 1/2 baths
- Basement foundation

Front Porch And Gable Add Style

Total Living Area: 988

- Pleasant covered porch entry
- The kitchen, living and dining areas are combined to maximize space
- Entry has convenient coat closet
- Laundry closet is located adjacent to bedrooms
- 3 bedrooms, 1 bath, 1-car garage
- Basement foundation, drawings also include crawl space foundation

TO ORDER SEE **PAGE 608** OR CALL TOLL-FREE 1-800-DREAM HOME (373-2646)

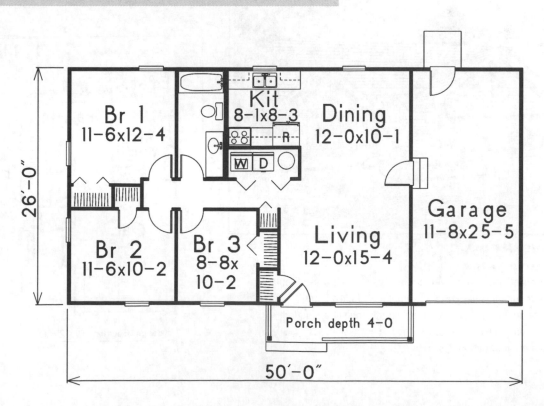

SMALL AND NARROW LOT

Bedroom 14'x 15'

WIC Balcony Bath

Second Floor 576 sq. ft.

Open To Below

Bedroom 12'4"x 11'

Width: 29'-10"
Depth: 58'-6"

WIC WIC

Master Bath

First Floor 1,281 sq. ft.

Covered Porch 15'x 6'

Master Bedroom 12'4"x 14'6"

Kitchen 9'6"x 14'8"

Dining 8'2"x 13'

Bath

Living 13'x 20'

Bedroom 12'4"x 11'

Porch 17'2"x 5'

Distinctive Style

Total Living Area: 1,857

- Master bedroom has double walk-in closets and a private bath
- Two-story living area has corner fireplace and overlooks dining area and kitchen
- Covered porch connects the dining area to the outdoors
- 4 bedrooms, 3 baths
- Slab foundation

SMALL AND NARROW LOT

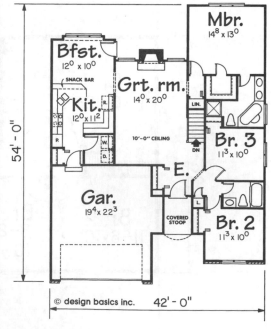

Mbr. 14⁸ x 13⁰

Bfst. 12⁰ x 10⁰

SNACK BAR

Grt. rm. 14⁰ x 20⁰

LIN.

Kit. 12⁰ x 11²

10'-0" CEILING

DN

Br. 3 11³ x 10⁰

54' - 0"

E.

Gar. 19⁴ x 22³

COVERED STOOP

Br. 2 11³ x 10⁰

© design basics inc. 42' - 0"

Simple And Cozy

Total Living Area: 1,392

- Centralized great room welcomes guests with a warm fireplace
- Master suite has separate entrance for added privacy
- Kitchen includes breakfast room, snack counter and laundry area
- 3 bedrooms, 2 baths, 2-car garage
- Basement foundation

TO ORDER SEE **PAGE 608** OR CALL TOLL-FREE 1-800-DREAM HOME (373-2646)

Luxurious Master Bath

Total Living Area: 1,456

- Open floor plan adds spaciousness to this design
- The study can easily be converted to a third bedroom
- Corner fireplace in great room is a terrific focal point
- 3 bedrooms, 2 baths, 2-car garage
- Basement foundation

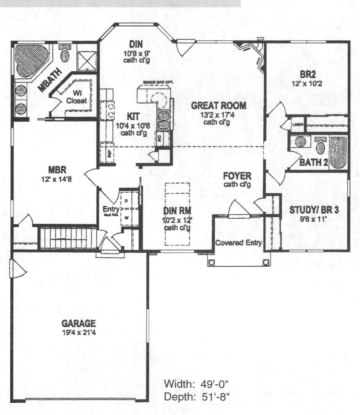

DIN
10'8 x 9'
cath cl'g

MBATH

WI Closet

SNACK BAR OPT.

KIT
10'4 x 10'6
cath cl'g

GREAT ROOM
13'2 x 17'4
cath cl'g

BR2
12' x 10'2

LINEN

BATH 2

MBR
12' x 14'8

Entry
Mud Rm.

D
W

DIN RM
10'2 x 12'
cath cl'g

FOYER
cath cl'g

STUDY/ BR 3
9'6 x 11'

Covered Entry

GARAGE
19'4 x 21'4

Width: 49'-0"
Depth: 51'-8"

SMALL AND NARROW LOT

247

Plan# 577-BF-1426

Price Code A

Central Living Room

Total Living Area: 1,420

- Energy efficient home with 2" x 6" exterior walls
- Living room has 12' ceiling, corner fireplace and atrium doors leading to covered porch
- Separate master suite has garden bath and walk-in closet
- 3 bedrooms, 2 baths, 2-car garage
- Slab or crawl space foundation, please specify when ordering

Plan# 577-DH-1716

Price Code B

SMALL AND NARROW LOT

Extra Large Porches

Total Living Area: 1,716

- Great room boasts a fireplace and access to the kitchen/breakfast area through a large arched opening
- Master bedroom includes a huge walk-in closet and French doors that lead onto an L-shaped porch
- Bedrooms #2 and #3 share a bath and linen closet
- 3 bedrooms, 2 baths, 2-car detached garage
- Crawl space or slab foundation, please specify when ordering

Plan# 577-1189

Price Code AA

Lovely Inviting Covered Porch

Total Living Area: 1,120

- Kitchen/family room creates a useful spacious area
- Rustic, colonial design perfect for many surroundings
- Oversized living room ideal for entertaining
- Carport includes functional storage area
- 3 bedrooms, 2 baths, 1-car carport
- Basement foundation, drawings also include crawl space and slab foundations

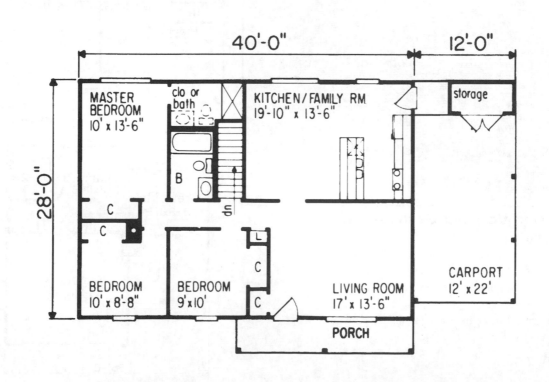

40'-0" 12'-0"

28'-0"

MASTER BEDROOM 10' x 13'-6"

clo or bath

KITCHEN/FAMILY RM. 19'-10" x 13'-6"

storage

B

C
C

BEDROOM 10' x 8'-8"

BEDROOM 9' x 10'

C

C

LIVING ROOM 17' x 13'-6"

CARPORT 12' x 22'

PORCH

SMALL AND NARROW LOT

Plan# 577-DR-2937

Price Code A

Second Floor
597 sq. ft.

10'-0" X 11'-0"
3,00 X 3,30

11'-0" X 15'-8"
3,30 X 4,70

First Floor
691 sq. ft.

12'-0" X 19'-0"
3,60 X 5,70

14'-0" X 20'-0"
4,20 X 6,00

12'-8" X 15'-8"
3,80 X 4,70

40'-0"
12,0 m

28'-0"
8,4 m

Cathedral Ceiling In Family Room
Total Living Area: 1,288

- Energy efficient home with 2" x 6" exterior walls
- Convenient snack bar in kitchen
- Half bath has laundry facilities on first floor
- Both second floor bedrooms easily access full bath
- 2 bedrooms, 1 1/2 baths, 1-car garage
- Basement foundation

SMALL AND NARROW LOT

Plan# 577-0487

Price Code AA

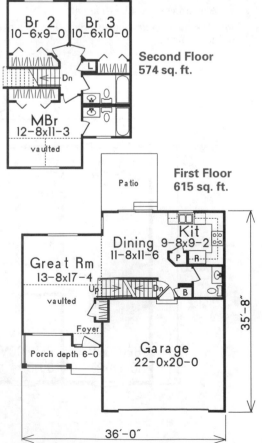

Br 2
10-6x9-0

Br 3
10-6x10-0

Second Floor
574 sq. ft.

Dn

MBr
12-8x11-3
vaulted

Patio

First Floor
615 sq. ft.

Kit

Dining
11-8x11-6

Great Rm
13-8x17-4
vaulted

Up

Dn

Foyer

Porch depth 6-0

Garage
22-0x20-0

35'-8"

36'-0"

Spacious Vaulted Great Room
Total Living Area: 1,189

- All bedrooms are located on the second floor
- Dining room and kitchen both have views of the patio
- Convenient half bath located near the kitchen
- Master bedroom has a private bath
- 3 bedrooms, 2 1/2 baths, 2-car garage
- Basement foundation

Space Creates Comfortable Atmosphere

Total Living Area: 1,000

- Bath includes convenient closeted laundry area
- Master bedroom includes double closets and private access to bath
- Foyer features handy coat closet
- L-shaped kitchen provides easy access outdoors
- 3 bedrooms, 1 bath
- Crawl space foundation, drawings also include basement and slab foundations

TO ORDER SEE **PAGE 608** OR CALL TOLL-FREE 1-800-DREAM HOME (373-2646)

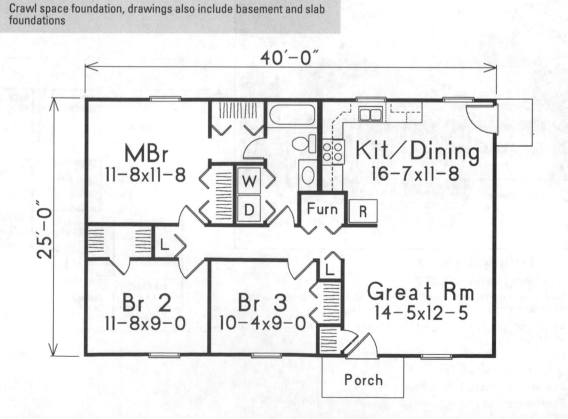

40'-0"

25'-0"

MBr
11-8x11-8

Kit/Dining
16-7x11-8

W
D

Furn

R

L

L

Br 2
11-8x9-0

Br 3
10-4x9-0

Great Rm
14-5x12-5

Porch

SMALL AND NARROW LOT

Plan# 577-AMD-2230E

Price Code E

Second Floor 1,100 sq. ft.

First Floor 1,220 sq. ft.

3 CAR VER. 49' WIDE

Cozy Loft On Second Floor

Total Living Area: 2,320

- Family room is flooded with sunlight from wall of windows
- Decorative columns help separate dining area from living area
- Breakfast nook has sliding glass doors leading to the outdoors
- 4 bedrooms, 2 1/2 baths, 2-car garage
- Crawl space foundation

Plan# 577-AP-1002

Price Code AA

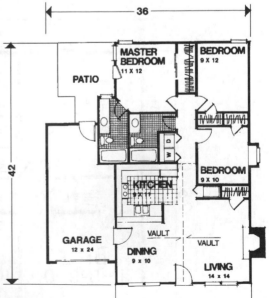

Open Living Spaces

Total Living Area: 1,050

- Master bedroom features a private bath and access outdoors onto a private patio
- Vaulted ceilings in the living and dining areas create a feeling of spaciousness
- Laundry closet is convenient to all bedrooms
- Efficient U-shaped kitchen
- 3 bedrooms, 2 baths, 1-car garage
- Basement or slab foundation, please specify when ordering

Gracious Living On A Small Lot

Total Living Area: 1,671

- Triple gables and stone facade create great curb appeal
- Two-story entry with hallway leads to a spacious family room, dining area with bay window and U-shaped kitchen
- Second floor features a large master bedroom with luxury bath, huge walk-in closet, overlook to entry and two secondary bedrooms with hall bath
- 3 bedrooms, 2 1/2 baths, 2-car garage
- Basement foundation

Second Floor
991 sq. ft

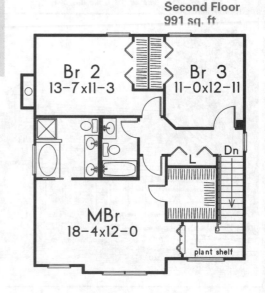

Br 2
13-7x11-3

Br 3
11-0x12-11

Dn

L

MBr
18-4x12-0

plant shelf

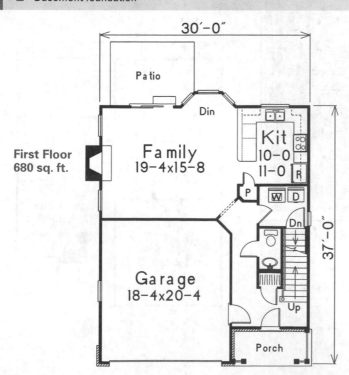

30'-0"

Patio

Din

First Floor
680 sq. ft.

Family
19-4x15-8

Kit
10-0
11-0

R

P

W   D

Dn

37'-0"

Garage
18-4x20-4

Up

Porch

SMALL AND NARROW LOT

253

Plan# 577-HDG-99004

Price Code A

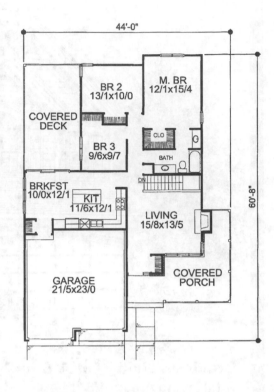

44'-0"

60'-8"

BR 2
13/1x10/0

M. BR
12/1x15/4

COVERED
DECK

CLO

BR 3
9/6x9/7

BATH

BRKFST
10/0x12/1

KIT
11/6x12/1

DN

LIVING
15/8x13/5

GARAGE
21/5x23/0

COVERED
PORCH

Covered Deck Off Breakfast Room
Total Living Area: 1,231

- Covered front porch
- Master bedroom has separate sink area
- Large island in kitchen for eat-in dining or preparation area
- 3 bedrooms, 1 bath, 2-car garage
- Basement foundation

Plan# 577-0273

Price Code AA

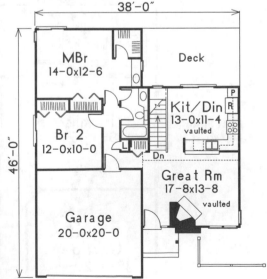

38'-0"

46'-0"

MBr
14-0x12-6

Deck

Br 2
12-0x10-0

Kit/Din
13-0x11-4
vaulted

Dn

Great Rm
17-8x13-8
vaulted

Garage
20-0x20-0

Compact Ranch Is An Ideal Starter Home
Total Living Area: 988

- Great room features corner fireplace
- Vaulted ceiling and corner windows add space and light in great room
- Eat-in kitchen with vaulted ceiling accesses deck for outdoor living
- Master bedroom features separate vanities and private access to the bath
- 2 bedrooms, 1 bath, 2-car garage
- Basement foundation

SMALL AND NARROW LOT

Covered Porch Surrounds Home

Total Living Area: 1,399

- Living room overlooks dining area through arched columns
- Laundry room contains handy half bath
- Spacious master bedroom includes sitting area, walk-in closet and plenty of sunlight
- 3 bedrooms, 1 1/2 baths, 1-car garage
- Basement foundation, drawings also include crawl space and slab foundations

Second Floor
667 sq. ft.

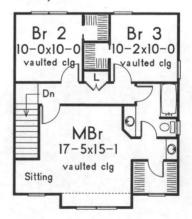

Br 2
10-0x10-0
vaulted clg

Br 3
10-2x10-0
vaulted clg

Dn

MBr
17-5x15-1
vaulted clg

Sitting

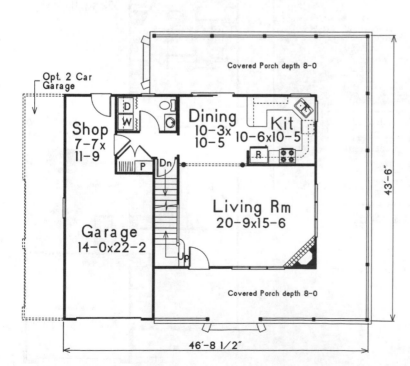

Opt. 2 Car Garage

Covered Porch depth 8-0

Shop
7-7x
11-9

Dining
10-3x
10-5

Kit
10-6x10-5

Dn

P

Living Rm
20-9x15-6

Garage
14-0x22-2

Up

Covered Porch depth 8-0

43'-6"

46'-8 1/2"

First Floor
732 sq. ft.

Plan# 577-DR-2250

Price Code AA

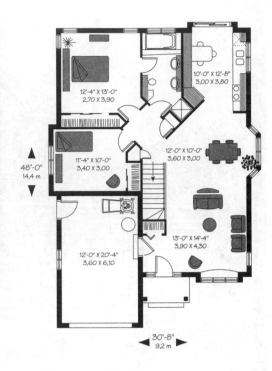

48'-0"
14,4 m

30'-8"
9,2 m

12'-4" X 13'-0"
2,70 X 3,90

10'-0" X 12'-8"
3,00 X 3,80

11'-4" X 10'-0"
3,40 X 3,00

12'-0" X 10'-0"
3,60 X 3,00

13'-0" X 14'-4"
3,90 X 4,30

12'-0" X 20'-4"
3,60 X 6,10

Country Feel With All The Comforts

Total Living Area: 1,103

- Energy efficient home with 2" x 6" exterior walls
- All bedrooms in one area of the house for privacy
- Bay window enhances dining area
- Living and dining areas combine for a spacious feeling
- Lots of storage throughout
- 2 bedrooms, 1 bath, 1-car garage
- Basement foundation

Plan# 577-HDS-1670

Price Code B

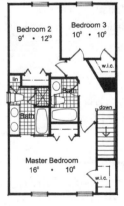

Bedroom 2
9⁴ • 12⁰

Bedroom 3
10⁰ • 10⁰

**Second Floor
692 sq. ft.**

lin

Bath

down

w.i.c.

Master Bedroom
16⁰ • 10⁰

w.i.c.

**First Floor
978 sq. ft.**

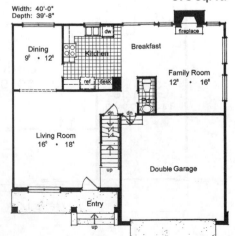

Width: 40'-0"
Depth: 39'-8"

Dining
9⁰ • 12⁰

Kitchen

dw

Breakfast

fireplace

ref desk

Family Room
12⁸ • 16⁸

dn   dn

Living Room
16⁰ • 18⁴

up

Double Garage

Entry

up

Charming Two-Story With Porch

Total Living Area: 1,670

- Lots of closet space throughout
- Family room is flooded with sunlight from many windows
- Open living areas make this home appear larger
- 4 bedrooms, 2 1/2 baths, 2-car garage
- Basement foundation

TO ORDER SEE **PAGE 608** OR CALL TOLL-FREE 1-800-DREAM HOME (373-2646)

Cozy And Functional Design

Total Living Area: 1,285

- Dining nook creates warm feeling with sunny box bay window
- Second floor loft perfect for recreation space or office hideaway
- Bedrooms include walk-in closets allowing extra storage space
- Kitchen, dining and living areas combine making perfect gathering place
- 2 bedrooms, 1 bath
- Crawl space foundation

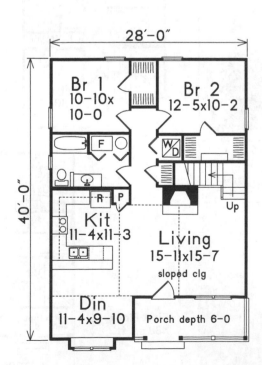

28'-0"

40'-0"

Br 1
10-10x
10-0

Br 2
12-5x10-2

F

W/D

R   P

Kit
11-4x11-3

Living
15-11x15-7
sloped clg

Up

Din
11-4x9-10   Porch depth 6-0

First Floor
1,032 sq. ft.

Loft
13-3x20-0
sloped clg

Dn

open to
below

Second Floor
253 sq. ft.

SMALL AND NARROW LOT

257

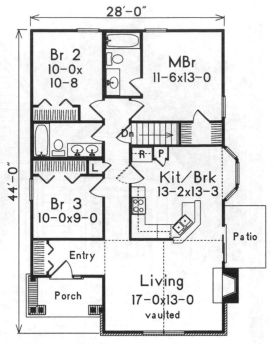

Three Bedroom Luxury In A Small Home

Total Living Area: 1,161

- Brickwork and feature window add elegance to home for a narrow lot
- Living room enjoys a vaulted ceiling, fireplace and opens to kitchen
- U-shaped kitchen offers a breakfast area with bay window, snack bar and built-in pantry
- 3 bedrooms, 2 baths
- Basement foundation

Plan# **577-0793**

Price Code AA

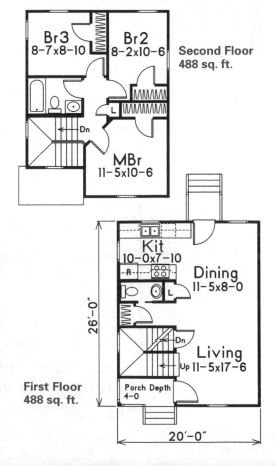

Open Layout Ensures Easy Living

Total Living Area: 976

- Cozy front porch opens into large living room
- Convenient half bath is located on first floor
- All bedrooms are located on second floor for privacy
- Dining room has access to the outdoors
- 3 bedrooms, 1 1/2 baths
- Basement foundation

SMALL AND NARROW LOT

Plan# 577-0518

Price Code B

Dormers Add Light, Space And Appeal

Total Living Area: 1,705

- Cozy design includes two bedrooms on first floor and two bedrooms on second floor for added privacy
- L-shaped kitchen provides easy access to dining room and outdoors
- Convenient first floor laundry area
- 4 bedrooms, 2 baths
- Crawl space foundation, drawings also include basement and slab foundations

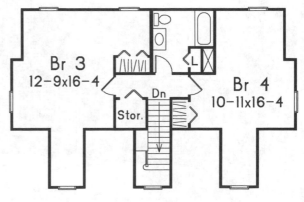

Second Floor
665 sq. ft.

Br 3
12-9x16-4

Dn

Stor.

Br 4
10-11x16-4

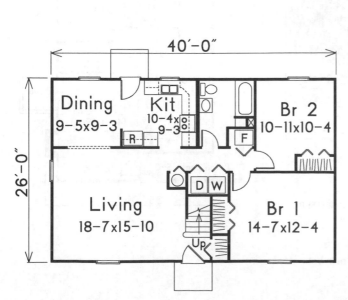

40'-0"

26'-0"

Dining
9-5x9-3

Kit
10-4x
9-3

R

Br 2
10-11x10-4

F

D W

Living
18-7x15-10

Up

Br 1
14-7x12-4

First Floor
1,040 sq. ft.

SMALL AND NARROW LOT

Plan # 577-0296

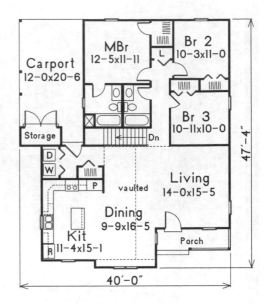

Carport 12-0x20-6
Storage
MBr 12-5x11-11
Br 2 10-3x11-0
Br 3 10-11x10-0
Dn
vaulted
Living 14-0x15-5
Dining 9-9x16-5
Kit 11-4x15-1
Porch
47'-4"
40'-0"

Compact Home With Functional Design

Total Living Area: 1,396

- Gabled front adds interest to facade
- Living and dining rooms share a vaulted ceiling
- Master bedroom features a walk-in closet and private bath
- Functional kitchen with a center work island and convenient pantry
- 3 bedrooms, 2 baths, 1-car carport
- Basement foundation, drawings also include crawl space foundation

Plan # 577-0809

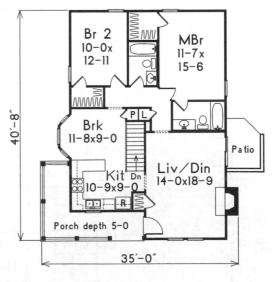

Br 2 10-0x 12-11
MBr 11-7x 15-6
Brk 11-8x9-0
Patio
Kit 10-9x9-0
Dn
Liv/Din 14-0x18-9
40'-8"
Porch depth 5-0
35'-0"

Stylish Retreat For A Narrow Lot

Total Living Area: 1,084

- Delightful country porch for quiet evenings
- The living room offers a front feature window which invites the sun and includes a fireplace and dining area with private patio
- The U-shaped kitchen features lots of cabinets and bayed breakfast room with built-in pantry
- Both bedrooms have walk-in closets and access to their own bath
- 2 bedrooms, 2 baths
- Basement foundation

Perfect Fit For A Narrow Site

Total Living Area: 1,270

- Spacious living area features angled stairs, vaulted ceiling, exciting fireplace and deck access
- Master bedroom includes a walk-in closet and private bath
- Dining and living rooms join to create an open atmosphere
- Eat-in kitchen with convenient pass-through to dining room
- 3 bedrooms, 2 baths, 2-car garage
- Basement foundation

38'-0"

54'-4"

Deck

MBr
12-4x12-0
vaulted

Br 3
10-0x
10-0

Living
12-0x18-0
vaulted

Dining
10-0x11-0

Br 2
12-4x11-0

Dn

Kit
11-0x
11-4

Garage
19-4x19-4

TO ORDER SEE **PAGE 608** OR CALL TOLL-FREE 1-800-DREAM HOME (373-2646)

SMALL AND NARROW LOT

Plan# 577-HP-C659

Price Code AA

Modern Rustic Design

Total Living Area: 1,118

- Roomy kitchen with bright windows and convenient storage
- Patio deck retreat extends the living area to the outdoors
- Built-in media center surrounds fireplace in great room
- 2 bedrooms, 2 baths, 2-car garage
- Slab foundation

Plan# 577-0495

Price Code AA

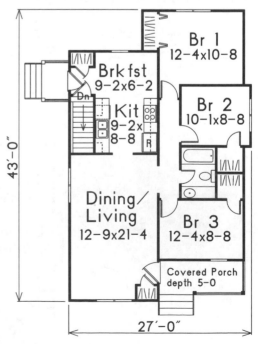

Compact Home Maximizes Space

Total Living Area: 987

- Galley kitchen opens into cozy breakfast room
- Convenient coat closets located by both entrances
- Dining/living room combined for expansive open area
- Breakfast room has access to the outdoors
- Front porch great for enjoying outdoor living
- 3 bedrooms, 1 bath
- Basement foundation

SMALL AND NARROW LOT

TO ORDER SEE **PAGE 608** OR CALL TOLL-FREE 1-800-DREAM HOME (373-2646)

Ornate Corner Porch Catches The Eye

Total Living Area: 1,550

- Impressive front entrance with a wrap-around covered porch and raised foyer
- Corner fireplace provides a focal point in the vaulted great room
- Loft is easily converted to a third bedroom or activity center
- Large family/kitchen area includes greenhouse windows and access to the deck and utility area
- Secondary bedroom has a large dormer and window seat
- 2 bedrooms, 2 1/2 baths, 2-car garage
- Basement foundation

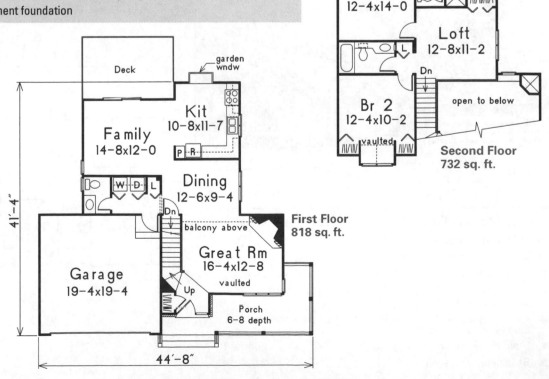

SMALL AND NARROW LOT

Plan# 577-CHD-11-27

Price Code AA

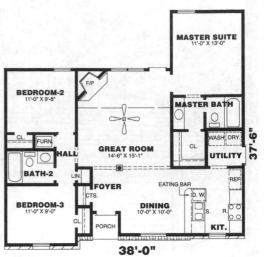

MASTER SUITE
11'-0" X 13'-0"

BEDROOM-2
11'-0" X 9'-8"

F/P

MASTER BATH

CL. FURN.

GREAT ROOM
14'-6" X 15'-1"

WASH. DRY.

CL.

UTILITY

BATH-2

LIN.

HALL

REF.

FOYER

EATING BAR

CTS.

BEDROOM-3
11'-0" X 9'-0"

D. W.

DINING
10'-0" X 10'-0"

CL.

PORCH

S.   R.

KIT.

37'-6"

38'-0"

Lovely Ranch Home

Total Living Area: 1,123

- Eating bar in kitchen extends dining area
- Dining area and great room flow together creating a sense of spaciousness
- Master suite has privacy from other bedrooms as well as a private bath
- Utility room is conveniently located near kitchen
- 3 bedrooms, 2 baths
- Crawl space or slab foundation, please specify when ordering

Plan# 577-0105

Price Code A

SMALL AND NARROW LOT

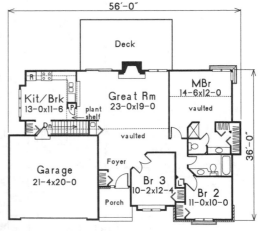

56'-0"

Deck

Kit/Brk
13-0x11-6

Great Rm
23-0x19-0

MBr
14-6x12-0
vaulted

plant
shelf

Dn

vaulted

Garage
21-4x20-0

Foyer

Br 3
10-2x12-4

Porch

Br 2
11-0x10-0

36'-0"

Distinctive Ranch Has A Larger Look

Total Living Area: 1,360

- Double-gabled front facade frames large windows
- Entry is open to vaulted great room, fireplace and rear deck
- Vaulted ceiling and large windows add openness to kitchen/ breakfast room
- Plan easily adapts to crawl space or slab construction, with the utilities replacing the stairs
- 3 bedrooms, 2 baths, 2-car garage
- Basement foundation

TO ORDER SEE **PAGE 608** OR CALL TOLL-FREE 1-800-DREAM HOME (373-2646)

Designed For Handicap Access

Total Living Area: 1,578

- Plenty of closet, linen and storage space
- Covered porches in the front and rear of home add charm to this design
- Open floor plan has unique angled layout
- 3 bedrooms, 2 baths, 2-car garage
- Bacomont foundation

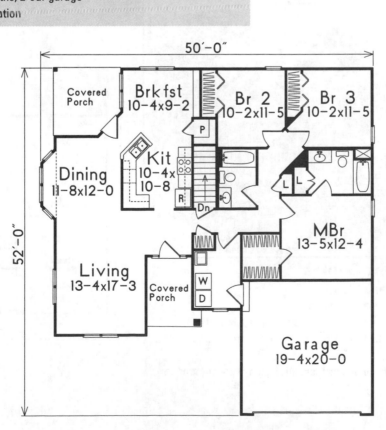

SMALL AND NARROW LOT

Plan# 577-DDI-95219

Price Code A

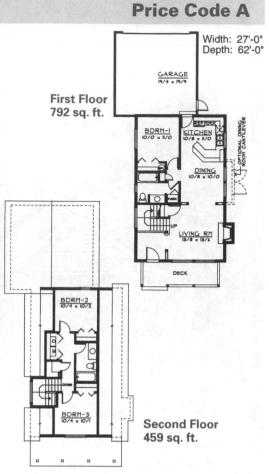

Width: 27'-0"
Depth: 62'-0"

First Floor
792 sq. ft.

Second Floor
459 sq. ft.

Country Cottage Styling
Total Living Area: 1,251

- Open living areas make this home feel larger
- Utility closet located on the second floor for convenience
- Lots of counterspace in kitchen
- 3 bedrooms, 2 baths, 2-car rear entry garage
- Crawl space foundation

Plan# 577-GH-24721

Price Code B

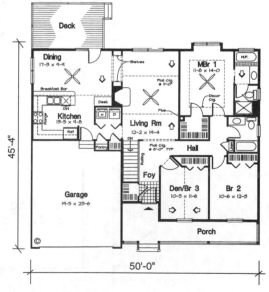

Shakes Accent Gables
Total Living Area: 1,539

- A tray ceiling tops the master bedroom
- The peninsula counter in the kitchen doubles as a breakfast bar
- A walk-in closet in the foyer has space for additional storage
- 3 bedrooms, 2 baths, 2-car garage
- Basement, crawl space or slab foundation, please specify when ordering

Inviting Victorian Details

Total Living Area: 947

- Efficiently designed kitchen/dining area accesses the outdoors onto a rear porch
- Future expansion plans included which allow the home to become 392 square feet larger with 3 bedrooms and 2 baths
- 2 bedrooms, 1 bath
- Crawl space or slab foundation, please specify when ordering

TO ORDER SEE **PAGE 608** OR CALL TOLL-FREE 1-800-DREAM HOME (373-2646)

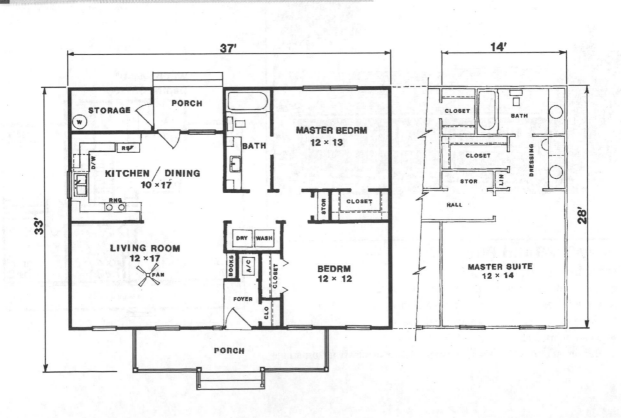

SMALL AND NARROW LOT

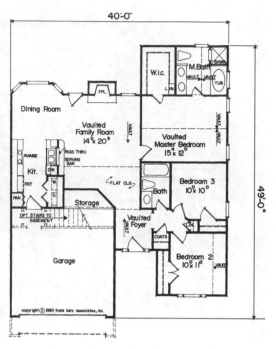

Sunny Bay In Dining Area

Total Living Area: 1,215

- Serving bar counter extends kitchen into living area
- Convenient front hall bath
- Vaulted master bedroom has spacious walk-in closet and private bath
- Efficient galley-styled kitchen has everything within reach
- 3 bedrooms, 2 baths, 2-car garage
- Crawl space, slab or walk-out basement foundation, please specify when ordering

---

Plan # **577-SH-SEA-023**

Price Code A

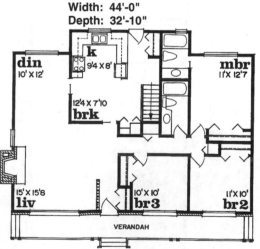

Easy-To-Build Plan

Total Living Area: 1,358

- Energy efficient home with 2" x 6" exterior walls
- Covered verandah invites outdoor relaxation
- Living room is warmed by masonry fireplace
- 3 bedrooms, 2 baths
- Basement or crawl space foundation, please specify when ordering

TO ORDER SEE **PAGE 608** OR CALL TOLL-FREE 1-800-DREAM HOME (373-2646)

Fireplace Highlights The Living Area

Total Living Area: 1,458

- Convenient snack bar joins kitchen with breakfast room
- Large living room has fireplace, plenty of windows, vaulted ceiling and nearby plant shelf
- Master bedroom offers a private bath with vaulted ceiling, walk-in closet, plant shelf and coffered ceiling
- Corner windows provide abundant light in breakfast room
- 3 bedrooms, 2 baths, 2-car garage
- Crawl space foundation, drawings also include slab foundation

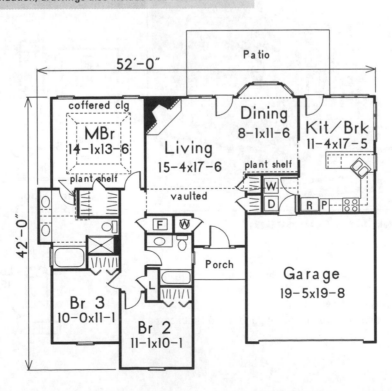

Plan # **577-NDG-675**

Price Code A

Open Living Areas
Total Living Area: 1,210

- Inviting covered porch leads to spacious great room
- Laundry room is centrally located for convenience
- Master suite comes with a private bath and a large walk-in closet
- 3 bedrooms, 2 baths, 2-car garage
- Crawl space or slab foundation, please specify when ordering

---

Plan # **577-0484**

Price Code A

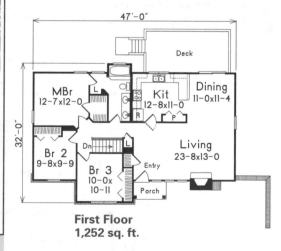

First Floor
1,252 sq. ft.

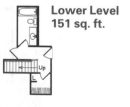

Lower Level
151 sq. ft.

Summer Home Or Year-Round
Total Living Area: 1,403

- Impressive living areas for a modest-sized home
- Special master/hall bath has linen storage, step-up tub and lots of window light
- Spacious closets everywhere you look
- 3 bedrooms, 2 baths, 2-car drive under garage and second bath on lower level
- Basement foundation

Plan# 577-0813

Price Code AAA

TO ORDER SEE **PAGE 608** OR CALL TOLL-FREE 1-800-DREAM HOME (373-2646)

Elegance In A Starter Or Retirement Home

Total Living Area: 888

- Home features an eye-catching exterior and includes a spacious porch
- The breakfast room with bay window is open to living room and adjoins kitchen with pass-through snack bar
- The bedrooms are quite roomy and feature walk-in closets and the master bedroom has double entry doors and access to rear patio
- The master bedroom has double entry doors and access to rear patio
- 2 bedrooms, 1 bath, 1-car garage
- Basement foundation

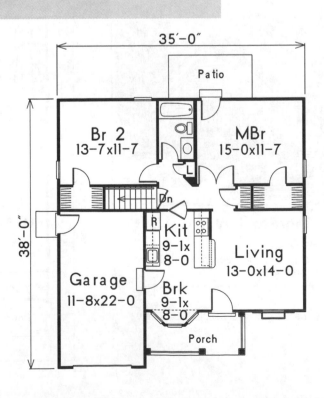

SMALL AND NARROW LOT

271

Plan# 577-DBI-8553

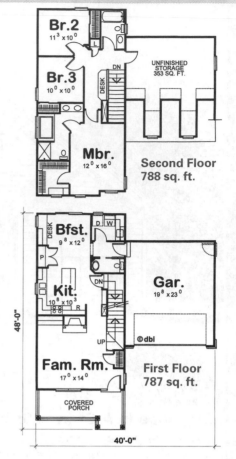

Second Floor
788 sq. ft.

First Floor
787 sq. ft.

Handsome Columns And Trim Details

Total Living Area: 1,575

- A half bath is tucked away in the laundry area for convenience
- Second floor hall has a handy desk
- Bonus area on the second floor has an additional 353 square feet of living area
- 3 bedrooms, 2 1/2 baths, 2-car garage
- Basement foundation

Plan# 577-0806

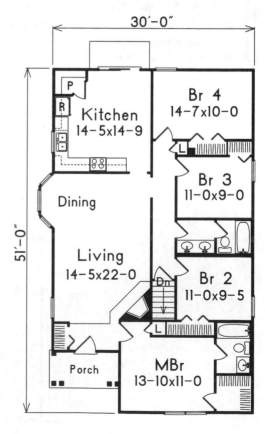

Four Bedroom Living For A Narrow Lot

Total Living Area: 1,452

- Large living room features cozy corner fireplace, bayed dining area and access from entry with guest closet
- Forward master bedroom suite enjoys having its own bath and linen closet
- Three additional bedrooms share a bath with double-bowl vanity
- 4 bedrooms, 2 baths
- Basement foundation

TO ORDER SEE **PAGE 608** OR CALL TOLL-FREE 1-800-DREAM HOME (373-2646)

Distinctive Home For Sloping Terrain

Total Living Area: 1,340

- Grand-sized vaulted living and dining rooms offer fireplace, wet bar and breakfast counter open to spacious kitchen
- Vaulted master suite features double entry doors, walk-in closet and elegant bath
- Basement includes a huge two-car garage and space for a bedroom/bath expansion
- 3 bedrooms, 2 baths, 2-car drive under garage with storage area
- Basement foundation

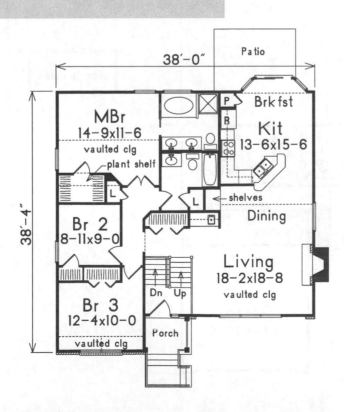

SMALL AND NARROW LOT

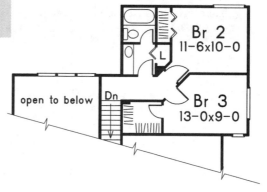

Window Expands Compact Two-Story

Total Living Area: 1,246

- Corner living room window adds openness and light
- Out-of-the-way kitchen with dining area accesses the outdoors
- Private first floor master bedroom with corner window
- Large walk-in closet is located in bedroom #3
- Easily built perimeter allows economical construction
- 3 bedrooms, 2 baths, 2-car garage
- Basement foundation

Second Floor
400 sq. ft.

Br 2
11-6x10-0

open to below   Dn

Br 3
13-0x9-0

36'-8"

Deck

Dining
9-0x9-6

Kit
12-0x
9-0

MBr
14-0x12-8

Dn

Living
12-4x17-0

vaulted

Up

plant shelf

Garage
20-0x20-0

38'-8"

First Floor
846 sq. ft.

SMALL AND NARROW LOT

TO ORDER SEE PAGE 608 OR CALL TOLL-FREE 1-800-DREAM HOME (373-2646)

Inviting Covered Corner Entry

Total Living Area: 1,747

- Entry opens into large family room with coat closet, angled fireplace and attractive plant shelf
- Kitchen and master bedroom access covered patio
- Functional kitchen includes ample workspace
- 4 bedrooms, 2 baths, 2-car garage
- Slab foundation

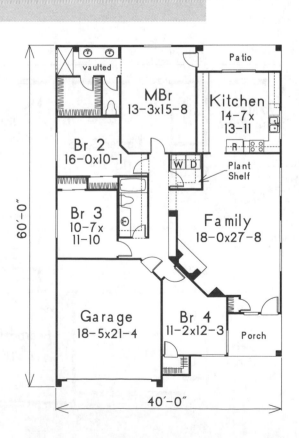

SMALL AND NARROW LOT

TO ORDER SEE PAGE 608 OR CALL TOLL-FREE 1-800-DREAM HOME (373-2646)

Loaded With Extras
Total Living Area: 1,281

- Spacious master suite with tray ceiling, double closets and private bath
- Vaulted family room has lots of sunlight and fireplace
- Plant shelf above kitchen and dining room is a nice decorative touch
- 3 bedrooms, 2 baths, 2-car drive under garage
- Walk-out basement foundation

SMALL AND NARROW LOT

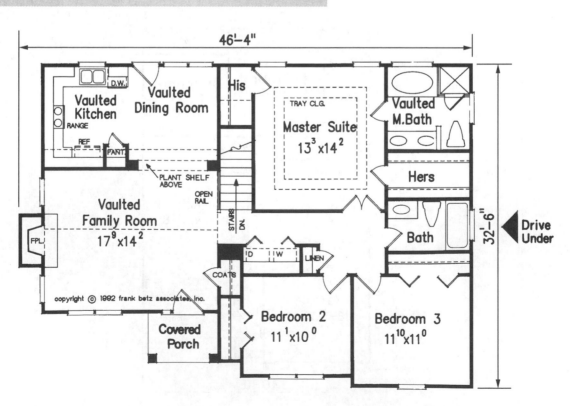

© 2003, Garrell Associates, Inc.

Great-Looking Gables Add Style

Total Living Area: 1,821

- 9' ceilings throughout first floor
- Master suite is secluded for privacy and has a spacious bath
- Sunny breakfast room features bay window
- Bonus room on the second floor has an additional 191 square feet of living area
- 3 bedrooms, 2 baths, 2-car side entry garage
- Basement or slab foundation, please specify when ordering

First Floor
1,821 sq. ft.

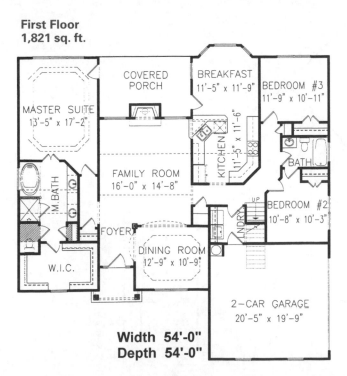

Width 54'-0"
Depth 54'-0"

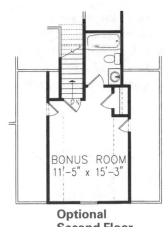

**Optional
Second Floor**

TO ORDER SEE **PAGE 608** OR CALL TOLL-FREE 1-800-DREAM HOME (373-2646)

Cozy Front Porch Welcomes Guests

Total Living Area: 1,393

- L-shaped kitchen features walk-in pantry, island cooktop and is convenient to laundry room and dining area
- Master bedroom features large walk-in closet and private bath with separate tub and shower
- Convenient storage/coat closet in hall
- View to the patio from the dining area
- 3 bedrooms, 2 baths, 2-car detached garage
- Crawl space foundation, drawings also include slab foundation

Plan# 577-0743

Price Code B

Efficient Kitchen Layout

Total Living Area: 1,598

- Additional storage area in garage
- Double-door entry into master bedroom with luxurious master bath
- Entry opens into large family room with vaulted ceiling and open stairway to basement
- 3 bedrooms, 2 baths, 2-car garage
- Basement foundation

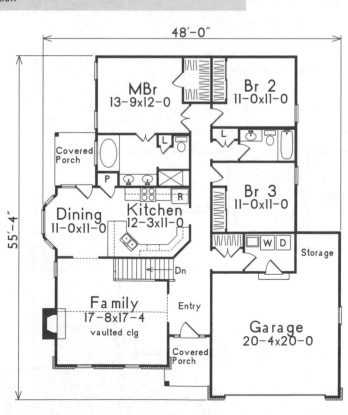

SMALL AND NARROW LOT

Compact Layout, Amenity Full

Total Living Area: 1,567

- Front gables and extended porch add charm to facade
- Large bay windows add brightness to breakfast and dining rooms
- The master bath boasts an oversized tub, separate shower, double sinks and large walk-in closet
- Living room features a vaulted ceiling and a prominent fireplace
- 3 bedrooms, 2 baths, 2-car drive under garage
- Basement foundation

SMALL AND NARROW LOT

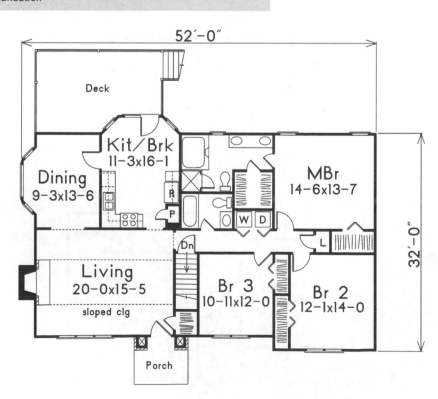

52'-0"

Deck

Kit/Brk
11-3x16-1

Dining
9-3x13-6

MBr
14-6x13-7

32'-0"

R

P

W D

Dn

L

Living
20-0x15-5

sloped clg

Br 3
10-11x12-0

Br 2
12-1x14-0

Porch

TO ORDER SEE **PAGE 608** OR CALL TOLL-FREE 1-800-DREAM HOME (373-2646)

Special Planning In This Compact Home

Total Living Area: 977

- Comfortable living room features a vaulted ceiling, fireplace, plant shelf and coat closet
- Both bedrooms are located on second floor and share a bath with double-bowl vanity and linen closet
- Sliding glass doors in dining room provide access to the deck
- 2 bedrooms, 1 1/2 baths, 1-car garage
- Basement foundation

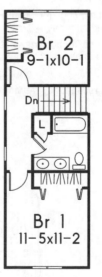

Br 2
9-1x10-1

Dn

L

Br 1
11-5x11-2

Second Floor
432 sq. ft.

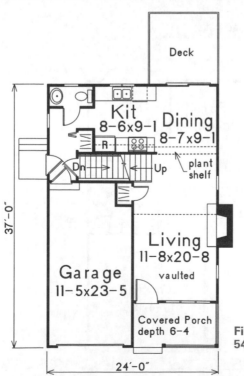

Deck

Kit
8-6x9-1

Dining
8-7x9-1

R

Dn   Up

plant shelf

Living
11-8x20-8
vaulted

Garage
11-5x23-5

Covered Porch
depth 6-4

First Floor
545 sq. ft.

37'-0"

24'-0"

SMALL AND NARROW LOT

Central Fireplace Focuses Family Living

Total Living Area: 1,408

- Handsome see-through fireplace offers a gathering point for the family room and kitchen/breakfast area
- Vaulted ceiling and large bay window in the master bedroom add charm to this room
- A dramatic angular wall and large windows add brightness to the kitchen/breakfast area
- Family room and kitchen/breakfast area have vaulted ceilings, adding to this central living area
- 3 bedrooms, 2 baths, 2-car garage
- Crawl space foundation, drawings also include slab foundation

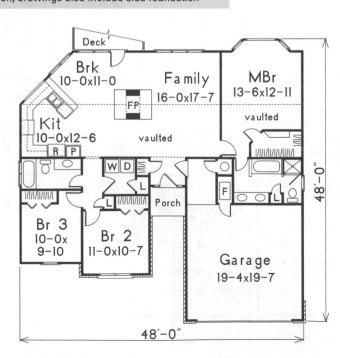

Deck

Brk
10-0x11-0

Family
16-0x17-7

MBr
13-6x12-11

vaulted

FP

Kit
10-0x12-6

vaulted

R P

W D

L

Porch

F

L

Br 3
10-0x
9-10

Br 2
11-0x10-7

Garage
19-4x19-7

48'-0"

48'-0"

Country Charm For A Small Lot

Total Living Area: 1,169

- Front facade features a distinctive country appeal
- Living room enjoys a wood-burning fireplace and pass-through to kitchen
- A stylish U-shaped kitchen offers an abundance of cabinet and counterspace with view to living room
- A large walk-in closet, access to rear patio and private bath are many features of the master bedroom
- 3 bedrooms, 2 baths, 1-car garage
- Basement foundation

TO ORDER SEE **PAGE 608** OR CALL TOLL-FREE 1-800-DREAM HOME (373-2646)

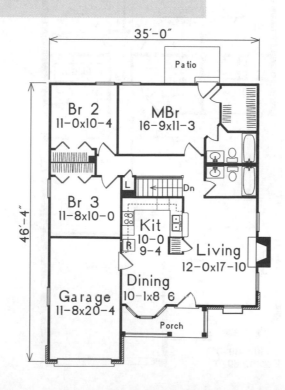

SMALL AND NARROW LOT

Bedrooms With Sloped Ceilings
Total Living Area: 1,710

■ Bedrooms have plenty of closet space

■ Laundry area located near bedrooms for efficiency

■ Corner fireplace warms large family room with 10' ceiling

■ 4 bedrooms, 2 baths, 2-car garage

■ Slab foundation

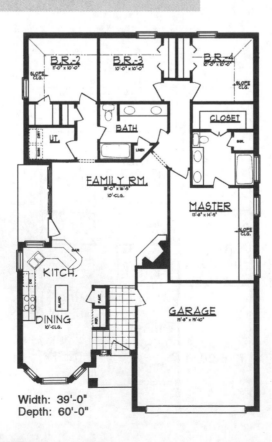

Width: 39'-0"
Depth: 60'-0"

TO ORDER SEE **PAGE 608** OR CALL TOLL-FREE 1-800-DREAM HOME (373-2646)

Flexible Design Is Popular

Total Living Area: 1,440

- Open floor plan with access to covered porches in front and back
- Lots of linen, pantry and closet space throughout
- Laundry/mud room between kitchen and garage is a convenient feature
- 2 bedrooms, 2 baths, 2-car side entry garage
- Basement foundation

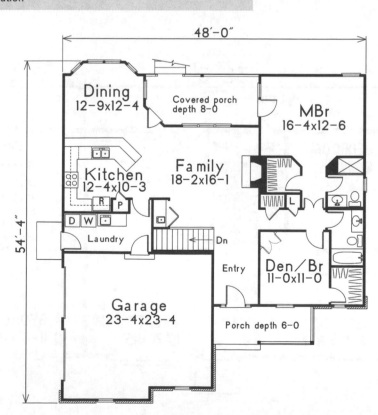

48'-0"

54'-4"

Dining
12-9x12-4

Covered porch
depth 8-0

MBr
16-4x12-6

Kitchen
12-4x10-3

Family
18-2x16-1

D W R P L

Laundry

Dn

Entry

Den/Br
11-0x11-0

Garage
23-4x23-4

Porch depth 6-0

SMALL AND NARROW LOT

285

Functional Livability In A Small Ranch

Total Living Area: 768

- Great room has an attractive box window for enjoying views
- Six closets provide great storage for a compact plan
- Plans include optional third bedroom with an additional 288 square feet of living area
- 2 bedrooms, 1 bath
- Basement foundation, drawings also include crawl space and slab foundations

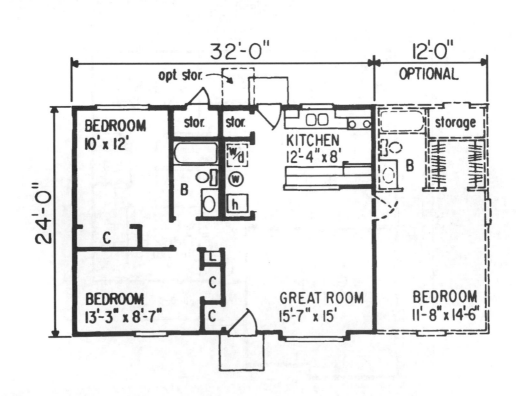

TO ORDER SEE **PAGE 608** OR CALL TOLL-FREE 1-800-DREAM HOME (373-2646)

Island Work Space

Total Living Area: 1,464

- Contemporary styled home has breathtaking two-story foyer and lovely open staircase
- Efficiently designed U-shaped kitchen
- Elegant great room has a cozy fireplace
- 3 bedrooms, 2 1/2 baths, 2-car garage
- Crawl space foundation

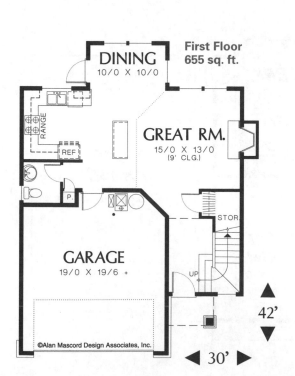

DINING
10/0 X 10/0

First Floor
655 sq. ft.

GREAT RM.
15/0 X 13/0
(9' CLG.)

RANGE

REF

P.

STOR.

UP

GARAGE
19/0 X 19/6 +

©Alan Mascord Design Associates, Inc.

42'

30'

MASTER
12/0 X 13/0

LINEN

W D

BR. 3
10/8 X 10/0

DN

FOYER
BELOW

BR. 2
11/0 X 11/8

Second Floor
809 sq. ft.

SMALL AND NARROW LOT

TO ORDER SEE PAGE 608 OR CALL TOLL-FREE 1-800-DREAM HOME (373-2646)

Arched Window Is A Focal Point

Total Living Area: 1,021

- 11' ceiling in great room expands living area
- Kitchen and breakfast room combine allowing easier preparation and cleanup
- Master suite features private bath and an oversized walk-in closet
- 3 bedrooms, 2 baths, optional 2-car garage
- Slab or crawl space foundation, please specify when ordering

SMALL AND NARROW LOT

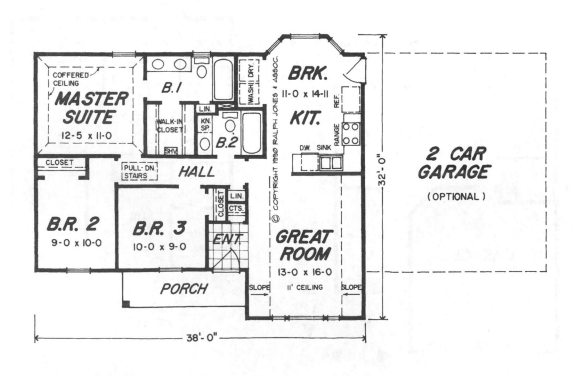

Spectacular Views From Window Wall

Total Living Area: 1,375

- Open U-shaped kitchen shares an eating bar with the dining room
- Two secondary bedrooms share a full bath
- Master bedroom provides a walk-in closet and private bath
- Loft on the second floor has an additional 284 square feet of optional living area
- 3 bedrooms, 2 baths
- Basement or crawl space foundation, please specify when ordering

Optional Second Floor

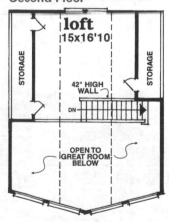

First Floor
1,375 sq. ft.

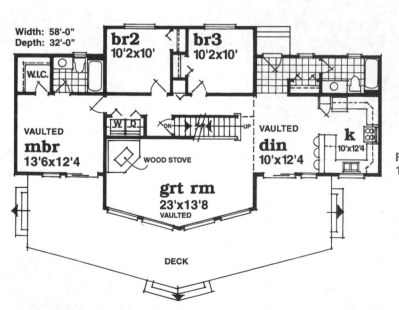

SMALL AND NARROW LOT

Plan# 577-MG-97099

Price Code AA

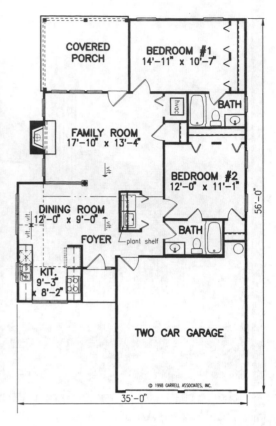

BEDROOM #1
14'-11" x 10'-7"

COVERED PORCH

BATH

FAMILY ROOM
17'-10" x 13'-4"

hvac

BEDROOM #2
12'-0" x 11'-1"

56'-0"

DINING ROOM
12'-0" x 9'-0"

FOYER

BATH

plant shelf

KIT.
9'-3"
x 8'-2"

TWO CAR GARAGE

© 1998 GARRELL ASSOCIATES, INC.

35'-0"

Narrow Lot Design

Total Living Area: 1,093

- Family room with fireplace overlooks large covered porch
- Vaulted family and dining rooms are adjacent to kitchen
- Bedroom #2 has its own entrance into bath
- Plant shelf accents vaulted foyer
- Centrally located laundry area
- 2 bedrooms, 2 baths, 2-car garage
- Slab foundation

Plan# 577-1120

Price Code A

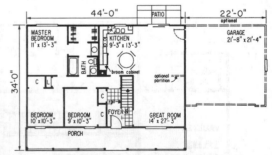

44'-0"

PATIO

22'-0"
optional

MASTER
BEDROOM
11' x 13'-3"

KITCHEN
9'-3" x 13'-3"

GARAGE
21'-8" x 21'-4"

34'-0"

BATH

broom cabinet

optional
partition

C

BEDROOM
10' x 10'-3"

BEDROOM
9' x 10'-3"

C

FOYER

GREAT ROOM
14' x 27'-3"

PORCH

Perfect Country Haven

Total Living Area: 1,232

- Ideal porch for quiet quality evenings
- Great room opens to dining room for those large dinner gatherings
- Functional L-shaped kitchen includes broom cabinet
- 3 bedrooms, 1 bath, optional 2-car garage
- Basement foundation, drawings also include crawl space and slab foundations

Enchanting One-Level Home

Total Living Area: 1,508

- Grand opening between rooms creates a spacious effect
- Additional room for quick meals or serving a larger crowd is provided at the breakfast bar
- Sunny dining area accesses the outdoors as well
- 3 bedrooms, 2 baths, 2-car garage
- Basement or crawl space foundation, please specify when ordering

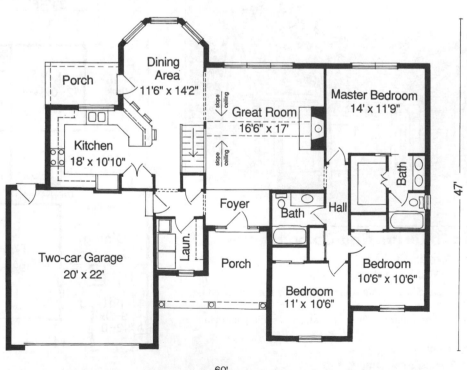

SMALL AND NARROW LOT

291

Plan # 577-RDD-1374-9

Price Code A

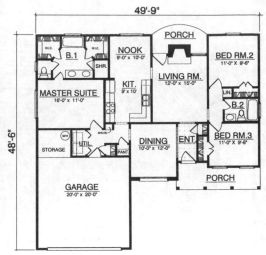

Scalloped Front Porch

Total Living Area: 1,374

- Garage has extra storage space
- Spacious living room has fireplace
- Well-designed kitchen with adjacent breakfast nook
- Separated master suite maintains privacy
- 3 bedrooms, 2 baths, 2-car garage
- Slab or crawl space foundation, please specify when ordering

Plan # 577-0277

Price Code AA

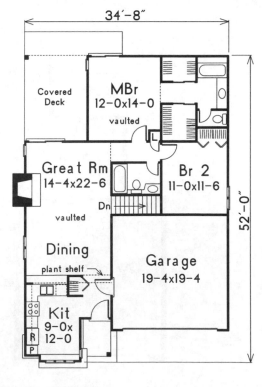

Charming Exterior And Cozy Interior

Total Living Area: 1,127

- Plant shelf joins kitchen and dining room
- Vaulted master suite has double walk-in closets, deck access and private bath
- Great room features vaulted ceiling, fireplace and sliding doors to covered deck
- Ideal home for a narrow lot
- 2 bedrooms, 2 baths, 2-car garage
- Basement foundation

SMALL AND NARROW LOT

Plan# 577-NDG-148

Price Code B

Bayed Dining Room
Total Living Area: 1,538

- Dining and great rooms highlighted in this design
- Master suite has many amenities
- Kitchen and laundry are accessible from any room in the house
- 3 bedrooms, 2 baths, 2-car garage
- Walk-out basement, basement, crawl space or slab foundation, please specify when ordering

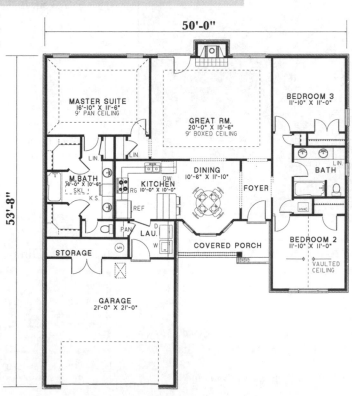

SMALL AND NARROW LOT

Plan# **577-DDI-95220**

Price Code B

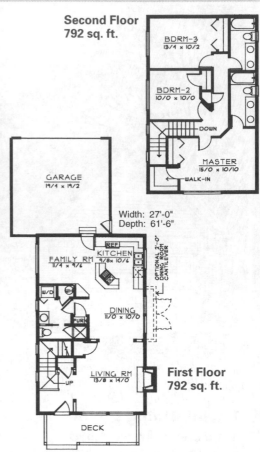

Second Floor 792 sq. ft.

Width: 27'-0"
Depth: 61'-6"

First Floor 792 sq. ft.

Open Living On First Floor

Total Living Area: 1,584

- Kitchen overlooks family room creating a natural gathering place
- Double vanity in master bath
- Dining room flows into living room
- 3 bedrooms, 2 1/2 baths, 2-car rear entry garage
- Crawl space foundation

Plan# **577-0479**

Price Code A

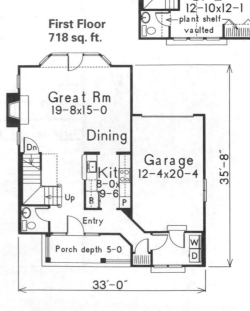

Second Floor 576 sq. ft.

First Floor 718 sq. ft.

Trendsetting Appeal For A Narrow Lot

Total Living Area: 1,294

- Great room has fireplace and large bay window and patio doors
- Enjoy a laundry room immersed in light with large windows, arched transom and attractive planter box
- Vaulted master bedroom with bay window and walk-in closets
- Bedroom #2 boasts a vaulted ceiling, plant shelf and half bath, perfect for a studio
- 2 bedrooms, 1 full bath, 2 half baths, 1-car rear entry garage
- Basement foundation

Front Porch Adds Style To This Ranch

Total Living Area: 1,496

- Master bedroom features coffered ceiling, walk-in closet and spacious bath
- Vaulted ceiling and fireplace grace family room
- Dining room is adjacent to kitchen and features access to rear porch
- Convenient access to utility room from kitchen
- 3 bedrooms, 2 baths, 2-car drive under garage
- Basement foundation

TO ORDER SEE **PAGE 608** OR CALL TOLL-FREE 1-800-DREAM HOME (373-2646)

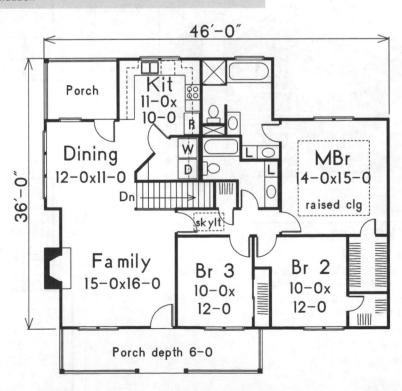

46'-0"

36'-0"

Porch

Kit
11-0x
10-0

Dining
12-0x11-0

Dn

skylt

Family
15-0x16-0

MBr
14-0x15-0
raised clg

Br 3
10-0x
12-0

Br 2
10-0x
12-0

Porch depth 6-0

SMALL AND NARROW LOT

Plan# 577-SH-SEA-226

Price Code B

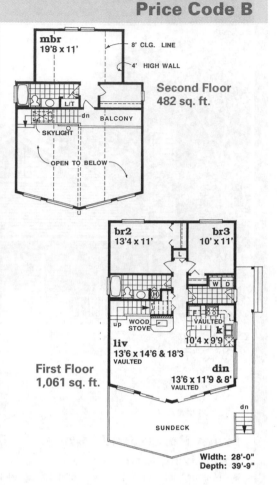

Second Floor 482 sq. ft.

First Floor 1,061 sq. ft.

Width: 28'-0"
Depth: 39'-9"

Expansive Glass Wall In Living Areas

Total Living Area: 1,543

- Enormous sundeck makes this a popular vacation style
- A woodstove warms the vaulted living and dining rooms
- A vaulted kitchen has a prep island and breakfast bar
- Second floor vaulted master bedroom has private bath and walk-in closet
- 3 bedrooms, 2 baths
- Crawl space foundation

Plan# 577-0415

Price Code A

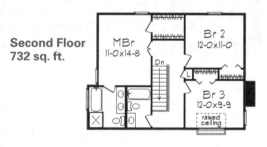

Second Floor 732 sq. ft.

First Floor 760 sq. ft.

Home Offers Wide Open Spaces

Total Living Area: 1,492

- Cleverly angled entry spills into living and dining rooms which share warmth of fireplace flanked by arched windows
- Master bedroom includes double-door entry, huge walk-in closet, shower and bath with picture window
- Stucco and dutch hipped roofs add warmth and charm to facade
- 3 bedrooms, 2 1/2 baths, 2-car garage
- Basement foundation

Great Room's Symmetry Steals The Show

Total Living Area: 1,985

- Charming design for a narrow lot
- Dramatic sunken great room features vaulted ceiling, large double-hung windows and transomed patio doors
- Grand master bedroom includes double entry doors, large closet, elegant bath and patio access
- 4 bedrooms, 3 1/2 baths, 2 car garage
- Basement foundation

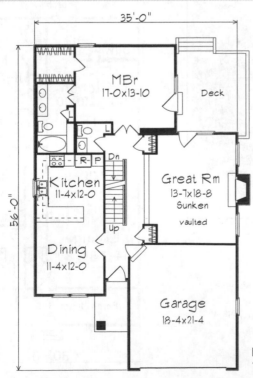

35'-0"

56'-0"

MBr
17-0x13-10

Deck

Kitchen
11-4x12-0

Great Rm
13-7x18-8
Sunken
vaulted

Dn

Up

R P

Dining
11-4x12-0

Garage
18-4x21-4

First Floor
1,114 sq. ft.

Br 3
12-4x12-5

Br 2
11-0x12-5

Dn

open to
below

Br 4
11-4x13-3

Second Floor
871 sq. ft.

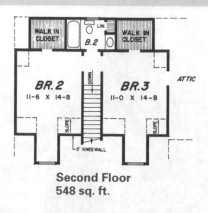

Second Floor
548 sq. ft.

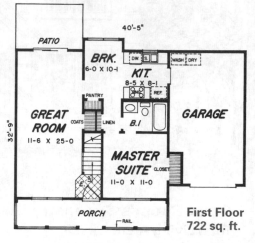

First Floor
722 sq. ft.

Lovely Front Dormers

Total Living Area: 1,270

- Convenient master suite on first floor
- Two secondary bedrooms on second floor each have a large walk-in closet and share a full bath
- Sunny breakfast room has lots of sunlight and easy access to great room and kitchen
- 3 bedrooms, 2 baths, 1-car garage
- Slab or crawl space foundation, please specify when ordering

Plan# **577-0297**

Price Code A

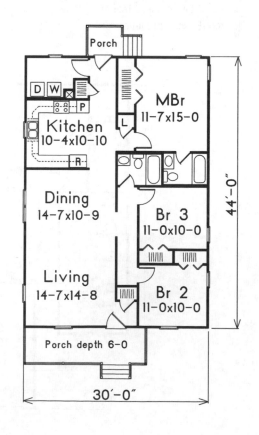

Gabled, Covered Front Porch

Total Living Area: 1,320

- Functional U-shaped kitchen features pantry
- Large living and dining areas join to create an open atmosphere
- Secluded master bedroom includes private full bath
- Covered front porch opens into large living area with convenient coat closet
- Utility/laundry room located near the kitchen
- 3 bedrooms, 2 baths
- Crawl space foundation

SMALL AND NARROW LOT

TO ORDER SEE **PAGE 608** OR CALL TOLL-FREE 1-800-DREAM HOME (373-2646)

Perfect For Escaping To The Outdoors

Total Living Area: 1,200

- Enjoy lazy summer evenings on this magnificent porch
- Activity area has fireplace and ascending stair from cozy loft
- Kitchen features built-in pantry
- Master suite enjoys large bath, walk-in closet and cozy loft overlooking room below
- 2 bedrooms, 2 baths
- Crawl space foundation

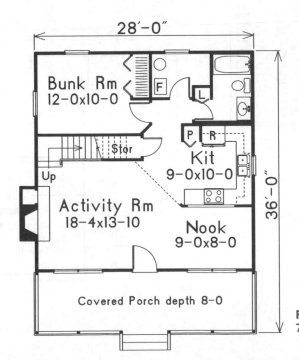

**First Floor
784 sq. ft.**

28'-0"

Bunk Rm
12-0x10-0

Stor

Up

Kit
9-0x10-0

Activity Rm
18-4x13-10

Nook
9-0x8-0

36'-0"

Covered Porch depth 8-0

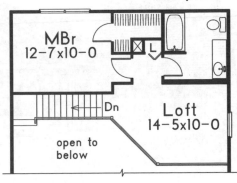

**Second Floor
416 sq. ft.**

MBr
12-7x10-0

Dn

Loft
14-5x10-0

open to
below

Exciting Features Throughout

Total Living Area: 1,315

- First floor laundry and kitchen are convenient work spaces
- Windows on both sides of the fireplace make the great room very pleasant for relaxing and enjoying views outdoors
- Open stairs to the lower level make it simple to finish the basement
- 3 bedrooms, 2 baths, 2-car side entry garage
- Walk-out basement or basement foundation, please specify when ordering

SMALL AND NARROW LOT

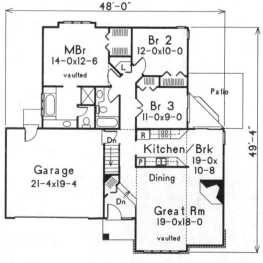

Great Room Window Adds Character

Total Living Area: 1,368

- Entry foyer steps down to open living area which combines great room and formal dining area
- Vaulted master suite includes box bay window, large vanity, separate tub and shower
- Cozy breakfast area features direct access to the patio and pass-through kitchen
- Handy linen closet located in hall
- 3 bedrooms, 2 baths, 2-car garage
- Basement foundation

Large Windows Grace This Split-Level
Total Living Area: 1,427

- Practical storage space situated in the garage
- Convenient laundry closet located on lower level
- Kitchen and dining area both have sliding doors that access the deck
- Large expansive space created by vaulted living and dining rooms
- 3 bedrooms, 2 baths, 2-car drive under garage
- Basement foundation

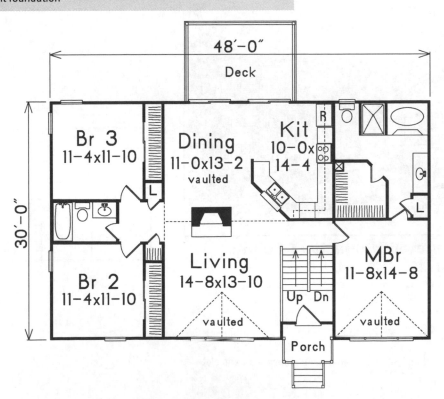

48'-0"

Deck

30'-0"

Br 3
11-4x11-10

Dining
11-0x13-2
vaulted

Kit
10-0x
14-4

Br 2
11-4x11-10

Living
14-8x13-10

vaulted

Up Dn

MBr
11-8x14-8

vaulted

Porch

SMALL AND NARROW LOT

Plan # 577-0209

Price Code B

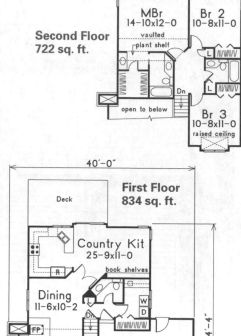

Second Floor 722 sq. ft.

MBr 14-10x12-0 vaulted plant shelf

Br 2 10-8x11-0

Br 3 10-8x11-0 raised ceiling

open to below

First Floor 834 sq. ft.

40'-0"

Deck

Country Kit 25-9x11-0

book shelves

Dining 11-6x10-2

Living 13-6x13-0 vaulted

Garage 20-0x23-6

Porch

44'-4"

Kitchen Center Of Living Activities

Total Living Area: 1,556

- A compact home with all the amenities
- Country kitchen combines practicality with access to other areas for eating and entertaining
- Two-way fireplace joins the dining and living areas
- Plant shelf and vaulted ceiling highlight the master bedroom
- 3 bedrooms, 2 1/2 baths, 2-car garage
- Basement foundation

Plan # 577-0507

Price Code AA

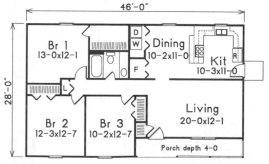

46'-0"

Br 1 13-0x12-1

Dining 10-2x11-0

Kit 10-3x11-0

Br 2 12-3x12-7

Br 3 10-2x12-7

Living 20-0x12-1

Porch depth 4-0

28'-0"

Country-Style With Spacious Rooms

Total Living Area: 1,197

- U-shaped kitchen includes ample work space, breakfast bar, laundry area and direct access to the outdoors
- Large living room with convenient coat closet
- Master bedroom features large walk-in closet
- 3 bedrooms, 1 bath
- Crawl space foundation, drawings also include basement and slab foundations

SMALL AND NARROW LOT

302

Covered Porch Adds To Country Charm

Total Living Area: 954

- Kitchen has cozy bayed eating area
- Master bedroom has a walk-in closet and private bath
- Large great room has access to the back porch
- Convenient coat closet near front entry
- 3 bedrooms, 2 baths
- Basement foundation

TO ORDER SEE **PAGE 608** OR CALL TOLL-FREE 1-800-DREAM HOME (373-2646)

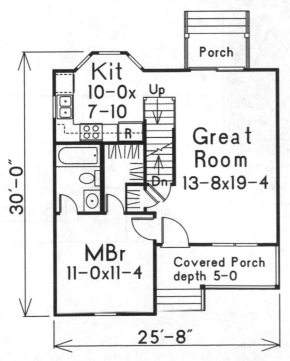

Porch

Kit
10-0x
7-10

Up

Great
Room
13-8x19-4

Dn

R

MBr
11-0x11-4

Covered Porch
depth 5-0

30'-0"

25'-8"

First Floor
618 sq. ft.

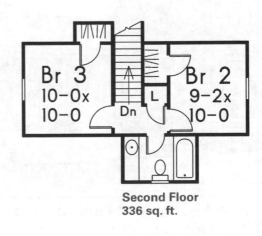

Br 3
10-0x
10-0

Dn

L

Br 2
9-2x
10-0

Second Floor
336 sq. ft.

SMALL AND NARROW LOT

303

Plan# 577-RJ-A10-50

Price Code AA

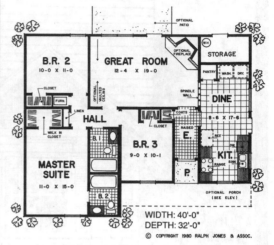

WIDTH: 40'-0"
DEPTH: 32'-0"

© COPYRIGHT 1980 RALPH JONES & ASSOC.

Country-Style Starter Home

Total Living Area: 1,084

- Raised floor in large formal entry
- Large kitchen open to dining area
- Great room has vaulted and sloped ceiling with optional fireplace
- Front porch with unique columns
- Master suite has walk-in closet
- 3 bedrooms, 2 baths, optional 2-car garage
- Slab or crawl space foundation, please specify when ordering

Plan# 577-0543

Price Code AA

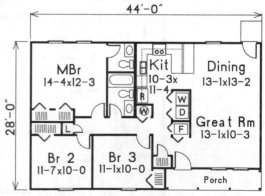

Large Living And Dining Areas

Total Living Area: 1,160

- U-shaped kitchen has breakfast bar and convenient laundry area
- Master bedroom features private half bath and large closet
- Dining room has outdoor access
- Dining and great rooms combine to create an open living atmosphere
- 3 bedrooms, 1 1/2 baths
- Crawl space foundation, drawings also include basement and slab foundations

A Charming Home Loaded With Extras

Total Living Area: 1,997

- Screened porch leads to a rear terrace with access to the breakfast room
- Living and dining rooms combine adding spaciousness
- Other welcome amenities include boxed windows in breakfast and dining rooms, a fireplace in living room and a pass-through snack bar in the kitchen
- 3 bedrooms, 2 1/2 baths
- Basement foundation

Second Floor
886 sq. ft.

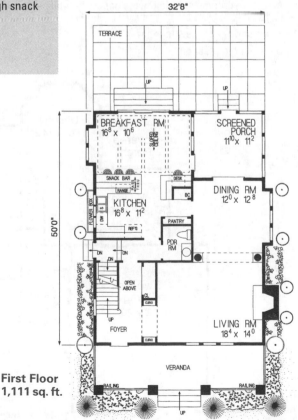

First Floor
1,111 sq. ft.

SMALL AND NARROW LOT

Stone Adds Charm To Exterior

Total Living Area: 1,509

- A grand opening between the great room and dining area visually expands the living space
- The kitchen is a delightful place to prepare meals with snack bar and large pantry
- Master bedroom enjoys a private bath with double-bowl vanity and large walk-in closet
- 3 bedrooms, 2 baths, 2-car garage
- Basement foundation

SMALL AND NARROW LOT

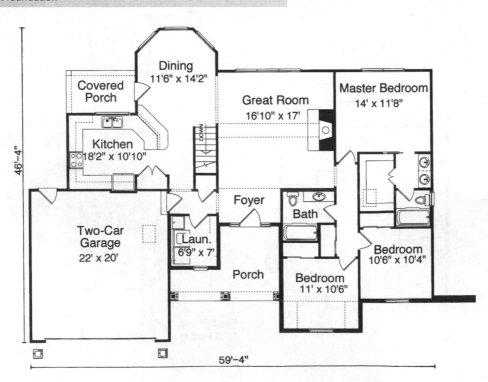

Bedrooms Separate From Rest Of Home
Total Living Area: 1,849

- Enormous laundry/mud room has many extras including storage area and half bath
- Lavish master bath has corner jacuzzi tub, double sinks, separate shower and walk-in closet
- Secondary bedrooms include walk-in closets
- Kitchen has wrap-around eating counter and is positioned between formal dining area and breakfast room for convenience
- 3 bedrooms, 2 1/2 baths, 2-car side entry garage
- Slab foundation, drawings also include crawl space foundation

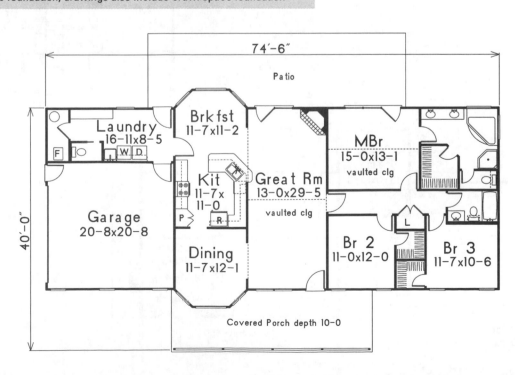

COUNTRY / VICTORIAN

TO ORDER SEE PAGE 608 OR CALL TOLL-FREE 1-800-DREAM HOME (373-2646)

Classic Rural Farmhouse
Total Living Area: 2,363

- Covered porches provide outdoor seating areas
- Corner fireplace becomes focal point of family room
- Kitchen features island cooktop and adjoining nook
- Energy efficient home with 2" x 6" exterior walls
- 3 bedrooms, 2 1/2 baths, 2-car garage
- Partial basement/crawl space foundation

COUNTRY / VICTORIAN

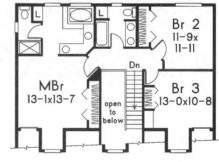

Second Floor
863 sq. ft.

Br 2
11-9x
11-11

MBr
13-1x13-7

Br 3
13-0x10-8

Dn

open to below

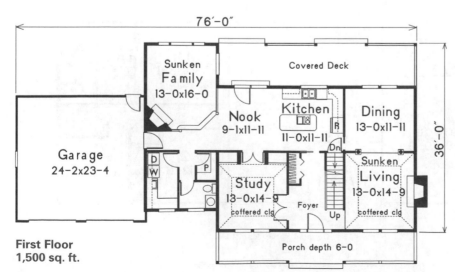

76'-0"

Sunken Family
13-0x16-0

Covered Deck

Nook
9-1x11-11

Kitchen
11-0x11-11

Dining
13-0x11-11

Garage
24-2x23-4

Study
13-0x14-9
coffered clg

Living
13-0x14-9
coffered clg

Sunken

Foyer

Up

Dn

36'-0"

Porch depth 6-0

First Floor
1,500 sq. ft.

Large Built-In Desk

Total Living Area: 1,815

- Second floor has built-in desk in hall; ideal as a computer work station or mini office area
- Two doors into laundry area make it handy from master bedroom and the rest of the home
- Inviting covered porch
- Lots of counterspace and cabinetry in kitchen
- 3 bedrooms, 2 1/2 baths, 2-car side entry garage
- Basement foundation

TO ORDER SEE **PAGE 608** OR CALL TOLL-FREE 1-800-DREAM HOME (373-2646)

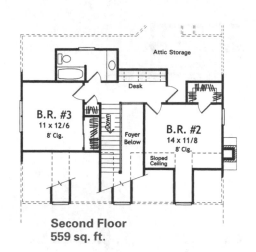

Second Floor
559 sq. ft.

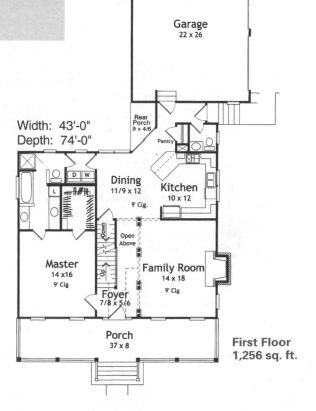

Width: 43'-0"
Depth: 74'-0"

Porch 37 x 8

First Floor
1,256 sq. ft.

COUNTRY / VICTORIAN

TO ORDER SEE **PAGE 608** OR CALL TOLL-FREE 1-800-DREAM HOME (373-2646)

Inviting Covered Verandas

Total Living Area: 1,830

- Inviting covered verandas in the front and rear of the home
- Great room has fireplace and cathedral ceiling
- Handy service porch allows easy access
- Master bedroom has vaulted ceiling and private bath
- 3 bedrooms, 2 baths, 3-car side entry garage
- Basement, crawl space or slab foundation, please specify when ordering

COUNTRY / VICTORIAN

Plan # 577-0143

Price Code E

Veranda Softens Country-Style Home

Total Living Area: 2,449

- Striking living area features fireplace flanked with windows, cathedral ceiling and balcony
- First floor master bedroom with twin walk-in closets and large linen storage
- Dormers add space for desks or seats
- 3 bedrooms, 2 1/2 baths, 2-car detached garage
- Slab foundation, drawings also include crawl space foundation

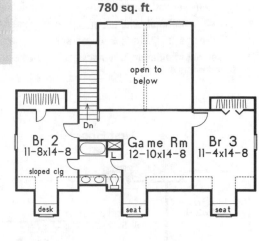

Second Floor
780 sq. ft.

open to below

Br 2
11-8x14-8

Game Rm
12-10x14-8

Br 3
11-4x14-8

Dn

sloped clg

desk

seat

seat

First Floor
1,669 sq. ft.

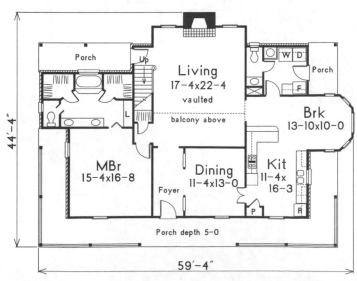

Porch

Up

Living
17-4x22-4
vaulted

balcony above

W D

F

Porch

Brk
13-10x10-0

L

MBr
15-4x16-8

Foyer

Dining
11-4x13-0

Kit
11-4x 16-3

P

R

Porch depth 5-0

44'-4"

59'-4"

Compact Design Offers Privacy

Total Living Area: 2,847

- Secluded first floor master bedroom includes an oversized window and a large walk-in closet
- Extensive attic storage and closet space
- Spacious second floor bedrooms, two of which share a private bath
- Great starter home with option to finish the second floor as needed
- 4 bedrooms, 3 1/2 baths, 2-car garage
- Basement foundation, drawings also include slab and crawl space foundations

COUNTRY/VICTORIAN

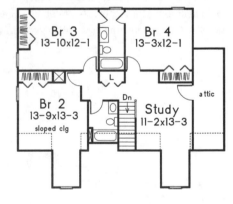

Second Floor
1,102 sq. ft.

Br 3
13-10x12-1

Br 4
13-3x12-1

Br 2
13-9x13-3

Study
11-2x13-3

sloped clg

attic

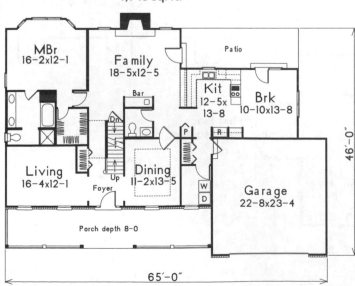

First Floor
1,745 sq. ft.

MBr
16-2x12-1

Family
18-5x12-5

Patio

Bar

Kit
12-5x
13-8

Brk
10-10x13-8

Living
16-4x12-1

Dining
11-2x13-5

Up

Foyer

Garage
22-8x23-4

Porch depth 8-0

46'-0"

65'-0"

TO ORDER SEE **PAGE 608** OR CALL TOLL-FREE 1-800-DREAM HOME (373-2646)

Terrific Layout For Family Living

Total Living Area: 1,409

- Striking fireplace in living room
- Eating bar off kitchen provides extra seating for dining
- Large master suite has its own bath
- 3 bedrooms, 2 baths, 2-car garage
- Slab or crawl space foundation, please specify when ordering

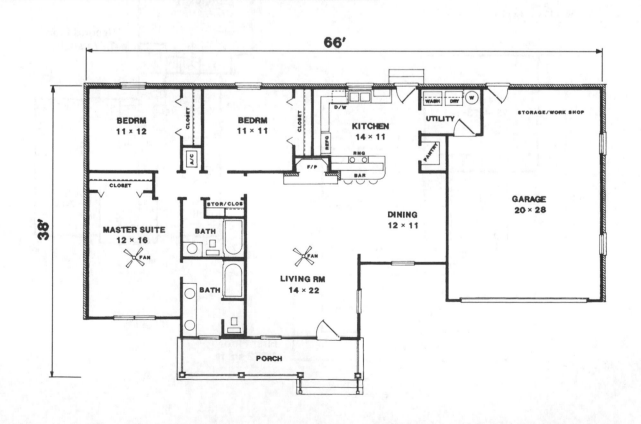

COUNTRY / VICTORIAN

TO ORDER SEE **PAGE 608** OR CALL TOLL-FREE 1-800-DREAM HOME (373-2646)

Country-Style Comfort

Total Living Area: 2,826

- Wrap-around covered porch is accessible from family and breakfast rooms in addition to front entrance
- Bonus room with separate entrance is suitable for an office or private accommodations
- Large, full-windowed breakfast room
- 4 bedrooms, 2 1/2 baths, 2-car side entry garage
- Basement foundation

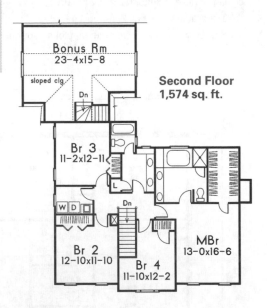

Bonus Rm
23-4x15-8

sloped clg.

Dn

Second Floor
1,574 sq. ft.

Br 3
11-2x12-11

W D

Br 2
12-10x11-10

Dn

Br 4
11-10x12-2

MBr
13-0x16-6

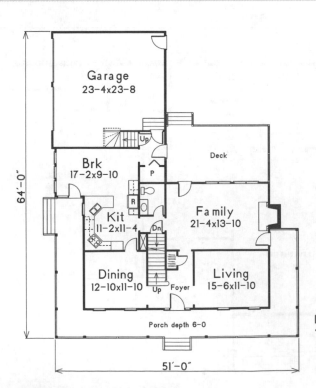

Garage
23-4x23-8

Up

Brk
17-2x9-10

Deck

P

R

Kit
11-2x11-4

Family
21-4x13-10

Dn

Dining
12-10x11-10

Up Foyer

Living
15-6x11-10

64'-0"

Porch depth 6-0

51'-0"

First Floor
1,252 sq. ft.

Plan# 577-0299

Price Code E

Comfortable Living At Its Finest

Total Living Area: 3,013

- Oversized rooms throughout
- Kitchen features island sink, large pantry and opens into sunny breakfast room
- Large family room with fireplace accesses rear deck and front porch
- Master bedroom includes large walk-in closet and private deluxe bath
- 4 bedrooms, 3 1/2 baths, 2-car side entry garage
- Basement foundation

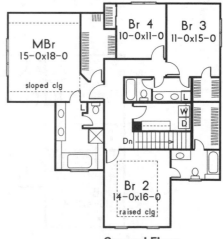

Second Floor
1,554 sq. ft.

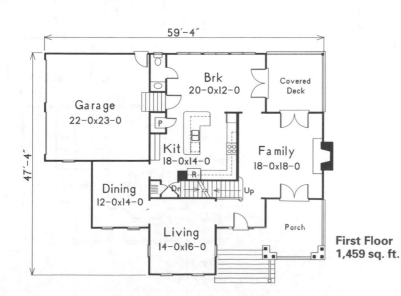

First Floor
1,459 sq. ft.

TO ORDER SEE **PAGE 608** OR CALL TOLL-FREE 1-800-DREAM HOME (373-2646)

COUNTRY / VICTORIAN

Outdoor Living Area Created By Veranda

Total Living Area: 2,213

■ Master bedroom features full bath with separate vanities, large walk-in closet and access to veranda

■ Living room enhanced by a fireplace, bay window and columns framing the gallery

■ 9' ceilings throughout home add to open feeling

■ 4 bedrooms, 2 1/2 baths, 2-car side entry garage

■ Slab foundation

COUNTRY / VICTORIAN

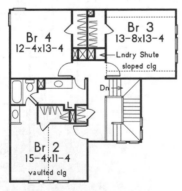

Second Floor
862 sq. ft.

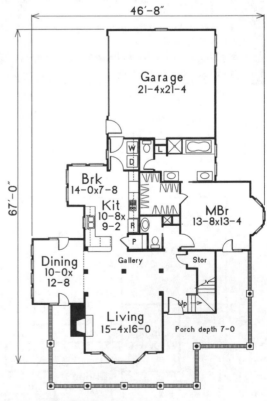

First Floor
1,351 sq. ft.

TO ORDER SEE **PAGE 608** OR CALL TOLL-FREE 1-800-DREAM HOME (373-2646)

Attractive Dormers Enhance Facade

Total Living Area: 2,112

- Double-door entrance from kitchen to dining area
- Nook located between family room and kitchen makes an ideal breakfast area
- Both baths on second floor feature skylights
- 3 bedrooms, 2 1/2 baths
- Basement foundation, drawings also include crawl space foundation

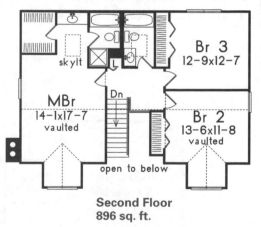

Second Floor
896 sq. ft.

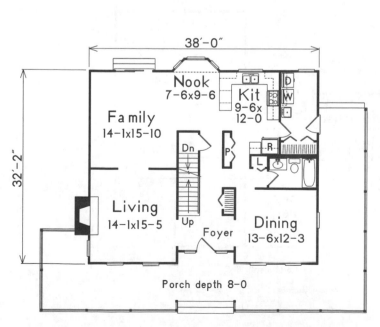

First Floor
1,216 sq. ft.

COUNTRY / VICTORIAN

317

TO ORDER SEE **PAGE 608** OR CALL TOLL-FREE 1-800-DREAM HOME (373-2646)

Covered Porch Adds Charm To Entrance

Total Living Area: 1,655

- Master bedroom features 9' ceiling, walk-in closet and bath with dressing area
- Oversized family room includes 10' ceiling and masonry see-through fireplace
- Island kitchen with convenient access to laundry room
- Handy covered walkway from garage to kitchen and dining area
- 3 bedrooms, 2 baths, 2-car garage
- Crawl space foundation

COUNTRY / VICTORIAN

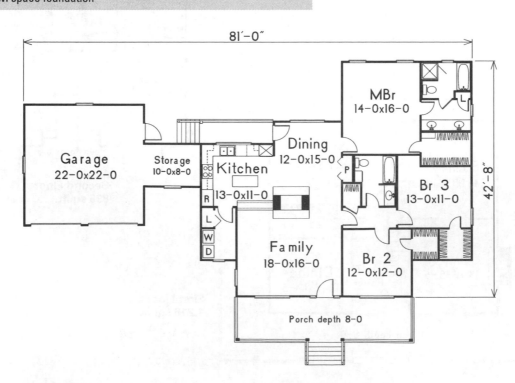

81'-0"

42'-8"

Garage
22-0x22-0

Storage
10-0x8-0

Kitchen
13-0x11-0

Dining
12-0x15-0

MBr
14-0x16-0

Br 3
13-0x11-0

Family
18-0x16-0

Br 2
12-0x12-0

Porch depth 8-0

Plan# 577-GSD-2825

Price Code F

Attractive Stone Accents

Total Living Area: 3,230

- Efficiently designed eating counter in kitchen for added dining
- Enormous deck surrounds the rear of this home making it perfect for entertaining
- Interesting two-sided fireplace in master bedroom
- Open living areas create a feeling of spaciousness
- 3 bedrooms, 2 1/2 baths
- Walk-out basement foundation

WIDTH: 66'-0"
DEPTH: 44'-0'

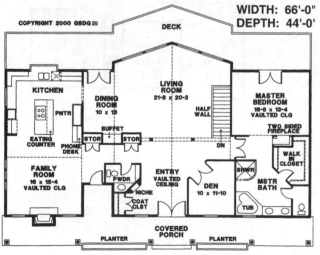

First Floor
2,169 sq. ft.

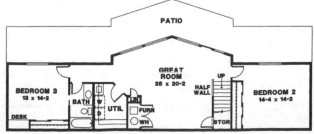

Lower Level
1,061 sq. ft.

COUNTRY / VICTORIAN

Victorian Has Unexpected Pleasures

Total Living Area: 2,935

- Gracious entry foyer with handsome stairway opens to separate living and dining rooms
- Kitchen has vaulted ceiling and skylight, island worktop, breakfast area with bay window and two separate pantries
- Large second floor master bedroom suite with fireplace, raised tub, dressing area with vaulted ceiling and skylight
- 4 bedrooms, 2 1/2 baths, 2-car side entry garage
- Basement foundation

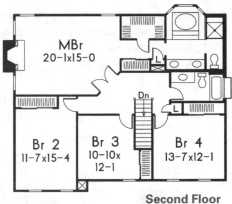

MBr
20-1x15-0

Br 2
11-7x15-4

Br 3
10-10x
12-1

Br 4
13-7x12-1

**Second Floor
1,320 sq. ft.**

Patio

Family
22-0x15-7

Kit/Brk
20-6x14-11

**First Floor
1,615 sq. ft.**

Bar

desk

Living
13-4x17-1

Dining
13-7x15-1

Garage
21-8x25-4

Foyer

Up

Porch

37'-8"

71'-0"

Lots Of Charm Inside And Out

Total Living Area: 2,431

- Octagon-shaped formal dining room makes an impact on the exterior of this home
- Angled walls add interest to the floor plan throughout this home
- Future playroom on the second floor has an additional 271 square feet of living area
- 4 bedrooms, 2 1/2 baths, 2-car side entry garage
- Slab foundation

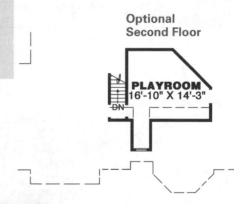

Optional
Second Floor

PLAYROOM
16'-10" X 14'-3"
DN

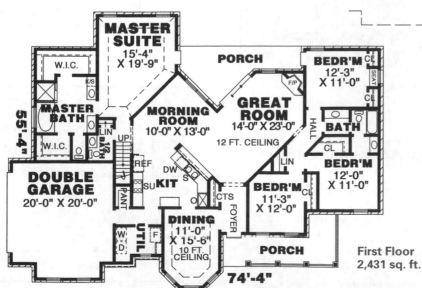

MASTER SUITE
15'-4"
X 19'-9"

W.I.C.

PORCH

BEDR'M
12'-3"
X 11'-0"

MASTER BATH

W.I.C.

MORNING ROOM
10'-0" X 13'-0"

GREAT ROOM
14'-0" X 23'-0"

12 FT. CEILING

BATH

55'-4"

LIN

UP

REF

KIT

DW
SU

BEDR'M
12'-0"
X 11'-0"

DOUBLE GARAGE
20'-0" X 20'-0"

PANT

CTS

FOYER

BEDR'M
11'-3"
X 12'-0"

W
D

UTIL

DINING
11'-0"
X 15'-6"
10 FT.
CEILING

PORCH

First Floor
2,431 sq. ft.

74'-4"

COUNTRY / VICTORIAN

321

Plan# **577-CHD-30-45**

Price Code F

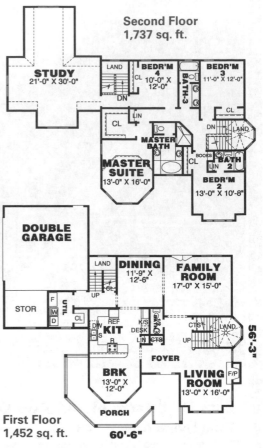

Second Floor
1,737 sq. ft.

STUDY
21'-0" X 30'-0"

LAND
DN

BEDR'M 4
10'-0" X 12'-0"

CL

BATH-3

BEDR'M 3
11'-0" X 12'-0"

CL

CL
LIN

MASTER BATH

DN
LAND

BOOKS
BATH 2

MASTER SUITE
13'-0" X 16'-0"

CL
LIN

BEDR'M 2
13'-0" X 10'-8"

DOUBLE GARAGE

STOR

LAND
UP

DINING
11'-9" X 12'-6"

FAMILY ROOM
17'-0" X 15'-0"

F
W
D

UTIL

CL

REF
K/S
DESK
LIN

CTS

CTS
LAND

UP

KIT

FOYER

LIVING ROOM
13'-0" X 16'-0"
F/P

BRK
13'-0" X 12'-0"

PORCH

56'-3"

60'-6"

First Floor
1,452 sq. ft.

Gorgeous Grand Victorian

Total Living Area: 3,189

- Enormous study on the second could easily be a home office or a children's play area
- Octagon-shaped landing in staircase is intriguing to the eye
- Intricate details on the covered front porch give this home a custom feel
- 4 bedrooms, 3 1/2 baths, 2-car side entry garage
- Slab foundation

Plan# **577-0213**

Price Code C

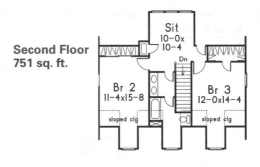

Second Floor
751 sq. ft.

Sit
10-0x 10-4

Dn

Br 2
11-4x15-8

Br 3
12-0x14-4

sloped clg

sloped clg

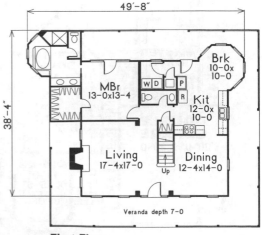

49'-8"

38'-4"

MBr
13-0x13-4

W D
P
R

Brk
10-0x 10-0

Kit
12-0x 10-0

Living
17-4x17-0

Up

Dining
12-4x14-0

Veranda depth 7-0

First Floor
1,308 sq. ft.

Country Charm Wrapped In A Veranda

Total Living Area: 2,059

- Octagon-shaped breakfast room offers plenty of windows and creates a view to the veranda
- First floor master bedroom has large walk-in closet and deluxe bath
- 9' ceilings throughout the home
- Secondary bedrooms and bath feature dormers
- 3 bedrooms, 2 1/2 baths, 2-car detached garage
- Slab foundation, drawings also include basement and crawl space foundations

Farmhouse Has Everything To Offer

Total Living Area: 2,571

- 9' ceilings throughout the first floor
- Office/guest bedroom #5 can easily be converted to either an office or bedroom depending on what is needed
- Elegant French doors lead from the kitchen into the formal dining area
- 4 bedrooms, 2 1/2 baths, 2-car side entry garage
- Basement, crawl space or slab foundation, please specify when ordering

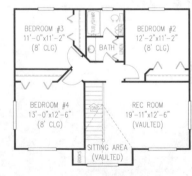

Second Floor
913 sq. ft.

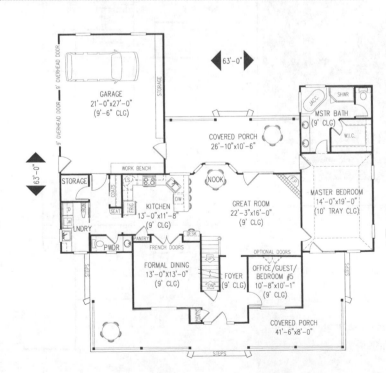

First Floor
1,658 sq. ft.

COUNTRY / VICTORIAN

Plan# 577-FB-1148

Price Code A

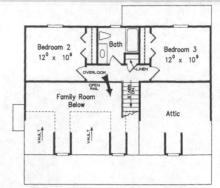

Second Floor
430 sq. ft.

DRIVE UNDER ▶

First Floor
1,061 sq. ft.

Southern Styling With Covered Porch

Total Living Area: 1,491

- Two-story family room has vaulted ceiling
- Well-organized kitchen has serving bar which overlooks family and dining rooms
- First floor master suite has tray ceiling, walk-in closet and master bath
- 3 bedrooms, 2 1/2 baths, 2-car drive under garage
- Walk-out basement foundation

Plan# 577-0413

Price Code D

Second Floor
1,070 sq. ft.

First Floor
1,112 sq. ft.

Distinctive Country Porch

Total Living Area: 2,182

- Meandering porch creates an inviting look
- Generous great room has four double-hung windows and gliding doors to exterior
- Highly functional kitchen features island/breakfast bar, menu desk and convenient pantry
- Each secondary bedroom includes generous closet and private bath
- 3 bedrooms, 3 1/2 baths, 2-car side entry garage
- Basement foundation

COUNTRY / VICTORIAN

TO ORDER SEE **PAGE 608** OR CALL TOLL-FREE 1-800-DREAM HOME (373-2646)

Easy Living

Total Living Area: 1,753

- Large front porch has charming appeal
- Kitchen with breakfast bar overlooks morning room and accesses covered porch
- Master suite with amenities like private bath, spacious closets and sunny bay window
- 3 bedrooms, 2 baths
- Slab or crawl space foundation, please specify when ordering

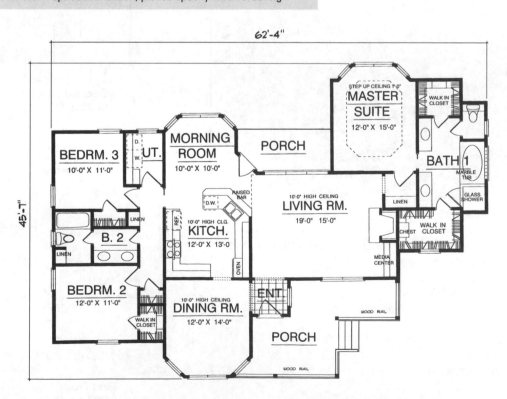

COUNTRY / VICTORIAN

Plan# **577-BF-DR1109**

Price Code AA

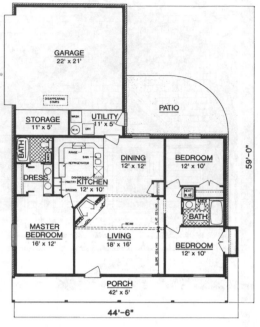

Quaint And Cozy

Total Living Area: 1,191

- Energy efficient home with 2" x 6" exterior walls
- Master bedroom located near living areas for maximum convenience
- Living room has cathedral ceiling and stone fireplace
- 3 bedrooms, 2 baths, 2-car side entry garage
- Slab or crawl space foundation, please specify when ordering

---

Plan# **577-HP-C675**

Price Code B

**Second Floor
580 sq. ft.**

Casual Country Home With Unique Loft

Total Living Area: 1,673

- Great room flows into the breakfast nook with outdoor access and beyond to an efficient kitchen
- Master bedroom on second floor has access to loft/study, private balcony and bath
- Covered porch surrounds the entire home for outdoor living area
- 3 bedrooms, 2 baths
- Crawl space foundation

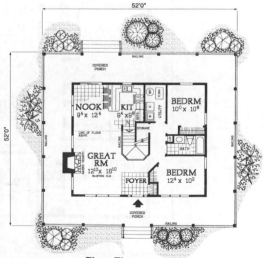

**First Floor
1,093 sq. ft.**

Wrap-Around Country Porch

Total Living Area: 1,875

- Country-style exterior with wrap-around porch and dormers
- Large second floor bedrooms share a dressing area and bath
- Master bedroom suite includes bay window, walk-in closet, dressing area and bath
- 3 bedrooms, 2 baths, 2-car side entry garage
- Crawl space foundation, drawings also include basement and slab foundations

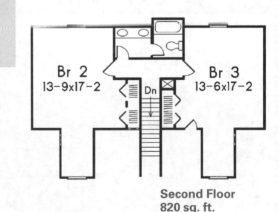

Br 2
13-9x17-2

Dn

Br 3
13-6x17-2

**Second Floor
820 sq. ft.**

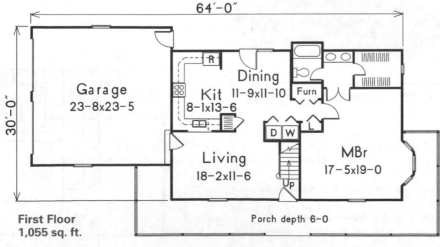

64'-0"

30'-0"

Garage
23-8x23-5

R

Dining
11-9x11-10

Kit
8-1x13-6

Furn

D W L

Living
18-2x11-6

Up

MBr
17-5x19-0

**First Floor
1,055 sq. ft.**

Porch depth 6-0

COUNTRY / VICTORIAN

327

Price Code C

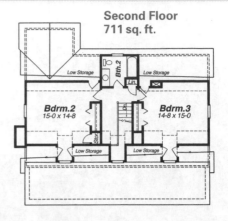

Second Floor
711 sq. ft.

Bdrm.2
15-0 x 14-8

Bdrm.3
14-8 x 15-0

Bth.2

Low Storage

First Floor
1,159 sq. ft.

Sundeck
16-0 x 12-0

Brkfst.
10-6 x 7-6

Kit.
10-6 x 10-0

Dining
10-10 x 8-10

Lav.

M.Bath

Living Area
20-6 x 13-6

Master
Bedroom
17-6 x 14-6

Entry

44-4

Ideal For Entertaining

Total Living Area: 1,870

- Kitchen is open to the living and dining areas
- Breakfast area has cathedral ceiling creating a sunroom effect
- Master bedroom is spacious with all the amenities
- Second floor bedrooms share hall bath
- 3 bedrooms, 2 1/2 baths, 2-car drive under garage
- Basement foundation

Plan# **577-0201**

Price Code D

COUNTRY / VICTORIAN

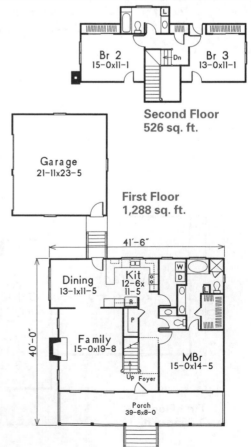

Br 2
15-0x11-1

Br 3
13-0x11-1

Dn

Second Floor
526 sq. ft.

Garage
21-11x23-5

First Floor
1,288 sq. ft.

41'-6"

Dining
13-1x11-5

Kit
12-6x
11-5

Family
15-0x19-8

MBr
15-0x14-5

Foyer

Up

Porch
39-6x8-0

40'-0"

Two-Story Foyer Adds Spacious Feeling

Total Living Area: 1,814

- Large master bedroom includes a spacious bath with garden tub, separate shower and large walk-in closet
- Spacious kitchen and dining area brightened by large windows and patio access
- Detached two-car garage with walkway leading to house adds charm to this country home
- 3 bedrooms, 2 1/2 baths, 2-car detached side entry garage
- Crawl space foundation, drawings also include slab foundation

Porch Creates A Comfortable Feel

Total Living Area: 2,266

- Great room includes fireplace flanked by built-in bookshelves and dining nook with bay window

- Unique media room includes double-door entrance, walk-in closet and access to full bath

- Master bedroom has lovely sitting area, walk-in closets and a private bath with step-up tub and double vanity

- 3 bedrooms, 3 baths, 2-car side entry garage

- Basement foundation, drawings also include crawl space foundation

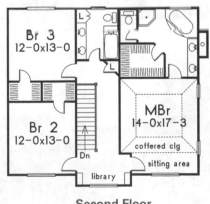

Second Floor
1,050 sq. ft.

Br 3
12-0x13-0

Br 2
12-0x13-0

MBr
14-0x17-3
coffered clg

sitting area

library

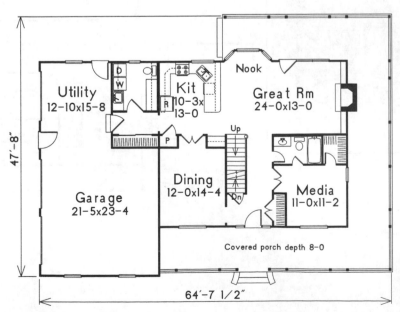

Utility
12-10x15-8

Kit
10-3x
13-0

Nook

Great Rm
24-0x13-0

Garage
21-5x23-4

Dining
12-0x14-4

Media
11-0x11-2

Covered porch depth 8-0

47'-8"

64'-7 1/2"

First Floor
1,216 sq. ft.

COUNTRY / VICTORIAN

Plan# 577-AX-5374

Price Code D

Wrap-Around Covered Porch

Total Living Area: 1,902

- Great room with fireplace is easily viewable from the kitchen and breakfast area
- Luxury master bedroom has a bay window and two walk-in closets
- 3 bedrooms, 2 baths, 2-car side entry garage
- Basement, crawl space or slab foundation, please specify when ordering

---

Plan# 577-GM-1253

Price Code A

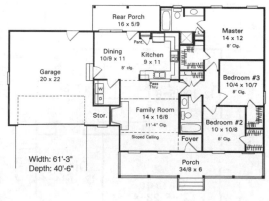

Covered Rear Porch

Total Living Area: 1,253

- Sloped ceiling and fireplace in family room add drama
- U-shaped kitchen is efficiently designed
- Large walk-in closets are found in all the bedrooms
- 3 bedrooms, 2 baths, 2-car garage
- Crawl space or slab foundation, please specify when ordering

COUNTRY / VICTORIAN

TO ORDER SEE **PAGE 608** OR CALL TOLL-FREE 1-800-DREAM HOME (373-2646)

Cozy Covered Front Porch

Total Living Area: 1,692

- Tray ceiling in master bedroom
- Breakfast bar overlooks vaulted great room
- Additional bedrooms are located away from master suite for privacy
- Bonus room above the garage has an additional 358 square feet of living area
- 3 bedrooms, 2 baths, 2-car garage
- Walk-out basement, slab or crawl space foundation, please specify when ordering

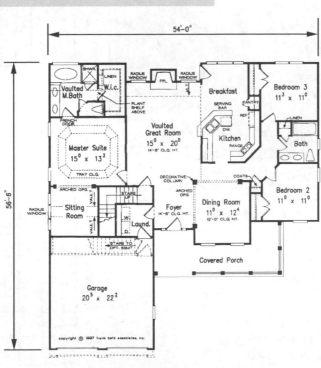

COUNTRY / VICTORIAN

Plan# **577-RDD-1815-8**   Price Code C

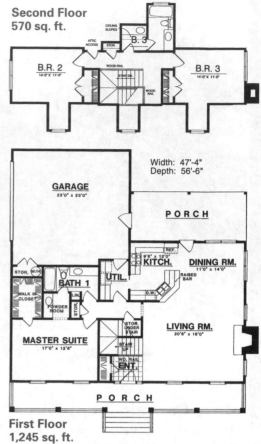

Second Floor
570 sq. ft.

Width: 47'-4"
Depth: 56'-6"

First Floor
1,245 sq. ft.

Kitchen Overlooks Living Area

Total Living Area: 1,815

- Well-designed kitchen opens to dining room and features raised breakfast bar
- First floor master suite has walk-in closet
- Front and back porches unite this home with the outdoors
- 3 bedrooms, 2 baths, 2-car side entry garage
- Basement, crawl space or slab foundation, please specify when ordering

Plan# **577-0492**   Price Code C

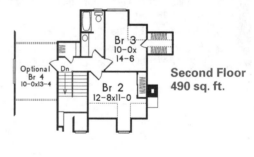

Second Floor
490 sq. ft.

56'-8"

54'-0"

First Floor
1,339 sq. ft.

Country Home With Plenty Of Style

Total Living Area: 1,829

- Entry foyer with coat closet opens to large family room with fireplace
- Two second floor bedrooms share a full bath
- Optional bedroom #4 on second floor can be finished as your family grows
- Cozy porch provides convenient side entrance into home
- 3 bedrooms, 2 1/2 baths, 2-car side entry garage
- Partial basement/crawl space foundation

COUNTRY / VICTORIAN

TO ORDER SEE **PAGE 608** OR CALL TOLL-FREE 1-800-DREAM HOME (373-2646)

Three Or Four Bedrooms

Total Living Area: 2,071

- Vaulted family room with fireplace
- Sunny breakfast room
- Private dining perfect for entertaining
- Second floor includes two bedrooms, a bath and an unfinished area that would be perfect as a fourth bedroom, office or play area
- 3 bedrooms, 2 1/2 baths, 2-car side entry garage
- Slab or crawl space foundation, please specify when ordering

Second Floor
676 sq. ft.

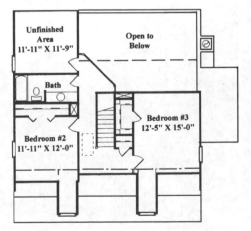

Unfinished Area
11'-11" X 11'-9"

Open to Below

Bath

Bedroom #3
12'-5" X 15'-0"

Bedroom #2
11'-11" X 12'-0"

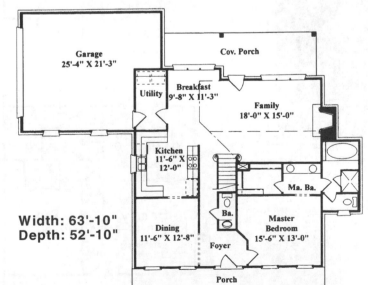

Garage
25'-4" X 21'-3"

Cov. Porch

Breakfast
9'-8" X 11'-3"

Utility

Family
18'-0" X 15'-0"

Kitchen
11'-6" X 12'-0"

Ma. Ba.

First Floor
1,395 sq. ft.

Ba.

Width: 63'-10"
Depth: 52'-10"

Dining
11'-6" X 12'-8"

Foyer

Master Bedroom
15'-6" X 13'-0"

Porch

COUNTRY / VICTORIAN

333

Plan# 577-HP-C681

Price Code B

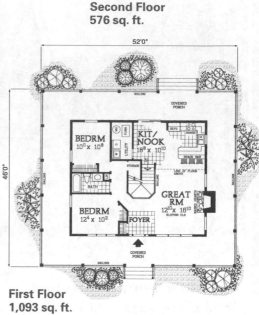

Second Floor
576 sq. ft.

First Floor
1,093 sq. ft.

52'0"

46'0"

A Great Country Farmhouse

Total Living Area: 1,669

- Generous use of windows add exciting visual elements to the exterior as well as plenty of natural light to the interior
- Two-story great room has a raised hearth
- Second floor loft/study would easily make a terrific home office
- 3 bedrooms, 2 baths
- Crawl space foundation

Plan# 577-0692

Price Code A

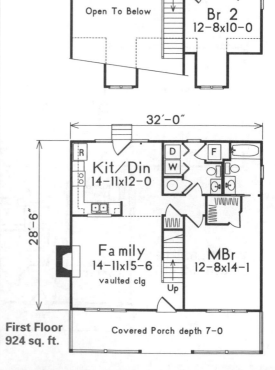

Second Floor
415 sq. ft.

Loft/ Br 3
10-7x11-11

Open To Below

Dn

Br 2
12-8x10-0

First Floor
924 sq. ft.

32'-0"

28'-6"

Kit/Din
14-11x12-0

Family
14-11x15-6
vaulted clg

MBr
12-8x14-1

Up

Covered Porch depth 7-0

Year-Round Or Weekend Getaway Home

Total Living Area: 1,339

- Full-length covered porch enhances front facade
- Vaulted ceiling and stone fireplace add drama to family room
- Walk-in closets in bedrooms provide ample storage space
- Combined kitchen/dining area adjoins family room for perfect entertaining space
- 3 bedrooms, 2 1/2 baths
- Crawl space foundation

COUNTRY / VICTORIAN

TO ORDER SEE PAGE 608 OR CALL TOLL-FREE 1-800-DREAM HOME (373-2646)

Two-Story, Charming Yet Practical

Total Living Area: 2,280

- Laundry area conveniently located on second floor
- Compact yet efficient kitchen
- Unique shaped dining room overlooks front porch
- Cozy living room enhanced with sloped ceiling and fireplace
- 4 bedrooms, 2 1/2 baths, 2-car side entry garage
- Basement foundation

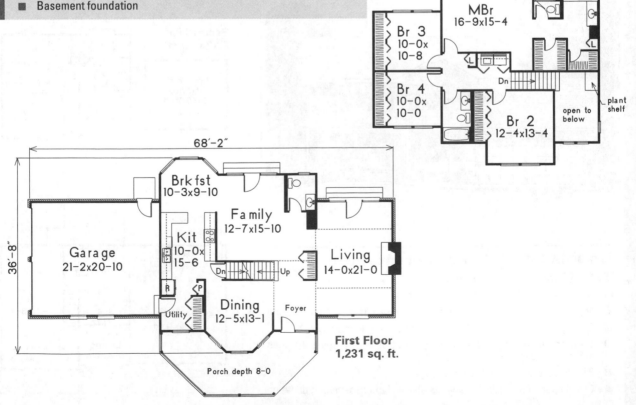

Second Floor
1,049 sq. ft.

MBr
16-9x15-4

Br 3
10-0x
10-8

Br 4
10-0x
10-0

Dn

L

plant shelf

open to below

Br 2
12-4x13-4

68'-2"

36'-8"

Brk fst
10-3x9-10

Family
12-7x15-10

Kit
10-0x
15-6

Garage
21-2x20-10

Living
14-0x21-0

Dn   Up

R   P

Utility

Dining
12-5x13-1

Foyer

First Floor
1,231 sq. ft.

Porch depth 8-0

COUNTRY / VICTORIAN

Plan# 577-0726

Price Code A

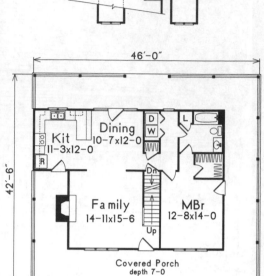

Second Floor 415 sq. ft.

Loft/Br 3 10-7x11-11

Open To Below

Dn

L

Br 2 12-8x10-0

46'-0"

42'-6"

Kit 11-3x12-0

Dining 10-7x12-0

D W

L

Dn

Family 14-11x15-6

MBr 12-8x14-0

Up

Covered Porch depth 7-0

First Floor 1,013 sq. ft.

Surrounding Porch For Country Views

Total Living Area: 1,428

- Large vaulted family room opens to dining area and kitchen with breakfast bar and access to surrounding porch
- First floor master suite offers large bath, walk-in closet and nearby laundry facilities
- A spacious loft/bedroom #3 overlooking family room and an additional bedroom and bath conclude the second floor
- 3 bedrooms, 2 baths
- Basement foundation

Plan# 577-0113

Price Code C

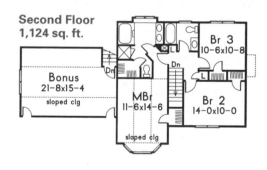

Second Floor 1,124 sq. ft.

Bonus 21-8x15-4 sloped clg

MBr 11-6x14-6 sloped clg

Dn

Br 3 10-6x10-8

L

Br 2 14-0x10-0

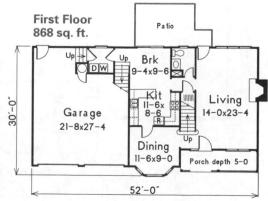

First Floor 868 sq. ft.

Patio

Up

D W

Brk 9-4x9-6

Up

Garage 21-8x27-4

Kit 11-6x 8-6

Living 14-0x23-4

R

Dining 11-6x9-0

Up

Porch depth 5-0

30'-0"

52'-0"

Double Bay Enhances Front Entry

Total Living Area: 1,992

- Distinct living, dining and breakfast areas
- Master bedroom boasts full end bay window and a cathedral ceiling
- Storage and laundry area located adjacent to the garage
- Bonus room for future office or playroom over the garage is included in the square footage
- 3 bedrooms, 2 1/2 baths, 2-car garage
- Crawl space foundation, drawings also include basement foundation

TO ORDER SEE **PAGE 608** OR CALL TOLL-FREE 1-800-DREAM HOME (373-2646)

Two-Story With Victorian Feel

Total Living Area: 1,982

- Spacious master bedroom has bath with corner whirlpool tub and sunny skylight above
- Breakfast area overlooks into great room
- Screened porch with skylight above extends the home outdoors and allows for entertainment area
- 4 bedrooms, 2 1/2 baths
- Crawl space or slab foundation, please specify when ordering

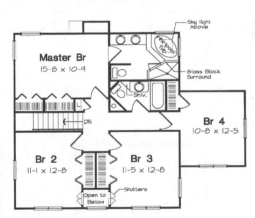

Second Floor
983 sq. ft.

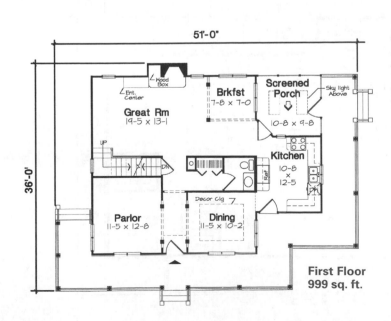

First Floor
999 sq. ft.

COUNTRY / VICTORIAN

337

Arched Touches On The Covered Porch

Total Living Area: 1,594

- Corner fireplace in the great room creates a cozy feel
- Spacious kitchen combines with the dining room creating a terrific gathering place
- A handy family and guest entrance is a casual and convenient way to enter the home
- 3 bedrooms, 2 baths, 2-car garage
- Slab or crawl space foundation, please specify when ordering

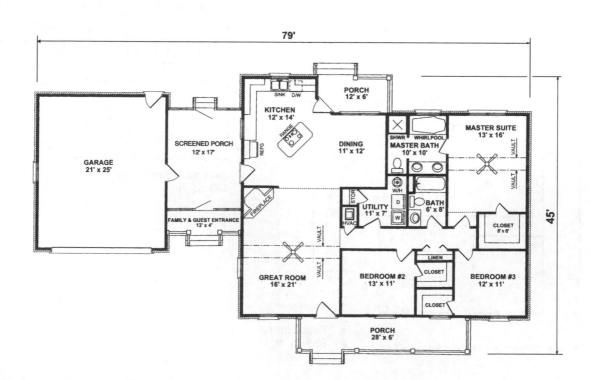

Inviting Home With Country Flavor

Total Living Area: 1,948

- Large elongated porch for moonlit evenings
- Stylish family room features beamed ceiling
- Skillfully designed kitchen convenient to an oversized laundry area
- Second floor bedrooms are all generously sized
- 3 bedrooms, 2 1/2 baths, 2-car garage
- Basement foundation, drawings also include crawl space foundation

Second Floor
868 sq. ft.

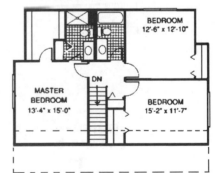

MASTER BEDROOM
13'-4" x 15'-0"

BEDROOM
12'-6" x 12'-10"

DN

BEDROOM
15'-2" x 11'-7"

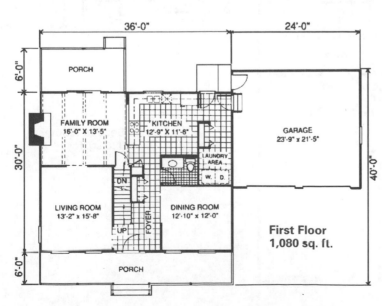

36'-0"

24'-0"

6'-0"

PORCH

FAMILY ROOM
16'-0" X 13'-5"

KITCHEN
12'-9" X 11'-6"

GARAGE
23'-9" x 21'-5"

30'-0"

40'-0"

DN

LAUNDRY AREA
W. D.

LIVING ROOM
13'-2" x 15'-8"

DINING ROOM
12'-10" x 12'-0"

UP

FOYER

First Floor
1,080 sq. ft.

6'-0"

PORCH

COUNTRY / VICTORIAN

339

Wood Beams Create A Tudor Feel

Total Living Area: 2,277

- Lots of windows in the great room create an inviting feeling
- First floor den/bedroom #4 would make an ideal home office
- Enormous dining area and kitchen combine to create a large gathering area overlooking into great room
- 4 bedrooms, 3 baths, 2-car garage
- Crawl space foundation

First Floor
1,349 sq. ft.

Second Floor
928 sq. ft.

©Alan Mascord Design Associates, Inc.

Vaulted Second Floor Sitting Area
Total Living Area: 2,433

- Two second floor bedrooms share a jack and jill bath
- Terrific covered porch has access into master bedroom or great room
- Snack bar in kitchen provides additional seating for dining
- 3 bedrooms, 2 1/2 baths, 2-car side entry garage
- Basement, crawl space or slab foundation, please specify when ordering

First Floor
1,590 sq. ft.

Second Floor
843 sq. ft.

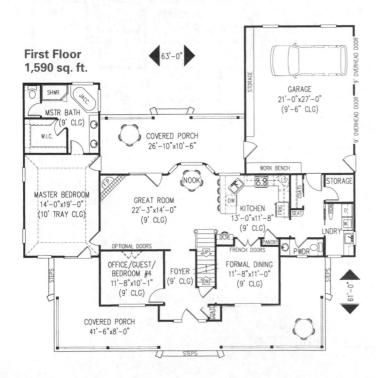

COUNTRY / VICTORIAN

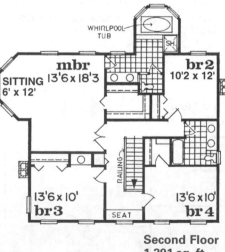

Farmhouse Feeling With This Home

Total Living Area: 2,582

- Both the family and living rooms are warmed by hearths
- The master suite on the second floor has a bayed sitting room and a private bath with whirlpool tub
- Old-fashioned window seat in second floor landing is a charming touch
- 4 bedrooms, 3 baths, 2-car side entry garage
- Basement or crawl space foundation, please specify when ordering

COUNTRY / VICTORIAN

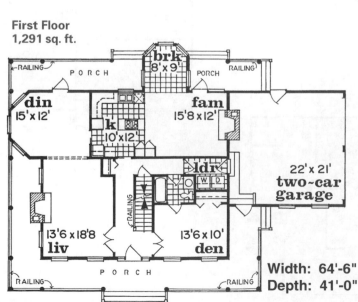

First Floor
1,291 sq. ft.

RAILING   PORCH   **brk** 8' x 9'   PORCH   RAILING

din 15' x 12'   **k** 10' x 12'   **fam** 15'8 x 12'

ldr W D

22' x 21' **two~car garage**

liv 13'6 x 18'8   **den** 13'6 x 10'

RAILING   PORCH   RAILING

Width: 64'-6"
Depth: 41'-0"

Second Floor
1,291 sq. ft.

WHIRLPOOL TUB   SH

mbr 13'6 x 18'3   SITTING 6' x 12'   **br 2** 10'2 x 12'

RAILING

br 3 13'6 x 10'   SEAT   **br 4** 13'6 x 10'

Two-Story With Terrific Curb Appeal

Total Living Area: 3,033

- Sunroom warmed by fireplace and brightened by lots of windows
- Bedroom #4 and bath #2 on second floor both lead to balcony through French doors
- 4 bedrooms, 3 1/2 baths, 2-car side entry garage
- Basement, crawl space, walk-out basement or slab foundation, please specify when ordering

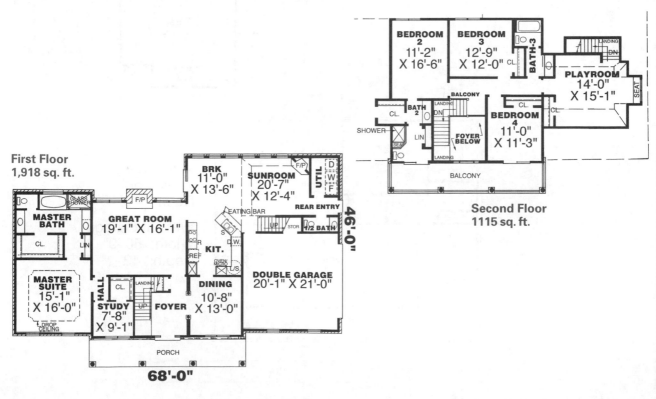

First Floor
1,918 sq. ft.

Second Floor
1115 sq. ft.

COUNTRY / VICTORIAN

Private Bedroom Area

Total Living Area: 1,550

- Wrap-around front porch is an ideal gathering place
- Handy snack bar is positioned so kitchen flows into family room
- Master bedroom has many amenities
- 3 bedrooms, 2 baths, 2-car detached side entry garage
- Slab or crawl space foundation, please specify when ordering

COUNTRY / VICTORIAN

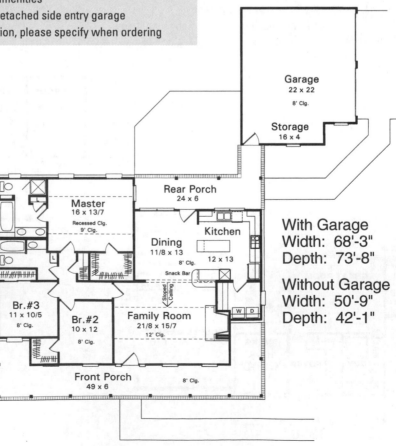

Garage
22 x 22
8' Clg.

Storage
16 x 4

Master
16 x 13/7
Recessed Clg.
9' Clg.

Rear Porch
24 x 6

Kitchen
12 x 13

Dining
11/8 x 13
8' Clg.

Snack Bar

Br.#3
11 x 10/5
8' Clg.

Br.#2
10 x 12
8' Clg.

Family Room
21/8 x 15/7
12' Clg.

Sloped Ceiling

W D

Front Porch
49 x 6   8' Clg.

With Garage
Width: 68'-3"
Depth: 73'-8"

Without Garage
Width: 50'-9"
Depth: 42'-1"

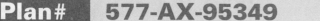

Plan# 577-AX-95349

Price Code G

TO ORDER SEE **PAGE 608** OR CALL TOLL-FREE 1-800-DREAM HOME (373-2646)

Spacious Country Charmer

Total Living Area: 2,874

- Openness characterizes the casual areas
- The kitchen is separated from the bayed breakfast nook by an island workspace
- Stunning great room has dramatic vaulted ceiling and a corner fireplace
- Unfinished loft on the second floor has an additional 300 square feet above the garage
- 4 bedrooms, 3 baths, 3-car side entry garage
- Basement, crawl space or slab foundation, please specify when ordering

First Floor
2,146 sq. ft.

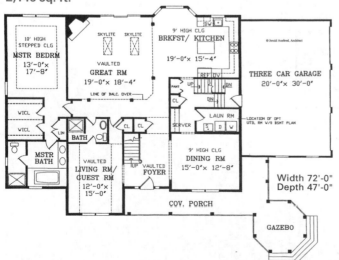

Second Floor
728 sq. ft.

Width 72'-0"
Depth 47'-0"

COUNTRY / VICTORIAN

345

Wrap-Around Porch Adds Curb Appeal

Total Living Area: 1,840

- All bedrooms located on the second floor for privacy
- Counter dining space provided in the kitchen
- Formal dining room connects to the kitchen through French doors
- 4 bedrooms, 2 1/2 baths, 2-car side entry garage with shop/storage
- Basement, crawl space or slab foundation, please specify when ordering

COUNTRY / VICTORIAN

First Floor
1,014 sq. ft.

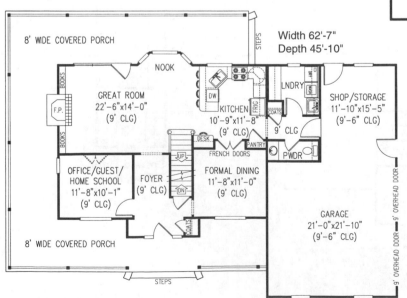

Width 62'-7"
Depth 45'-10"

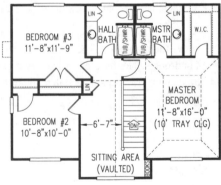

Second Floor
826 sq. ft.

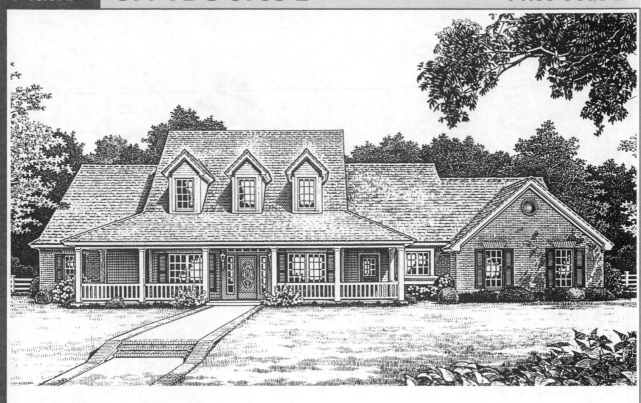

Impressive Gallery
Total Living Area: 2,674

- First floor master bedroom has convenient location
- Kitchen and breakfast area have island and access to covered front porch
- Second floor bedrooms have dormer window seats for added charm
- Optional future rooms on second floor have an additional 520 square feet of living area
- 4 bedrooms, 3 baths, 3-car side entry garage
- Basement or slab foundation, please specify when ordering

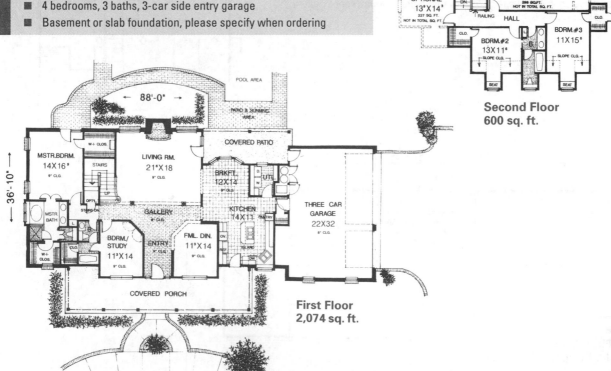

Second Floor
600 sq. ft.

First Floor
2,074 sq. ft.

COUNTRY / VICTORIAN

Screened Area Makes A Place To Relax

Total Living Area: 1,434

- Private second floor master bedroom features a private bath and a roomy walk-in closet
- A country kitchen with peninsula counter adjoins the living room creating a larger living area
- The living room has a warm fireplace and a volume ceiling
- 3 bedrooms, 2 baths, 2-car garage
- Basement, crawl space or slab foundation, please specify when ordering

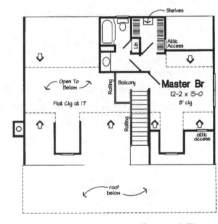

Second Floor
416 sq. ft.

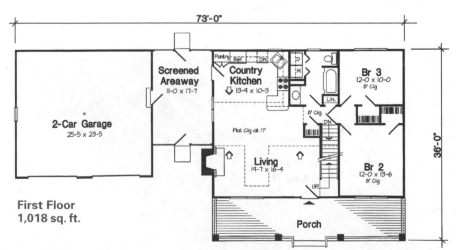

First Floor
1,018 sq. ft.

Optimal Family Living Layout

Total Living Area: 1,926

- Large covered rear porch is spacious enough for entertaining
- L-shaped kitchen is compact yet efficient and includes a snack bar for extra dining
- Oversized utility room has counterspace, extra shelves and space for a second refridgerator
- Secluded master suite has a private bath and a large walk-in closet
- 3 bedrooms, 2 baths, 2-car side entry garage
- Slab or crawl space foundation, please specify when ordering

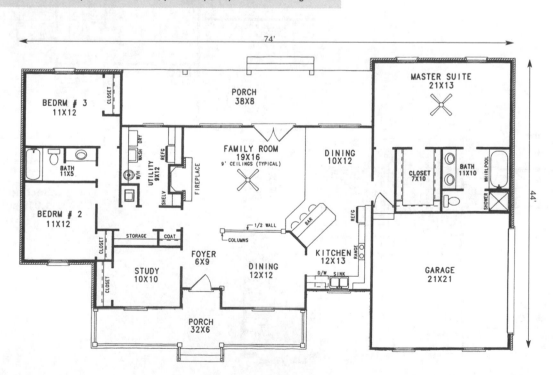

COUNTRY / VICTORIAN

TO ORDER SEE PAGE 608 OR CALL TOLL-FREE 1-800-DREAM HOME (373-2646)

Fireplaces In Family And Living Rooms

Total Living Area: 2,170

- Energy efficient home with 2" x 6" exterior walls
- Barrel vaulted two-story entrance foyer leads to an angled gallery
- Kitchen features a sunny bay window
- Bonus room with private staircase has an additional 390 square feet of living area
- 3 bedrooms, 2 1/2 baths, 2-car garage
- Basement foundation

COUNTRY / VICTORIAN

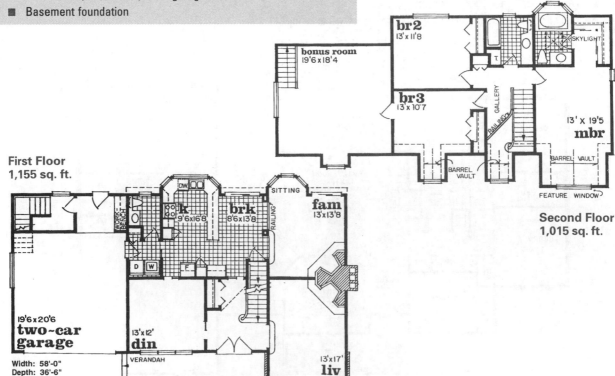

Second Floor
1,015 sq. ft.

br2
13'x 11'8

bonus room
19'6 x 18'4

br3
13' x 10'7

13' X 19'5
mbr

SKYLIGHT

GALLERY

RAILING

BARREL VAULT

BARREL VAULT

FEATURE WINDOW

First Floor
1,155 sq. ft.

DW

k
9'6x6'8

brk
8'6x13'8

SITTING

fam
13'x13'8

RAILING

D   W

F

two-car
garage
19'6x20'6

13'x12'
din

VERANDAH

13'x17'
liv

WORK BENCH

Width: 58'-0"
Depth: 36'-6"

Dormers Create A Charming Feel

Total Living Area: 2,802

- Formal dining area flows into large family room making great use of space
- Cozy nook off kitchen would make an ideal breakfast dining area
- Covered patio attaches to master bedroom and family room
- Framing - only concrete block available
- 4 bedrooms, 2 baths, 2-car side entry garage
- Slab foundation

Second Floor
509 sq. ft.

First Floor
2,293 sq. ft.

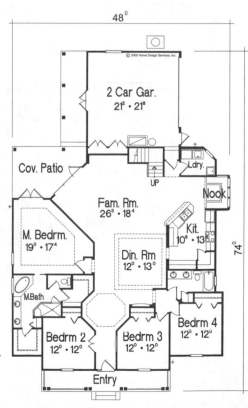

COUNTRY / VICTORIAN

Layout Created By Victorian Turret

Total Living Area: 2,050

- Large kitchen and dining area have access to garage and porch
- Master bedroom suite features unique turret design, private bath and large walk-in closet
- Laundry facilities conveniently located near bedrooms
- 3 bedrooms, 2 1/2 baths, 2-car side entry garage
- Basement foundation, drawings also include crawl space and slab foundations

COUNTRY / VICTORIAN

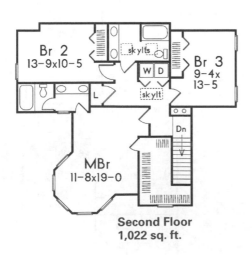

Br 2
13-9x10-5

skylts

W D

Br 3
9-4x
13-5

skylt

L

Dn

MBr
11-8x19-0

Second Floor
1,022 sq. ft.

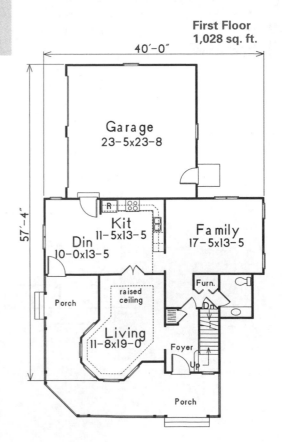

First Floor
1,028 sq. ft.

40'-0"

Garage
23-5x23-8

57'-4"

R

Kit
11-5x13-5

Din
10-0x13-5

Family
17-5x13-5

Furn.

raised
ceiling

Dn

Living
11-8x19-0

Foyer

Up

Porch

Porch

Kitchen With Island Sink

Total Living Area: 2,010

- Oversized kitchen is a great gathering place with eat-in island bar, dining area nearby and built-in desk
- First floor master bedroom has privacy
- Unique second floor kid's living area for playroom
- Optional bonus room above the garage has an additional 313 square feet of living area
- 3 bedrooms, 2 1/2 baths, 2-car side entry garage
- Basement foundation

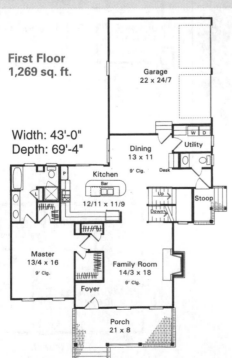

First Floor
1,269 sq. ft.

Width: 43'-0"
Depth: 69'-4"

Garage
22 x 24/7

Dining
13 x 11
9' Clg.

Utility
W D
Desk

Kitchen
Bar
12/11 x 11/9

Up
Downs
Stoop

Master
13/4 x 16
9' Clg.

Family Room
14/3 x 18
9' Clg.

Foyer

Porch
21 x 8

Second Floor
741 sq. ft.

Optional Bonus
24/7 x 11/4

Kid's Living
10/8 x 11/3
8' Clg.

Attic Storage

Rail
Downs

Bedroom #3
13/4 x 11
8' Clg.

Sloped Clg.

Linen

Bedroom #2
14/4 x 15/7
8' Clg.

COUNTRY / VICTORIAN

Plan# 577-CHD-20-51

Price Code C

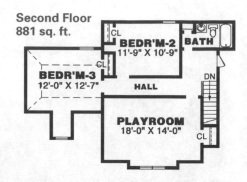

Second Floor 881 sq. ft.

BEDR'M-2 11'-9" X 10'-9"
BATH
BEDR'M-3 12'-0" X 12'-7"
HALL
DN
PLAYROOM 18'-0" X 14'-0"

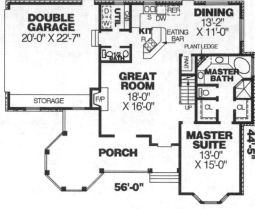

First Floor 1,203 sq. ft.

DOUBLE GARAGE 20'-0" X 22'-7"
DINING 13'-2" X 11'-0"
KIT
EATING BAR
PLANT LEDGE
STORAGE
F/P
GREAT ROOM 18'-0" X 16'-0"
MASTER BATH
UP
MASTER SUITE 13'-0" X 15'-0"
PORCH
56'-0"
44'-5"

Victorian Gazebo Enhances Front Porch

Total Living Area: 2,084

- Charming bay window in master suite allows sunlight in as well as style
- Great room accesses front covered porch extending the living area to the outdoors
- Large playroom on second floor is ideal for family living
- 3 bedrooms, 2 1/2 baths, 2-car side entry garage
- Slab, crawl space or basement foundation, please specify when ordering

Plan# 577-JV-1735A

Price Code B

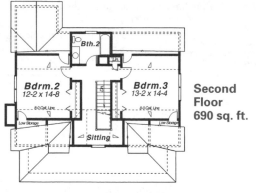

Bth.2
Bdrm.2 12-2 x 14-8
Bdrm.3 13-2 x 14-4
Sitting

Second Floor 690 sq. ft.

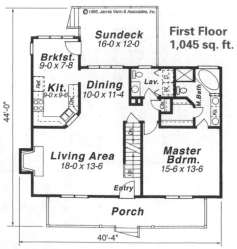

Sundeck 16-0 x 12-0
Brkfst. 9-0 x 7-8
Kit. 9-0 x 9-6
Dining 10-0 x 11-4
Lav.
Living Area 18-0 x 13-6
Master Bdrm. 15-6 x 13-6
Entry
Porch
44'-0"
40'-4"

First Floor 1,045 sq. ft.

Quaint Porch Adds Charm

Total Living Area: 1,735

- Angled kitchen wall expands space into the dining room
- Second floor has a cozy sitting area with cheerful window
- Two spacious bedrooms on second floor share a bath
- 3 bedrooms, 2 1/2 baths, 2-car drive under garage
- Basement foundation

Home With Rear Entry Garage

Total Living Area: 2,707

- Double-doors lead into handsome study
- Kitchen and breakfast room flow into great room creating terrific gathering place
- Second floor includes bonus room perfect for a game room
- 4 bedrooms, 3 baths, 2-car rear entry garage
- Crawl space or slab foundation, please specify when ordering

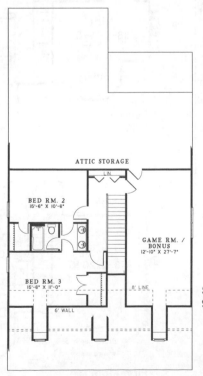

Second Floor
994 sq. ft.

ATTIC STORAGE

BED RM. 2
15'-6" X 10'-6"

GAME RM. / BONUS
12'-10" X 27'-7"

BED RM. 3
15'-6" X 11'-0"

First Floor
1,713 sq. ft.

37'-0"

73'-0"

GARAGE
19'-4" X 20'-0"

GRILLING PORCH
16'-8" X 8'-0"

GREAT RM.
10' BOXED CEILING
16'-8" X 14'-8"

M. BATH
8'-5" X 14'-6"

WHP TUB

MASTER SUITE
10' BOXED CEILING
14'-7" X 13'-0"

BREAKFAST AREA
16'-8" X 10'-0"

COMPUTER DESK

PANTRY

KITCHEN

BATH

GUEST RM. / STUDY
12'-3" X 10'-0"

FOYER
7'-6" X 11'-0"

DINING RM.
13'-3" X 11'-0"

COVERED PORCH
37'-0" X 8'-0"

COUNTRY / VICTORIAN

Plan# 577-0768

Price Code C

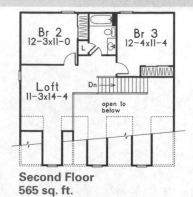

Second Floor
565 sq. ft.

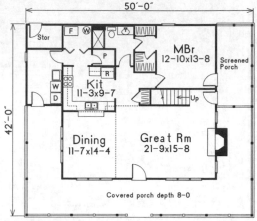

First Floor
1,314 sq. ft.

Charming Wrap-Around Porch

Total Living Area: 1,879

- Open floor plan on both floors makes home appear larger
- Loft area overlooks great room or can become an optional fourth bedroom
- Large walk-in pantry in kitchen and large storage in rear of home has access from exterior
- 3 bedrooms, 2 baths
- Crawl space foundation

Plan# 577-0234

Price Code C

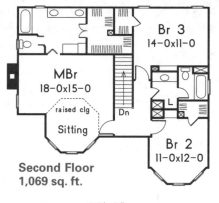

Second Floor
1,069 sq. ft.

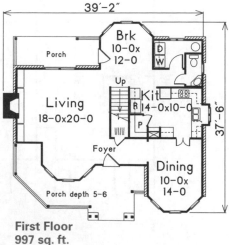

First Floor
997 sq. ft.

Home Features Double Bays

Total Living Area: 2,066

- Large master bedroom includes sitting area and private bath
- Open living room features a fireplace with built-in bookshelves
- Spacious kitchen accesses formal dining area and breakfast room
- 3 bedrooms, 2 1/2 baths
- Slab foundation

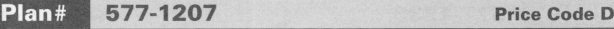

Plan# 577-1207

Price Code D

Charming Style With Accents
Total Living Area: 2,360

- Ample-sized living and dining rooms directly off foyer
- Family room enhanced with built-in bookshelves and cozy fireplace
- Master suite complemented with spacious walk-in closet and private bath with skylight
- 4 bedrooms, 2 1/2 baths, 2-car garage
- Partial basement/crawl space foundation, drawings also include crawl space and slab foundations

Second Floor
727 sq. ft.

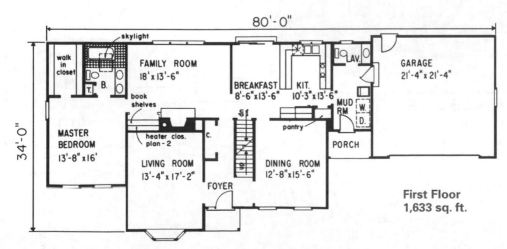

First Floor
1,633 sq. ft.

Plan# 577-1336

Price Code A

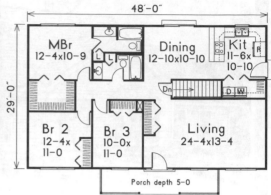

48'-0"

29'-0"

MBr
12-4x10-9

Dining
12-10x10-10

Kit
11-6x
10-10

Dn

D W

Br 2
12-4x
11-0

Br 3
10-0x
11-0

Living
24-4x13-4

Porch depth 5-0

Efficient Ranch With Country Charm

Total Living Area: 1,364

- Master suite features spacious walk-in closet and private bath
- Great room highlighted with several windows
- Kitchen with snack bar adjacent to dining area
- Plenty of storage space throughout
- 3 bedrooms, 2 baths, optional   2-car garage
- Basement foundation, drawings also include crawl space foundation

Plan# 577-HDS-1963

Price Code C

2 Car Garage
21' · 21'

Width: 58'-0"
Depth: 66'-8"

Laundry

Stor

Nook

Covered Patio

Mstr. Bath

Bedroom 2
11' · 11'

pan.

Kitchen

w.i.c.

Bath 2

Dining Rm.
14' · 11'

Family Room
15' · 26'

Master Bedroom
14' · 18'

Bedroom 3
12' · 12'

Covered Porch

Charming Covered Porch

Total Living Area: 1,963

- Spacious breakfast nook is a great gathering place
- Master bedroom has its own wing with private bath and lots of closet space
- Large laundry room with closet and sink
- 3 bedrooms, 2 baths, 2-car side entry garage
- Slab or crawl space foundation, please specify when ordering

COUNTRY / VICTORIAN

Eye-Catching Wrap-Around Porch

Total Living Area: 2,594

- Snack bar in kitchen creates an extra place for dining
- Master bath has interesting bayed whirlpool bath
- A wonderful sun room extends off the breakfast room creating a beautiful area for gathering
- 4 bedrooms, 2 1/2 baths, 2 car side entry garage
- Basement foundation

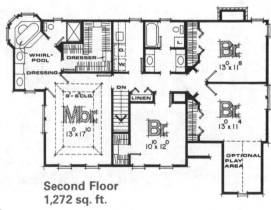

Second Floor
1,272 sq. ft.

First Floor
1,322 sq. ft.

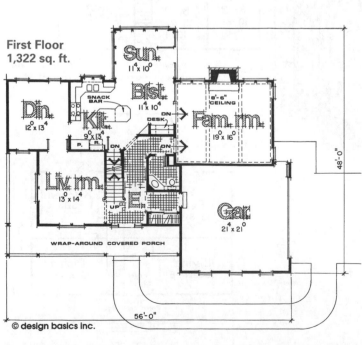

© design basics inc.

Plan# 577-0293

Price Code B

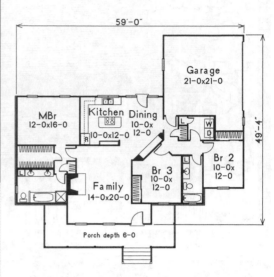

59'-0"

Garage
21-0x21-0

49'-4"

MBr
12-0x16-0

Kitchen

Dining
10-0x
12-0

10-0x12-0

W
D

Br 2
10-0x
12-0

Family
14-0x20-0

Br 3
10-0x
12-0

Porch depth 6-0

Covered Porch Is Focal Point Of Entry

Total Living Area: 1,595

- Dining room has convenient built-in desk and provides access to the outdoors
- L-shaped kitchen area features island cooktop
- Family room has high ceiling and a fireplace
- Private master suite includes large walk-in closet and bath with separate tub and shower units
- 3 bedrooms, 2 baths, 2-car side entry garage
- Slab foundation, drawings also include crawl space foundation

Plan# 577-0134

Price Code D

COUNTRY / VICTORIAN

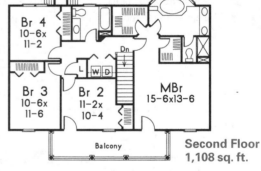

Br 4
10-6x
11-2

L W D

Dn

MBr
15-6x13-6

Br 3
10-6x
11-6

Br 2
11-2x
10-4

Balcony

Second Floor
1,108 sq. ft.

First Floor
1,108 sq. ft.

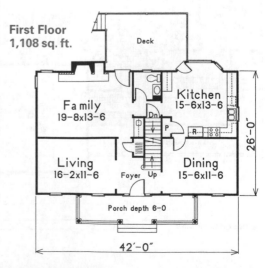

Deck

Family
19-8x13-6

Kitchen
15-6x13-6

Dn

P

R

Living
16-2x11-6

Foyer

Up

Dining
15-6x11-6

Porch depth 6-0

26'-0"

42'-0"

Lots Of Windows In Great Room

Total Living Area: 2,216

- Luxury master bedroom suite features full-windowed bathtub bay, double walk-in closets and access to the front balcony
- Spacious kitchen/breakfast room combination
- Second floor laundry facility
- 4 bedrooms, 2 1/2 baths, 2-car drive under garage
- Basement foundation

Plan# 577-VL-3038 — Price Code E

Plan#	**577-VL-3038**	Price Code E

An Open Feel To A Classic Country Home

Total Living Area: 3,038

- Second floor bedrooms each have their own dressing areas while sharing a central bath
- Two sets of double-doors brighten a spacious great room while leading to an outdoor porch
- Large kitchen has a center island and an angled snack bar which overlooks into the breakfast room
- 3 bedrooms, 2 1/2 baths, 2-car garage
- Slab or crawl space foundation, please specify when ordering

Second Floor
836 sq. ft.

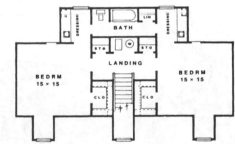

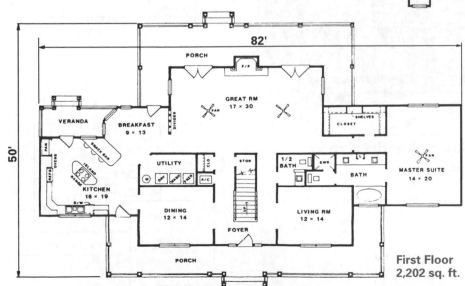

First Floor
2,202 sq. ft.

Plan# 577-GH-34003

Price Code AA

Oversized Front Porch

Total Living Area: 1,146

- Master bedroom has private bath
- Well-organized kitchen is loaded with cabinetry
- Sloped ceiling in living room and dining room creates a comfortable atmosphere
- 3 bedrooms, 2 baths
- Basement, slab or crawl space foundation, please specify when ordering

Plan# 577-0177

Price Code D

Separate Living Areas Lend Privacy

Total Living Area: 2,562

- Large, open foyer creates a grand entrance
- Convenient open breakfast area includes peninsula counter, bay window and easy access to the sundeck
- Dining and living rooms flow together for expanded entertaining space
- 3 bedrooms, 2 1/2 baths, 2-car side entry garage
- Basement foundation, drawings also include slab and crawl space foundations

Second Floor
1,434 sq. ft.

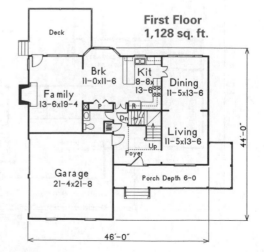

First Floor
1,128 sq. ft.

COUNTRY / VICTORIAN

Distinct Country Look And Feel

Total Living Area: 2,253

- Great room joined by covered porch
- Secluded parlor provides area for peace and quiet or private office
- Sloped ceiling adds drama to master suite
- Great room and kitchen/breakfast area combine for large open living
- 3 bedrooms, 2 1/2 baths, 2-car garage
- Basement foundation

First Floor
1,203 sq. ft.

Second Floor
1,050 sq. ft.

Plan# 577-0515

Price Code A

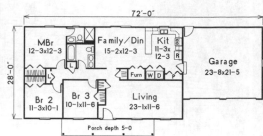

Stylish Ranch With Rustic Charm

Total Living Area: 1,344

- Family/dining room has sliding door
- Master bedroom includes private bath with shower
- Hall bath includes double vanity for added convenience
- Kitchen features U-shaped design, large pantry and laundry area
- 3 bedrooms, 2 baths, 2-car garage
- Crawl space foundation, drawings also include basement and slab foundations

Plan# 577-0227

Price Code B

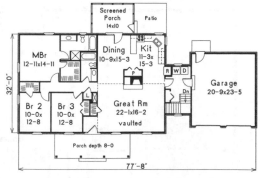

COUNTRY / VICTORIAN

Roof Line And Facade Add Charm

Total Living Area: 1,674

- Great room, dining area and kitchen, surrounded with vaulted ceiling, central fireplace and log bin
- Laundry/mud room is located between the garage and family area
- Easily expandable screened porch is adjacent to patio
- Master bedroom has a full bath with tub and a separate shower
- 3 bedrooms, 2 baths, 2-car garage
- Basement foundation, drawings also include crawl space and slab foundations

Plan# 577-1305

Price Code C

TO ORDER SEE **PAGE 608** OR CALL TOLL-FREE 1-800-DREAM HOME (373-2646)

Extra Amenities Enhance Living

Total Living Area: 2,009

- Spacious master bedroom has dramatic sloped ceiling and private bath with double sinks and walk-in closet
- Bedroom #3 has extra storage inside closet
- Versatile screened porch is ideal for entertaining year-round
- Sunny breakfast area located near kitchen and screened porch for convenience
- 3 bedrooms, 2 1/2 baths
- Basement foundation

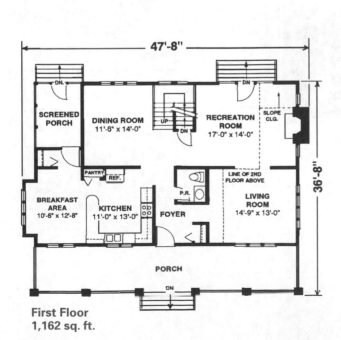

First Floor
1,162 sq. ft.

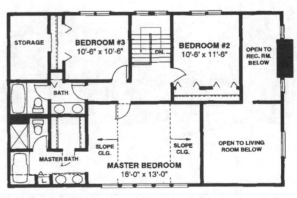

Second Floor
847 sq. ft.

COUNTRY / VICTORIAN

365

Plan# **577-CHP-1733-A-7**

Price Code B

Second Floor
499 sq. ft.

Width: 36'-0"
Depth: 49'-0"

First Floor
1,238 sq. ft.

Quaint Country Home

Total Living Area: 1,737

- U-shaped kitchen, sunny bayed breakfast room and living area become one large gathering area
- Living area has sloped ceilings and a balcony overlook from second floor
- Second floor includes lots of storage area
- 3 bedrooms, 2 1/2 baths
- Slab or crawl space foundation, please specify when ordering

Plan# **577-1220**

Price Code B

Cheerful And Sunny Kitchen

Total Living Area: 1,540

- Porch entrance into foyer leads to an impressive dining area with full window and a half-circle window above
- Kitchen/breakfast room has a center island and cathedral ceiling
- Great room has cathedral ceiling and exposed beams
- Master bedroom includes full bath and walk-in closet
- 3 bedrooms, 2 baths, 2-car garage
- Basement foundation, drawings also include crawl space and slab foundations

COUNTRY / VICTORIAN

366

Porch Adds To Farmhouse Style

Total Living Area: 1,793

- Beautiful foyer leads into the great room that has a fireplace flanked by two sets of beautifully transomed doors both leading to a large covered porch
- Dramatic eat-in kitchen includes an abundance of cabinets and workspace in an exciting angled shape
- Delightful master suite has many amenities
- Optional bonus room has an additional 779 square feet of living area
- 3 bedrooms, 2 baths, 2-car side entry garage
- Basement, crawl space or slab foundation, please specify when ordering

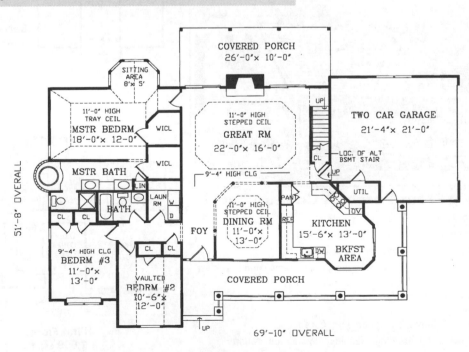

COUNTRY / VICTORIAN

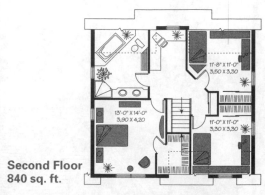

Second Floor
840 sq. ft.

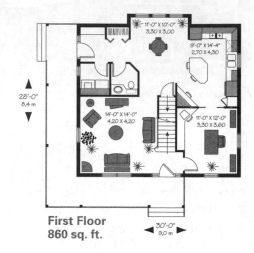

28'-0"
8,4 m

First Floor
860 sq. ft.

30'-0"
9,0 m

Charming Wrap-Around Porch
Total Living Area: 1,700

- Energy efficient home with 2" x 6" exterior walls
- Cozy living area has plenty of space for entertaining
- Snack bar in kitchen provides extra dining area
- 3 bedrooms, 1 1/2 baths
- Basement foundation

COUNTRY / VICTORIAN

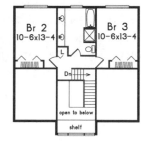

Second Floor
534 sq. ft.

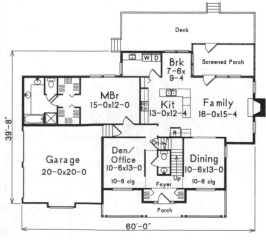

39'-8"

60'-0"

First Floor
1,509 sq. ft.

Welcoming Front Porch, A Country Touch
Total Living Area: 2,043

- Energy efficient home with 2" x 6" exterior walls
- Two-story central foyer includes two coat closets
- Large combined space provided by the kitchen, family and breakfast rooms
- Breakfast nook for informal dining looks out to the deck and screened porch
- 3 bedrooms, 2 1/2 baths, 2-car side entry garage
- Basement foundation, drawings also include slab foundation

©Alan Mascord Design Associates, Inc.

Dramatic U-Shaped Stairs

Total Living Area: 2,287

- Wrap-around porch creates an inviting feeling
- First floor windows have transom windows above
- Den has see-through fireplace into the family area
- 3 bedrooms, 2 1/2 baths, 2-car side entry garage
- Crawl space foundation

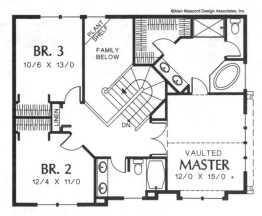

©Alan Mascord Design Associates, Inc.

BR. 3
10/6 X 13/0

PLANT SHELF

FAMILY BELOW

DN.

LINEN

BR. 2
12/4 X 11/0

VAULTED
MASTER
12/0 X 15/0 +

Second Floor
916 sq. ft.

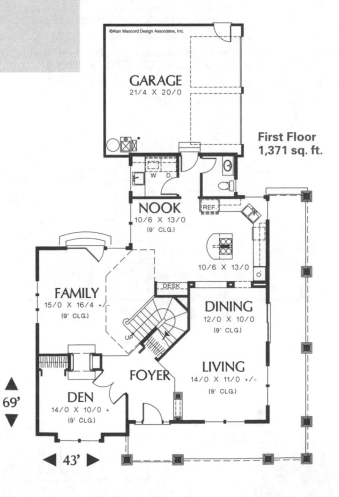

©Alan Mascord Design Associates, Inc.

GARAGE
21/4 X 20/0

W   D

First Floor
1,371 sq. ft.

NOOK
10/6 X 13/0
(9' CLG.)

REF.

10/6 X 13/0

FAMILY
15/0 X 16/4 +/-
(9' CLG.)

DESK

DINING
12/0 X 10/0
(9' CLG.)

UP

FOYER

LIVING
14/0 X 11/0 +/-
(9' CLG.)

DEN
14/0 X 10/0 +
(9' CLG.)

69'

43'

COUNTRY / VICTORIAN

Dramatic Country Architecture

Total Living Area: 2,100

- Courtyard has stone walls, lantern columns and covered porch
- Great room features a stone fireplace, built-in shelves, vaulted ceilings and atrium with dramatic staircase and a window wall
- Vaulted ceiling with plant shelf adorn the master bedroom
- 1,391 square feet of optional living area on the lower level with family room, walk-in bar, sitting area, bedroom #3 and a bath
- 3 bedrooms, 3 baths, 3-car side entry garage
- Walk-out basement foundation

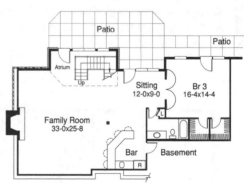

Optional Lower Level

First Floor
2,100 sq. ft.

KOIZUMI

Graceful Southern Hospitality
Total Living Area: 1,771

- Efficient country kitchen shares space with a bayed eating area
- Two-story family/great room is warmed by a fireplace in winter and open to outdoor country comfort in the summer with double French doors
- First floor master suite offers a bay window and access to the porch through French doors
- 3 bedrooms, 2 1/2 baths, optional 2-car detached garage
- Basement foundation

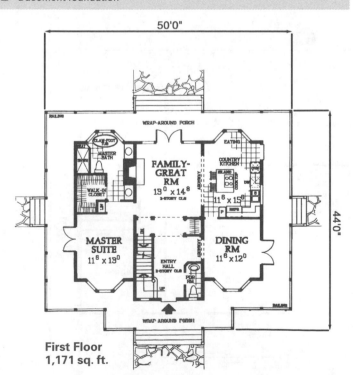

First Floor
1,171 sq. ft.

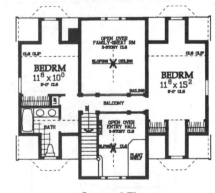

Second Floor
600 sq. ft.

Private Master Suite

Total Living Area: 1,458

- Divider wall allows for some privacy in the formal dining area
- Two secondary bedrooms share a full bath
- Covered front and rear porches create enjoyable outdoor living spaces
- 3 bedrooms, 2 baths, 2-car garage
- Slab or crawl space foundation, please specify when ordering

COUNTRY / VICTORIAN

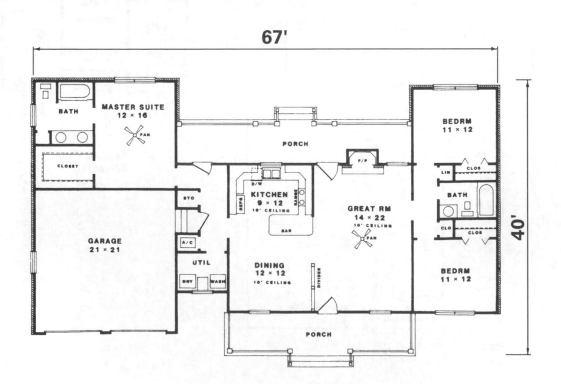

TO ORDER SEE **PAGE 608** OR CALL TOLL-FREE 1-800-DREAM HOME (373-2646)

Grand Victorian Home

Total Living Area: 2,590

- Energy efficient home with 2" x 6" exterior walls
- Utility room is located on the second floor for convenience
- Master bedroom has private bath with double vanity, oversized shower and freestanding tub in bay window
- Bonus room above the garage has an additional 459 square feet of living area
- 3 bedrooms, 2 1/2 baths, 2-car garage
- Basement foundation

Second Floor
1,238 sq. ft.

First Floor
1,352 sq. ft.

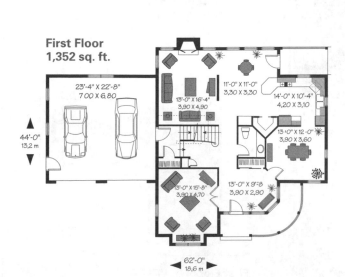

COUNTRY / VICTORIAN

Plan# 577-RJ-B1416

Price Code A

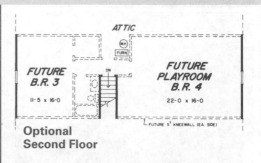

Optional Second Floor

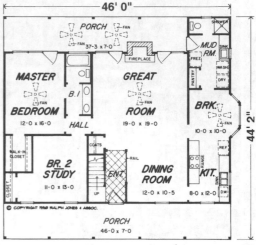

First Floor 1,455 sq. ft.

Decorative Accents On Front Porch

Total Living Area: 1,455

- Spacious mud room has a large pantry, space for a freezer, sink/counter area and bath with shower
- Bedroom #2 can easily be converted to a study or office area
- Optional second floor bedroom and playroom have an additional 744 square feet of living area
- 2 bedrooms, 2 baths
- Slab or crawl space foundation, please specify when ordering

---

Plan# 577-0396

Price Code C

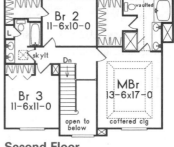

Second Floor 899 sq. ft.

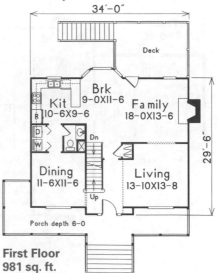

First Floor 981 sq. ft.

Extras Add Character To This Home

Total Living Area: 1,880

- Master suite enhanced with coffered ceiling
- Generous family and breakfast areas are modern and functional
- Front porch complements front facade
- 3 bedrooms, 2 1/2 baths, 2-car drive under garage
- Basement foundation

Optional Media Room

Total Living Area: 3,706

- Master suite has walk-in closets, a private bath and an exercise/hobby room that accesses a sun room
- Breakfast room with counter seating joins kitchen and dining area
- 3 bedrooms, 2 1/2 baths, 3-car detached garage
- Crawl space or slab foundation, please specify when ordering

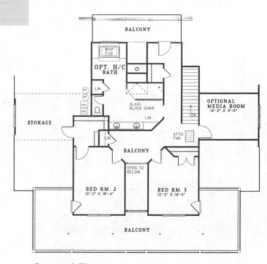

Second Floor
1,233 sq. ft.

First Floor
2,473 sq. ft.

Second Floor
1,085 sq. ft.

Br 2
10-6x11-2

Br 3
10-6x11-6

Br 4
10-0x11-6

MBr
13-5x17-6

Dn

Deck

First Floor
1,129 sq. ft.

45'-0"

26'-0"

Deck

Brk
10-2x
13-6

Kit
8-3x
13-6

Family
19-6x13-6

Dining
13-6x11-6

Living
13-6x11-6

Foyer

Dn

Up

Covered Porch

Turret Provides Dramatic Focus

Total Living Area: 2,214

- Victorian accents dominate facade
- Covered porches and decks fan out to connect front and rear entries and add to outdoor living space
- Elegant master bedroom suite features a five-sided windowed alcove and private deck
- Corner kitchen with a sink-top peninsula
- 4 bedrooms, 2 1/2 baths, 2-car drive under garage
- Basement foundation

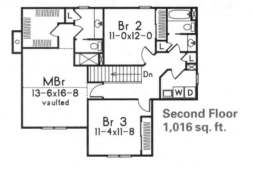

MBr
13-6x16-8
vaulted

Br 2
11-0x12-0

Br 3
11-4x11-8

Dn

W D

L

Second Floor
1,016 sq. ft.

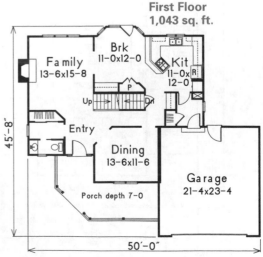

First Floor
1,043 sq. ft.

Family
13-6x15-8

Brk
11-0x12-0

Kit
11-0x
12-0

Up

Dn

Entry

Dining
13-6x11-6

Garage
21-4x23-4

Porch depth 7-0

45'-8"

50'-0"

Angled Porch Greets Guests

Total Living Area: 2,059

- Large desk and pantry add to the breakfast room
- Laundry is located on second floor near bedrooms
- Vaulted ceiling in master suite
- Mud room is conveniently located near garage
- 3 bedrooms, 2 1/2 baths, 2-car garage
- Basement foundation

COUNTRY / VICTORIAN

TO ORDER SEE **PAGE 608** OR CALL TOLL-FREE 1-800-DREAM HOME (373-2646)

Spacious Country Home

Total Living Area: 2,123

- L-shaped porch extends the entire length of this home creating lots of extra space for outdoor living
- Master bedroom is secluded for privacy and has double closets, double vanity in bath and a double-door entry onto covered porch
- Efficiently designed kitchen
- 3 bedrooms, 2 1/2 baths
- Crawl space foundation

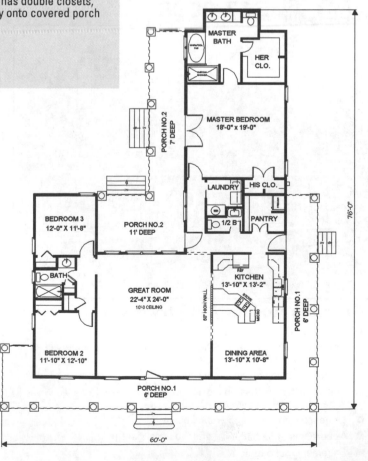

COUNTRY / VICTORIAN

Plan# 577-0765

Price Code AA

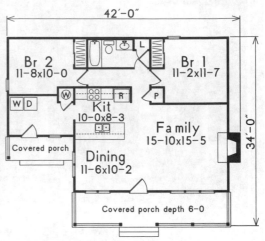

42'-0"

34'-0"

Br 2
11-8x10-0

Br 1
11-2x11-7

W D

W

L

R

P

Kit
10-0x8-3

Family
15-10x15-5

Covered porch

Dining
11-6x10-2

Covered porch depth 6-0

Rustic Design With Modern Features

Total Living Area: 1,000

- Large mud room with separate covered porch entrance
- Full-length covered front porch
- Bedrooms on opposite sides of the home for privacy
- Vaulted ceiling creates an open and spacious feeling
- 2 bedrooms, 1 bath
- Crawl space foundation

COUNTRY / VICTORIAN

Plan# 577-0598

Price Code C

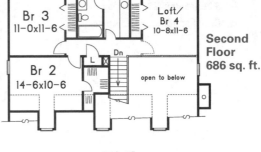

Br 3
11-0x11-6

Loft/
Br 4
10-8x11-6

L

Dn

Br 2
14-6x10-6

open to below

Second Floor 686 sq. ft.

38'-0"

32'-0"

Deck

Brk
8-2x
8-2

Kit
9-4x
13-6

Dining
13-6x11-6

W D

R

Dn

Living
13-6x15-6

vaulted

MBr
14-6x13-6

Up

Porch depth 6-0

First Floor 1,132 sq. ft.

Dormers Accent Country Home

Total Living Area: 1,818

- Breakfast room is tucked behind the kitchen and has laundry closet and deck access
- Living and dining areas share vaulted ceiling and fireplace
- Master bedroom has two closets, large double-bowl vanity, separate tub and shower
- Large front porch wraps around home
- 4 bedrooms, 2 1/2 baths, 2-car drive under garage
- Basement foundation

Victorian With Custom-Feel Interior

Total Living Area: 3,323

■ Cozy den has two walls of bookshelves making it a quiet retreat

■ A useful screened porch is located off dining room for dining and entertaining outdoors

■ Varied ceiling heights throughout bedrooms on second floor add interest

■ 4 bedrooms, 2 1/2 baths, 2-car side entry garage

■ Basement foundation

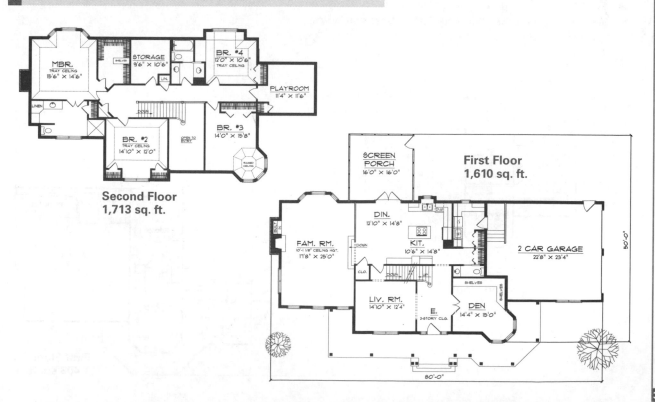

Second Floor
1,713 sq. ft.

First Floor
1,610 sq. ft.

COUNTRY / VICTORIAN

Unique Octagon-Shaped Porch

Total Living Area: 2,044

- Formal dining area easily accesses kitchen through double-doors
- Two-car garage features a workshop area for projects or extra storage
- Second floor includes loft space ideal for office area and a handy computer center
- Colossal master bedroom with double walk-in closets and a private bath with a bay window seat
- 3 bedrooms, 2 1/2 baths, 2-car side entry garage
- Basement, crawl space or slab foundation, please specify when ordering

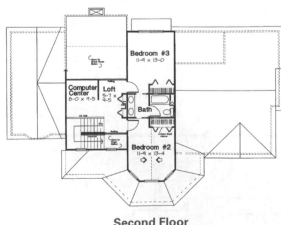

Second Floor
641 sq. ft.

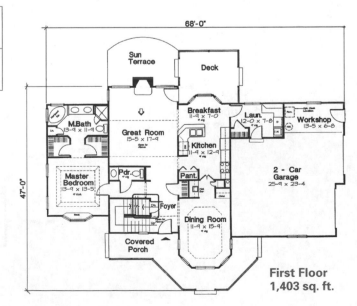

First Floor
1,403 sq. ft.

COUNTRY / VICTORIAN

Porch And Turret Accent Design

Total Living Area: 3,556

- Jack and jill bath located between two of the bedrooms on the second floor
- Second floor features three bedrooms and overlooks the great room
- Formal entrance and additional family entrance from covered porch to laundry/mud room
- First floor master suite features coffered ceiling, his and hers walk-in closets, luxury bath and direct access to study
- 4 bedrooms, 3 1/2 baths, 3-car side entry garage
- Basement foundation

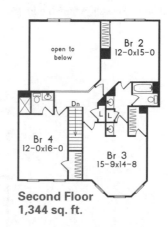

open to below

Br 2
12-0x15-0

Dn

Br 4
12-0x16-0

Br 3
15-9x14-8

Second Floor
1,344 sq. ft.

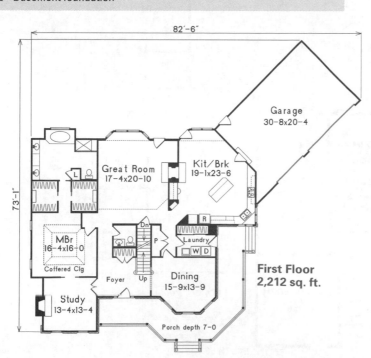

82'-6"

Garage
30-8x20-4

73'-1"

Great Room
17-4x20-10

Kit/Brk
19-1x23-6

MBr
16-4x16-0

Coffered Clg

Laundry

W D

R

Foyer

Up

Dn

P

Dining
15-9x13-9

First Floor
2,212 sq. ft.

Study
13-4x13-4

Porch depth 7-0

COUNTRY / VICTORIAN

TO ORDER SEE PAGE 608 OR CALL TOLL-FREE 1-800-DREAM HOME (373-2646)

Covered Porches All Around

Total Living Area:　1,725

- ■ Spectacular arches when entering foyer
- ■ Dining room has double-doors leading to kitchen
- ■ Unique desk area off kitchen ideal for computer work station
- ■ 3 bedrooms, 2 baths, 2-car side entry garage
- ■ Slab or crawl space foundation, please specify when ordering

COUNTRY / VICTORIAN

COPYRIGHT LARRY E. BELK

GARAGE

UTIL

REAR ENTRY

PORCH

BRKFST RM
10-4 X 10-0
11 FT VAULTED CLG

DEPTH 72-8

BEDRM 2
11-0 X 12-6
9 FT CLG

BEDRM 3
11-0 X 10-0
9 FT CLG

GREAT RM
17-0 X 17-0
11 FT CLG

KITCHEN
8-6 X 17-0
9 FT CLG

BATH 2

ARCH　ARCH

DINING RM
12-0 X 12-6
11 FT CLG

LEDGE　LEDGE

MASTER BATH
9 FT CLG

FOYER
11 FT CLG

PANTRY

DESK

HK S L

LIN

MASTER BEDRM
13-0 X 14-8
9 FT CLG

PORCH

SEAT

WIDTH 56-4

TO ORDER SEE **PAGE 608** OR CALL TOLL-FREE **1-800-DREAM HOME** (373-2646)

Country Charm With Style

Total Living Area: 2,245

- Covered wrap-around porch and arched windows
- Great room with an 18' vaulted ceiling has a fireplace set into a media wall
- Master bedroom has a 10' ceiling and bay window
- 3 bedrooms, 2 1/2 baths, 2-car side entry garage
- Basement, crawl space or slab foundation, please specify when ordering

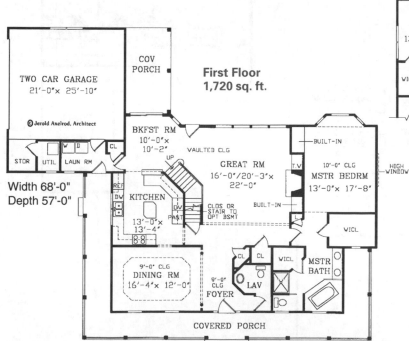

First Floor
1,720 sq. ft.

Width 68'-0"
Depth 57'-0"

Second Floor
525 sq. ft.

COUNTRY / VICTORIAN

383

Convenient First Floor Master Suite

Total Living Area: 2,504

- Efficient kitchen boasts a peninsula counter adding workspace as well as an eating bar
- The nook and kitchen blend nicely into the great room for family gathering
- The utility room has a soaking sink, extra counterspace and plenty of room for an additional refrigerator
- 4 bedrooms, 2 1/2 baths, 3-car garage
- Basement foundation

COUNTRY / VICTORIAN

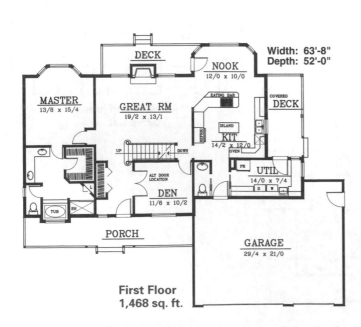

Width: 63'-8"
Depth: 52'-0"

DECK

NOOK
12/0 x 10/0

MASTER
13/8 x 15/4

GREAT RM
19/2 x 13/1

EATING BAR

COVERED DECK

REFRIG

ISLAND

KIT
14/2 x 12/0

OVEN

UP

DOWN

ALT DOOR LOCATION

FR

UTIL
14/0 x 7/4

D W

DEN
11/6 x 10/2

TUB   SH

PORCH

GARAGE
29/4 x 21/0

**First Floor
1,468 sq. ft.**

OPEN TO BELOW

BDRM 3
10/6 x 10/9

BDRM 4
10/6 x 10/9

DOWN

PLANT LEDGE

LINEN

LIN

TUB

BDRM 2
11/6 x 10/10

BONUS
13/8 x 24/3

**Second Floor
1,036 sq. ft.**

TO ORDER SEE **PAGE 608** OR CALL TOLL-FREE 1-800-DREAM HOME (373-2646)

Plenty Of Seating At Breakfast Bar

Total Living Area: 2,544

- Central family room becomes gathering place
- Second floor recreation room is a great game room for children
- First floor master suite secluded from main living areas
- 3 bedrooms, 2 1/2 baths, 2-car side entry garage
- Basement foundation, drawings also include crawl space and slab foundations

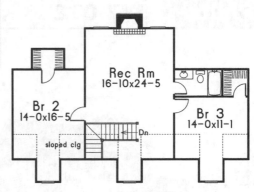

Second Floor
951 sq. ft.

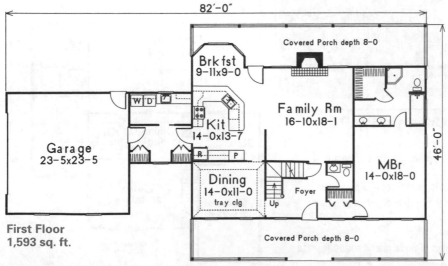

First Floor
1,593 sq. ft.

COUNTRY / VICTORIAN

Plan # 577-0686

Price Code B

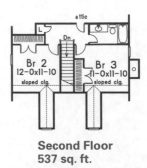

Second Floor
537 sq. ft.

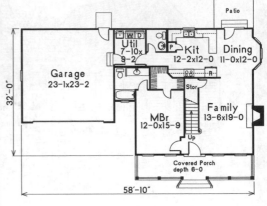

First Floor
1,072 sq. ft.

Charming Home Arranged For Open Living

Total Living Area: 1,609

- Kitchen captures full use of space with pantry, ample cabinets and workspace
- Master bedroom is well-secluded with walk-in closet and private bath
- Large utility room includes sink and extra storage
- Attractive bay window in dining area provides light
- 3 bedrooms, 2 1/2 baths, 2-car garage
- Slab foundation

Plan # 577-0723

Price Code B

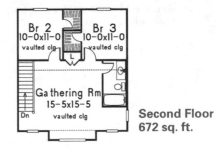

Second Floor
672 sq. ft.

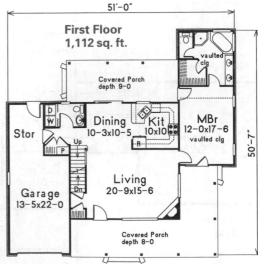

Outdoor Living Area Created By Porch

Total Living Area: 1,784

- Spacious living area with corner fireplace offers a cheerful atmosphere with large windows
- Large second floor gathering room is great for kid's play area
- Secluded master suite has separate porch entrances and large master bath with walk-in closet
- 3 bedrooms, 2 1/2 baths, 1-car garage
- Basement foundation, drawings also include crawl space foundation

COUNTRY / VICTORIAN

TO ORDER SEE **PAGE 608** OR CALL TOLL-FREE **1-800-DREAM HOME** (373-2646)

Classic, Modern Features Abound

Total Living Area: 3,035

- Front facade includes large porch
- Private master bedroom with windowed sitting area, walk-in closet, sloped ceiling and skylight
- Formal living and dining rooms adjoin the family room through attractive French doors
- Energy efficient home with 2" x 6" exterior walls
- 4 bedrooms, 3 1/2 baths, 2-car side entry garage
- Crawl space foundation, drawings also include slab and basement foundations

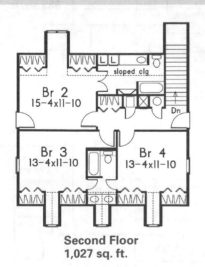

Second Floor
1,027 sq. ft.

First Floor
2,008 sq. ft.

ELEGANT HOMES

387

Second Floor
588 sq. ft.

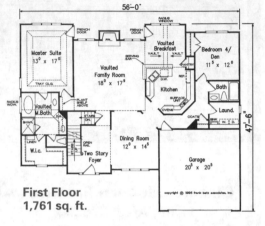

First Floor
1,761 sq. ft.

Bright And Beautiful

Total Living Area: 2,349

- Open and airy with two-story foyer and family room
- Den is secluded from the rest of the home and ideal as an office space
- Second floor bedrooms have walk-in closets and share a bath
- Optional bonus room has an additional 276 square feet of living area
- 4 bedrooms, 3 baths, 2-car garage
- Walk-out basement, slab or crawl space foundation, please specify when ordering

---

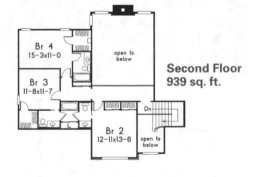

Second Floor
939 sq. ft.

First Floor
2,221 sq. ft.

Magnificent Manor Home

Total Living Area: 3,160

- Covered entry porch leading into magnificent two-story foyer which accesses formal rooms on either side
- Main floor master suite features his and her closets and large master bath
- Efficiently designed kitchen includes island cooktop and pass-through to breakfast room
- 4 bedrooms, 3 1/2 baths, 3-car side entry garage
- Basement foundation

ELEGANT HOMES

Angled Den With Built-Ins

Total Living Area: 3,158

- Coffered ceiling in entry
- Vaulted ceilings in living room, master bedroom and family room
- Interior columns accent the entry, living and dining areas
- Kitchen island has eating bar adding extra seating
- Master bath has garden tub and a separate shower
- 3 bedrooms, 2 1/2 baths, 3-car garage
- Crawl space foundation

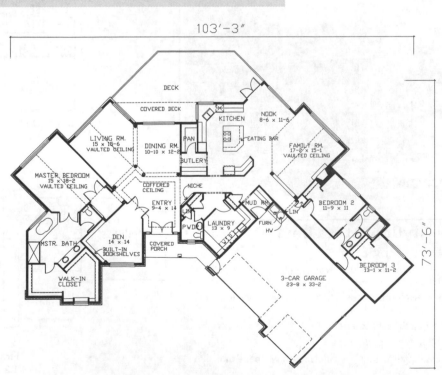

ELEGANT HOMES

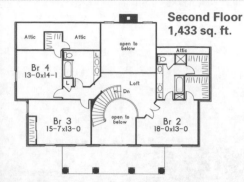

Second Floor 1,433 sq. ft.

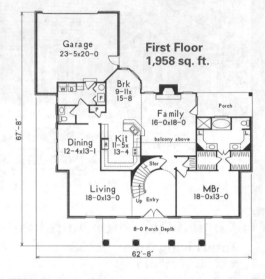

First Floor 1,958 sq. ft.

Dramatic Entry With Soaring Staircase

Total Living Area: 3,391

- Magnificent first floor master suite has two walk-in closets and double vanities
- Generous secondary bedrooms
- Bedroom #2 has private bath and plenty of closet space
- Two-story family room with fireplace and balcony above
- 4 bedrooms, 3 1/2 baths, 2-car rear entry garage
- Crawl space foundation, drawings also include slab foundation

ELEGANT HOMES

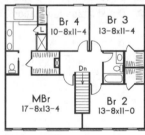

Second Floor 1,140 sq. ft.

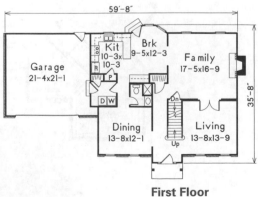

Traditional Styling At Its Best

Total Living Area: 2,358

- U-shaped kitchen provides an ideal layout, adjoining breakfast room allows for casual dining
- Formal dining and living rooms have attractive floor-to-ceiling windows
- Master bedroom includes deluxe bath
- 4 bedrooms, 2 1/2 baths, 2-car garage
- Basement foundation, drawings also include crawl space and slab foundations

First Floor 1,218 sq. ft.

TO ORDER SEE **PAGE 608** OR CALL TOLL-FREE 1-800-DREAM HOME (373-2646)

Formal And Informal Living

Total Living Area: 2,591

- Formal living area has a nice view extending past the covered patio
- Family room is adjacent to breakfast area and has a vaulted ceiling and fireplace creating a cozy atmosphere
- Master suite has a private sitting area and large master bath
- Gallery adds interest to entry
- 4 bedrooms, 3 baths, 3-car side entry garage
- Slab foundation

ELEGANT HOMES

391

Plan# 577-CHP-3054-B-3

Price Code H

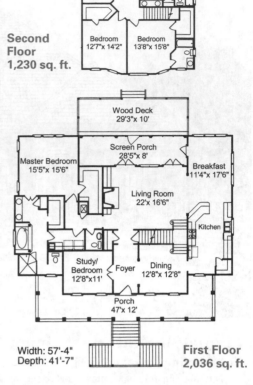

Second Floor 1,230 sq. ft.

First Floor 2,036 sq. ft.

Width: 57'-4"
Depth: 41'-7"

Beautiful Entrance Is Graced With Charm

Total Living Area: 3,266

- Screened porch has double-door entrances from living room
- Sunny breakfast room has lots of windows for a cheerful atmosphere
- All bedrooms on second floor have spacious walk-in closets
- Multimedia room makes a great casual family room
- 5 bedrooms, 3 1/2 baths, 2-car drive under garage
- Two-story pier foundation

Plan# 577-0708

Price Code E

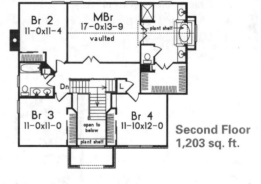

Second Floor 1,203 sq. ft.

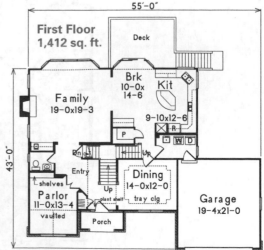

First Floor 1,412 sq. ft.

55'-0"

43'-0"

Stately Front Entrance With Style

Total Living Area: 2,615

- Grand two-story entry features majestic palladian window, double French doors to parlor and access to powder room
- State-of-the-art kitchen has corner sink with two large archtop windows, island snack bar, menu desk and walk-in pantry
- Master bath is vaulted and offers a luxurious step-up tub, palladian window, built-in shelves and columns with plant shelf
- 4 bedrooms, 2 1/2 baths, 2-car garage
- Basement foundation

ELEGANT HOMES

Rich With Victorian Details

Total Living Area: 2,632

- Energy efficient home with 2" x 6" exterior walls
- Master bedroom has cheerful octagon-shaped sitting area
- Arched entrances create a distinctive living room with a lovely tray ceiling and help define the dining room
- 4 bedrooms, 2 1/2 baths, 2-car garage
- Basement or crawl space foundation, please specify when ordering

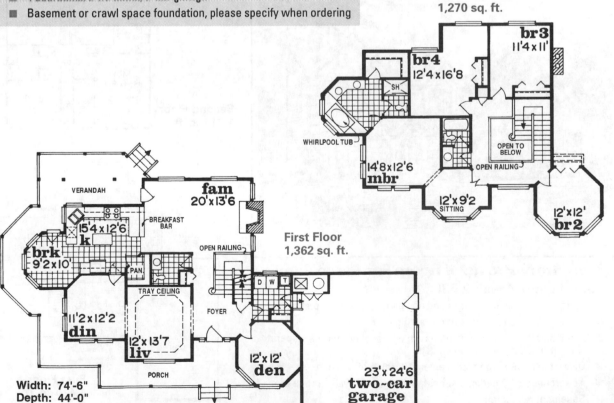

Second Floor
1,270 sq. ft.

br3
11'4 x 11'

br4
12'4 x 16'8

SH

WHIRLPOOL TUB

14'8 x 12'6
mbr

OPEN TO BELOW

OPEN RAILING

12' x 9'2
SITTING

12' x 12'
br2

VERANDAH

fam
20' x 13'6

BREAKFAST BAR

15'4 x 12'6
k

OPEN RAILING

First Floor
1,362 sq. ft.

PAN.

brk
9'2 x 10'

D W T

TRAY CEILING

FOYER

11'2 x 12'2
din

12' x 13'7
liv

12' x 12'
den

23' x 24'6
two-car garage

PORCH

Width: 74'-6"
Depth: 44'-0"

Plan# 577-0159

Price Code F

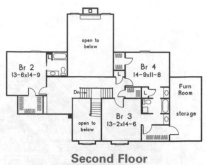

Second Floor
1,218 sq. ft.

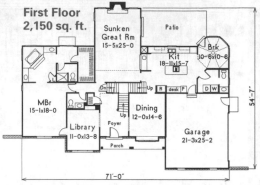

First Floor
2,150 sq. ft.

A Great House, Spacious Inside And Out

Total Living Area: 3,368

- Sunken great room with cathedral ceiling, wooden beams, skylights and a masonry fireplace
- Octagon-shaped breakfast room has domed ceiling with beams, large windows and door to patio
- Private master bedroom has a deluxe bath and dressing area
- Oversized walk-in closets and storage areas in each bedroom
- 4 bedrooms, 3 full baths, 2 half baths, 2-car side entry garage
- Basement foundation

Plan# 577-0691

Price Code E

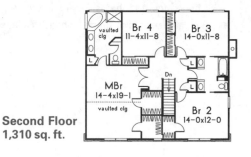

Second Floor
1,310 sq. ft.

First Floor
1,420 sq. ft.

Two-Story Provides Room For Large Family

Total Living Area: 2,730

- Spacious kitchen features island and generous walk-in pantry
- Covered deck offers private retreat to the outdoors
- Large master bedroom and bath with whirlpool corner tub, separate shower and double walk-in closets
- Oversized laundry room conveniently located off kitchen
- 4 bedrooms, 2 1/2 baths, 3-car side entry garage with storage area
- Basement foundation

ELEGANT HOMES

A Country Home Loaded With Amenities
Total Living Area: 3,818

- A covered patio wraps around the rear of the home providing extra outdoor living area
- Master suite is separated from other bedrooms for privacy
- 459 square feet of additional living area available in the bonus room
- Framing - only concrete block available
- 4 bedrooms, 3 1/2 baths, 3-car side entry garage
- Slab foundation

First Floor
3,359 sq. ft.

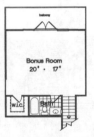

Optional Second Floor

Plan# 577-0184

Price Code D

Study 11-5x11-8
Br 3 11-11x10-0
MBr 13-8x15-4
open to below
vaulted
Br 2 13-8x11-0

Second Floor 1,118 sq. ft.

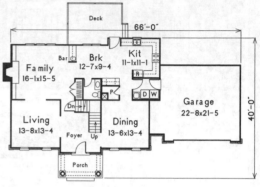

Deck
66'-0"
Bar
Brk 12-7x9-4
Kit 11-1x11-1
Family 16-1x15-5
Garage 22-8x21-5
40'-0"
Living 13-8x13-4
Dn
Dining 13-6x13-4
Foyer Up
D W
Porch

First Floor 1,293 sq. ft.

Impressive Front Balcony

Total Living Area: 2,411

- Elegant entrance features a two-story vaulted foyer
- Large family room enhanced by masonry fireplace and wet bar
- Master bedroom suite includes walk-in closet, oversized tub and separate shower
- Second floor study could easily convert to a fourth bedroom
- 3 bedrooms, 2 1/2 baths, 2-car garage
- Basement foundation, drawings also include slab and crawl space foundations

Plan# 577-0391

Price Code E

MBr 19-8x13-0 vaulted
Br 3 12-8x14-8
plant shelf
Dn
open to below
plant shelf
Br 4 11-8x11-4 raised ceiling
Br 2 12-8x13-8 window seat

Second Floor 1,325 sq. ft.

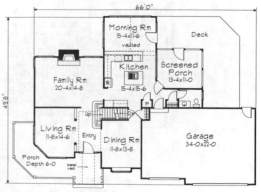

66'0"
Morning Rm 15-4x11-6 vaulted
Deck
Kitchen 15-4x15-6
Screened Porch 13-4x11-0
Family Rm 20-4x14-8
49'8"
Living Rm 11-8x14-6
Up
Entry
Dining Rm 11-8x13-8
Garage 34-0x22-0
Porch Depth 6-0
barrel vault

First Floor 1,360 sq. ft.

Outdoor Exposure Front And Back

Total Living Area: 2,685

- 9' ceilings throughout first floor
- Vaulted master bedroom, isolated for privacy, boasts magnificent bath with garden tub, separate shower and two closets
- Laundry area near bedrooms
- Screened porch and morning room both located off well-planned kitchen
- 4 bedrooms, 2 1/2 baths, 3-car garage
- Basement foundation

ELEGANT HOMES

Triple Dormers Add Curb Appeal

Total Living Area: 3,383

- Large vaulted activity center on the second floor has a built-in entertainment center perfect for computer or media center
- First floor includes a secluded home office off the master suite that has direct access to the outdoors
- A large fireplace divides the dining room from the great room while maintaining a feeling of openness
- 4 bedrooms, 3 1/2 baths, 2-car side entry garage
- Slab or crawl space foundation, please specify when ordering

Second Floor
1,132 sq. ft.

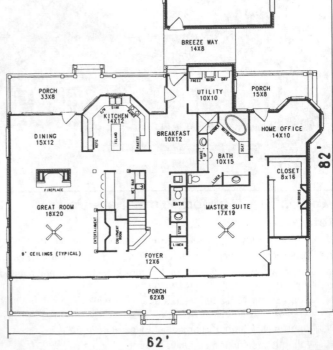

First Floor
2,251 sq. ft.

ELEGANT HOMES

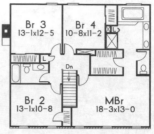

Br 3
13-1x12-5

Br 4
10-8x11-2

Br 2
13-1x10-8

MBr
18-3x13-0

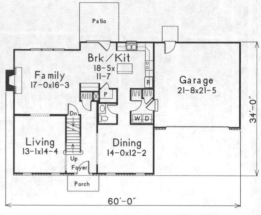

**Second Floor
1,140 sq. ft.**

Clean, Practical Colonial

Total Living Area: 2,328

- Formal living and dining rooms feature floor-to-ceiling windows
- Kitchen with island counter and pantry makes cooking a delight
- Expansive master bedroom has luxury bath with double vanity and walk-in closet
- 4 bedrooms, 2 1/2 baths, 2-car garage
- Basement foundation, drawings also include slab and crawl space foundations

Patio

Brk/Kit
18-5x
11-7

Family
17-0x16-3

Garage
21-8x21-5

Living
13-1x14-4

Dining
14-0x12-2

Up
Foyer

Porch

34'-0"

60'-0"

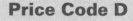

**First Floor
1,188 sq. ft.**

68'-0"

Deck

MBr
16-4x13-8

Brkfst
11-0x13-3

open to below

Br 2
13-1x13-8

Kitchen
13-4x11-0

Great Rm
16-8x20-0
vaulted clg

Dining
13-4x12-8
coffered Clg

Foyer

plant shelf

Garage
23-4x30-0

Covered Porch depth 6-0

Br 3
11-0x12-1

Br 4
11-0x12-8

52'-4"

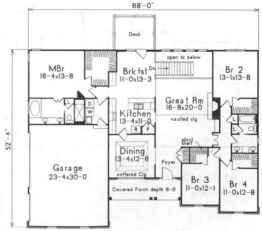

ELEGANT HOMES

Appealing Gabled Front Facade

Total Living Area: 2,412

- Coffered ceiling in dining room adds character and spaciousness
- Great room enhanced by vaulted ceiling and atrium window wall
- Spacious well-planned kitchen includes breakfast bar and overlooks breakfast room and beyond to deck
- Luxurious master suite features enormous walk-in closet, private bath and easy access to laundry area
- 4 bedrooms, 2 baths, 3-car side entry garage
- Walk-out basement foundation

Stately Colonial Entry

Total Living Area: 4,652

- A grand foyer introduces a formal dining room and library with beamed ceiling and built-ins
- Covered porches at the rear offer splendid views
- The magnificent master bedroom has a 10' ceiling, a private sitting area and a luxurious dressing room with walk-in closet
- Secondary bedrooms have window seats, large closets and private bath access
- 4 bedrooms, 3 1/2 baths, 3-car side entry garage
- Walk-out basement or basement foundation, please specify when ordering

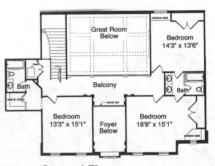

Second Floor
1,238 sq. ft.

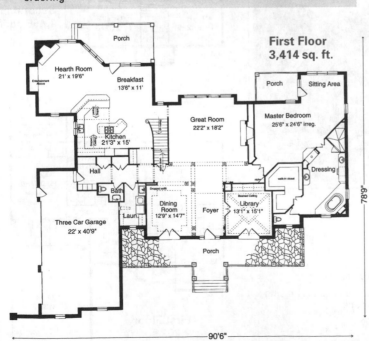

First Floor
3,414 sq. ft.

Plan # 577-0821

Price Code E

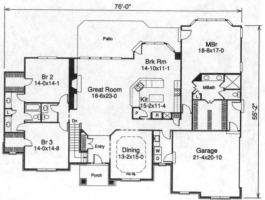

Spacious One-Story With French Flavor

Total Living Area: 2,695

- A grandscale great room features a fireplace with flanking shelves, handsome entry foyer with staircase and opens to large kitchen and breakfast room
- Roomy master bedroom has a bay window, huge walk-in closet and bath with a shower built for two
- Bedrooms #2 and #3 are generously oversized with walk-in closets and a jack and jill style bath
- 3 bedrooms, 2 1/2 baths, 2-car side entry garage
- Basement foundation

Plan # 577-0735

Price Code F

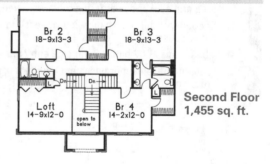

Second Floor
1,455 sq. ft.

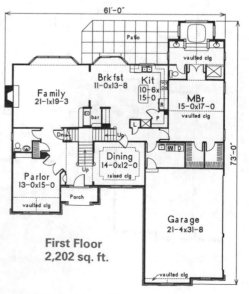

First Floor
2,202 sq. ft.

Stately Elegance

Total Living Area: 3,657

- Dramatic two-story foyer has a stylish niche, a convenient powder room and French doors leading to parlor
- Kitchen includes a large walk-in pantry, breakfast island, computer center and 40' vista through family room with walk-in wet bar
- Vaulted master bath has marble steps and Roman columns leading to a majestic-sized whirlpool tub with marble deck
- 4 bedrooms, 3 1/2 baths, 3-car side entry garage
- Basement foundation

ELEGANT HOMES

COPYRIGHT LARRY E. BELK

Step Up Into Master Bath Tub

Total Living Area: 2,678

- Elegant arched opening graces entrance
- Kitchen has double ovens, walk-in pantry and an eating bar
- Master bedroom has beautiful bath spotlighting a step up tub
- 4 bedrooms, 2 1/2 baths, 2-car side entry garage
- Crawl space or slab foundation, please specify when ordering

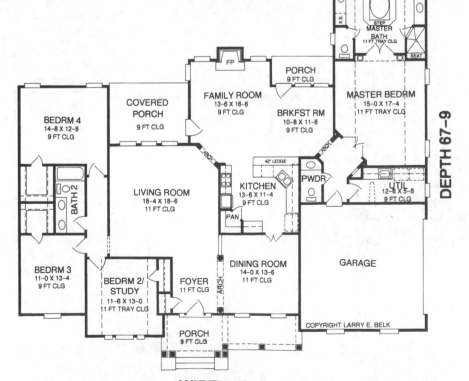

COPYRIGHT LARRY E. BELK

WIDTH 70-2

DEPTH 67-9

ELEGANT HOMES

Staircase Makes A Beautiful Entrance

Total Living Area: 2,889

- Energy efficient home with 2" x 6" exterior walls
- Cathedral ceiling in family room is impressive
- 9' ceilings throughout first floor
- Private home office located away from traffic flow
- 4 bedrooms, 3 1/2 baths, 2-car side entry garage
- Basement foundation

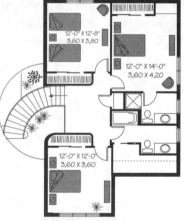

Second Floor
962 sq. ft.

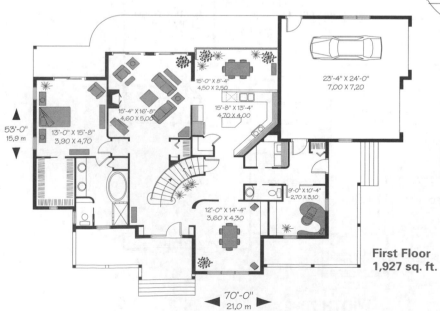

First Floor
1,927 sq. ft.

53'-0"
15,9 m

70'-0"
21,0 m

ELEGANT HOMES

A Touch Of Old World Charm

Total Living Area: 2,320

- From the foyer, there is a panoramic view of the dramatic great room and formal dining room
- A butler's pantry is strategically placed between the formal dining room and kitchen and breakfast room
- French doors add light and style to the breakfast room
- 4 bedrooms, 2 1/2 baths, 2-car garage
- Basement foundation

Second Floor
725 sq. ft.

First Floor
1,595 sq. ft.

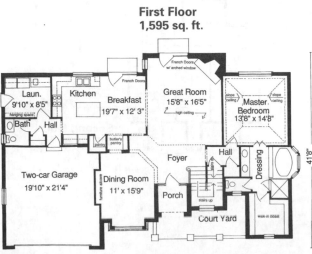

ELEGANT HOMES

Plenty Of Built-Ins

Total Living Area: 3,012

- ■ Master suite has sitting area with entertainment center/library
- ■ Utility room has a sink and includes lots of storage and counterspace
- ■ Future space above garage has an additional 336 square feet of living area
- ■ 4 bedrooms, 3 1/2 baths, 2-car side entry garage
- ■ Crawl space, slab or basement foundation, please specify when ordering

First Floor
2,202 sq. ft.

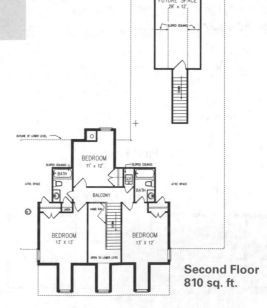

Second Floor
810 sq. ft.

ELEGANT HOMES

Superb Victorian Details

Total Living Area: 2,420

- Master suite filled with extras like unique master bath and lots of storage
- Extending off great room is a bright sunroom with access to a deck
- Compact kitchen with nook creates useful breakfast area
- Cozy built-in table in breakfast area
- 4 bedrooms, 2 1/2 baths, 2-car garage
- Basement foundation

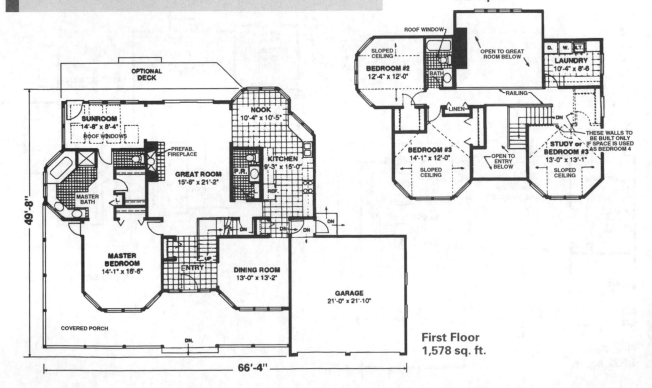

Second Floor
842 sq. ft.

ROOF WINDOW

SLOPED CEILING

BEDROOM #2
12'-4" x 12'-0"

BATH

OPEN TO GREAT ROOM BELOW

D. W. LT.

LAUNDRY
10'-4" x 8'-6"

LINEN

RAILING

BEDROOM #3
14'-1" x 12'-0"

SLOPED CEILING

OPEN TO ENTRY BELOW

DN

STUDY or BEDROOM #3
13'-0" x 13'-1"

SLOPED CEILING

THESE WALLS TO BE BUILT ONLY IF SPACE IS USED AS BEDROOM 4

OPTIONAL DECK

SUNROOM
14'-8" x 8'-4"
ROOF WINDOWS

PREFAB. FIREPLACE

NOOK
10'-4" x 10'-5"

KITCHEN
9'-3" x 15'-0"

GREAT ROOM
15'-6" x 21'-2"

P.R.

REF.

MASTER BATH

MASTER BEDROOM
14'-1" x 16'-6"

ENTRY

UP

DN

DN

DN

DINING ROOM
13'-0" x 13'-2"

GARAGE
21'-0" x 21'-10"

COVERED PORCH

DN.

49'-8"

66'-4"

First Floor
1,578 sq. ft.

ELEGANT HOMES

405

Brick Traditional

Total Living Area: 2,737

- T-stairs make any room easily accessible
- Two-story foyer and grand room create spacious feeling
- Master bedroom has gorgeous bay window and a sitting area
- Bedroom #4 has its own private bath
- 5 bedrooms, 4 baths, 2-car side entry garage
- Basement foundation

ELEGANT HOMES

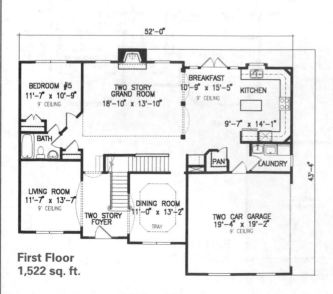

First Floor
1,522 sq. ft.

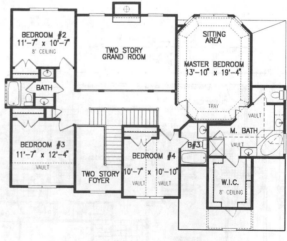

Second Floor
1,215 sq. ft.

TO ORDER SEE **PAGE 608** OR CALL TOLL-FREE 1-800-DREAM HOME (373-2646)

Delightful Dormers Add Drama

Total Living Area: 3,231

- Breakfast nook and kitchen combine creating a large open dining space
- A cozy and private study is convenient to the master bedroom perfect for an office
- Decorative columns enhance the formal dining room
- Bonus room included in the the square footage for the second floor, would make a great children's play room
- 4 bedrooms, 2 1/2 baths, 3-car garage
- Crawl space foundation

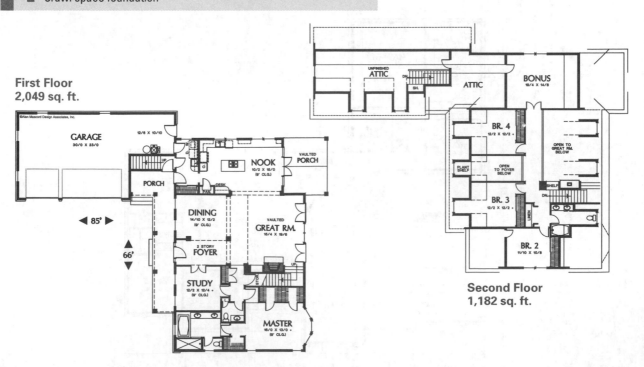

First Floor
2,049 sq. ft.

©Alan Mascord Design Associates, Inc.

GARAGE
30/0 X 23/0

12/8 X 10/10

NOOK
10/2 X 16/0
(9' CLG.)

VAULTED
PORCH

PORCH

DESK

DINING
14/10 X 12/2
(9' CLG.)

VAULTED
GREAT RM.
18/4 X 19/6

◄ 85' ►

2 STORY
FOYER

66'

STUDY
12/2 X 12/4 +
(9' CLG.)

MASTER
18/0 X 13/0 +
(9' CLG.)

Second Floor
1,182 sq. ft.

UNFINISHED
ATTIC

ATTIC

BONUS
18/4 X 14/8

BR. 4
12/2 X 12/2

OPEN TO
GREAT RM.
BELOW

PLANT
SHELF

OPEN
TO FOYER
BELOW

SHELF

BR. 3
12/2 X 12/2 +

LINEN

BR. 2
11/10 X 10/8

© Copyright MCMXCVIII – Ralph Jones

Elegant European Styling

Total Living Area: 2,600

- Formal entry with large opening to dining area and great room with coffered ceiling
- Great room has coffered ceiling, corner fireplace and atrium doors leading to rear covered porch
- Morning room with rear view and angled eating bar
- Exercise room, or office, or computer room near master suite
- 4 bedrooms, 2 1/2 baths, 3-car side entry garage
- Slab or crawl space foundation, please specify when ordering

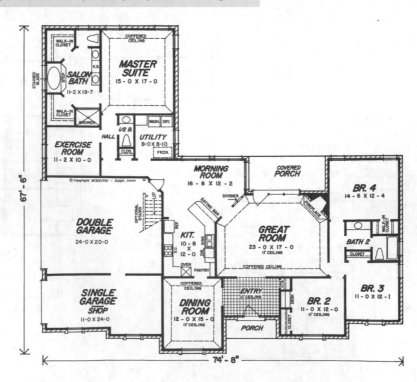

Striking Front Facade With Arched Entry

Total Living Area: 2,718

- Master suite has tray ceiling, access to the rear deck, walk-in closet and an impressive private bath
- Dining and living rooms flank the foyer and both feature tray ceilings
- Spacious family room features 12' ceiling, fireplace and access to the rear deck
- Kitchen has a 9' ceiling, large pantry and bar overlooking the breakfast room
- 4 bedrooms, 2 1/2 baths, 2-car side entry garage
- Basement foundation

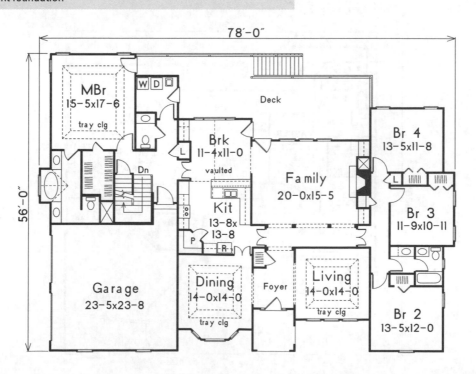

ELEGANT HOMES

409

Multiple See-Through Fireplaces

Total Living Area: 2,900

- Stately arched entry with double-doors is inviting to guests
- Decorative columns through entry, dining area and great room add look of elegance
- Octagon-shaped breakfast room with intricate tray ceiling looks out to screened-in porch and large rear deck
- 9' ceilings in bedrooms and kitchen area
- 2 bedrooms, 2 1/2 baths, 3-car garage with golf cart storage
- Walk-out basement or basement foundation, please specify when ordering

ELEGANT HOMES

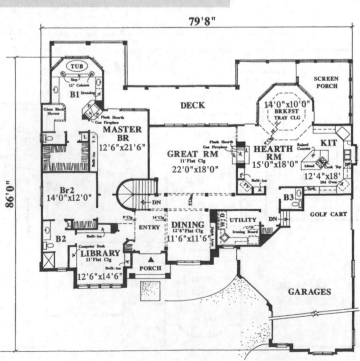

J.N. HANSEN RTL.

Magnificent Facade

Total Living Area: 2,887

- Columned foyer opens into living room which has sunken wet bar that extends into pool area
- Stunning master bedroom accesses patio and offers view of pool through curved window wall
- Dining room boasts window walls
- Second floor includes two bedrooms, bath and shared balcony deck overlooking pool area
- 4 bedrooms, 2 1/2 baths, 2-car garage
- Slab foundation

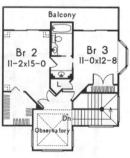

Second Floor
675 sq. ft.

Balcony

Br 2
11-2x15-0

Br 3
11-0x12-8

Observatory

Dn

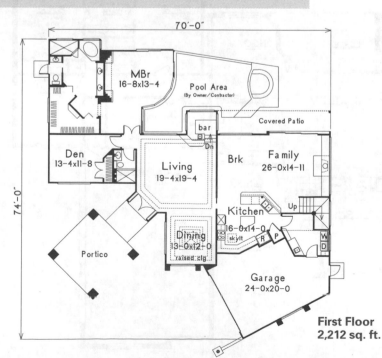

70'-0"

74'-0"

MBr
16-8x13-4

Pool Area
(By Owner/Contractor)

Covered Patio

bar
Dn

Den
13-4x11-8

Living
19-4x19-4

Brk

Family
26-0x14-11

Kitchen
16-0x14-0
skylt

Up

R   P

W D

Dining
13-0x12-0
raised clg

Portico

Garage
24-0x20-0

First Floor
2,212 sq. ft.

Elaborate Stonework Adds Charm

Total Living Area: 2,560

- See-through fireplace surrounded with shelving warms both family room and living room
- Tall ceilings in living areas
- Bedrooms maintain privacy
- 4 bedrooms, 3 baths, 3-car side entry garage
- Slab foundation

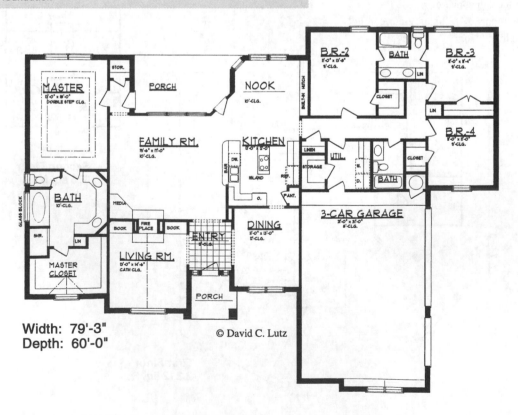

Width: 79'-3"
Depth: 60'-0"

© David C. Lutz

ELEGANT HOMES

TO ORDER SEE PAGE 608 OR CALL TOLL-FREE 1-800-DREAM HOME (373-2646)

Colossal Southern Colonial

Total Living Area: 4,187

- 10' ceilings on first floor and 9' ceilings on the second floor
- Private first floor bedroom accesses bath
- Second floor sitting area accesses balcony through French doors
- Octagon-shaped breakfast room is a nice focal point
- Future gameroom over garage has an additional 551 square feet of living area
- 5 bedrooms, 4 1/2 baths, 3-car side entry garage
- Slab foundation

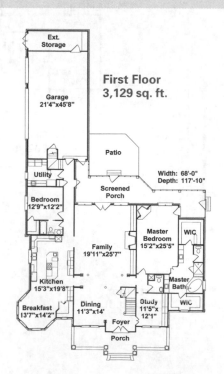

First Floor
3,129 sq. ft.

Width: 68'-0"
Depth: 117'-10"

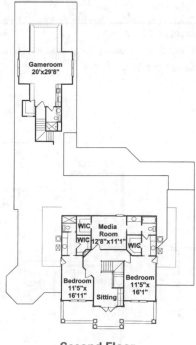

Second Floor
1,058 sq. ft.

ELEGANT HOMES

413

Tudor Style Has Old World Feel

Total Living Area: 3,420

- Master bedroom has cozy fireplace flanked by windows and a private bath
- Living and dining rooms adjoin for maximum convenience and versatility
- Special amenities include first floor library and second floor family room and study area
- 4 bedrooms, 3 baths, 2-car side entry garage
- Basement foundation

ELEGANT HOMES

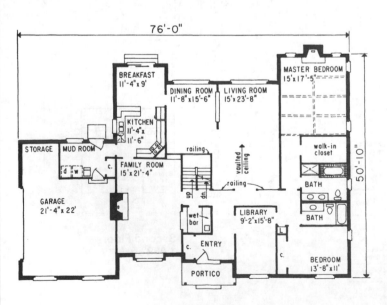

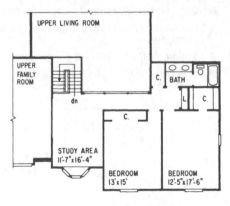

Second Floor
902 sq. ft.

First Floor
2,665 sq. ft.

Central Gathering Room

Total Living Area: 3,272

- Living room with fireplace accesses rear patio and wrap-around front porch
- Large formal dining room
- Master bedroom has walk-in closet and deluxe bath
- 4 bedrooms, 3 full baths, 2 half baths, 2 car side entry garage
- Basement, crawl space or slab foundation, please specify when ordering

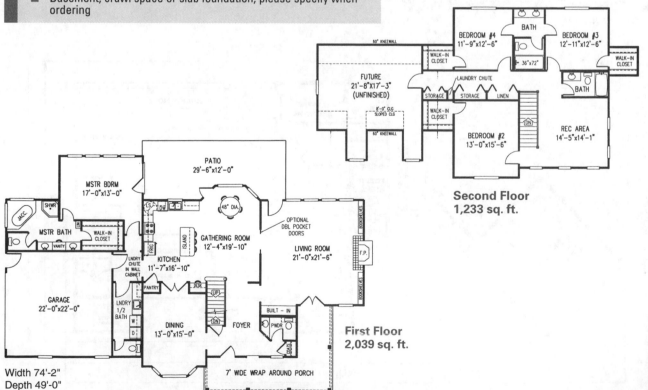

Second Floor
1,233 sq. ft.

First Floor
2,039 sq. ft.

Width 74'-2"
Depth 49'-0"

ELEGANT HOMES

Sprawling Ranch Design

Total Living Area: 2,421

- Charming courtyard on the side of the home easily accesses the porch leading into the breakfast area
- French doors throughout home create a sunny atmosphere
- Master bedroom accesses covered porch
- 4 bedrooms, 2 baths, optional 2-car garage
- Crawl space or slab foundation, please specify when ordering

ELEGANT HOMES

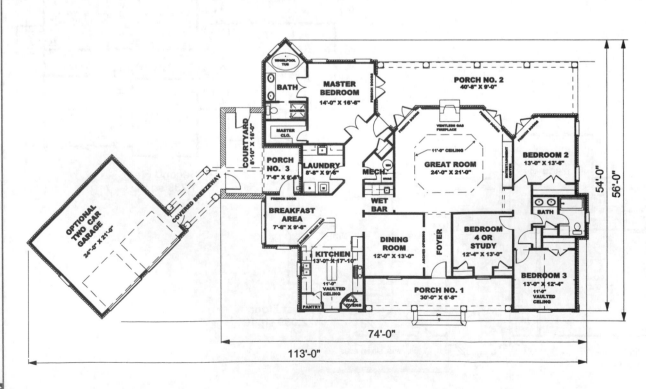

Plan# 577-0677

Price Code E

TO ORDER SEE **PAGE 608** OR CALL TOLL-FREE 1-800-DREAM HOME (373-2646)

Spacious Room Around A Central Foyer

Total Living Area: 3,006

- Energy efficient home with 2" x 6" exterior walls
- Large all purpose room and bath on third floor
- Efficient U-shaped kitchen includes a pantry and adjacent planning desk
- 4 bedrooms, 3 1/2 baths, 2-car side entry garage
- Basement foundation, drawings also include slab foundation

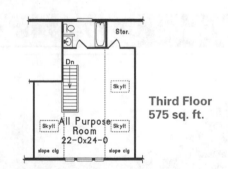

Third Floor
575 sq. ft.

All Purpose Room 22-0x24-0

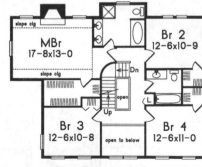

MBr 17-8x13-0
Br 2 12-6x10-9
Br 3 12-6x10-8
Br 4 12-6x11-0

Second Floor
1,138 sq. ft.

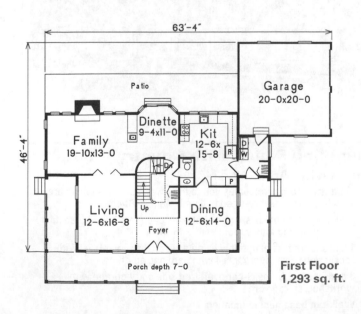

63'-4"
46'-4"
Patio
Family 19-10x13-0
Dinette 9-4x11-0
Kit 12-6x 15-8
Garage 20-0x20-0
Living 12-6x16-8
Dining 12-6x14-0
Foyer
Up
Porch depth 7-0

First Floor
1,293 sq. ft.

ELEGANT HOMES

Plan# 577-0338

Price Code E

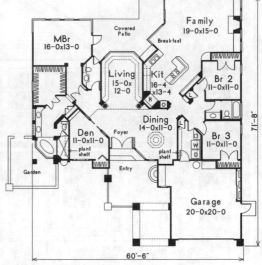

Fountain Graces Entry

Total Living Area: 2,397

- Covered entrance with fountain leads to double-door entry and foyer
- Kitchen features two pantries and opens into breakfast and family rooms
- Master bath features huge walk-in closet, electric clothes carousel, double-bowl vanity and corner tub
- 3 bedrooms, 2 1/2 baths, 2-car garage
- Slab foundation

Plan# 577-0748

Price Code D

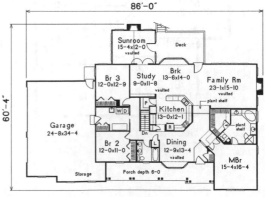

Rambling Ranch With Country Charm

Total Living Area: 2,514

- Expansive porch welcomes you to the foyer, spacious dining area with bay and a gallery-sized hall with plant shelf above
- A highly functional U-shaped kitchen is open to a bayed breakfast room, study and family room with a 46' vista
- 1,509 square feet of optional living area on the lower level with recreation room, bedroom #4 with bath and an office
- 3 bedrooms, 2 baths, 3-car oversized side entry garage with workshop/storage area
- Walk-out basement foundation

ELEGANT HOMES

Plan# **577-0713**

Price Code E

Double Atrium Embraces The Sun

Total Living Area: 3,199

- Grand scale kitchen features bay-shaped cabinetry built over atrium that overlooks two-story window wall
- A second atrium dominates the master bedroom which boasts a sitting area with bay window and luxurious bath, which has whirlpool tub open to the garden atrium and lower level study
- 3 bedrooms, 2 1/2 baths, 3-car side entry garage
- Walk-out basement foundation

Rear View

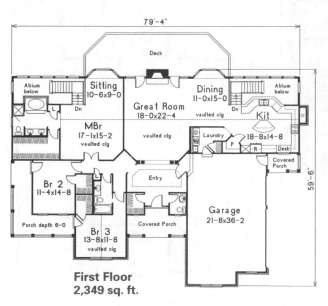

79'-4"

Deck

| Atrium below | Sitting 10-6x9-0 | | Dining 11-0x15-0 | Atrium below |

Great Room 18-0x22-4
vaulted clg

MBr 17-1x15-2
vaulted clg

Kit 18-8x14-8

vaulted clg

Laundry

Desk

Covered Porch

Entry

Br 2 11-4x14-8

Porch depth 6-0

Br 3 13-8x11-8
vaulted clg

Covered Porch

Garage 21-8x36-2

59'-6"

First Floor
2,349 sq. ft.

Lower Level
850 sq. ft.

Up

Up

Study 16-7x21-4

Unfinished Basement

Family Room 18-4x19-4

ELEGANT HOMES

Plan# **577-0738**

Price Code G

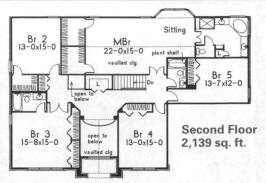

Br 2
13-0x15-0

MBr
22-0x15-0
vaulted clg

Sitting

plant shelf

Br 5
13-7x12-0

open to below

Br 3
15-8x15-0

open to below
vaulted clg

Br 4
13-0x15-0

Second Floor
2,139 sq. ft.

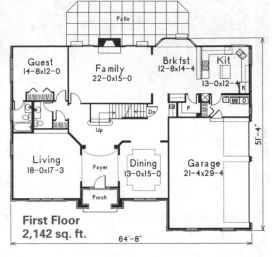

Patio

Guest
14-8x12-0

Family
22-0x15-0

Brk fst
12-8x14-4

Kit
13-0x12-4

Up

Living
18-0x17-3

Foyer

Dining
13-0x15-0

Garage
21-4x29-4

Porch

51'-4"

First Floor
2,142 sq. ft.

64'-8"

Elegance In A Five Bedroom Home

Total Living Area: 4,281

- The classic foyer with marble tile enjoys a two-story vaulted ceiling, a dramatic second floor balcony and views through a 6' x 9' elliptical window
- First floor features large-sized living, dining and family rooms plus a convenient guest bedroom
- Second floor master bedroom suite includes two huge walk-in closets, sitting room with bay window and luxury bath
- 5 bedrooms, 4 1/2 baths, 3-car side entry garage
- Basement foundation

Plan# **577-0721**

Price Code D

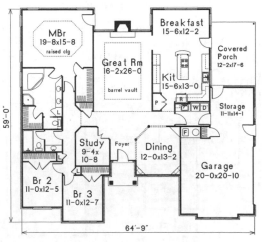

MBr
19-8x15-8
raised clg

Great Rm
16-2x26-0
barrel vault

Breakfast
15-6x12-2

Kit
15-6x13-0

Covered Porch
12-2x17-6

Storage
11-1Ix14-1

Study
9-4x
10-8

Foyer

Dining
12-0x13-2

Garage
20-0x20-10

Br 2
11-0x12-5

Br 3
11-0x12-7

59'-0"

64'-9"

Well-Designed Plan Has Many Extras

Total Living Area: 2,437

- Spacious breakfast area with access to the covered porch is adjacent to kitchen and great room
- Dining area has columned entrance and built-in corner cabinets
- Cozy study has handsome double-door entrance off a large foyer
- Raised ceiling and lots of windows in master suite create a spacious, open feel
- 3 bedrooms, 2 baths, 2-car side entry garage
- Slab foundation, drawings also include crawl space foundation

Brick Ranch Has It All

Total Living Area: 2,671

- Spacious master suite has luxurious bath with whirlpool tub, oversized shower and walk-in closet
- Great room and breakfast room both access the grilling porch perfect for entertaining
- Laundry room is conveniently located near all secondary bedrooms
- 4 bedrooms, 2 1/2 baths, 2-car side entry garage
- Crawl space or slab foundation, please specify when ordering

ELEGANT HOMES

Plan # 577-0351

Price Code F

Second Floor
1,620 sq. ft.

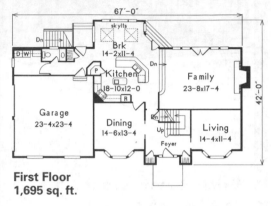

First Floor
1,695 sq. ft.

Two-Story Sunken Family Room

Total Living Area: 3,315

- Island kitchen, breakfast room and two-story sunken family room combine for convenient family dining or entertaining
- Two-story foyer opens into bay windowed formal dining and living rooms
- Master bedroom features sitting area, double walk-in closets and a deluxe bath
- 4 bedrooms, 3 1/2 baths, 2-car side entry garage
- Basement foundation

Plan # 577-0319

Price Code F

First Floor
2,436 sq. ft.

Spectacular View From The Great Room

Total Living Area: 3,796

- Entry foyer leads directly to great room with fireplace and wonderful view through wall of windows
- Kitchen and breakfast room feature a large island cooktop, pantry and easy access outdoors
- Master bedroom includes vaulted ceiling and pocket door entrance into master bath that features double-bowl vanity and large tub
- 4 bedrooms, 3 1/2 baths, 2-car garage
- Basement foundation

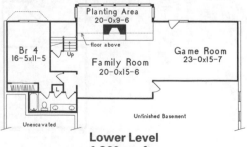

Lower Level
1,360 sq. ft.

ELEGANT HOMES

TO ORDER SEE **PAGE 608** OR CALL TOLL-FREE 1-800-DREAM HOME (373-2646)

Handsome Facade, Spacious Living

Total Living Area: 2,396

- Generously wide entry welcomes guests
- Central living area with a 12' ceiling and large fireplace serves as a convenient traffic hub
- Kitchen is secluded, yet has easy access to the living, dining and breakfast areas
- Deluxe master bedroom suite has a walk-in closet, oversized tub, shower and other amenities
- Energy efficient home with 2" x 6" exterior walls
- 4 bedrooms, 2 baths, 2-car garage
- Slab foundation, drawings also include basement and crawl space foundations

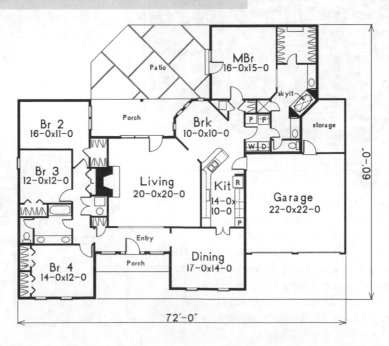

ELEGANT HOMES

Plan# 577-0405

Price Code F

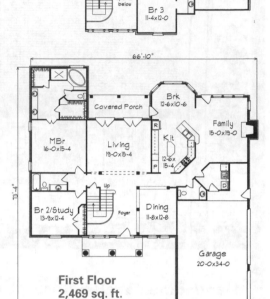

Second Floor 1,025 sq. ft.

Br 4 12-6x16-0

open to below

Balcony

Game Rm 14-6x17-4

open to below

Br 3 11-4x12-0

First Floor 2,469 sq. ft.

66'-10"

Covered Porch

Brk 12-6x10-6

Family 15-0x19-0

MBr 16-0x15-4

Living 19-0x15-4

Kit 12-6x 15-4

73'-4"

Br 2/Study 13-9x12-4

Foyer

Dining 11-8x12-8

Garage 20-0x34-0

Striking Double Arched Entry

Total Living Area: 3,494

- Majestic two-story foyer opens into living and dining rooms, both framed by arched columns
- Balcony overlooks large living area featuring French doors to covered porch
- Luxurious master suite
- Convenient game room supports lots of activities
- 4 bedrooms, 3 1/2 baths, 3-car side entry garage
- Slab foundation, drawings also include crawl space foundation

---

Plan# 577-0236

Price Code F

sloped clg

open to below

Br 2 13-5x13-0

Balcony 11-6x9-7

Dn

Br 3 13-5x11-1

Br 4 11-4x11-11

open

Second Floor 983 sq. ft.

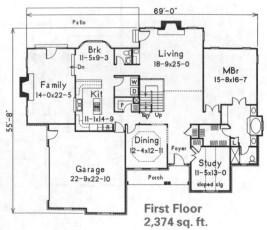

69'-0"

Patio

Brk 11-5x9-3

Living 18-9x25-0

MBr 15-8x16-7

Family 14-0x22-5

Kit 11-1x14-9

55'-8"

Dining 12-4x12-11

Foyer

Garage 22-9x22-10

Porch

Study 11-5x13-0

sloped clg

First Floor 2,374 sq. ft.

Elegant Entrance

Total Living Area: 3,357

- Attractive balcony overlooks entry foyer and living area
- Balcony area could easily convert to a fifth bedroom
- Spacious kitchen also opens into sunken family room with a fireplace
- First floor master suite boasts large walk-in closet and dressing area
- Central laundry room with laundry chute from second floor
- 4 bedrooms, 2 full baths, 2 half baths, 2-car side entry garage
- Basement foundation, drawings also include crawl space and slab foundations

ELEGANT HOMES

Duo Atrium For Fantastic Views

Total Living Area: 2,125

- A cozy porch leads to the vaulted great room with fireplace through the entry which has a walk-in closet and bath

- Large and well-arranged kitchen offers spectacular views from its cantilevered sink cabinetry through a two-story atrium window wall

- Master bedroom boasts a sitting room, large walk-in closet and bath with garden tub overhanging a brightly lit atrium

- 1,047 square feet of optional living area on the lower level featuring a study and family room with walk-in bar and full bath below the kitchen

- 3 bedrooms, 2 1/2 baths, 2-car side entry garage

- Walk-out basement foundation

TO ORDER SEE **PAGE 608** OR CALL TOLL-FREE 1-800-DREAM HOME (373-2646)

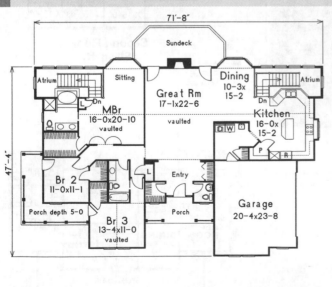

First Floor
2,125 sq. ft.

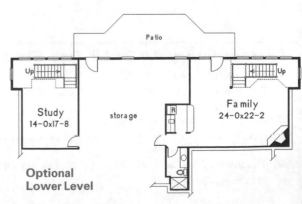

Optional
Lower Level

ELEGANT HOMES

Plan# 577-CHD-30-49

Price Code E

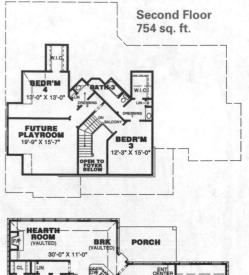

Second Floor
754 sq. ft.

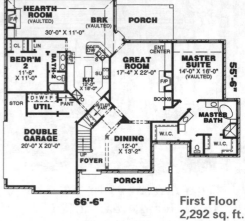

First Floor
2,292 sq. ft.

Stylish And Functional

Total Living Area: 3,046

- Secluded hearth room is tucked away from main living areas creating a cozy feeling
- Master suite maintains lots of privacy and has a luxurious feel
- Future playroom on the second floor has an additional 298 square feet of living area
- 4 bedrooms, 3 baths, 2-car side entry garage
- Slab foundation

Plan# 577-CHD-40-10

Price Code F

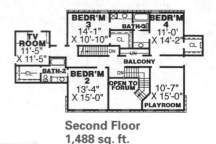

Second Floor
1,488 sq. ft.

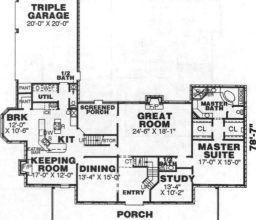

First Floor
2,570 sq. ft.

Extraordinary All Brick Two-Story

Total Living Area: 4,058

- T.V. room on the second floor is secluded so not to disturb the bedrooms
- Screened porch is a relaxing escape
- Keeping room directly off kitchen has a cozy fireplace warming these casual living areas
- 4 bedrooms, 3 full baths, 2 half baths, 3-car side entry garage
- Slab foundation

ELEGANT HOMES

Atrium Ranch With True Pizzazz

Total Living Area: 2,397

- A grand entry leads to a dramatic vaulted foyer with plant shelf
- Great room has a 12' vaulted ceiling, atrium featuring 2 1/2 story windows and fireplace with flanking bookshelves
- Convenient sunroom and side porch adjoin the breakfast room
- 898 square feet of optional living area on the lower level with family room, bedroom #4 and bath
- 3 bedrooms, 2 baths, 3-car side entry garage
- Walk-out basement foundation

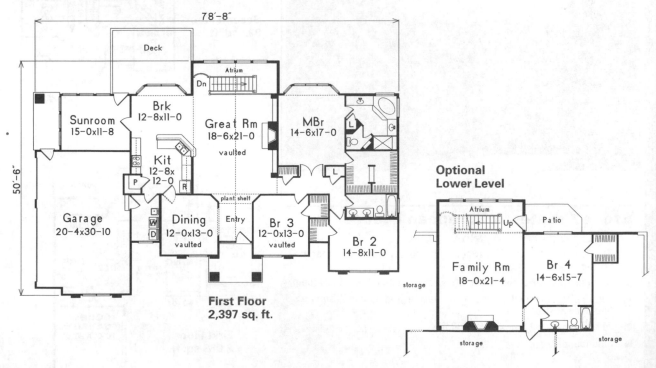

First Floor
2,397 sq. ft.

Optional Lower Level

ELEGANT HOMES

427

Plan#' 577-AP-2520

Price Code D

Grand Arched Entry

Total Living Area: 2,564

■ Hearth room is surrounded by kitchen, dining and breakfast rooms making it the focal point of the living areas

■ Escape to the master bedroom which has a luxurious private bath and a sitting area leading to the deck outdoors

■ The secondary bedrooms share a jack and jill bath and both have walk-in closets

■ 3 bedrooms, 2 1/2 baths, 2-car side entry garage

■ Basement, crawl space or slab foundation, please specify when ordering

Plan# 577-CHD-29-38

Price Code E

Second Floor
822 sq. ft.

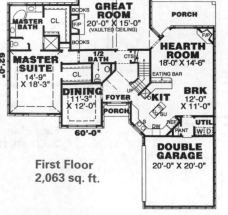

Stone Creates A European Feel

Total Living Area: 2,885

■ Spacious hearth room is warmed by corner fireplace and creates a terrific casual living area

■ Octagon-shaped second floor loft is big enough to be a family room

■ Future playroom on the second floor has an additional 302 square feet of living area

■ 3 bedrooms, 3 1/2 baths, 2-car garage

■ Slab foundation

First Floor
2,063 sq. ft.

ELEGANT HOMES

COPYRIGHT LARRY E. BELK

Striking Great Room

Total Living Area: 2,586

- Great room has impressive tray ceiling and see-through fireplace into bayed breakfast room
- Master bedroom has walk-in closet and private bath
- 4 bedrooms, 3 baths, 2-car side entry garage
- Basement, crawl space or slab foundation, please specify when ordering

WIDTH 64'-10"

DEPTH 61'-0"

First Floor
2,028 sq. ft.

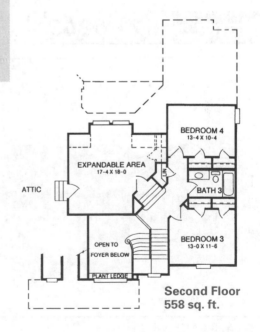

Second Floor
558 sq. ft.

ELEGANT HOMES

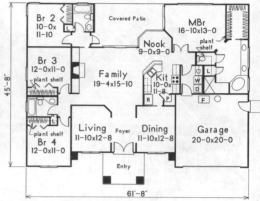

Stately Covered Front Entry

Total Living Area: 2,089

- Family room features fireplace, built-in bookshelves and triple sliders opening to covered patio
- Kitchen overlooks family room and features pantry and desk
- Separated from the three secondary bedrooms, the master bedroom becomes a quiet retreat with patio access
- Master bath has a walk-in closet and corner tub
- 4 bedrooms, 3 baths, 2-car garage
- Slab foundation

Grand-Sized Living

Total Living Area: 3,366

- Wonderful covered patio off secluded study and breakfast area
- Separate dining area for entertaining
- Spacious master suite has enormous private bath with walk-in closet
- 4 bedrooms, 3 1/2 baths, 2-car side entry garage
- Crawl space foundation, drawings also include slab foundation

ELEGANT HOMES

Plan# 577-HDS-3098

Price Code F

Stucco And Stone Home

Total Living Area: 3,947

- Master bedroom is ultra luxurious with private bath, enormous walk-in closet and sitting area leading to the lanai
- Vaulted family room has lots of windows and a corner fireplace
- Secluded study has double closets and built-ins
- Framing - only concrete block available
- 4 bedrooms, 4 baths, 3-car side entry garage
- Slab foundation

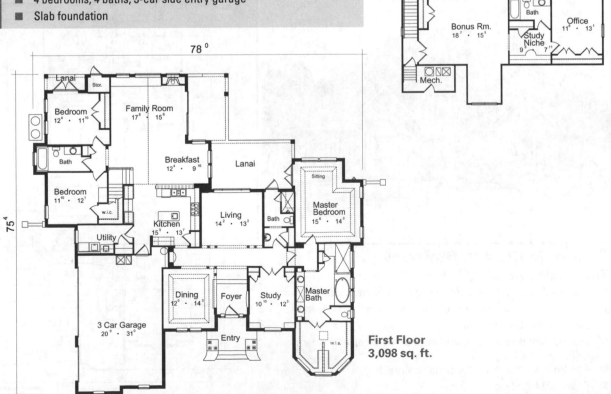

Second Floor
849 sq ft

Bonus Rm.
18⁷ · 15⁵

Bath

Office
11⁵ · 13¹

Study Niche
9³ · 7¹¹

Mech.

First Floor
3,098 sq. ft.

78⁰

75⁴

Lanai

Stor.

Bedroom
12⁴ · 11¹⁰

Family Room
17⁶ · 15⁶

Bath

Bedroom
11¹⁰ · 12¹

w.i.c.

Breakfast
12⁴ · 9¹⁰

Lanai

Utility

Kitchen
15³ · 13⁷

Living
14² · 13²

Bath

Master Bedroom
15⁶ · 14⁸

Sitting

Dining
12⁰ · 14⁴

Foyer

Study
10¹⁰ · 12³

Master Bath

3 Car Garage
20⁰ · 31⁰

Entry

ELEGANT HOMES

431

Plan# 577-0716

Price Code F

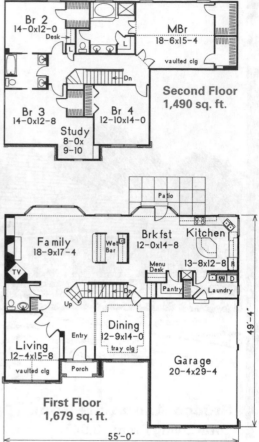

Second Floor
1,490 sq. ft.

First Floor
1,679 sq. ft.

Grandscale Elegance

Total Living Area: 3,169

- Formal areas include entry with handcrafted stairway and powder room, French doors to living room and dining area with tray ceiling
- Informal areas consist of a large family room with bay window, fireplace, walk-in wet bar and kitchen open to breakfast room
- Stylish master suite is located on second floor for privacy
- Front secondary bedroom includes a private study
- 4 bedrooms, 2 1/2 baths, 3-car side entry garage
- Basement foundation

Plan# 577-DBI-2332

Price Code F

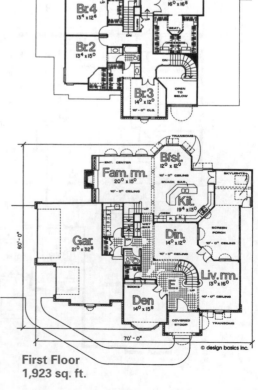

Second Floor
1,852 sq. ft.

First Floor
1,923 sq. ft.

Dramatic Curved Stairway

Total Living Area: 3,775

- Screened porch off living and dining areas brings the outdoors in
- Bookshelves flank each side of the fireplace in the family room
- Built-in bookshelves in den
- Second floor master suite has bayed sitting area and a wonderful bath
- 4 bedrooms, 3 1/2 baths, 3-car side entry garage
- Basement foundation

Second Floor Terrace

Total Living Area: 2,300

- Cozy fireplace in master suite
- 9' ceiling on first floor
- Energy efficient home with 2" x 6" exterior walls
- 3 bedrooms, 2 1/2 baths, 2-car side entry garage
- Basement foundation

TO ORDER SEE **PAGE 608** OR CALL TOLL-FREE 1-800-DREAM HOME (373-2646)

Second Floor
1,233 sq. ft.

First Floor
1,067 sq. ft.

ELEGANT HOMES

ARTLINE

See-Through Fireplace In Family Room

Total Living Area: 3,502

- 12' ceiling in dining room
- Interior column accents and display niches
- Living and family rooms share a see-through fireplace
- Master bath has a double walk-in closet
- 4 bedrooms, 2 full baths, 2 half baths, 3-car side entry garage
- Basement or crawl space foundation, please specify when ordering

Second Floor
782 sq. ft.

BEDROOM 3
15 X 9-8

OPEN TO BELOW

PLANT SHELF

BATH

BEDROOM 2
10-2 X 13

SEAT

LIN

VAULTED CEILING

BONUS ROOM
17-6 X 18-8

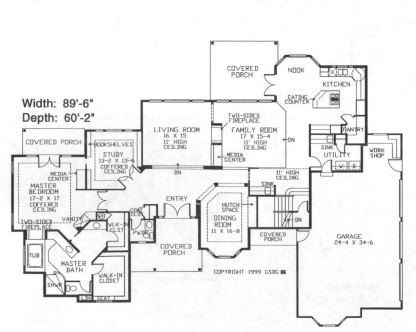

Width: 89'-6"
Depth: 60'-2"

COVERED PORCH

NOOK

KITCHEN

EATING COUNTER

COVERED PORCH

TWO-SIDED FIREPLACE

BOOKSHELVES

STUDY
13-2 X 13-6
COFFERED CEILING

LIVING ROOM
16 X 15
11' HIGH CEILING

FAMILY ROOM
17 X 15-4
11' HIGH CEILING

MEDIA CENTER

DN

PANTRY

SINK
UTILITY

WORK SHOP

MEDIA CENTER

MASTER BEDROOM
17-2 X 17
COFFERED CEILING

TWO-SIDED FIREPLACE

VANITY

WH

WLK-IN CLST

COAT CLS.

PWDR

ENTRY

DN

11' HIGH CEILING

SINK

DN

TUB

MASTER BATH

WALK-IN CLOSET

COVERED PORCH

HUTCH SPACE

DINING ROOM
11 X 16-8

COVERED PORCH

GARAGE
24-4 X 34-6

SHWR

LIN SEAT

COPYRIGHT 1999 GSDG

First Floor
2,720 sq. ft.

ELEGANT HOMES

Large Butler's Pantry

Total Living Area: 3,008

- Oversized rooms throughout
- Large kitchen area
- Future space above the garage has an additional 381 square feet of living area
- Spacious master suite with private bath and walk-in closet
- 3 bedrooms, 2 1/2 baths, 3-car side entry garage
- Basement, crawl space and slab foundation, please specify when ordering

Second Floor
1,315 sq. ft.

BEDROOM #3
11'-0"x12'-4"

MASTER BATH

MASTER BEDROOM
18'-0"x14'-10"

W.I.C.

FUTURE
18'-4"x18'-8"

LAUNDRY CHUTE

LINEN

BATH

BEDROOM #2
15'-0"x12'-5"

W.I.C.

PLANT SHELF

OPEN TO BELOW

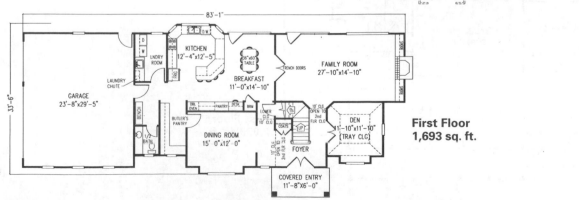

83'-1"

33'-6"

KITCHEN
12'-4"x12'-5"

LNDRY ROOM

LAUNDRY CHUTE

FAMILY ROOM
27'-10"x14'-10"

GARAGE
23'-8"x29'-5"

BREAKFAST
11'-0"x14'-10"

BUTLER'S PANTRY

PANTRY

1/2 BATH

DINING ROOM
15'-0"x12'-0"

COATS

DEN
11'-10"x11'-10"
(TRAY CLG)

FOYER

First Floor
1,693 sq. ft.

COVERED ENTRY
11'-8"x6'-0"

ELEGANT HOMES

435

Outdoor Living Created By Decks
Total Living Area: 3,149

- 10' ceilings on first floor and 9' ceilings on second floor
- All bedrooms include walk-in closets
- Formal living and dining rooms flank two-story foyer
- 4 bedrooms, 3 1/2 baths, 2-car detached garage
- Slab foundation, drawings also include crawl space foundation

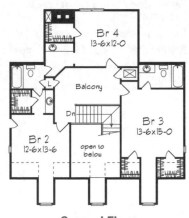

Second Floor
1,116 sq. ft.

Br 4
13-6x12-0

Balcony

Br 3
13-6x15-0

Br 2
12-6x13-6

Dn

open to below

66'-0"

40'-0"

Deck

Deck

Porch

Porch

Brk
13-8x9-0

Great Rm
23-6x17-6

Kit
13-6x
13-6

MBr
13-6x18-10

raised ceiling

Porch

Dining
12-6x15-6

Foyer

up

Living
13-6x12-8

Porch

Porch

First Floor
2,033 sq. ft.

E. Nelson
DESIGN GROUP, LLC

Varied Ceiling Heights

Total Living Area: 2,439

- Enter columned gallery area just before reaching family room with see-through fireplace
- Master suite has a corner whirlpool tub
- Double-door entrance into study
- 4 bedrooms, 3 baths, 2-car garage
- Slab, crawl space, basement or walk-out basement foundation, please specify when ordering

ELEGANT HOMES

Large Kitchen Is Centrally Located

Total Living Area: 2,731

- Isolated master bedroom with double walk-in closets, coffered ceiling and elegant bath
- Both dining and living rooms feature coffered ceilings and bay windows
- Breakfast room includes dramatic vaulted ceiling and plenty of windows
- Family room features fireplace flanked by shelves, vaulted ceiling and access to rear deck
- Secondary bedrooms separate from living areas
- 4 bedrooms, 3 1/2 baths, 2-car side entry garage
- Basement foundation

ELEGANT HOMES

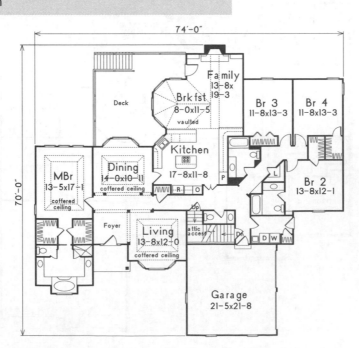

Plan# 577-0730

Price Code D

TO ORDER SEE PAGE 608 OR CALL TOLL-FREE 1-800-DREAM HOME (373-2646)

Mother-In-Law Suite

Total Living Area: 2,408

- Large vaulted great room overlooks atrium and window wall, adjoins dining room, spacious breakfast room with bay and pass-through kitchen
- A special private bedroom with bath, separate from other bedrooms, is perfect for mother-in-law suite or children home from college
- Atrium open to 1,100 square feet of optional living area below
- 4 bedrooms, 3 baths, 3-car side entry garage
- Walk-out basement foundation

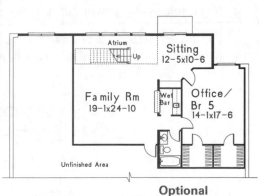

**Optional
Lower Level**

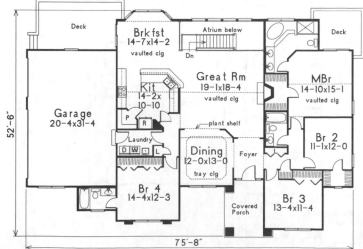

**First Floor
2,408 sq. ft.**

ELEGANT HOMES

439

Southern Elegance

Total Living Area: 2,669

- Nice-sized corner pantry in kitchen
- Guest bedroom located off the great room with a full bath would make an excellent office
- Master bath has double walk-in closets, whirlpool bath and a large shower
- 3 bedrooms, 3 1/2 baths, 2-car side entry garage
- Basement or slab foundation, please specify when ordering

ELEGANT HOMES

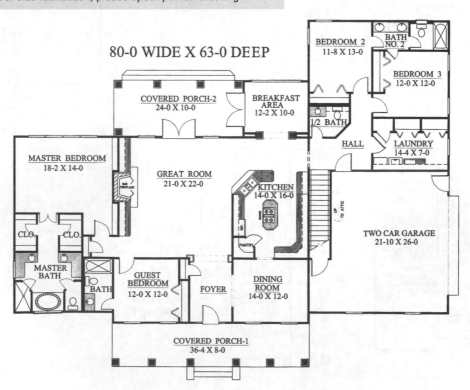

80-0 WIDE X 63-0 DEEP

Two-Story Solarium Welcomes The Sun

Total Living Area: 3,850

- Entry, with balcony above, leads into a splendid great room with sunken solarium
- Kitchen layout boasts a half-circle bar and cooktop island with banquet-sized dining nearby
- Solarium features U-shaped stairs with balcony and arched window
- Master suite includes luxurious bath and large study with bay window
- 5 bedrooms, 3 1/2 baths, 3-car garage
- Basement foundation

Interior View

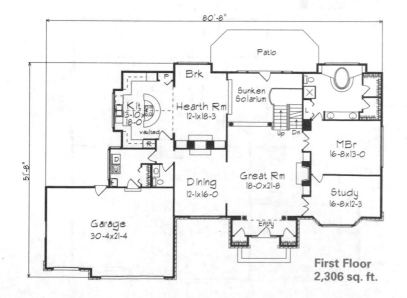

First Floor
2,306 sq. ft.

80'-8"
51'-8"

Patio

Brk

Kit
13-10x15-9
18-0

Hearth Rm
12-1x18-3

Sunken Solarium

MBr
16-8x13-0

Dining
12-1x16-0

Great Rm
18-0x21-8

Study
16-8x12-3

Garage
30-4x21-4

Entry

vaulted

Up   Dn

Second Floor
1,544 sq. ft.

Br 5
12-1x14-3

Sunken Solarium Below

Br 2
13-11x15-9

Loft

Dn

Br 4
12-1x12-0

Library
15-8x9-8

Br 3
15-5x12-0

open to below

ELEGANT HOMES

Ranch Has Luxurious Master Suite

Total Living Area: 2,523

- Entry with high ceiling leads to massive vaulted great room with wet bar, plant shelves, pillars and fireplace with a harmonious window trio
- Elaborate kitchen with bay and breakfast bar adjoins morning room with fireplace-in-a-bay
- Vaulted master bedroom features fireplace, book and plant shelves, large walk-in closet and double baths
- 3 bedrooms, 2 baths, 3-car garage
- Basement foundation

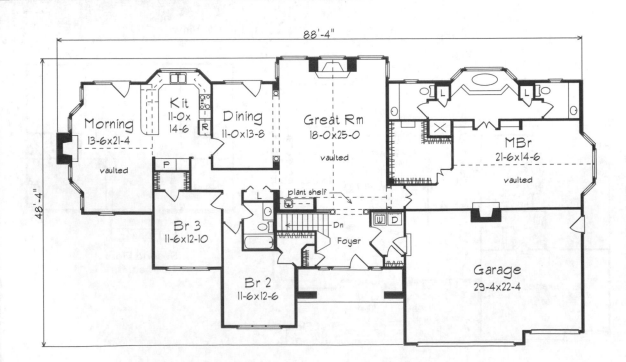

TO ORDER SEE **PAGE 608** OR CALL TOLL-FREE 1-800-DREAM HOME (373-2646)

Expansive Family Room

Total Living Area: 3,671

- 14' high entry ceiling with display niches
- 11'-9" ceiling in nook, den, dining and sitting rooms
- Kitchen has island eating counter, pantry and built-in desk
- Fireplace in master suite
- 3 bedrooms, 2 full baths, 2 half baths, 4-car garage
- Crawl space foundation

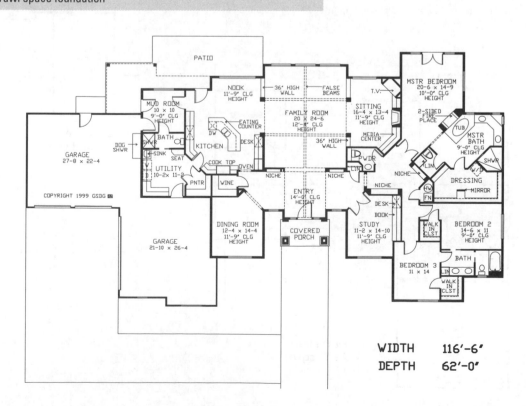

WIDTH   116'-6'
DEPTH   62'-0'

ELEGANT HOMES

TO ORDER SEE **PAGE 608** OR CALL TOLL-FREE 1-800-DREAM HOME (373-2646)

Comfortable Living

Total Living Area: 2,311

- Fireplaces warm master suite and family room
- Vaulted breakfast room near kitchen
- Formal living room near dining room
- Optional bonus room on second floor has an additional 425 square feet of living area
- 3 bedrooms, 2 1/2 baths, 2-car side entry garage
- Walk-out basement, slab or crawl space foundation, please specify when ordering

ELEGANT HOMES

61'-0"

65'-4"

Sitting Area

TRAY CLG.

Master Suite
17⁹ x 20⁰

PLANT SHELF ABOVE

Hers

Vaulted M.Bath

PLANT SHELF ABOVE

SHWR.

LINEN

His

K.S.

w. D.

Lqund.

Pwdr.

COATS

STAIRS TO OPT. BSMT.

FPL.

Vaulted Breakfast

VAULT

VAULT

VAULT

RANGE

DW.

Kitchen

REF.

PANTRY

PLANT SHELF ABOVE

PASS THRU

FRENCH DOOR

RADIUS WINDOW

Vaulted Family Room
16⁰ x 22⁶
15'-0" HIGH CEILING

VAULT

FPL.

LINEN

Bedroom 2
12² x 11⁶

Bath

Bedroom 3
11⁰ x 11⁰

COATS

ARCHED OPENINGS

Dining Room
12⁹ x 12⁸
15'-0" HIGH CEILING

Foyer
15'-0" HIGH CEILING

COVERED PORCH

Vaulted Living Room/ Opt. Bedroom 4
12⁵ x 12⁹

Garage
22⁵ x 21⁰

First Floor
2,311 sq. ft.

copyright © 1996 frank betz associates, inc.

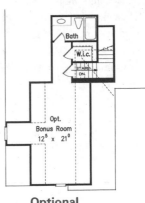

Bath

W.i.c.

STAIRS DN.

Opt. Bonus Room
12⁵ x 21⁰

Optional Second Floor

Countless Amenities Throughout

Total Living Area: 6,544

- Master bedroom has an octagon-shaped sitting area drenched in sunlight as well as a cozy fireplace
- A butler's pantry/wet bar connects the living room to the kitchen
- A circular staircase is accessible from the master sitting area to the second floor game room which features an oversized bar area with sink and a fireplace
- Framing - only concrete block available
- Bonus room on the second floor has an additional 453 square feet of living area
- 6 bedrooms, 6 full baths, 2 half baths, 3-car side entry garage
- Slab foundation

Second Floor
2,228 sq. ft.

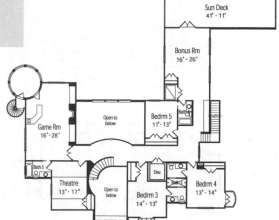

First Floor
4,318 sq. ft.

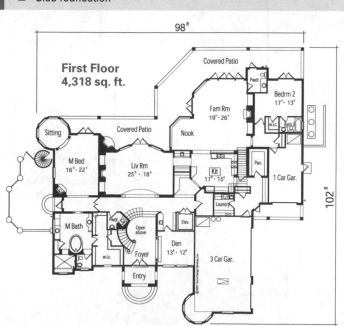

ELEGANT HOMES

445

Gables Add Interest To Facade

Total Living Area: 3,398

- Large built-in media center in family room perfect for relaxing
- Large and luxurious master bedroom features a beautiful bath
- Second floor library nook is a quiet retreat
- 4 bedrooms, 2 1/2 baths, 3-car garage
- Crawl space foundation

ELEGANT HOMES

Second Floor
1,577 sq. ft.

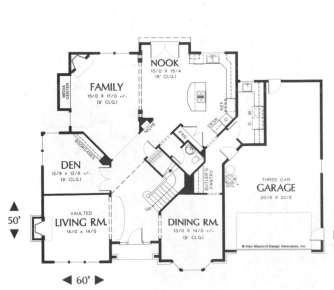

First Floor
1,821 sq. ft.

Plan# 577-FDG-8576-L

Price Code E

Private First Floor Master Suite

Total Living Area: 3,017

- Impressive two-story entry has curved staircase
- Family room has unique elliptical vault above window
- Master suite includes a private covered patio and bath with walk-in closet
- Breakfast area overlooks great room
- Bonus room on the second floor has an additional 234 square feet of living area
- 4 bedrooms, 3 1/2 baths, 3-car side entry garage
- Slab foundation

Second Floor
978 sq. ft.

First Floor
2,039 sq. ft.

ELEGANT HOMES

447

Sunny Sitting Area In Master Suite
Total Living Area: 2,545

- Beautiful covered front porch gives country appeal
- Open family room has 10' ceiling
- Kitchen has abundant counterspace
- 4 bedrooms, 2 1/2 baths, 3-car side entry garage
- Slab foundation

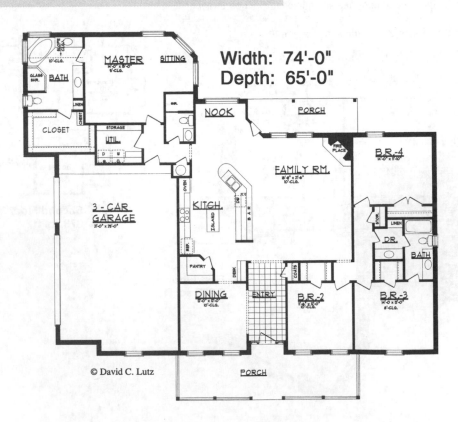

Width: 74'-0"
Depth: 65'-0"

© David C. Lutz

Lots Of Outdoor Living Area On Porches

Total Living Area: 2,775

- Oversized laundry room is ideal for family living and includes plenty of extra closetspace
- Kitchen and great room combine creating plenty of space for entertaining
- Cozy breakfast room is sunny and bright with lots of windows and double-doors to a screened porch
- 3 bedrooms, 3 baths, 2-car side entry garage
- Slab foundation

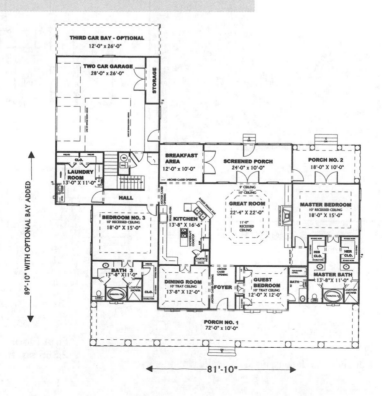

ELEGANT HOMES

Plan# 577-0445

Price Code F

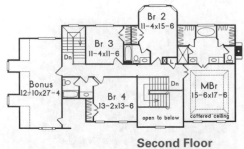

Second Floor
1,874 sq. ft.

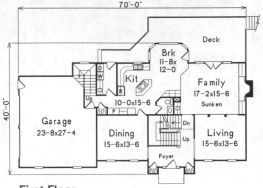

First Floor
1,553 sq. ft.

Stately Two-Story

Total Living Area: 3,427

- 10' ceilings on first floor
- Elaborate master bedroom features coffered ceiling and luxurious private bath
- Two-story showplace foyer flanked by dining and living rooms
- 4 bedrooms, 3 1/2 baths, 2-car side entry garage
- Basement foundation

Plan# 577-FD7507

Price Code F

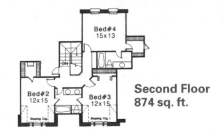

Second Floor
874 sq. ft.

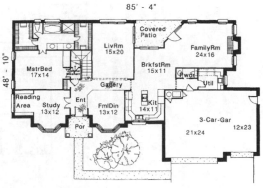

First Floor
2,365 sq. ft.

European Style Creates Elegant Facade

Total Living Area: 3,239

- Private study has a secluded reading area
- Casual family room has access to covered patio
- Gallery area is elegant and creates a formal atmosphere entering the living room
- 4 bedrooms, 3 1/2 baths, 3-car garage
- 9' ceilings on the first floor
- Basement, crawl space or slab foundations, please specify when ordering

ELEGANT HOMES

Lower Level Ideal For An In-Law Suite

Total Living Area: 4,380

- 11' ceilings on first floor and 9' ceilings on second floor
- Intricate porch details display one-of-a-kind craftsmanship
- Impressive foyer has curved staircase creating a grand entry
- Second floor bedroom accesses private balcony for easy outdoor relaxation
- Optional lower level has an additional 1,275 square feet of living area
- 4 bedrooms, 3 1/2 baths, 3-car drive under garage
- Walk-out basement foundation

Second Floor
1,406 sq. ft.

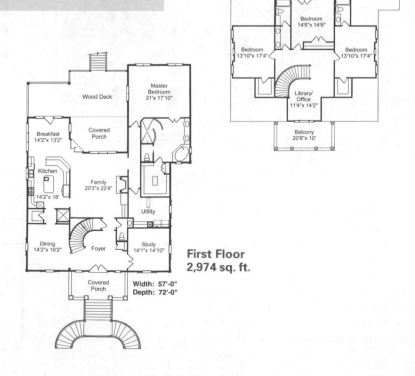

Optional
Lower Level

First Floor
2,974 sq. ft.

Width: 57'-0"
Depth: 72'-0"

ELEGANT HOMES

Plan# 577-0720

Price Code E

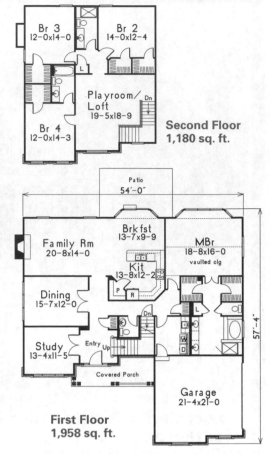

Second Floor 1,180 sq. ft.

First Floor 1,958 sq. ft.

Distinctive Two-Level Living

Total Living Area: 3,138

- Impressive stair descends into large entry and study through double-doors
- Private dining is spacious and secluded
- Family room, master suite and laundry are among the many generously-sized rooms
- Three large bedrooms, two baths and four walk-in closets compose the second floor
- 4 bedrooms, 3 1/2 baths, 2-car side entry garage
- Basement foundation

Plan# 577-0302

Price Code D

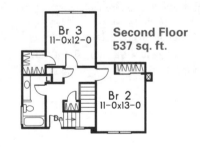

Second Floor 537 sq. ft.

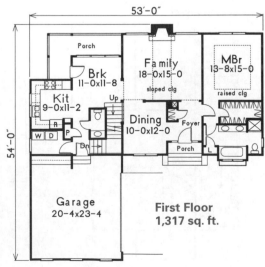

First Floor 1,317 sq. ft.

Stucco And Stone Add Charm To Facade

Total Living Area: 1,854

- Front entrance enhanced by arched transom windows and rustic stone
- Isolated master bedroom with dressing area and walk-in closet
- Family room features high, sloped ceilings and large fireplace
- Breakfast area accesses covered rear porch
- 3 bedrooms, 2 1/2 baths, 2-car side entry garage
- Basement foundation

ELEGANT HOMES

Plan# 577-0101

Price Code AA

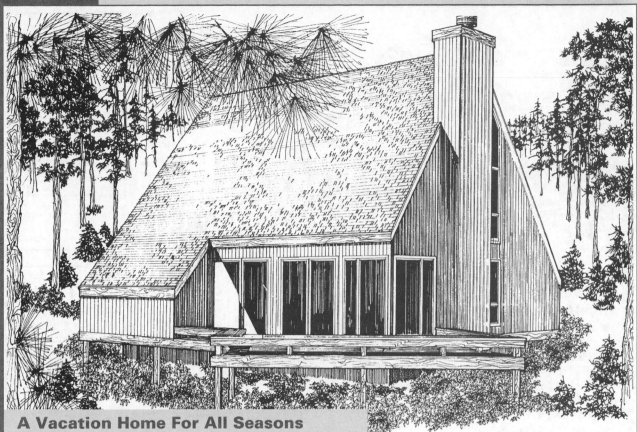

A Vacation Home For All Seasons
Total Living Area: 1,039

- Cathedral construction provides the maximum in living area openness
- Expansive glass viewing walls
- Two decks, front and back
- Charming second story loft arrangement
- Simple, low-maintenance construction
- 2 bedrooms, 1 1/2 baths
- Crawl space foundation

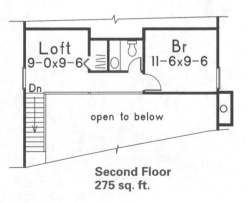

Second Floor
275 sq. ft.

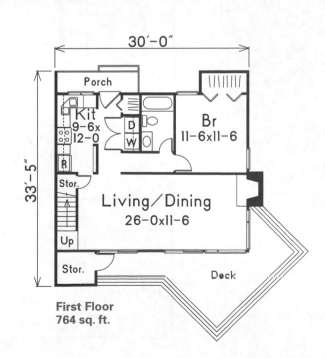

First Floor
764 sq. ft.

Plan # 577-SH-SEA-001

Price Code B

Second Floor 576 sq. ft.

br2 11'2 X 8'4

STORAGE

br3 11'2 X 8'5

OPEN TO BELOW

16'x11' **fam**

PATIO

First Floor 1,094 sq. ft.

43' (13.1m)

35'4 (10.8m)

VERANDAH

mbr 11'x13'10

ldr

VERANDAH

8'8 X 12'2

k

23'2x14'4 **liv**

9'10x10'10 **din**

VERANDAH

This Home Has Alpine Appeal

Total Living Area: 1,670

- Living and dining areas combine making an ideal space for entertaining
- Master bedroom accesses rear verandah through sliding glass doors
- Second floor includes cozy family room with patio deck just outside of the secondary bedrooms
- 3 bedrooms, 2 baths
- Crawl space foundation

Plan # 577-0475

Price Code B

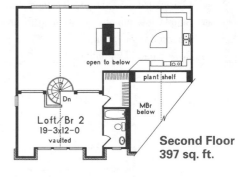

open to below

plant shelf

Dn

MBr below

Loft / Br 2 19-3x12-0 vaulted

Second Floor 397 sq. ft.

40'-0"

First Floor 1,314 sq. ft.

Deck

34'-0"

Great Rm 19-3x18-6 vaulted

Kit/Brk 17-3x 14-0

Up

Dn

Entry

MBr 13-7x14-7 vaulted

Porch

Ideal For Lake, Mountains Or Seaside

Total Living Area: 1,711

- Colossal entry leads to a vaulted great room with exposed beams, two-story window wall, brick fireplace, wet bar and balcony
- Bayed breakfast room shares the fireplace and joins a sun-drenched kitchen and sundeck
- Master bedroom has double entry doors, closets and bookshelves
- Spiral stair and balcony dramatizes a loft that doubles as a spacious second bedroom
- 2 bedrooms, 2 1/2 baths
- Basement foundation

VACATION

454

TO ORDER SEE PAGE 608 OR CALL TOLL-FREE 1-800-DREAM HOME (373-2646)

Abundance Of Walk-In Closets

Total Living Area: 1,474

- Kitchen and dining area include center eat-in island and large pantry
- Laundry facilities and hall bath are roomy
- Secondary bedrooms both have walk-in closets
- 3 bedrooms, 2 baths, 2-car detached garage
- Slab or crawl space foundation, please specify when ordering

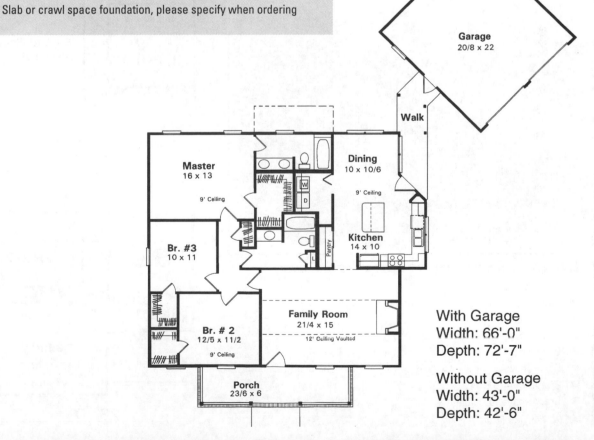

Garage
20/8 x 22

Walk

Master
16 x 13
9' Ceiling

Dining
10 x 10/6
9' Ceiling

Br. #3
10 x 11

Kitchen
14 x 10

W
D
Pantry

Br. # 2
12/5 x 11/2
9' Ceiling

Family Room
21/4 x 15
12' Ceiling Vaulted

Porch
23/6 x 6

With Garage
Width: 66'-0"
Depth: 72'-7"

Without Garage
Width: 43'-0"
Depth: 42'-6"

VACATION

455

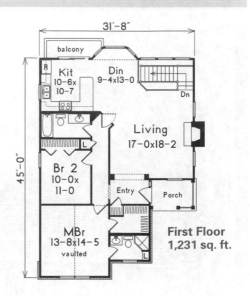

First Floor
1,231 sq. ft.

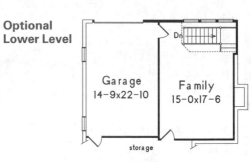

Optional
Lower Level

Atrium Living For Views On A Narrow Lot

Total Living Area: 1,231

- Dutch gables and stone accents provide an enchanting appearance
- The spacious living room offers a masonry fireplace, atrium with window wall and is open to a dining area with bay window
- A breakfast counter, lots of cabinet space and glass sliding doors to a walk-out balcony create a sensational kitchen
- 380 square feet of optional living area on the lower level
- 2 bedrooms, 2 baths, 1-car drive under garage
- Walk-out basement foundation

Plan# 577-0461
Price Code AAA

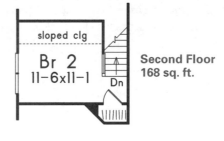

Second Floor
168 sq. ft.

First Floor
660 sq. ft.

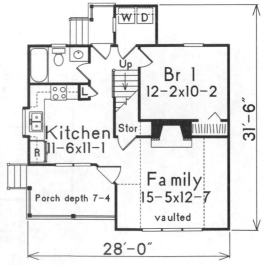

Cottage-Style, Appealing And Cozy

Total Living Area: 828

- Vaulted ceiling in living area enhances space
- Convenient laundry room
- Sloped ceiling creates unique style in bedroom #2
- Efficient storage space under the stairs
- Covered entry porch provides cozy sitting area and plenty of shade
- 2 bedrooms, 1 bath
- Crawl space foundation

VACATION

Ski Chalet With Style
Total Living Area: 1,680

- Highly functional lower level includes wet hall with storage, laundry area, work shop and cozy ski lounge with enormous fireplace
- First floor warmed by large fireplace in living/dining area which features spacious wrap-around deck
- Lots of sleeping space for guests or a large family
- 5 bedrooms, 2 1/2 baths
- Basement foundation

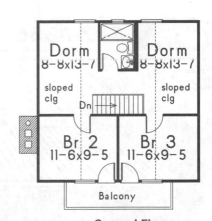

Second Floor
528 sq. ft.

Lower Level
576 sq. ft.

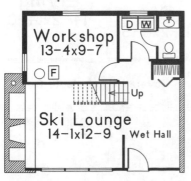

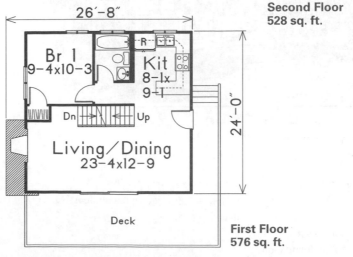

First Floor
576 sq. ft.

Plan# 577-DR-2160

Price Code AA

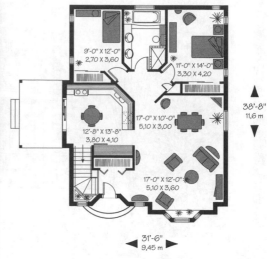

9'-0" X 12'-0"
2,70 X 3,60

11'-0" X 14'-0"
3,30 X 4,20

17'-0" X 10'-0"
5,10 X 3,00

12'-8" X 13'-8"
3,80 X 4,10

17'-0" X 12'-0"
5,10 X 3,60

38'-8"
11,6 m

31'-6"
9,45 m

Views Of Terrace From Dining Area

Total Living Area: 1,199

- Energy efficient home with 2" x 6" exterior walls
- Open living is ideal for entertaining
- Spacious kitchen has lots of extra counterspace
- Nice-sized bedrooms are separated by bath
- 2 bedrooms, 1 bath
- Basement foundation

Plan# 577-0696

Price Code AAA

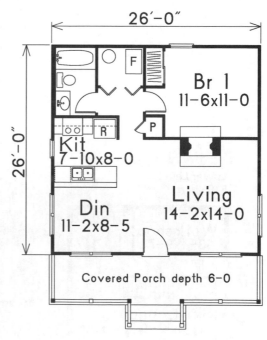

26'-0"

26'-0"

Br 1
11-6x11-0

Kit
7-10x8-0

Din
11-2x8-5

Living
14-2x14-0

Covered Porch depth 6-0

Small And Cozy Cabin

Total Living Area: 676

- See-through fireplace between bedroom and living area adds character
- Combined dining and living areas create an open feeling
- Full-length front covered porch perfect for enjoying the outdoors
- Additional storage available in utility room
- 1 bedroom, 1 bath
- Crawl space foundation

VACATION

TO ORDER SEE PAGE 608 OR CALL TOLL-FREE 1-800-DREAM HOME (373-2646)

English Cottage With Modern Amenities
Total Living Area: 1,816

- Two-way living room fireplace with large nearby window seat
- Wrap-around dining room windows create sunroom appearance
- Master bedroom has abundant closet and storage space
- Rear dormers, closets and desk areas create interesting and functional second floor
- 3 bedrooms, 2 1/2 baths, 2-car detached garage
- Slab foundation, drawings also include crawl space foundation

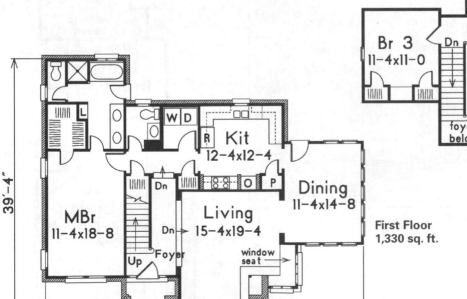

Br 3
11-4x11-0

balcony

Dn

Br 2
10-4x11-4

desk

foyer
below

Second Floor
486 sq. ft.

39'-4"

MBr
11-4x18-8

Kit
12-4x12-4

W D

R

Dn

O P

Dining
11-4x14-8

Dn

Living
15-4x19-4

Foyer

Up

window seat

First Floor
1,330 sq. ft.

47'-4"

Plan# **577-0693**

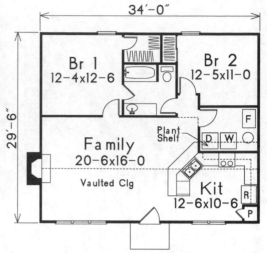

Ideal Home Or Retirement Retreat

Total Living Area: 1,013

- Vaulted ceiling in both family room and kitchen with dining area just beyond breakfast bar
- Plant shelf above kitchen is a special feature
- Oversized utility room has space for full-size washer and dryer
- Hall bath is centrally located with easy access from both bedrooms
- 2 bedrooms, 1 bath
- Slab foundation

Plan# **577-0243**

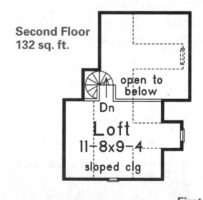

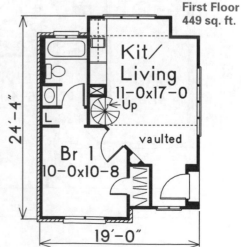

Dormers Accent This Vacation Retreat

Total Living Area: 581

- Kitchen/living room features space for dining and spiral steps leading to the loft area
- Large loft space can easily be converted to a bedroom or work area
- Entry space has a unique built-in display niche
- 1 bedroom, 1 bath
- Slab foundation

VACATION

Porch And Deck Allow Terrific Views

Total Living Area: 1,649

- Enormous two-story living room has lots of windows and a double-door access onto a spacious porch
- Master bedroom is separated from other bedrooms for privacy
- Well-organized kitchen has oversized counterspace for serving and dining
- 3 bedrooms, 2 baths
- Pier foundation

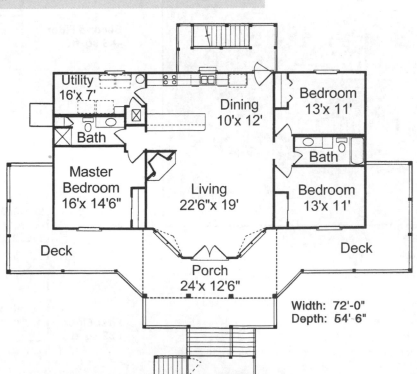

Width: 72'-0"
Depth: 54' 6"

VACATION

461

Second Floor
584 sq. ft.

26' (7.9m)

30' (9.1m)

First Floor
780 sq. ft.

Sensational Chalet

Total Living Area: 1,364

- First floor master bedroom is convenient to all living areas
- Large deck connects the first floor to the outdoors, while a lovely balcony connects the second floor
- Secondary bedrooms share a bath on the second floor
- 3 bedrooms, 1 1/2 baths
- Crawl space foundation

Plan# **577-N015**

Price Code A

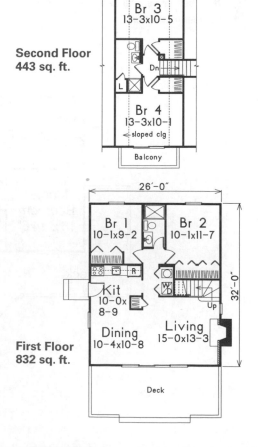

Second Floor
443 sq. ft.

26'-0"

32'-0"

First Floor
832 sq. ft.

Rustic Haven

Total Living Area: 1,275

- Wall shingles and stone veneer fireplace all fashion an irresistible rustic appeal
- Living area features fireplace and opens to an efficient kitchen
- Two bedrooms on second floor
- 4 bedrooms, 2 baths
- Basement foundation, drawings also include crawl space and slab foundations

VACATION

TO ORDER SEE **PAGE 608** OR CALL TOLL-FREE 1-800-DREAM HOME (373-2646)

An Open Feel With Vaulted Ceilings

Total Living Area: 1,470

- Vaulted breakfast room is cheerful and sunny
- Private second floor master bedroom with bath and walk-in closet
- Large utility room has access to the outdoors
- 3 bedrooms, 2 baths
- Basement, crawl space or slab foundation, please specify when ordering

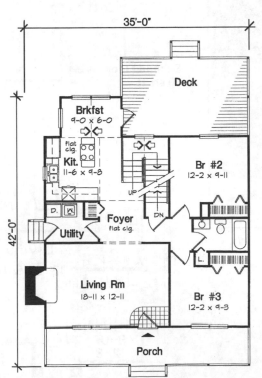

Rear View

First Floor plan (35'-0" × 42'-0"):
- Deck
- Brkfst 9-0 × 6-0
- Kit. 11-6 × 9-8 (Flat clg.)
- Br #2 12-2 × 9-11
- UP
- DN
- Foyer flat clg.
- Utility
- D.
- W.
- Living Rm 18-11 × 12-11
- Br #3 12-2 × 9-3
- Porch

First Floor
1,035 sq. ft.

Second Floor plan:
- open to below
- DN
- Master Br 14-3 × 12-11

Second Floor
435 sq. ft.

VACATION

463

Plan # 577-0650

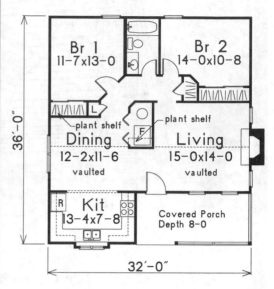

Br 1
11-7x13-0

Br 2
14-0x10-8

plant shelf   plant shelf

Dining
12-2x11-6
vaulted

Living
15-0x14-0
vaulted

Kit
13-4x7-8

R

Covered Porch
Depth 8-0

36'-0"

32'-0"

Quaint Cottage With Inviting Front Porch

Total Living Area: 1,020

- Living room is warmed by a fireplace
- Dining and living rooms are enhanced by vaulted ceilings and plant shelves
- U-shaped kitchen with large window over the sink
- 2 bedrooms, 1 bath
- Slab foundation

Plan # 577-0242

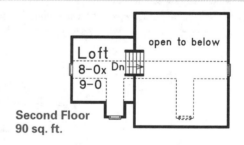

Loft
8-0x
9-0

Dn

open to below

**Second Floor
90 sq. ft.**

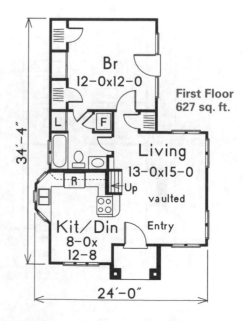

Br
12-0x12-0

L   F

**First Floor
627 sq. ft.**

Living
13-0x15-0
vaulted

Up

Kit/Din
8-0x
12-8

R

Entry

34'-4"

24'-0"

Stone Entry Provides A Unique Accent

Total Living Area: 717

- Incline ladder leads up to cozy loft area
- Living room features plenty of windows and vaulted ceiling
- U-shaped kitchen includes a small bay window at the sink
- 1 bedroom, 1 bath
- Slab foundation

TO ORDER SEE **PAGE 608** OR CALL TO

Cottage Retreat

Total Living Area: 960

- Cozy, yet open floor plan is perfect for a vacation getaway or a guest house
- Spacious kitchen features peninsula cooktop with breakfast bar that overlooks the large living room
- Bath is complete with laundry facilities
- Front deck is ideal for enjoying views or outdoor entertaining
- 2 bedrooms, 1 bath
- Crawl space foundation

VACATION

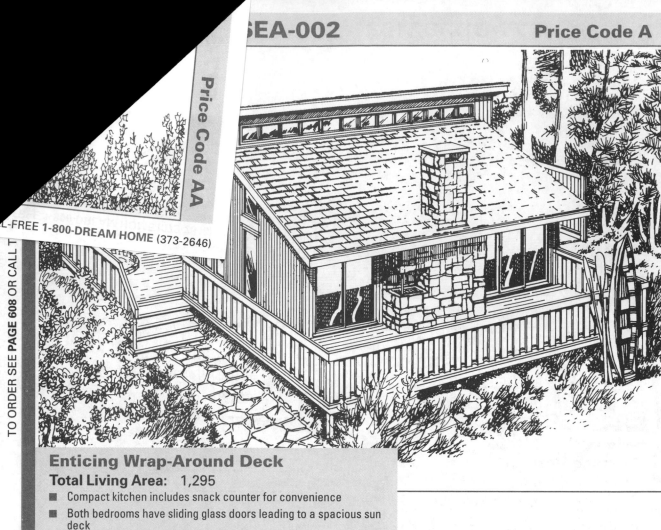

TO ORDER SEE **PAGE 608** OR CALL TOLL-FREE 1-800-DREAM HOME (373-2646)

Enticing Wrap-Around Deck

Total Living Area: 1,295

- Compact kitchen includes snack counter for convenience
- Both bedrooms have sliding glass doors leading to a spacious sun deck
- Vaulted living area is sunny and bright with double sliding glass doors accessing the outdoors
- 2 bedrooms, 1 bath, 1-car carport
- Crawl space foundation

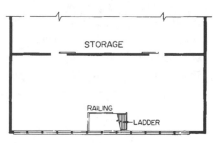

Second Floor
358 sq. ft.

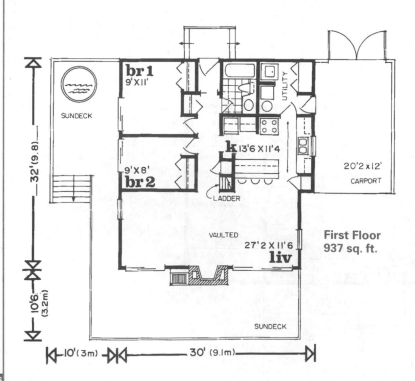

First Floor
937 sq. ft.

VACATION

Terrific Design Loaded With Extras

Total Living Area: 865

- Central living area provides an enormous amount of space for gathering around the fireplace
- Outdoor ladder on wrap-around deck connects top deck with main deck
- Kitchen is bright and cheerful with lots of windows and access to deck
- 2 bedrooms, 1 bath
- Pier foundation

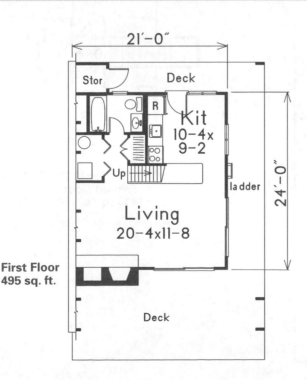

First Floor
495 sq. ft.

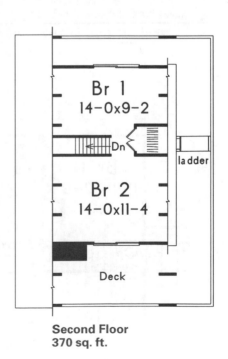

Second Floor
370 sq. ft.

Open Living Area

Total Living Area: 1,154

- U-shaped kitchen with large breakfast bar and handy laundry area
- Private second floor bedrooms share half bath
- Large living/dining area opens to deck
- 3 bedrooms, 1 1/2 baths
- Crawl space foundation, drawings also include slab foundation

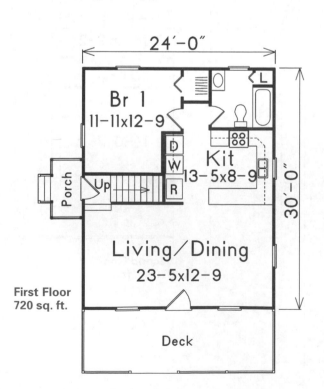

First Floor
720 sq. ft.

24'-0"

Br 1
11-11x12-9

Kit
13-5x8-9

Porch

Up

D
W
R

30'-0"

Living/Dining
23-5x12-9

Deck

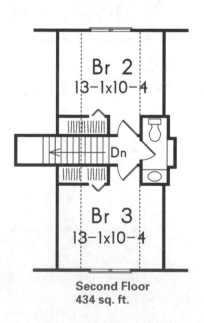

Br 2
13-1x10-4

Dn

Br 3
13-1x10-4

Second Floor
434 sq. ft.

Quaint Alpine Style
Total Living Area: 1,563

- Centrally located utility room
- Double sliding glass doors add drama to living room
- Plenty of storage throughout
- Master bedroom is located on second floor for privacy and includes amenities such as a private rear balcony, dressing area and bath with front balcony
- 3 bedrooms, 2 baths
- Basement, crawl space or slab foundation, please specify when ordering

Second Floor
419 sq. ft.

First Floor
1,144 sq. ft.

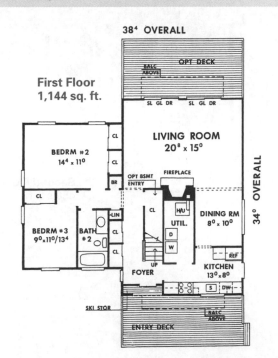

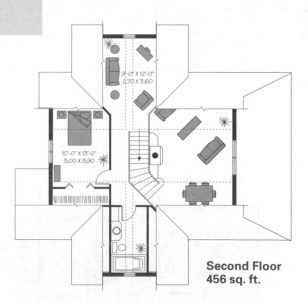

Covered Porch Adds Appeal

Total Living Area: 1,480

- Energy efficient home with 2" x 6" exterior walls
- Cathedral ceiling in family and dining rooms
- Master bedroom has walk-in closet and access to bath
- 2 bedrooms, 2 baths
- Basement foundation

Second Floor
456 sq. ft.

14'-8" X 12'-0"
4,40 X 3,60

14'-0" X 22'-8"
4,20 X 6,80

40'-0"
12,0 m

14'-8" X 12'-0"
4,40 X 3,60

First Floor
1,024 sq. ft.

32'-0"
9,6 m

9'-0" X 12'-0"
2,70 X 3,60

10'-0" X 13'-0"
3,00 X 3,90

VACATION

Breathtaking Balcony Overlook

Total Living Area: 1,299

- Convenient storage for skis, etc. located outside front entrance
- Kitchen and dining room receive light from box bay window
- Large vaulted living room features cozy fireplace and overlook from second floor balcony
- Two second floor bedrooms share jack and jill bath
- Second floor balcony extends over entire length of living room below
- 3 bedrooms, 2 baths
- Crawl space foundation, drawings also include slab foundation

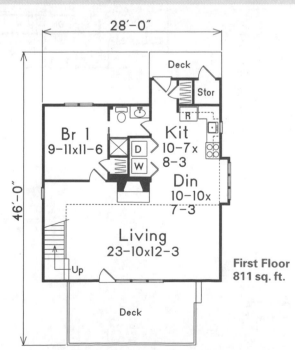

First Floor
811 sq. ft.

28'-0"
46'-0"

Deck
Stor
Br 1
9-11x11-6
Kit
10-7x
8-3
Din
10-10x
7-3
Living
23-10x12-3
Up
Deck

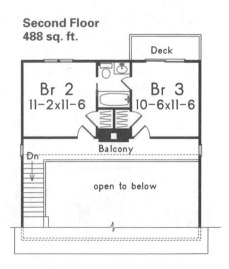

Second Floor
488 sq. ft.

Deck
Br 2
11-2x11-6
Br 3
10-6x11-6
Balcony
Dn
open to below

VACATION

TO ORDER SEE PAGE 608 OR CALL TOLL-FREE 1

Spacious A-Frame
Total Living Area: 1,769

- Living room boasts elegant cathedral ceiling and fireplace
- U-shaped kitchen and dining area combine for easy living
- Secondary bedrooms include double closets
- Secluded master bedroom with sloped ceiling, large walk-in closet and private bath
- 3 bedrooms, 2 baths
- Basement foundation, drawings also include crawl space and slab foundations

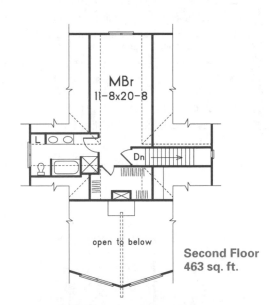

Second Floor
463 sq. ft.

MBr
11-8x20-8

open to below

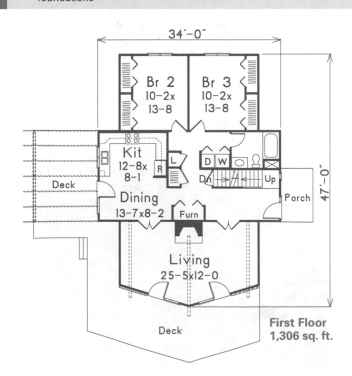

34'-0"
47'-0"

Br 2
10-2x
13-8

Br 3
10-2x
13-8

Kit
12-8x
8-1

Deck

Dining
13-7x8-2

Furn

Living
25-5x12-0

Porch

Deck

First Floor
1,306 sq. ft.

VACATION

472

Price Co

TO ORDER SEE **PAGE 608** OR CALL TOLL-FREE 1-8

Comfortable Home Has Character

Total Living Area: 1,482

- Energy efficient home with 2" x 6" exterior walls
- Corner fireplace warms living area
- Screened is spacious and connects to other living areas in the home
- Two bedrooms on second floor share a spacious bath
- 2 bedrooms, 1 1/2 baths
- Basement foundation

Second Floor
587 sq. ft.

First Floor
895 sq. ft.

36'-0"
10,8 m

12'-0" X 9'-0"
3,60 X 2,70

24'-8" X 12'-4"
7,40 X 3,70

11'-4" X 13'-8"
3,40 X 4,10

38'-0"
11,4 m

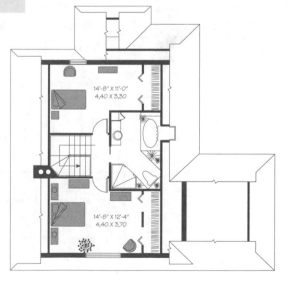

14'-8" X 11'-0"
4,40 X 3,30

14'-8" X 12'-4"
4,40 X 3,70

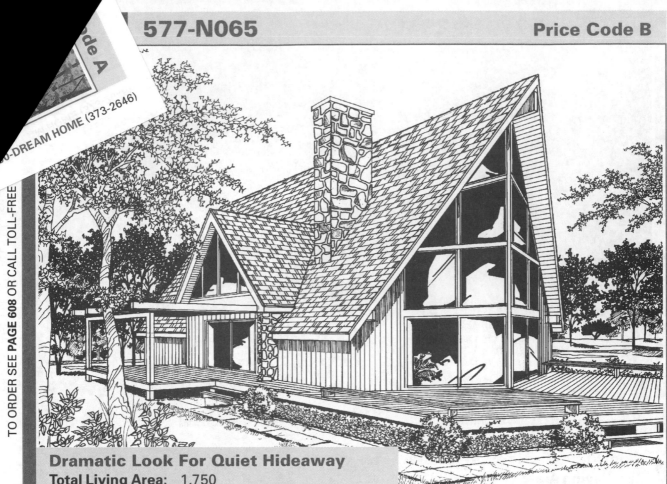

TO ORDER SEE **PAGE 608** OR CALL TOLL-FREE 0-DREAM HOME (373-2646)

Dramatic Look For Quiet Hideaway

Total Living Area: 1,750

- Family room brightened by floor-to-ceiling windows and sliding doors providing access to large deck
- Second floor sitting area perfect for game room or entertaining
- Kitchen includes eat-in dining area plus outdoor dining patio as a bonus
- Plenty of closet and storage space throughout
- 3 bedrooms, 2 baths
- Basement foundation, drawings also include crawl space and slab foundations

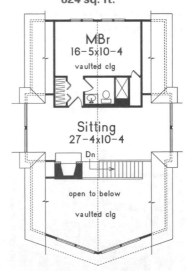

Second Floor
624 sq. ft.

MBr
16-5x10-4
vaulted clg

Sitting
27-4x10-4

Dn

open to below

vaulted clg

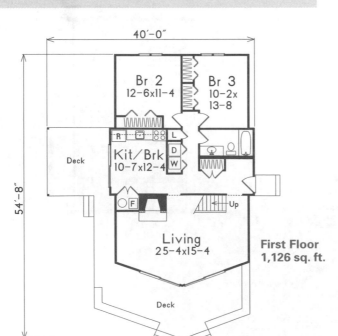

40'-0"

Br 2
12-6x11-4

Br 3
10-2x 13-8

Deck

Kit/Brk
10-7x12-4

54'-8"

Up

Living
25-4x15-4

First Floor
1,126 sq. ft.

Deck

Alpine Style Creates Cozy Cabin Feel

Total Living Area: 1,577

- Large living area is a great gathering place with enormous stone fireplace, cathedral ceiling and kitchen with snack bar nearby
- Second floor loft has half-wall creating an open atmosphere
- 3 bedrooms, 2 1/2 baths
- Crawl space foundation

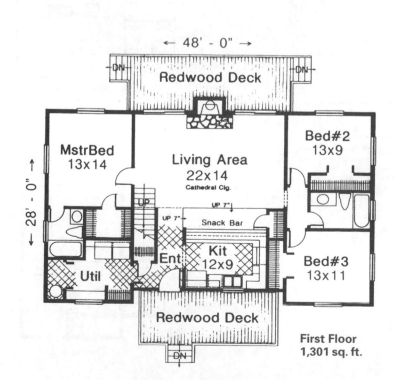

← 48' - 0" →

28' - 0"

Redwood Deck

DN

MstrBed
13x14

Living Area
22x14
Cathedral Clg.

Bed#2
13x9

UP

UP 7"

UP 7"
Snack Bar

Ent

Kit
12x9

Bed#3
13x11

Util

Redwood Deck

DN

First Floor
1,301 sq. ft.

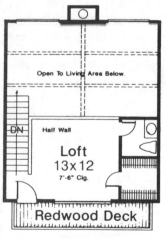

Open To Living Area Below.

DN

Half Wall

Loft
13x12
7'-6" Clg.

Redwood Deck

Second Floor
276 sq. ft.

VACATION

Roomy Vacation Retreat

Total Living Area: 2,652

- Multiple levels provide many areas for entertaining
- Oversized living room features enormous fireplace
- Large balcony ideal for admiring views
- Compact, yet efficient kitchen includes breakfast bar
- Plenty of closet space for sports equipment and patio furniture storage
- 3 bedrooms, 2 1/2 baths, 2-car garage
- Basement foundation

Second Floor
504 sq. ft.

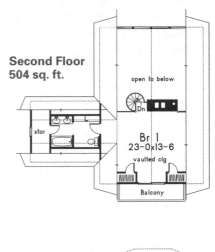

open to below

Dn

Br 1
23-0x13-6
vaulted clg

stor

Balcony

VACATION

First Floor
1,074 sq. ft.

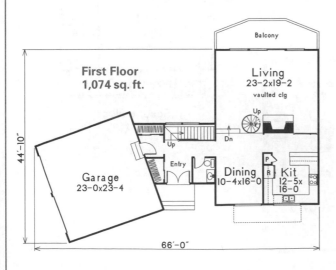

Balcony

Living
23-2x19-2
vaulted clg

Up

Up   Dn

Garage
23-0x23-4

Entry

Dining
10-4x16-0

Kit
12-5x
16-0

44'-10"

66'-0"

Lower Level
1,074 sq. ft.

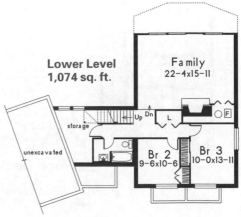

Family
22-4x15-11

storage

Up Dn   L

F

unexcavated

Br 2
9-6x10-6

Br 3
10-0x13-11

Screened Porch Adds To This Plan

Total Living Area: 1,496

- Energy efficient home with 2" x 6" exterior walls
- Great room includes oversized stone fireplace for cozy gatherings
- Second floor includes den/studio making an ideal home office
- 3 bedrooms, 2 baths, 1-car rear entry garage
- Basement, crawl space or slab foundation, please specify when ordering foundation

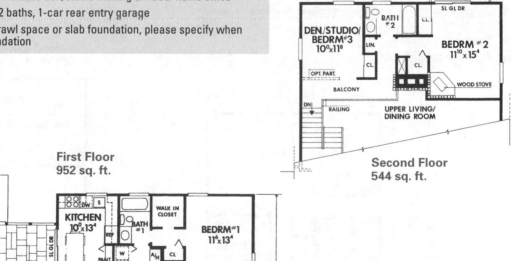

Second Floor
544 sq. ft.

First Floor
952 sq. ft.

VACATION

477

Unique Yet Functional Design

Total Living Area: 1,316

- Massive vaulted family/living room is accented with fireplace and views to outdoors through sliding glass doors
- Galley-style kitchen is centrally located
- Unique separate shower room near bath doubles as a convenient mud room
- 3 bedrooms, 1 bath
- Crawl space foundation

Second Floor
328 sq. ft.

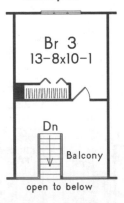

Br 3
13-8x10-1

Dn

Balcony

open to below

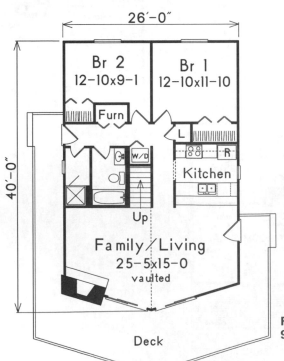

26'-0"

40'-0"

Br 2
12-10x9-1

Br 1
12-10x11-10

Furn

W/D

L

R

Kitchen

Up

Family/Living
25-5x15-0
vaulted

First Floor
988 sq. ft.

Deck

VACATION

TO ORDER SEE **PAGE 608** OR CALL TOLL-FREE 1-800-DREAM HOME (373-2646)

Bedrooms Separated From Living Areas

Total Living Area: 1,292

- Master bedroom has access to the outdoors onto deck and a private bath
- Prominent woodstove enhances vaulted living/dining area
- Two secondary bedrooms share a bath
- Kitchen has a convenient snack counter
- 3 bedrooms, 2 baths
- Crawl space foundation

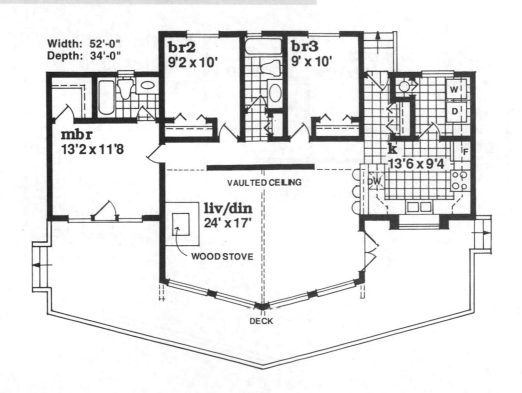

Width: 52'-0"
Depth: 34'-0"

br2
9'2 x 10'

br3
9' x 10'

W
D

mbr
13'2 x 11'8

k
13'6 x 9'4

F

DW

VAULTED CEILING

liv/din
24' x 17'

WOOD STOVE

DECK

VACATION

479

Home Designed For Outdoor Lifestyle

Total Living Area: 1,230

- Full-width deck creates plenty of outdoor living area
- The master bedroom accesses the deck through sliding glass doors and features a private bath
- Vaulted living room has a woodstove
- 3 bedrooms, 2 baths
- Crawl space or basement foundation, please specify when ordering

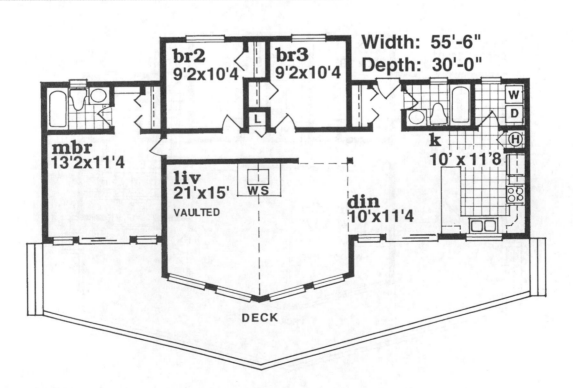

Width: 55'-6"
Depth: 30'-0"

br2 9'2x10'4

br3 9'2x10'4

mbr 13'2x11'4

liv 21'x15' VAULTED

W S

din 10'x11'4

k 10' x 11'8

W D H

L

DECK

VACATION

KURT KAUSS
ORLANDO

Contemporary Elegance With Efficiency

Total Living Area: 1,321

- Rear garage and elongated brick wall adds to appealing facade
- Dramatic vaulted living room includes corner fireplace and towering feature windows
- Kitchen/breakfast room is immersed in light from two large windows and glass sliding doors
- 3 bedrooms, 2 baths, 1-car rear entry garage
- Basement foundation

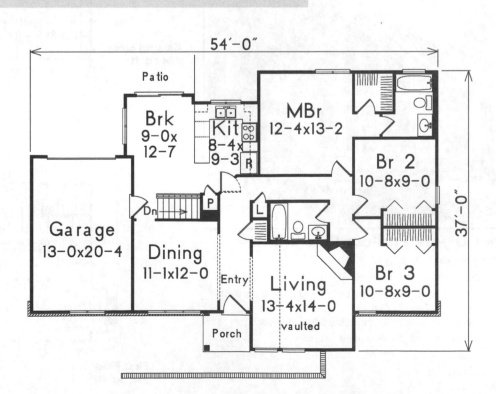

54'-0"

Patio

Brk
9-0x
12-7

Kit
8-4x
9-3

R

MBr
12-4x13-2

Br 2
10-8x9-0

37'-0"

Dn

P

L

Garage
13-0x20-4

Dining
11-1x12-0

Entry

Living
13-4x14-0
vaulted

Br 3
10-8x9-0

Porch

VACATION

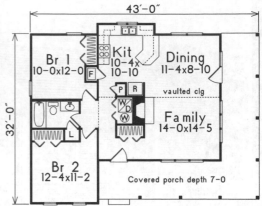

Vaulted Ceiling Adds Spaciousness

Total Living Area: 990

- Wrap-around porch on two sides of this home
- Private and efficiently designed
- Space for efficiency washer and dryer unit for convenience
- 2 bedrooms, 1 bath
- Crawl space foundation

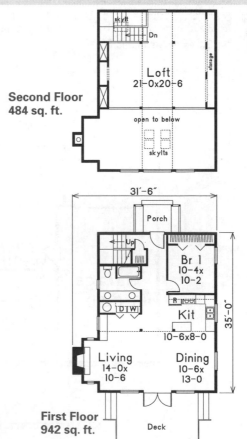

Second Floor 484 sq. ft.

First Floor 942 sq. ft.

Loft Area Offers Endless Possibilities

Total Living Area: 1,426

- Large front deck invites outdoor relaxation
- Expansive windows, skylights, vaulted ceiling and fireplace enhance the living/dining combination
- Nook, adjacent to the living room, has a cozy window seat
- Kitchen becomes a part of the living/dining area
- 1 bedroom, 1 bath
- Crawl space foundation

VACATION

Large Patio Adds Outdoor Appeal

Total Living Area: 1,056

- Energy efficient home with 2" x 6" exterior walls
- Unique fireplace becomes focal point in living and dining areas
- Three-season room off living area is cheerful and bright
- Galley-style kitchen is efficiently designed
- 2 bedrooms, 1 1/2 baths
- Basement foundation

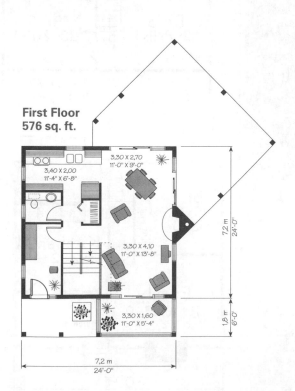

First Floor
576 sq. ft.

3,30 X 2,70
11'-0" X 9'-0"

3,40 X 2,00
11'-4" X 6'-8"

3,30 X 4,10
11'-0" X 13'-8"

3,30 X 1,60
11'-0" X 5'-4"

7,2 m
24'-0"

1,8 m
6'-0"

7,2 m
24'-0"

2,80 X 3,20
9'-4" X 10'-8"

3,20 X 4,90
10'-8" X 16'-4"

Second Floor
480 sq. ft.

VACATION

Plan# 577-DH-864G

Price Code AAA

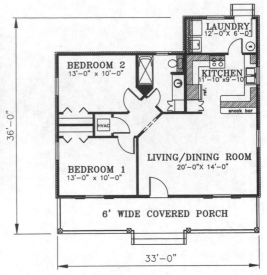

LAUNDRY
12'-0" X 6'-0"

BEDROOM 2
13'-0" x 10'-0"

KITCHEN
11'-10"x9'-10

HVAC

snack bar

BEDROOM 1
13'-0" x 10'-0"

LIVING/DINING ROOM
20'-0"X 14'-0"

36'-0"

6' WIDE COVERED PORCH

33'-0"

Charming Country Cottage

Total Living Area: 864

- Large laundry area accesses the outdoors as well as the kitchen
- Front covered porch creates an ideal outdoor living area
- Snack bar in kitchen creates a quick and easy dining area
- 2 bedrooms, 1 bath
- Crawl space or slab foundation, please specify when ordering

Plan# 577-0462

Price Code AA

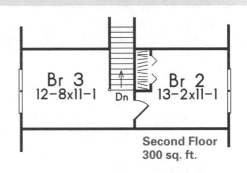

Br 3
12-8x11-1

Dn

Br 2
13-2x11-1

**Second Floor
300 sq. ft.**

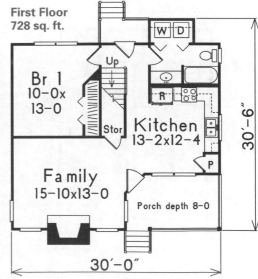

**First Floor
728 sq. ft.**

W D

Br 1
10-0x
13-0

Up

R

Stor

Kitchen
13-2x12-4

P

30'-6"

Family
15-10x13-0

Porch depth 8-0

30'-0"

Quaint Country Home Is Ideal

Total Living Area: 1,028

- Master bedroom conveniently located on first floor
- Well-designed bath contains laundry facilities
- L-shaped kitchen has a handy pantry
- Tall windows flank family room fireplace
- Cozy covered porch provides unique angled entry into home
- 3 bedrooms, 1 bath
- Crawl space foundation

VACATION

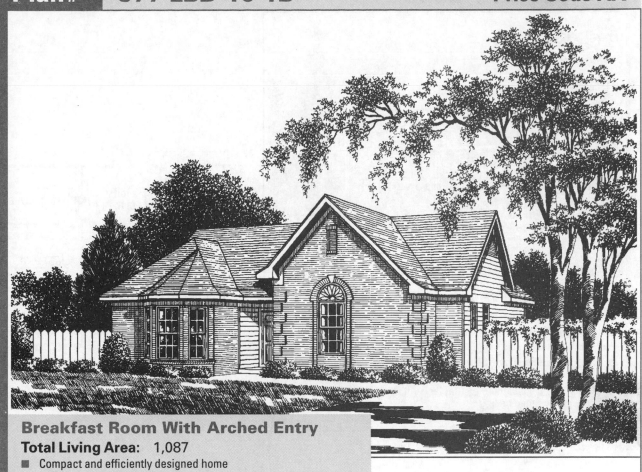

Breakfast Room With Arched Entry

Total Living Area: 1,087

- Compact and efficiently designed home
- Master bedroom separate from other bedrooms for privacy
- 10' ceiling in great room
- 3 bedrooms, 2 baths
- Slab or crawl space foundation, please specify when ordering

DOOR

STOR

BEDRM 2
10-0 X 10-0

BATH
2

MASTER
BATH

SHLV

GREAT ROOM
13-8 X 15-6
10 FT CEILING

BEDRM 3
10-0 X 10-0

DEPTH 42-2

ENTRY

PAN

COPYRIGHT   LARRY E. BELK

ARCH

KITCHEN
17-8 X 11-6

MASTER BEDRM
11-4 X 15-0

PORCH

BRKFST

WIDTH 35-10

VACATION

485

Plan# 577-0699

Price Code AA

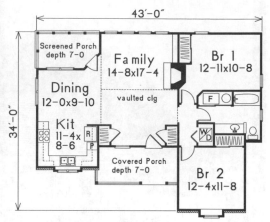

Comfortable Vacation Retreat

Total Living Area: 1,073

- Home includes lovely covered front porch and a screened porch off dining area
- Space for efficiency washer and dryer located conveniently between bedrooms
- Family room spotlighted by fireplace with flanking bookshelves and spacious vaulted ceiling
- 2 bedrooms, 1 bath
- Crawl space foundation

Plan# 577-N114

Price Code AAA

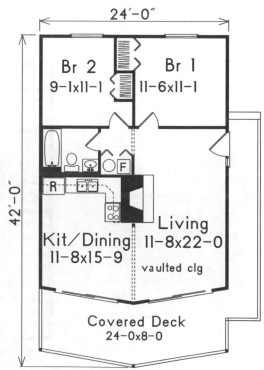

Riverside Views From Covered Deck

Total Living Area: 792

- Attractive exterior features wood posts and beams, wrap-around deck with railing and glass sliding doors with transoms
- Kitchen, living and dining areas enjoy sloped ceilings, cozy fireplace and views over deck
- Two bedrooms share a bath just off the hall
- 2 bedrooms, 1 bath
- Crawl space foundation, drawings also include slab foundation

VACATION

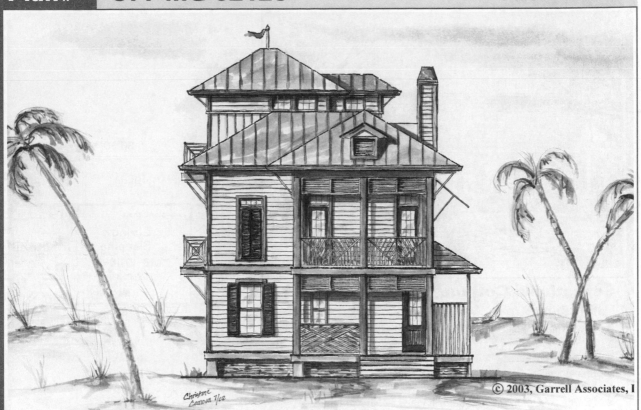

© 2003, Garrell Associates, I

Terrific Home For Views

Total Living Area: 2,136

- 9' ceilings on first floor, 10' ceilings on second floor and 9' ceilings on the third floor
- Unique third floor loft has space for sleeping as well as a balcony for enjoying views
- Open living areas allow plenty of space for entertaining
- Terrific master bedroom has private bath, cozy fireplace and two sets of double-doors leading onto covered porch
- 2 bedrooms, 3 1/2 baths
- Crawl space foundation

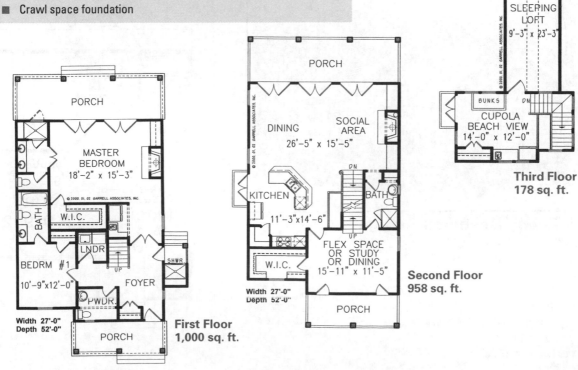

First Floor
1,000 sq. ft.

Width 27'-0"
Depth 52'-0"

Second Floor
958 sq. ft.

Width 27'-0"
Depth 52'-0"

Third Floor
178 sq. ft.

VACATION

487

Plan# **577-0658**

Price Code AAA

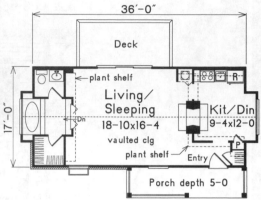

Sensational Cottage Retreat

Total Living Area: 647

- Large vaulted room for living/sleeping with plant shelves on each end, stone fireplace and wide glass doors for views
- Roomy kitchen is vaulted and has a bayed dining area and fireplace
- Step down into a sunken and vaulted bath featuring a 6'-0" whirlpool tub-in-a-bay with shelves at each end for storage
- A large palladian window adorns each end of the cottage
- 1 living/sleeping room, 1 bath
- Crawl space foundation

Plan# **577-N118**

Price Code AAA

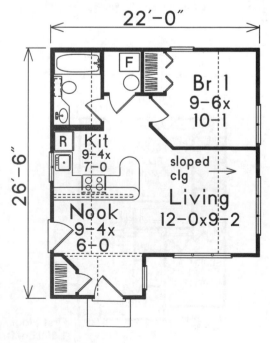

Graciously Designed Refuge

Total Living Area: 527

- Cleverly arranged home has it all
- Foyer spills into the dining nook with access to side views
- An excellent kitchen offers a long breakfast bar and borders the living room with free-standing fireplace
- A cozy bedroom has a full bath just across the hall
- 1 bedroom, 1 bath
- Crawl space foundation

VACATION

Appealing Lattice Detail And Brickwork

Total Living Area: 1,560

- Two-story master bedroom has sunny dormer above, large walk-in closet and private bath
- Great room has unique two-story ceiling with dormers
- Spacious kitchen has large center island creating a ideal work space
- 3 bedrooms, 2 1/2 baths
- Basement, crawl space or slab foundation, please specify when ordering

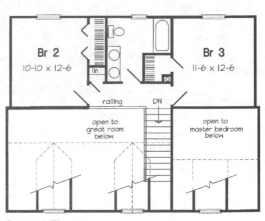

Rear View

First Floor
1,061 sq. ft.

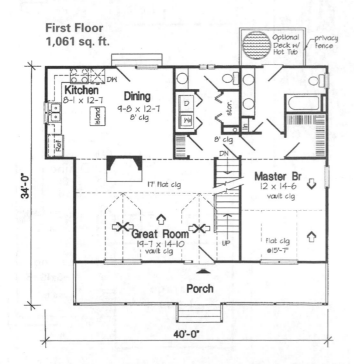

Optional Deck w/ Hot Tub
privacy fence

Kitchen
8-1 x 12-7

Dining
9-8 x 12-7
8' clg

Island

DW

Ref

D

W

stor.

8' clg

DN

Master Br
12 x 14-6
vault clg

17' Flat clg

Great Room
19-7 x 14-10
vault clg

flat clg
@15'-7"

UP

34'-0"

40'-0"

Porch

Br 2
10-10 x 12-6

Br 3
11-6 x 12-6

railing

DN

open to great room below

open to master bedroom below

Second Floor
499 sq. ft.

VACATION

489

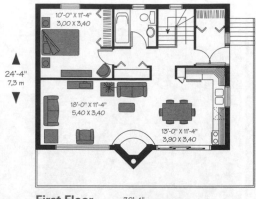

First Floor
787 sq. ft.

Lower Level
787 sq. ft.

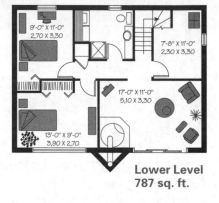

Enormous Fireplace Is The Focal Point

Total Living Area: 1,574

- Energy efficient home with 2" x 6" exterior walls
- Private bedroom on first floor has plenty of privacy
- Lower level has an additional living area which is convenient to secondary bedrooms
- 3 bedrooms, 2 baths
- Basement foundation

TO ORDER SEE **PAGE 608** OR CALL TOLL-FREE 1-800-DREAM HOME (373-2646)

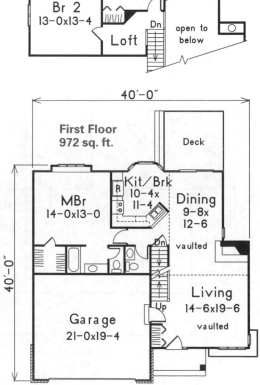

Second Floor
476 sq. ft.

Br 3
11-0x10-6

Br 2
13-0x13-4

Loft

Dn open to below

40'-0"

First Floor
972 sq. ft.

Deck

MBr
14-0x13-0

Kit/Brk
10-4x
11-4

Dining
9-8x
12-6

vaulted

Living
14-6x19-6

vaulted

Garage
21-0x19-4

Up

40'-0"

Vaulted Living With Corner Fireplace

Total Living Area: 1,448

- Dining room conveniently adjoins kitchen and accesses rear deck
- Private first floor master bedroom
- Secondary bedrooms share a bath and cozy loft area
- 3 bedrooms, 2 1/2 baths, 2-car garage
- Basement foundation

VACATION

Corner Windows Grace Library

Total Living Area: 1,824

- Living room features 10' ceiling, fireplace and media center
- Dining room includes bay window and convenient kitchen access
- Master bedroom features large walk-in closet and double-doors leading into master bath
- Modified U-shaped kitchen features pantry and bar
- 3 bedrooms, 2 baths, 2-car detached garage
- Slab foundation

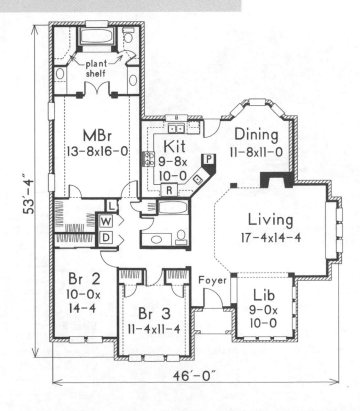

plant shelf

MBr 13-8x16-0

Kit 9-8x 10-0

Dining 11-8x11-0

Living 17-4x14-4

Br 2 10-0x 14-4

Br 3 11-4x11-4

Foyer

Lib 9-0x 10-0

53'-4"

46'-0"

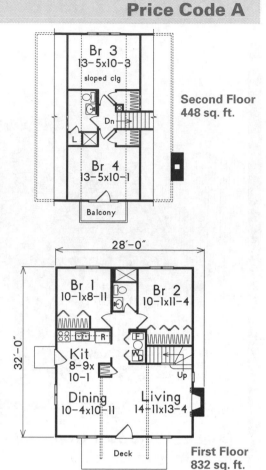

Second Floor
448 sq. ft.

First Floor
832 sq. ft.

A Chalet For Lakeside Living

Total Living Area: 1,280

- Attention to architectural detail has created the look of an authentic Swiss cottage
- Spacious living room including adjacent kitchenette and dining area, enjoy views to the front deck
- Hall bath shared by two sizable bedrooms is included on first and second floors
- 4 bedrooms, 2 baths
- Crawl space foundation, drawings also include basement and slab foundations

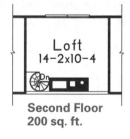

Second Floor
200 sq. ft.

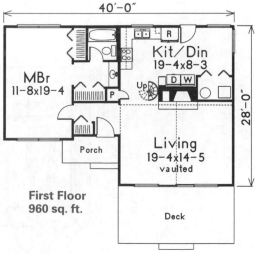

First Floor
960 sq. ft.

Large Master Bedroom Is Private

Total Living Area: 1,160

- Kitchen/dining area combines with laundry area creating a functional organized area
- Spacious vaulted living area has large fireplace and is brightened by glass doors accessing large deck
- Ascend to second floor loft by spiral stairs and find a cozy hideaway
- Master suite includes private bath and double closets
- 1 bedroom, 1 bath
- Crawl space foundation

TO ORDER SEE PAGE 608 OR CALL TOLL-FREE 1-800-DREAM HOME (373-2646)

Exciting Living For A Narrow Sloping Lot

Total Living Area: 1,200

- Entry leads to a large dining area which opens to kitchen and sun drenched living room
- An expansive window wall in the two-story atrium lends space and light to living room with fireplace
- The large kitchen features a breakfast bar, built in pantry and storage galore
- 697 square feet of optional living area on the lower level includes a family room, bedroom #3 and a bath
- 2 bedrooms, 1 bath
- Walk-out basement foundation

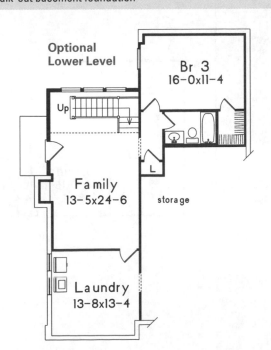

Optional Lower Level

Br 3
16-0x11-4

Up

Family
13-5x24-6

storage

L

Laundry
13-8x13-4

31'-8"

MBr
16-8x12-0

Atrium

Dn

48'-0"

Living
14-0x18-0

Br 2
10-11x 10-7

L

Porch

Kit
11-2x 13-4

Dining
10-6x11-4

R

P

First Floor
1,200 sq. ft.

VACATION

493

Plan# 577-SH-SEA-008

Price Code AA

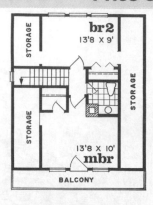

Second Floor
401 sq. ft.

Width: 24'-0"
Depth: 36'-0"

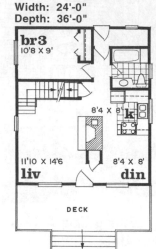

First Floor
672 sq. ft.

Chalet Cottage

Total Living Area: 1,073

- The front-facing deck and covered balcony add to outdoor living areas
- The fireplace is the main focus in the living room, separating the living room from the dining room
- Three large storage areas are found on the second floor
- 3 bedrooms, 1 1/2 baths
- Basement or crawl space foundation, please specify when ordering

Plan# 577-N064

Price Code AA

Clerestory Windows Enhance Facade

Total Living Area: 1,176

- Efficient kitchen offers plenty of storage, a dining area and a stylish eating bar
- A gathering space is created by the large central living room
- Closet and storage space throughout helps keep sporting equipment organized and easily accessible
- Each end of home is comprised of two bedrooms and full bath
- 4 bedrooms, 2 baths
- Crawl space foundation, drawings also include slab foundation

VACATION

TO ORDER SEE **PAGE 608** OR CALL TOLL-FREE 1-800-DREAM HOME (373-2646)

Truly Unique Design

Total Living Area: 2,104

- 9' ceilings on the first floor
- Living room opens onto deck through double French doors
- Second floor includes large storage room
- 3 bedrooms, 2 baths, 2-car garage
- Crawl space foundation

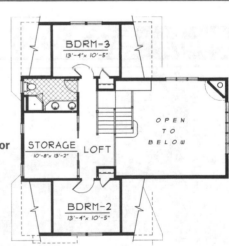

Second Floor
669 sq. ft.

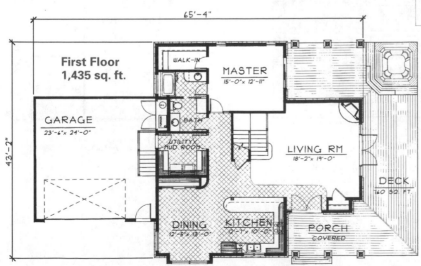

First Floor
1,435 sq. ft.

VACATION

Plan# **577-0653**

Price Code B

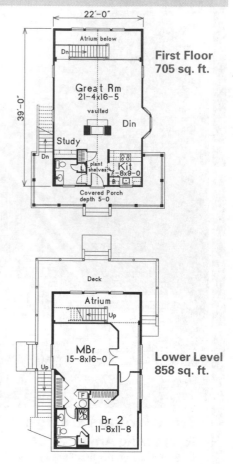

22'-0"

Atrium below

Dn

Great Rm
21-4x16-5

vaulted

Din

Study

Dn

plant shelves

Kit
8x9-0

39'-0"

Covered Porch
depth 5-0

**First Floor
705 sq. ft.**

Deck

Atrium

Up

MBr
15-8x16-0

Up

F

Br 2
11-8x11-8

L

**Lower Level
858 sq. ft.**

Irresistible Paradise Retreat

Total Living Area: 1,563

- Enjoyable wrap-around porch and lower sundeck
- Vaulted entry is adorned with palladian window, plant shelves, stone floor and fireplace
- Huge vaulted great room has magnificient views through a two-story atrium window wall
- 2 bedrooms, 1 1/2 baths
- Basement foundation

Plan# **577-N010**

Price Code AAA

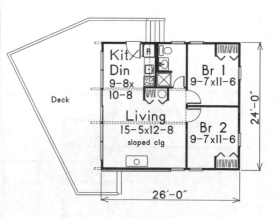

**Kit
Din**
9-8x
10-8

R

Br 1
9-7x11-6

Deck

Living
15-5x12-8
sloped clg

Br 2
9-7x11-6

24'-0"

26'-0"

Designed For Seclusion

Total Living Area: 624

- The combination of stone, vertical siding, lots of glass and a low roof line creates a cozy retreat
- Vaulted living area features free-standing fireplace that heats adjacent stone wall for warmth
- Efficient kitchen includes dining area and view to angular deck
- Two bedrooms share a hall bath with shower
- 2 bedrooms, 1 bath
- Pier foundation

VACATION

Skylights Brighten Living Area

Total Living Area: 1,487

- Kitchen has pass-through counter with space for dining
- First floor bedroom can easily be converted to a den with spacious walk-in closet and access to deck outdoors
- Second floor bedroom also has a private deck
- 3 bedroom, 1 1/2 baths
- Basement foundation

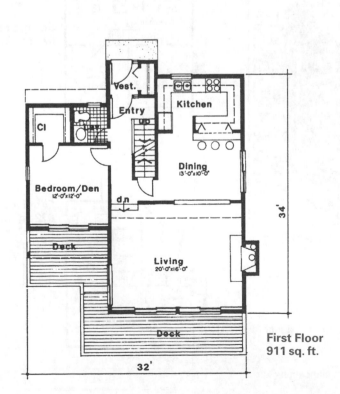

First Floor
911 sq. ft.

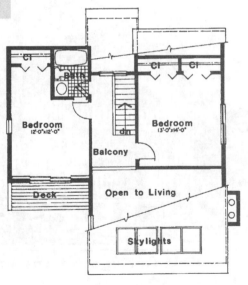

Second Floor
576 sq. ft.

VACATION

TO ORDER SEE PAGE 608 OR CALL TOLL-FREE 1-800-DREAM HOME (373-2646)

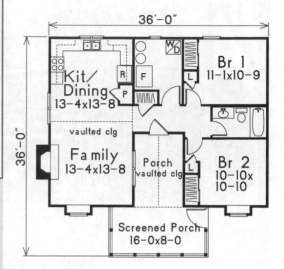

Excellent For Weekend Entertaining

Total Living Area: 924

- Box bay window seats brighten interior while enhancing front facade
- Spacious kitchen with lots of cabinet space and large pantry
- T-shaped covered porch is screened in for added enjoyment
- Plenty of closet space throughout with linen closets in both bedrooms
- 2 bedrooms, 1 bath
- Slab foundation

Plan# **577-N127**

Price Code A

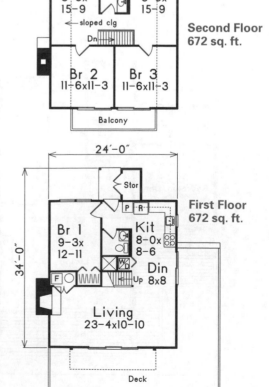

VACATION

Irresistible Cottage Adorns Any Setting

Total Living Area: 1,344

- Beautiful stone fireplace, bracketed balcony and surrounding deck create appealing atmosphere
- Enormous living room, open to dining area, enjoys views to deck through two large sliding doors
- Second floor delivers lots of sleeping area and views from exterior balcony
- 5 bedrooms, 2 baths
- Crawl space foundation, drawings also include slab foundation

Handsome Stonework

Total Living Area: 1,124

- Varied ceiling heights throughout this home
- Enormous bayed breakfast room overlooks great room with fireplace
- Conveniently located washer and dryer closet
- 3 bedrooms, 2 baths, 2-car drive under garage
- Walk-out basement foundation

TO ORDER SEE **PAGE 608** OR CALL TOLL-FREE 1-800-DREAM HOME (373-2646)

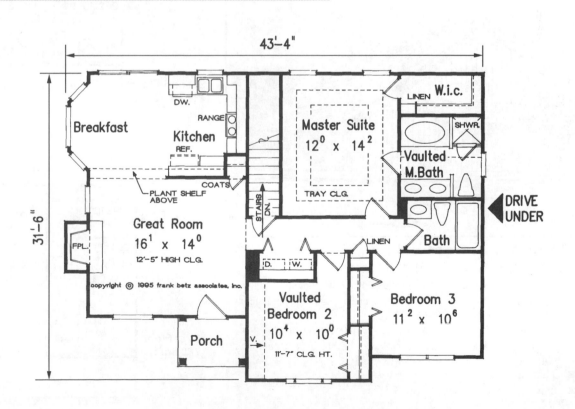

VACATION

499

Plan# **577-N087**

Corner Window Wall Dominates Design

Total Living Area: 784

- Outdoor relaxation will be enjoyed with this home's huge wraparound wood deck
- Upon entering the spacious living area, a cozy free-standing fireplace, sloped ceiling and corner window wall catch the eye
- Charming kitchen features pass-through peninsula to dining area
- 3 bedrooms, 1 bath
- Pier foundation

Plan# **577-N006**

Price Code A

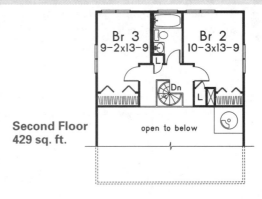

Second Floor
429 sq. ft.

Mountain Retreat

Total Living Area: 1,209

- Bracketed shed roof and ski storage add charm to vacation home
- Living and dining rooms enjoy a sloped ceiling, second floor balcony overlook and view to a large deck
- Kitchen has snack bar and accesses second floor via circular stair
- Second floor includes two bedrooms with sizable closets, center hall bath and balcony overlooking rooms below
- 3 bedrooms, 2 baths
- Crawl space foundation

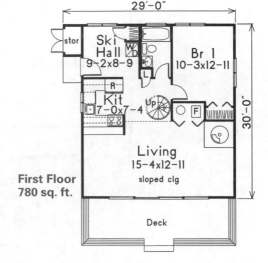

First Floor
780 sq. ft.

VACATION

TO ORDER SEE **PAGE 608** OR CALL TOLL-FREE 1-800-DREAM HOME (373-2646)

Attractive A-Frame

Total Living Area: 1,416

- Second floor has a bedroom and bath secluded for privacy
- Efficiently designed kitchen accesses deck through sliding glass doors
- Wall of windows in dining/living area brightens interior
- Enormous wrap-around deck provides plenty of outdoor living area
- 3 bedrooms, 2 baths
- Basement, crawl space or slab foundation, please specify when ordering

**Second Floor
400 sq. ft.**

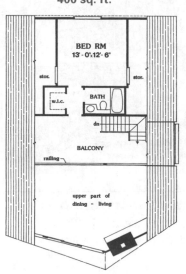

24' - 0"

BED RM
12'-6"x11'-6"

BED RM
12'-6"x11'-6"

under roof

cl

cl

BATH

htr.

up

laundry

UTIL

hw

lin.

d. w.

ref

dw

cl

range

KITCHEN
11'-6" x 9'-0"

FOYER

railing

up

covered porch

balcony above

DECK

DINING - LIVING
23'-4" x 16'-0"
cathedral ceiling

sl. gl. dr.

fireplace

sl. gl. dr.

up

DECK

rail

**First Floor
1,016 sq. ft.**

44'-4"

BED RM
13'-0"x12'-6"

stor.

stor.

w.l.c.

BATH

dn.

BALCONY

railing

upper part of
dining - living

Plan# 577-N026

Price Code AA

Dorm
14-0x12-0
vaulted clg

Dn

Balcony
14-0x6-6

open to
below

**Second Floor
314 sq. ft.**

22'-0"

Br 1
12-0x11-5

R

F

Up

Kitchen
11-5x11-4

36'-0"

Living
20-0x11-6
vaulted clg

**First Floor
792 sq. ft.**

Deck

A Vacation Oasis

Total Living Area: 1,106

- Delightful A-frame provides exciting vacation style living all year long
- Sundeck accesses large living room with open soaring ceiling
- Enormous sleeping area is provided on second floor with balcony overlook to living room below
- 2 bedrooms, 1 bath
- Pier foundation

Plan# 577-N119

Price Code A

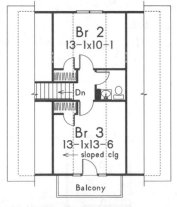

Br 2
13-1x10-1

Dn

Br 3
13-1x13-6
← sloped clg

Balcony

**Second Floor
420 sq. ft.**

26'-0"

R

Br 1
9-4x12-6

Kit
10-1x
9-5

30'-0"

Up

F
P

Living
25-4x13-2

**First Floor
780 sq. ft.**

Deck

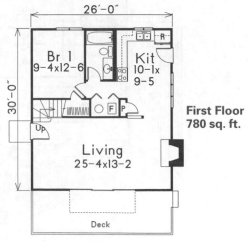

Roughing It In Luxury

Total Living Area: 1,200

- Ornate ranch-style railing enhances exterior while the stone fireplace provides a visual anchor
- Spectacular living room features inviting fireplace and adjoins a charming kitchen with dining area
- First floor bedroom, hall bath and two second floor bedrooms with half bath and exterior balcony complete the home
- 3 bedrooms, 1 1/2 baths
- Crawl space foundation, drawings also include slab foundation

VACATION

Dramatic Expanse Of Windows

Total Living Area: 1,660

- Convenient gear and equipment room
- Spacious living and dining rooms look even larger with the openness of the foyer and kitchen
- Large wrap-around deck, a great plus for outdoor living
- Broad balcony overlooks living and dining rooms
- 3 bedrooms, 3 baths
- Partial basement/crawl space foundation, drawings also include slab foundation

TO ORDER SEE **PAGE 608** OR CALL TOLL-FREE 1-800-DREAM HOME (373-2646)

Second Floor
368 sq. ft.

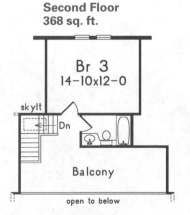

Br 3
14-10x12-0

skylt

Dn

Balcony

open to below

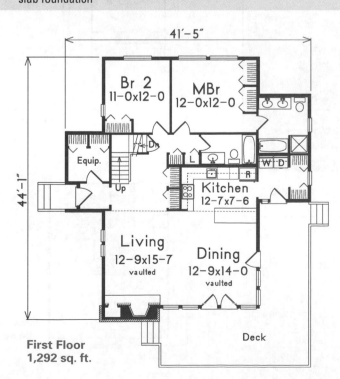

Br 2
11-0x12-0

MBr
12-0x12-0

41'-5"

Equip.

Up

W D

Kitchen
12-7x7-6

44'-1"

Living
12-9x15-7
vaulted

Dining
12-9x14-0
vaulted

Deck

First Floor
1,292 sq. ft.

VACATION

Plan# 577-DR-3900

Price Code AAA

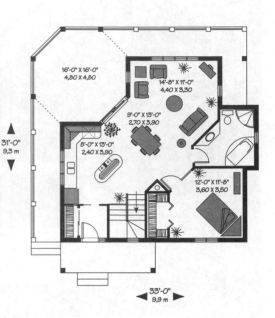

31'-0"
9,3 m

33'-0"
9,9 m

16'-0" X 16'-0"
4,80 X 4,80

14'-8" X 11'-0"
4,40 X 3,30

9'-0" X 13'-0"
2,70 X 3,90

8'-0" X 13'-0"
2,40 X 3,90

12'-0" X 11'-8"
3,60 X 3,50

Casual Open Living

Total Living Area: 840

- Energy efficient home with 2" x 6" exterior walls
- Prominent gazebo located in the rear of the home for superb outdoor living
- Enormous bath has corner oversized tub
- Lots of windows create a cheerful and sunny atmosphere
- 1 bedroom, 1 bath
- Walk-out basement foundation

Plan# 577-N057

Price Code A

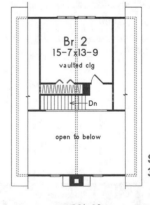

Br 2
15-7x13-9
vaulted clg

Dn

open to below

Second Floor
327 sq. ft.

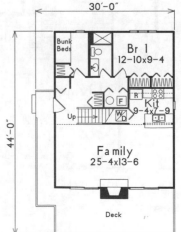

30'-0"

44'-0"

Bunk Beds

Br 1
12-10x9-4

Kit
9-4x7-9

Up

Family
25-4x13-6

Deck

First Floor
884 sq. ft.

Country Retreat For Quiet Times

Total Living Area: 1,211

- Extraordinary views are enjoyed in family room through sliding doors
- Functional kitchen features snack bar and laundry closet
- Bedroom and bunk room on the first floor for convenience
- Additional plan for second floor creates 223 square feet of additional bedroom space
- 3 bedrooms, 1 bath
- Crawl space foundation, drawings also include basement foundation

VACATION

TO ORDER SEE **PAGE 608** OR CALL TOLL-FREE **1-800-DREAM HOME** (373-2646)

Cozy Ranch Home

Total Living Area: 950

- Deck adjacent to kitchen for outdoor dining
- Vaulted ceiling, open stairway and fireplace complement great room
- Secondary bedroom with sloped ceiling and box bay window can convert to den
- Master bedroom with walk-in closet, plant shelf, separate dressing area and private access to bath
- Kitchen has garage access and opens to great room
- 2 bedrooms, 1 bath, 1-car garage
- Basement foundation

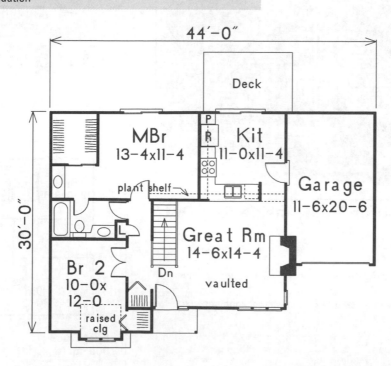

VACATION

Plan# 577-SH-SEA-285

Price Code B

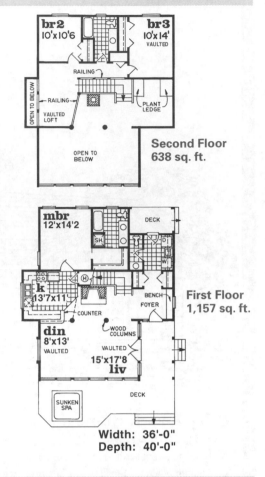

Second Floor
638 sq. ft.

First Floor
1,157 sq. ft.

br2 10'x10'6
br3 10'x14' VAULTED
RAILING
OPEN TO BELOW
RAILING
VAULTED LOFT
PLANT LEDGE
OPEN TO BELOW

mbr 12'x14'2
DECK
SH
k 13'7"x11'
din 8'x13' VAULTED
COUNTER
WOOD COLUMNS
BENCH FOYER
VAULTED 15'x17'8 liv
SUNKEN SPA
DECK

Width: 36'-0"
Depth: 40'-0"

Deck Enhances Outdoor Living Areas

Total Living Area: 1,795

- Window wall in living and dining areas brings the outdoors in
- Master bedroom has a full bath and walk-in closet
- Vaulted loft on second floor is a unique feature
- 3 bedrooms, 2 1/2 baths
- Basement or crawl space foundation, please specify when ordering

---

Plan# 577-N113

Price Code A

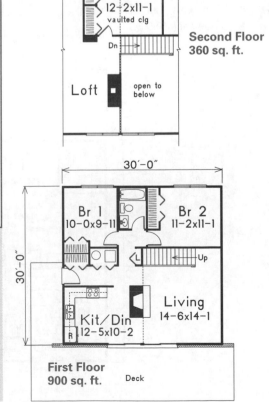

Second Floor
360 sq. ft.

Br 3 12-2x11-1 vaulted clg
Dn
Loft
open to below

30'-0"

Br 1 10-0x9-11
Br 2 11-2x11-1
Up
30'-0"
Living 14-6x14-1
Kit/Din 12-5x10-2
R

First Floor
900 sq. ft.
Deck

Windows Brighten Home Inside And Out

Total Living Area: 1,260

- Living area features enormous stone fireplace and sliding glass doors for accessing deck
- Kitchen/dining area is organized with lots of cabinet and counter space
- Second bedroom is vaulted and has closet space along one entire wall
- 3 bedrooms, 1 bath
- Crawl space foundation

Rustic Styling Enhances This Ranch

Total Living Area: 1,398

- Country kitchen has vaulted ceiling, spacious eating bar and lots of extra space for dining
- Enormous vaulted great room has cozy fireplace flanked by windows and ceiling beams for an added rustic appeal
- Master suite bath has shower and step-up tub with stained glass ledge and plant niche accents
- 3 bedrooms, 2 baths, 2-car garage
- Slab or crawl space foundation, please specify when ordering

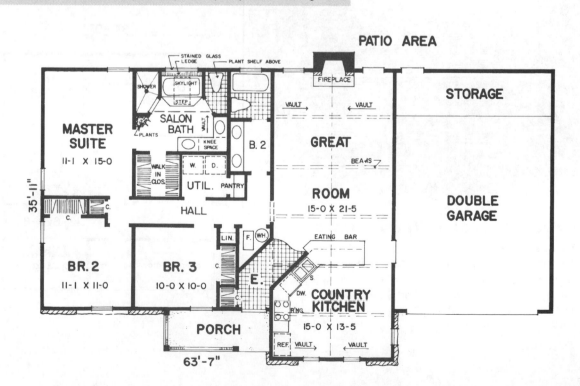

PATIO AREA

STAINED GLASS LEDGE — PLANT SHELF ABOVE

FIREPLACE

SKYLIGHT

SHOWER

STEP

VAULT → ← VAULT

STORAGE

MASTER SUITE
11-1 X 15-0

SALON BATH

PLANTS

KNEE SPACE

B. 2

GREAT

ROOM
15-0 X 21-5

BEAMS

DOUBLE GARAGE

35'-11"

WALK IN CLOS.

W. D.

UTIL.   PANTRY

HALL

C.

EATING BAR

LIN.   F.   WH

BR. 2
11-1 X 11-0

BR. 3
10-0 X 10-0

C.

E.

S

DW.

COUNTRY KITCHEN
15-0 X 13-5

R'NG

PORCH

63'-7"

REF.   VAULT →   ← VAULT

VACATION

Plan# **577-AX-94322**

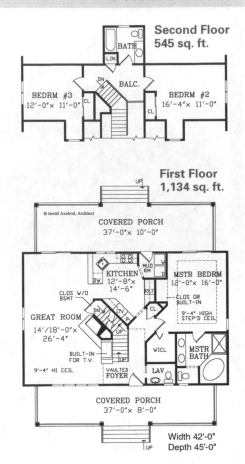

Second Floor
545 sq. ft.

BATH
LIN

DN BALC.

BEDRM #3
12'-0"× 11'-0"
CL

BEDRM #2
16'-4"× 11'-0"
CL

First Floor
1,134 sq. ft.

UP

© Jerold Axelrod, Architect

COVERED PORCH
37'-0"× 10'-0"

KITCHEN
12'-8"×
14'-6"

MUD RM

MSTR BEDRM
12'-0"× 16'-0"

CLOS W/D BSMT

CLOS OR BUILT-IN

9'-4" HIGH STEP'D CEIL

GREAT ROOM
14'/18'-0"×
26'-4"

DN

CL

WICL

MSTR BATH

BUILT-IN FOR T.V.

UP

9'-4" HI CEIL

VAULTED FOYER

LAV

COVERED PORCH
37'-0"× 8'-0"

UP

Width 42'-0"
Depth 45'-0"

Rustic Informality

Total Living Area: 1,679

- Wide, angled spaces in both the great room and the master bedroom create roomy appeal and year-round comfort
- Amenities in the luxurious master bedroom include a large walk-in closet, a whirlpool bath and double-vanity
- The nicely appointed kitchen offers nearby laundry facilities and porch access
- 3 bedrooms, 2 1/2 baths, 2-car drive under garage
- Basement, crawl space or slab foundation, please specify when ordering

Plan# **577-0698**

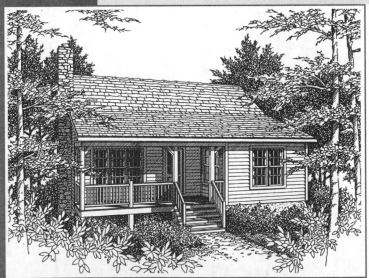

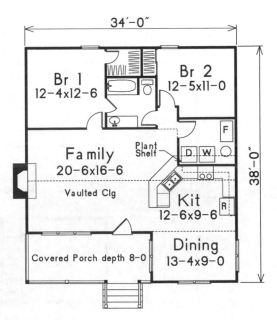

34'-0"

Br 1
12-4x12-6

Br 2
12-5x11-0

Family
20-6x16-6

Plant Shelf

D W F

Vaulted Clg

Kit
12-6x9-6

R

38'-0"

Covered Porch depth 8-0

Dining
13-4x9-0

Flexible Layout For Various Uses

Total Living Area: 1,143

- Enormous stone fireplace in family room adds warmth and character
- Spacious kitchen with breakfast bar overlooks family room
- Separate dining area great for entertaining
- Vaulted family room and kitchen create an open atmosphere
- 2 bedrooms, 1 bath
- Crawl space foundation

VACATION

Price Code A

TO ORDER SEE **PAGE 608** OR CALL TOLL-FREE 1-800-DREAM HOME (373-2646)

Fantastic A-Frame Get-Away

Total Living Area: 1,224

- Get away to this cozy A-frame featuring three bedrooms
- Living/dining room with free-standing fireplace walks out onto a large deck
- U-shaped kitchen has a unique built-in table at end of counter for intimate gatherings
- Both second floor bedrooms enjoy their own private balcony
- 3 bedrooms, 1 bath
- Crawl space foundation

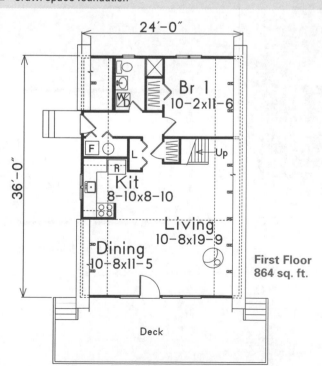

First Floor
864 sq. ft.

24'-0"

36'-0"

Br 1
10-2x11-6

Up

F   L

Kit
8-10x8-10

R

Living
10-8x19-9

Dining
10-8x11-5

Deck

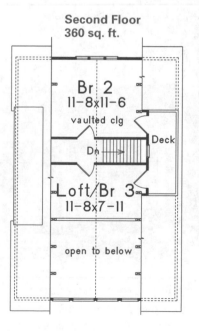

Second Floor
360 sq. ft.

Br 2
11-8x11-6
vaulted clg

Deck

Dn

Loft/Br 3
11-8x7-11

open to below

VACATION

Plan # **577-CHP-1642-A-10**

Price Code B

Second Floor 528 sq. ft.

Bedroom 14'x 11'2"

Ma. Ba.

Master Bedroom 13'x 13'6"

Open to Below

Width: 37'-0"
Depth: 52'-0"

First Floor 1,122 sq. ft.

Porch 12'x 9'5"

Kitchen 8'8"x 18'

Dining 11'6"x 18'

Bedroom 13'x 10'11"

Living 16'6"x 14'5"

Bath

Bedroom 13'x 10'9"

Porch 20'6"x 5'

Deck 34'x 10'

Ideal Vacation Style For Views

Total Living Area: 1,650

- Master bedroom located on second floor for privacy
- Open living space connects to dining area
- Two-story living area features lots of windows for views to the outdoors and a large fireplace
- Efficiently designed kitchen
- 4 bedrooms, 2 baths
- Pier foundation

Plan # **577-0700**

Price Code AAA

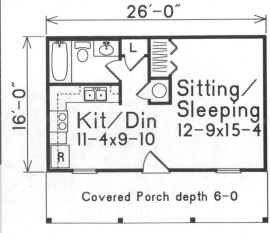

26'-0"

16'-0"

L

Sitting/ Sleeping 12-9x15-4

Kit/Din 11-4x9-10

R

Covered Porch depth 6-0

Year-Round Hideaway

Total Living Area: 416

- Open floor plan creates spacious feeling
- Covered porch has rustic appeal
- Plenty of cabinetry and workspace in kitchen
- Large linen closet centrally located and close to bath
- Sleeping area, 1 bath
- Slab foundation

TO ORDER SEE **PAGE 608** OR CALL TOLL-FREE 1-800-DREAM HOME (373-2646)

Multiple Decks Surround Home

Total Living Area: 1,267

- Triple sets of sliding glass doors leading to sun deck brighten living room
- Oversized mud room has lots of extra closet space for convenience
- Centrally located heat circulating fireplace creates a focal point while warming the home
- 3 bedrooms, 2 baths
- Basement or crawl space foundation, please specify when ordering

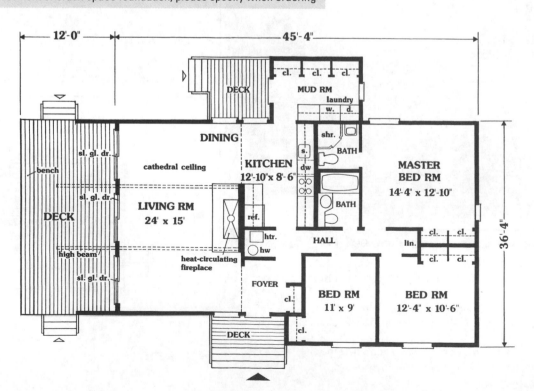

VACATION

Plan# 577-RJ-A921

Price Code AA

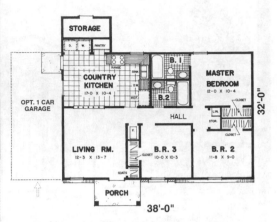

Stone Accents Create A Tudor Feel

Total Living Area: 977

- Large storage closet ideal for patio furniture storage or lawn equipment
- Large kitchen with enough room for dining looks into oversized living room
- Front covered porch adds charm
- 3 bedrooms, 2 baths, optional 1-car garage
- Slab or crawl space foundation, please specify when ordering

Plan# 577-0292

Price Code A

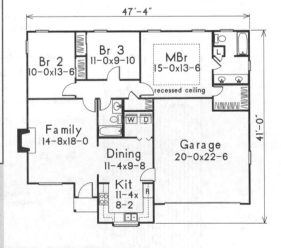

Gable Facade Adds Appeal To This Ranch

Total Living Area: 1,304

- Covered entrance leads into family room with 10' ceiling and fireplace
- 10' ceilings in kitchen, dining and family rooms
- Master bedroom features coffered ceiling, walk-in closet and private bath
- Efficient kitchen includes large window over the sink
- 3 bedrooms, 2 baths, 2-car garage
- Slab foundation

VACATION

Retreat With Attractive A-Frame Styling

Total Living Area: 1,312

- Expansive deck extends directly off living area
- L-shaped kitchen is organized and efficient
- Bedroom to the left of the kitchen makes a great quiet retreat or office
- Living area flanked with windows for light
- 3 bedrooms, 1 1/2 baths
- Pier foundation

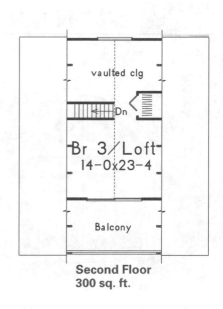

**Second Floor
300 sq. ft.**

Br 3/Loft
14-0x23-4

vaulted clg

Dn

Balcony

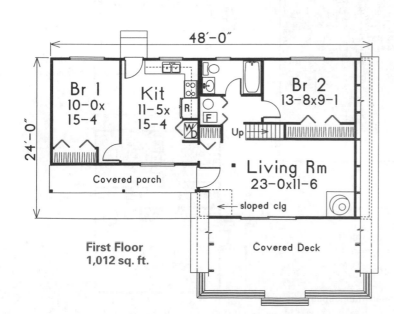

48'-0"

24'-0"

Br 1
10-0x
15-4

Kit
11-5x
15-4

R

F

W
D

Br 2
13-8x9-1

Covered porch

Up

Living Rm
23-0x11-6

sloped clg

Covered Deck

**First Floor
1,012 sq. ft.**

Plan# 577-N130

Price Code B

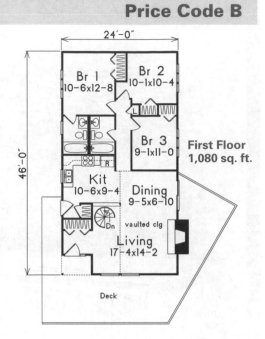

24'-0"

Br 1
10-6x12-8

Br 2
10-1x10-4

L

Br 3
9-1x11-0

**First Floor
1,080 sq. ft.**

46'-0"

Kit
10-6x9-4

Dining
9-5x6-10

R

vaulted clg

Dn

Living
17-4x14-2

Deck

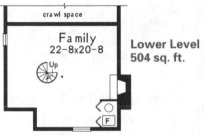

crawl space

Family
22-8x20-8

**Lower Level
504 sq. ft.**

Up

Nestled Oasis Romances The Sun

Total Living Area: 1,584

- Vaulted living/dining room features stone fireplace, ascending spiral stair and separate vestibule with guest closet
- Space saving kitchen has an eat-in area and access to the deck
- Master bedroom adjoins a full bath
- 3 bedrooms, 2 baths
- Basement foundation, drawings also include crawl space and slab foundations

Plan# 577-N049

Price Code A

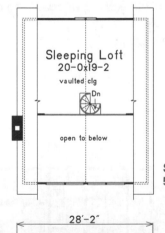

Sleeping Loft
20-0x19-2

vaulted clg

Dn

open to below

**Second Floor
507 sq. ft.**

28'-2"

Br 2
11-4x10-3

Br 1
11-3x11-5

F

R

Kit
9-1x7-9

**First Floor
884 sq. ft.**

34'-0"

Up

Living
25-4x13-8

Deck

Cozy Vacation Retreat

Total Living Area: 1,391

- Large living room with masonry fireplace features soaring vaulted ceiling
- A spiral staircase in hall leads to huge loft area overlooking living room below
- Two first floor bedrooms share a full bath
- 2 bedrooms, 1 bath
- Pier foundation, drawings also include crawl space foundation

VACATION

Unique A-Frame Detailing Has Appeal

Total Living Area: 1,272

- Stone fireplace accents living room
- Spacious kitchen includes snack bar overlooking living room
- First floor bedroom roomy and secluded
- Plenty of closet space for second floor bedrooms plus a generous balcony which wraps around second floor
- 3 bedrooms, 1 1/2 baths
- Crawl space foundation

Second Floor
480 sq. ft.

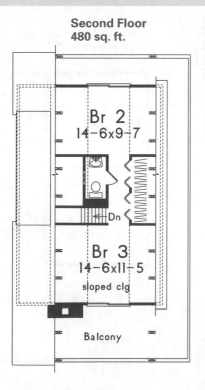

Br 2
14-6x9-7

Dn

Br 3
14-6x11-5
sloped clg

Balcony

First Floor
702 sq. ft.

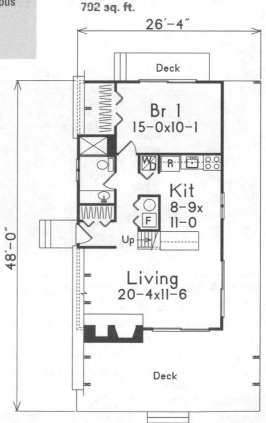

26'-4"

Deck

Br 1
15-0x10-1

W/D   R

Kit
8-9x
11-0

F

Up

48'-0"

Living
20-4x11-6

Deck

VACATION

515

Plan# 577-0651

Price Code AA

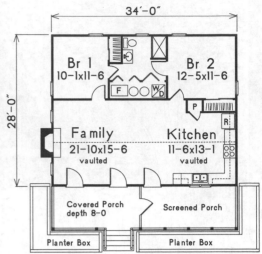

Large Vaulted Living Space

Total Living Area: 962

- Both the kitchen and family room share warmth from the fireplace
- Charming facade features covered porch on one side, screened porch on the other and attractive planter boxes
- L-shaped kitchen boasts convenient pantry
- 2 bedrooms, 1 bath
- Crawl space foundation

Plan# 577-N131

Price Code AAA

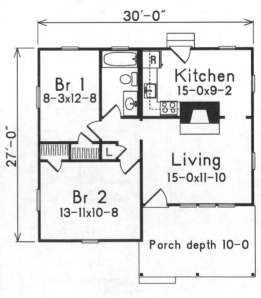

Porch Adds To Perfect Outdoor Getaway

Total Living Area: 733

- Bedrooms separate from kitchen and living area for privacy
- Lots of closet space throughout this home
- Centrally located bath is easily accessible
- Kitchen features door to rear of home and a door separating it from the rest of the home
- 2 bedrooms, 1 bath
- Pier foundation

VACATION

TO ORDER SEE **PAGE 608** OR CALL TOLL-FREE 1-800-DREAM HOME (373-2646)

Vacation Paradise
Total Living Area: 960

- Interesting roof and wood beams overhang a generous-sized deck
- Family room area is vaulted and opens to dining and kitchen
- Pullman-style kitchen has been skillfully designed
- Two bedrooms and hall bath are located at the rear of home
- 2 bedrooms, 1 bath
- Crawl space foundation

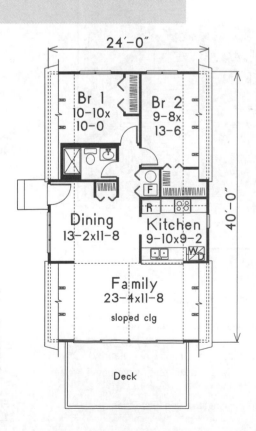

24'-0"

40'-0"

Br 1
10-10x
10-0

Br 2
9-8x
13-6

Dining
13-2x11-8

Kitchen
9-10x9-2

F

R

W D

Family
23-4x11-8

sloped clg

Deck

VACATION

Plan# 577-0547

Price Code AAA

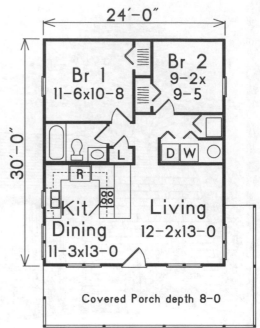

24'-0"

30'-0"

Br 1
11-6x10-8

Br 2
9-2x
9-5

L

D W

R

Kit/
Dining
11-3x13-0

Living
12-2x13-0

Covered Porch depth 8-0

Designed For Comfort And Utility

Total Living Area: 720

- Abundant windows in living and dining rooms provide generous sunlight
- Secluded laundry area with handy storage closet
- U-shaped kitchen with large breakfast bar opens into living area
- Large covered deck offers plenty of outdoor living space
- 2 bedrooms, 1 bath
- Crawl space foundation, drawings also include slab foundation

Plan# 577-N020

Price Code C

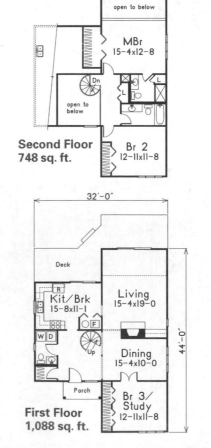

open to below

MBr
15-4x12-8

Dn

L

L

open to below

Second Floor
748 sq. ft.

Br 2
12-11x11-8

32'-0"

Deck

R

Kit/Brk
15-8x11-1

Living
15-4x19-0

W D

F

Up

Dining
15-4x10-0

44'-0"

Porch

Br 3/
Study
12-11x11-8

First Floor
1,088 sq. ft.

Contemporary Escape

Total Living Area: 1,836

- Foyer sparkles with spiral stair, sloped ceilings and celestial windows
- Living room has fireplace with bookshelves and views to the outdoors
- U-shaped kitchen includes eat-in breakfast area and dining nearby
- Master suite revels in having a balcony overlooking the living room
- 3 bedrooms, 2 1/2 baths
- Crawl space foundation, drawings also include slab foundation

VACATION

A Home Designed For Hillside Views
Total Living Area: 1,806

- Wrap-around deck, great for entertaining, enhances appearance
- Side entry foyer accesses two rear bedrooms, hall bath and living and dining area
- L-shaped kitchen is open to dining area
- Lots of living area is provided on the lower level, including a spacious family room with fireplace and sliding doors to patio under deck
- 3 bedrooms, 2 baths
- Basement foundation

Lower Level
1,064 sq. ft.

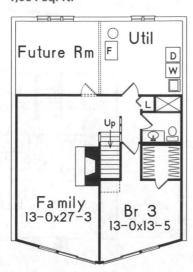

Future Rm

Util
F

D
W

L

Up

Family
13-0x27-3

Br 3
13-0x13-5

28'-0"

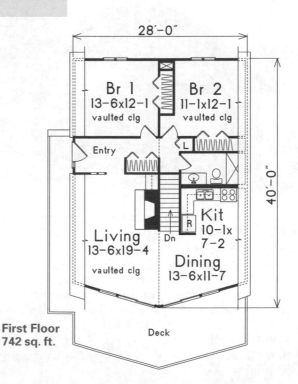

Br 1
13-6x12-1
vaulted clg

Br 2
11-1x12-1
vaulted clg

Entry

L

40'-0"

Living
13-6x19-4

vaulted clg

Dn

R

Kit
10-1x
7-2

Dining
13-6x11-7

First Floor
742 sq. ft.

Deck

VACATION

Plan# **577-0680**

Price Code B

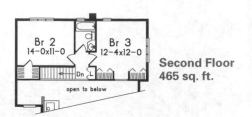

Br 2
14-0x11-0

Br 3
12-4x12-0

**Second Floor
465 sq. ft.**

open to below

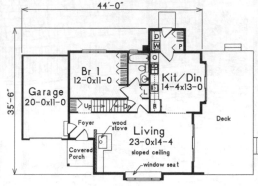

44'-0"

35'-6"

Garage
20-0x11-0

Br 1
12-0x11-0

Kit/Din
14-4x13-0

Foyer

wood
stove

Deck

Living
23-0x14-4

sloped ceiling

Covered
Porch

window seat

**First Floor
967 sq. ft.**

Dramatic Sloping Ceiling In Living Room

Total Living Area: 1,432

- Enter the two-story foyer from covered porch or garage
- Living room has square bay and window seat, glazed end wall with floor-to-ceiling windows and access to the deck
- Kitchen/dining room also opens to the deck for added convenience
- 3 bedrooms, 2 baths, 1-car garage
- Basement foundation, drawings also include slab foundation

Plan# **577-N149**

Price Code A

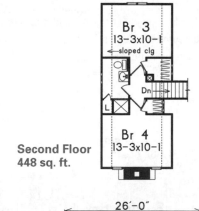

Br 3
13-3x10-1

sloped clg

Dn

L

Br 4
13-3x10-1

**Second Floor
448 sq. ft.**

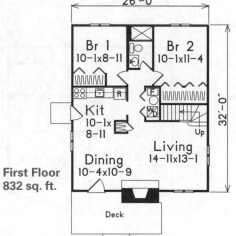

26'-0"

32'-0"

Br 1
10-1x8-11

Br 2
10-1x11-4

Kit
10-1x
8-11

R

Living
14-11x13-1

Up

Dining
10-4x10-9

**First Floor
832 sq. ft.**

Deck

Cozy Cottage Living

Total Living Area: 1,280

- A front porch deck, ornate porch roof, massive stone fireplace and old English windows all generate inviting appeal
- Large living room accesses kitchen with spacious dining area
- Two spacious bedrooms with ample closet space comprise second floor
- 4 bedrooms, 2 baths
- Basement foundation, drawings also include slab and crawl space foundations

VACATION

Entrance Opens To Stylish Features

Total Living Area: 1,661

- Large open foyer with angled wall arrangement and high ceiling adds to spacious living room
- Kitchen and dining area have impressive cathedral ceilings and French door allowing access to the patio
- Utility room conveniently located near kitchen
- Secluded master bedroom has large walk-in closets, unique brick wall arrangement and 10' ceiling
- 3 bedrooms, 2 baths, 2-car garage
- Slab foundation

VACATION

Plan# 577-0549

Price Code A

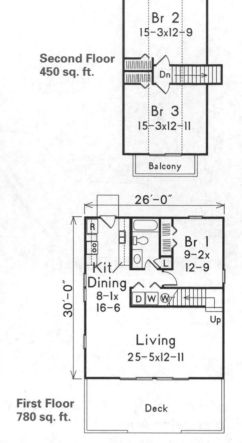

Second Floor 450 sq. ft.

Br 2
15-3x12-9

Dn

Br 3
15-3x12-11

Balcony

26'-0"

R

Kit

Dining
8-1x
16-6

Br 1
9-2x
12-9

DW W

Living
25-5x12-11

Up

30'-0"

First Floor 780 sq. ft.

Deck

Perfect Vacation Home

Total Living Area: 1,230

- Spacious living room accesses huge sun deck
- Bedroom #3 features a balcony overlooking the deck
- Kitchen with dining area accesses the outdoors
- Washer and dryer tucked under stairs
- 3 bedrooms, 1 bath
- Crawl space foundation, drawings also include slab foundation

---

Plan# 577-N145

Price Code AAA

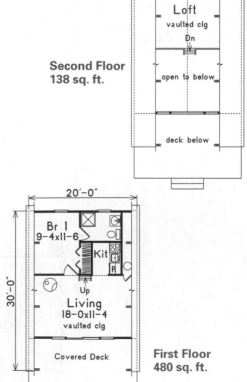

Second Floor 138 sq. ft.

Loft
vaulted clg

Dn

open to below

deck below

20'-0"

Br 1
9-4x11-6

Kit

Up

Living
18-0x11-4
vaulted clg

30'-0"

Covered Deck

First Floor 480 sq. ft.

An A-Frame For Every Environment

Total Living Area: 618

- Memorable family events are certain to be enjoyed on this fabulous partially covered sundeck
- Equally impressive is the living area with its cathedral ceiling and exposed rafters
- A kitchenette, bedroom and bath conclude the first floor with a delightful sleeping loft above bedroom and bath
- 1 bedroom, 1 bath
- Pier foundation

VACATION

TO ORDER SEE **PAGE 608** OR CALL TOLL-FREE 1-800-DREAM HOME (373-2646)

Trendsetting Contemporary Retreat

Total Living Area: 1,528

- Large deck complements handsome exterior
- Family room provides a welcome space for family get-togethers and includes a sloped ceiling and access to studio/loft
- Kitchen features dining space and view to deck
- A hall bath is shared by two bedrooms on first floor which have ample closet space
- 2 bedrooms, 1 bath
- Crawl space foundation

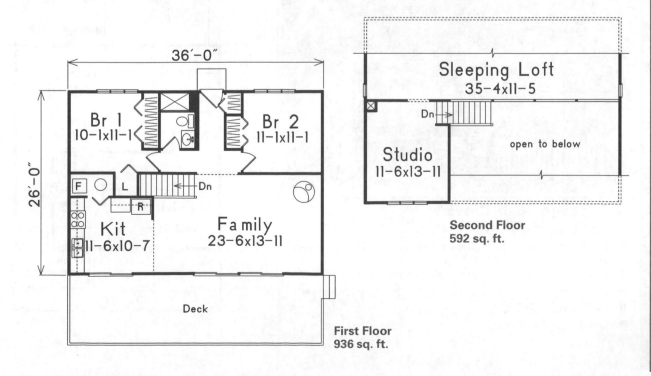

36'-0"

Br 1
10-1x11-1

Br 2
11-1x11-1

26'-0"

F

L

R

Dn

Kit
11-6x10-7

Family
23-6x13-11

Deck

First Floor
936 sq. ft.

Sleeping Loft
35-4x11-5

Dn

open to below

Studio
11-6x13-11

Second Floor
592 sq. ft.

VACATION

523

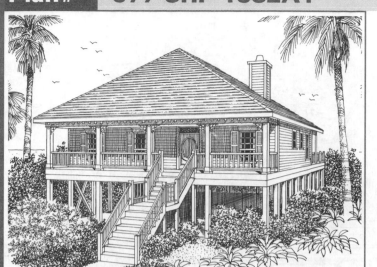

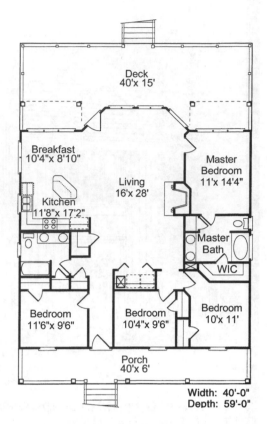

Deck
40'x 15'

Breakfast
10'4"x 8'10"

Living
16'x 28'

Master
Bedroom
11'x 14'4"

Kitchen
11'8"x 17'2"

Master
Bath

WIC

Bedroom
11'6"x 9'6"

Bedroom
10'4"x 9'6"

Bedroom
10'x 11'

Porch
40'x 6'

Width: 40'-0"
Depth: 59'-0"

Great Relaxed Styled Plan

Total Living Area: 1,520

- 9' ceilings throughout this home
- Living room has fireplace and large bay window that connects to an oversized deck
- Master bedroom has wall of windows and terrific views to the outdoors
- 4 bedrooms, 2 baths
- Pier foundation

TO ORDER SEE PAGE 608 OR CALL TOLL-FREE 1-800-DREAM HOME (373-2646)

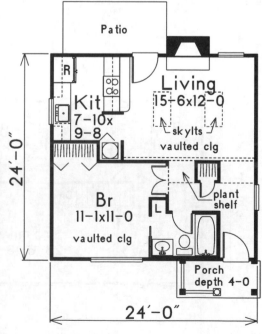

Patio

R

Living
15-6x12-0

skylts

vaulted clg

Kit
7-10x
9-8

plant
shelf

Br
11-1x11-0

L

vaulted clg

Porch
depth 4-0

24'-0"

24'-0"

A Cottage With Class

Total Living Area: 576

- Perfect country retreat features vaulted living room and entry with skylights and plant shelf above
- Double-doors enter a vaulted bedroom with bath access
- Kitchen offers generous storage and pass-through breakfast bar
- 1 bedroom, 1 bath
- Crawl space foundation

VACATION

TO ORDER SEE **PAGE 608** OR CALL TOLL-FREE 1-800-DREAM HOME (373-2646)

Leisure Living With Interior Surprise

Total Living Area: 1,354

- Soaring ceilings highlight the kitchen, living and dining areas creating dramatic excitement
- A spectacular large deck surrounds the front and both sides of home
- An impressive U-shaped kitchen has wrap-around breakfast bar and shares fantastic views with both the first and second floors through an awesome wall of glass
- Two bedrooms with a bath, a loft for sleeping and second floor balcony overlooking living area, complete the home
- 3 bedrooms, 1 bath
- Crawl space foundation

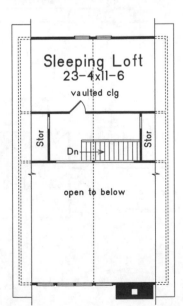

Second Floor
394 sq. ft.

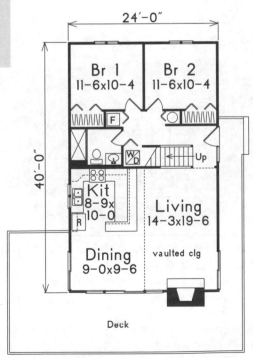

First Floor
960 sq. ft.

VACATION

577-0808

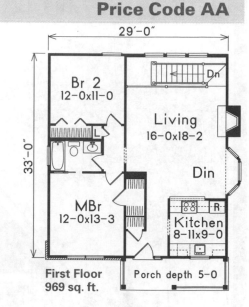

29'-0"

33'-0"

Br 2
12-0x11-0

Living
16-0x18-2

Dn

MBr
12-0x13-3

Din

Kitchen
8-11x9-0

R

L

First Floor
969 sq. ft.

Porch depth 5-0

Cottage With Atrium
Total Living Area: 969

- Eye-pleasing facade enjoys stone accents with country porch for quiet evenings
- A bayed dining area, cozy fireplace and atrium with sunny two-story windows are the many features of the living room
- Step-saver kitchen includes a pass-through snack bar
- 325 square feet of optional living area on the lower level
- 2 bedrooms, 1 bath, 1-car rear entry garage
- Walk-out basement foundation

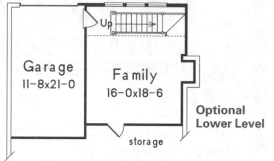

Up

Garage
11-8x21-0

Family
16-0x18-6

Optional
Lower Level

storage

577-0767

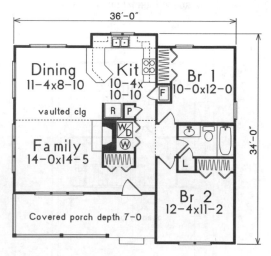

36'-0"

34'-0"

Dining
11-4x8-10

Kit
10-4x
10-10

Br 1
10-0x12-0

vaulted clg

R P

F

W
D

Family
14-0x14-5

W

Br 2
12-4x11-2

L

Covered porch depth 7-0

Vacation Home Or Year-Round Living
Total Living Area: 990

- Covered front porch adds charming feel
- Vaulted ceilings in kitchen, family and dining rooms creates a spacious feel
- Large linen, pantry and storage closets throughout
- 2 bedrooms, 1 bath
- Crawl space foundation

VACATION

Cozy Swiss Chalet Cottage

Total Living Area: 1,286

- Living room has warm fireplace and a dining room with a snack bar counter through to the kitchen
- U-shaped kitchen has a window sink
- The master bedroom has a private balcony and a full bath
- Lots of storage throughout this home
- 3 bedrooms, 2 baths
- Crawl space foundation

br3
10'3 x 9'

STORAGE

F

k
9'11 x 8'

13'7 x 15'1
liv

10'5 x 10'2
din

VERANDAH

First Floor
725 sq. ft.

Width: 25'-0"
Depth: 36'-6"

br2
13'4 x 10'6

STORAGE

STORAGE

13'4 x 12'
mbr

BALCONY

Second Floor
561 sq. ft.

TO ORDER SEE **PAGE 608** OR CALL TOLL-FREE 1-800-DREAM HOME (373-2646)

VACATION

Plan# 577-DDI-96217

Price Code B

BALCONY

MASTER
18/4 x 23/4

O P E N   T O   B E L O W

Second Floor
677 sq. ft.

First Floor
1,093 sq. ft.

Width: 28'-0"
Depth: 40'-9"

BDRM-2
11/10 x 10/4

KITCHEN
11/0 x 10/10

DINING RM.
11/10 x 10/2

DECK

GREAT RM.
27/0 x 16/0

Modern A-Frame Style

Total Living Area: 1,770

■ Private master bedroom on second floor has balcony, bath and large walk-in closet

■ Oversized laundry room has extra storage and counter space

■ Dining room adjacent to kitchen making entertaining easy

■ 2 bedrooms, 2 baths

■ Basement or walk-out basement foundation, please specify when ordering

Plan# 577-DR-2919

Price Code AA

11'-0" X 10'-4"
3.30 X 3.10

Second Floor
395 sq. ft.

11'-8" X 11'-8"
3.50 X 3.50

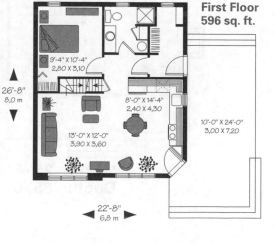

First Floor
596 sq. ft.

9'-4" X 10'-4"
2.80 X 3.10

26'-8"
8.0 m

8'-0" X 14'-4"
2.40 X 4.30

10'-0" X 24'-0"
3.00 X 7.20

13'-0" X 12'-0"
3.90 X 3.60

22'-8"
6.8 m

Charming Country Cottage

Total Living Area: 991

■ Energy efficient home with 2" x 6" exterior walls

■ Master bedroom has large walk-in closet

■ Large and open kitchen is well-organized

■ 2 bedrooms, 2 baths

■ Basement or crawl space foundation, please specify when ordering

VACATION

2-Car Garage Apartment - Cape Cod

Total Living Area: 566

- Building height - 22'-0"
- Roof pitch - 12/12, 4.5/12
- Ceiling heights-
  First floor - 8'-0"   Second floor - 7'-7"
- Two 9' x 7' overhead doors
- Charming dormers add appeal to this design
- Comfortable open living area
- Complete list of materials
- Step-by-step instructions

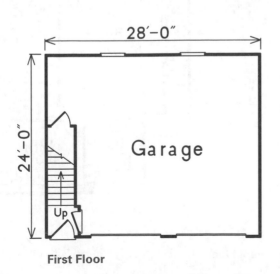

28'-0"

24'-0"

Garage

Up

First Floor

Second Floor

Dn

Studio
18-2x18-4

R

APARTMENT GARAGES

3-Car Apartment Garage With Flair

Total Living Area: 929

- Building height - 27'-0"
- Roof pitch - 6.5/12, 10/12
- Ceiling heights -
  First floor - 9'-0"   Second floor - 8'-0"
- 16' x 8', 9' x 8' overhead doors
- 2 bedrooms, 1 bath, 3-car side entry garage
- Slab foundation
- Spacious living room with dining area has access to 8' x 12' deck through glass sliding doors
- Complete list of materials

APARTMENT GARAGES

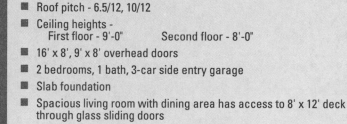

Patio

Util

Sto

Up

W D

Entry

Garage
23-4x29-4

35'-0"

Covered porch depth 5-0

31'-0"

First Floor

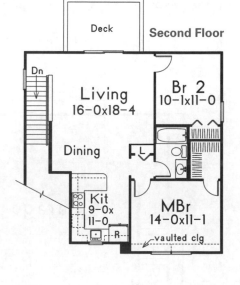

Deck   **Second Floor**

Dn

Living
16-0x18-4

Br 2
10-1x11-0

Dining

L

Kit
9-0x
11-0

MBr
14-0x11-1

vaulted clg

R

TO ORDER SEE PAGE 608 OR CALL TOLL-FREE 1-800-DREAM HOME (373-2646)

3-Car Garage Apartment
Total Living Area: 974

- Building height - 23'-2"
- Roof pitch - 5/12
- Ceiling height - 8'-0"
- 2 bedrooms, 1 bath
- Three 9' x 7' overhead doors
- Kitchen and breakfast room combine living area for spaciousness
- Complete list of materials

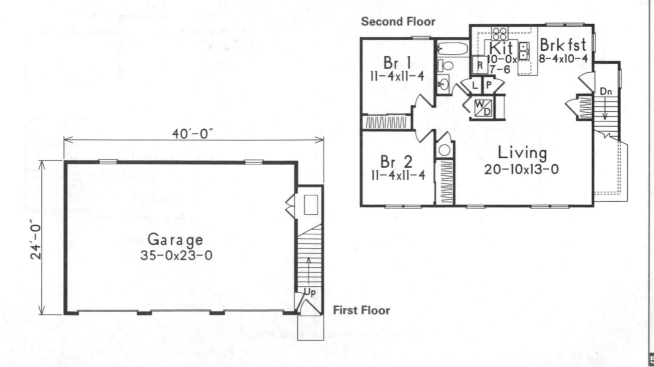

Second Floor

Br 1
11-4x11-4

Kit
10-0x7-6

Brkfst
8-4x10-4

R

L P

W/D

Dn

Br 2
11-4x11-4

Living
20-10x13-0

40'-0"

24'-0"

Garage
35-0x23-0

Up

First Floor

2-Car Garage Apartment

Total Living Area: 628

- Building height - 26'-6"
- Roof pitch - 8/12, 9/12
- Ceiling heights -
  First floor - 9'-0"   Second floor - 8'-0"
- 16' x 7' overhead door
- 1 bedroom, 1 bath
- Cozy living room offers vaulted ceiling, fireplace and a pass-through kitchen
- Complete list of materials

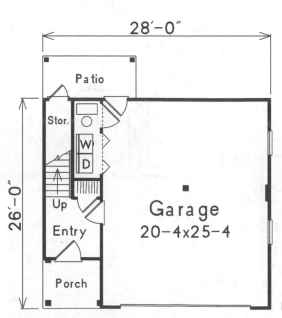

First Floor

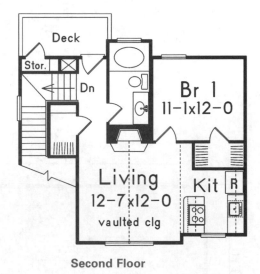

Second Floor

Plan # 577-15030

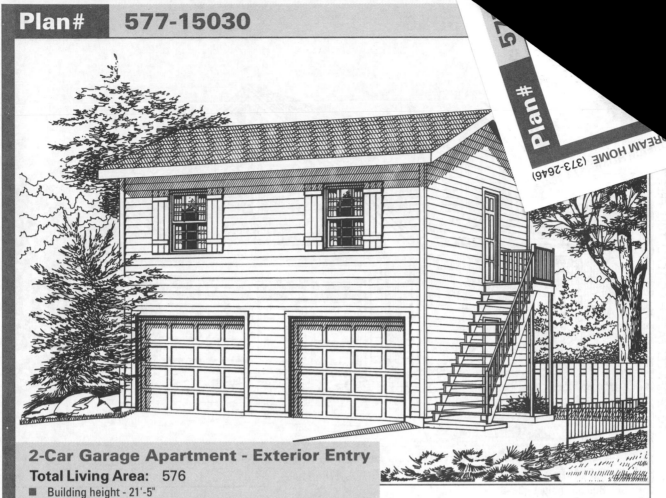

TO ORDER SEE **PAGE 608** OR CALL TOLL-FREE 1

2-Car Garage Apartment - Exterior Entry

Total Living Area: 576

- Building height - 21'-5"
- Roof pitch - 4/12
- Ceiling height - 8'-0"
- Two 9' x 7' overhead doors
- 1 bedroom, 1 bath
- Loft has roomy kitchen and dining area
- Private side exterior entrance
- Style complements many types of homes
- Complete list of materials
- Step-by-step instructions

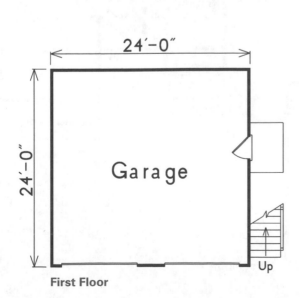

24'-0"

24'-0"

Garage

Up

First Floor

Kit/Dining
17-11x9-1

R

Dn

Br
11-5x11-8

Living
11-8x14-4

Second Floor

3-Car Garage Apartment
Total Living Area: 676

- Building height - 22'-0"
- Roof pitch - 12/12
- Ceiling height - 8'-0"
- 1 bedroom, 1 bath
- Complete list of materials

APARTMENT GARAGES

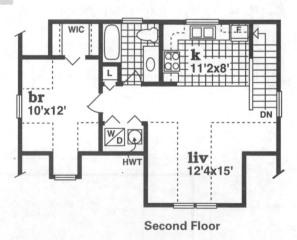

Second Floor

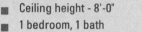

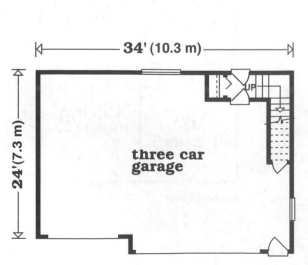

First Floor

Plan# 577-15034

Price Code P13

2-Car Garage Apartment

Total Living Area: 654

- Building height - 24'-0"
- Roof pitch - 7/12
- Ceiling height - 8'-0"
- 16' x 7' overhead door
- 1 bedroom, 1 bath
- Vaulted living room is open to a pass-through kitchen and breakfast bar with an overhead plant shelf and sliding glass doors to an outside balcony
- Complete list of materials

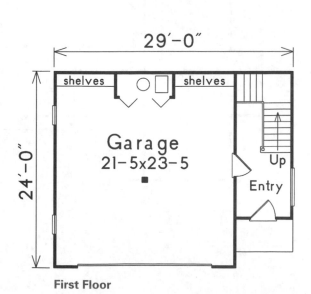

29'-0"

24'-0"

shelves ○ ▢ shelves

Garage 21-5x23-5

Up

Entry

First Floor

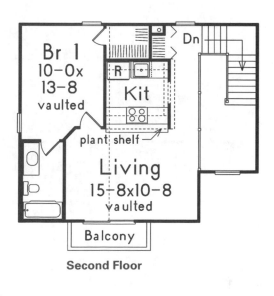

Br 1 10-0x 13-8 vaulted

Dn

R

Kit

plant shelf

Living 15-8x10-8 vaulted

Balcony

Second Floor

APARTMENT GARAGES

3-Car Garage With Bonus Room

Total Living Area: 686

- Building height - 25'-6"
- Roof pitch - 10/12
- Ceiling heights -
  First floor - 12'-0"   Second floor - 8'-0"
- Three 9' x 10' overhead doors
- Vaulted bonus room would make an ideal home office or hobby area
- Complete list of materials

APARTMENT GARAGES

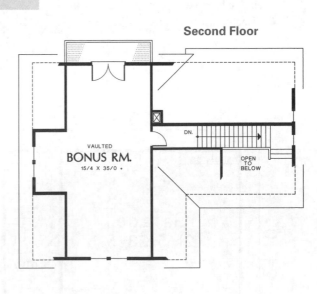

Second Floor

VAULTED
BONUS RM.
15/4 X 35/0 +

DN.

OPEN
TO
BELOW

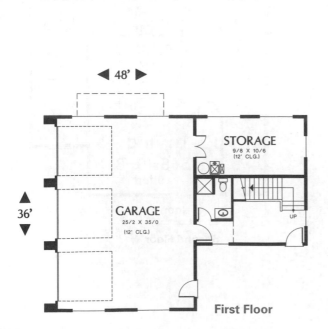

◄ 48' ►

36'

STORAGE
9/8 X 10/6
(12' CLG.)

GARAGE
25/2 X 35/0
(12' CLG.)

UP

First Floor

3-Car Garage Apartment

Total Living Area: 1,032

- Building height - 24'-0"
- Roof pitch - 5/12, 10/12
- Ceiling heights - 8'-0"
- 2 bedrooms, 1 bath
- Spacious family room flows into kitchen/breakfast area
- Two sunny bedrooms share a bath
- Complete list of materials

TO ORDER SEE **PAGE 608** OR CALL TOLL-FREE 1-800-DREAM HOME (373-2646)

APARTMENT GARAGES

Second Floor

Br 1
11-8x12-0

Kit./Brk
21-0x10-4

Br 2
12-1x11-7

Family
20-0x15-7

40'-0"

30'-0"

40'-0"

26'-0"

3-Car Garage

8' Ceiling

9'x7' Door 9'x7' Door 9'x7' Door

Up

F

Conc. Stoop

First Floor

3-Car Garage Apartment

Total Living Area: 1,040

- Building height - 23'-0"
- Roof pitch - 5/12
- Ceiling height - 8'-0"
- Three 9' x 7' overhead doors
- 2 bedrooms, 1 bath
- Large rooms offer comfortable living with second floor laundry, ample cabinets and sliding doors to deck
- Complete list of materials

APARTMENT GARAGES

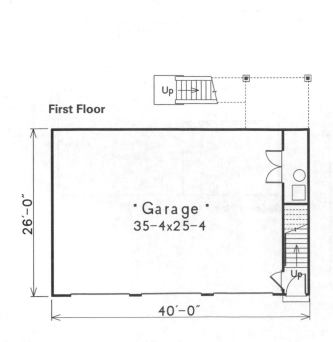

First Floor

Up

Garage
35-4x25-4

26'-0"

40'-0"

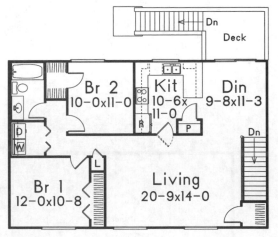

Dn

Deck

Br 2
10-0x11-0

Kit
10-6x
11-0

Din
9-8x11-3

Dn

Br 1
12-0x10-8

Living
20-9x14-0

Second Floor

Plan# 577-15514

2-Car Garage Apartment With Dormers

Total Living Area: 652

- Building height - 23'-0"
- Ceiling height - 8'-0"
- Roof pitch - 3 1/2/12, 11/12
- 1 bedroom, 1 bath
- Complete list of materials

TO ORDER SEE PAGE 608 OR CALL TOLL-F

Width: 28'-0"
Depth: 26'-0"

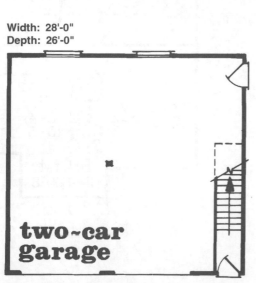

two-car
garage

First Floor

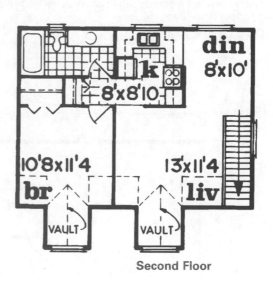

din
8'x10'

k
8'x8'10

10'8x11'4
br

13x11'4
liv

VAULT   VAULT

Second Floor

APARTMENT GARAGES

539

Pric

3-Car Garage Apantment With Storage

Total Living Area: 973

- Building height - 24'-8"
- Roof pitch - 6/12
- Ceiling height - 8'-0"
- 2 bedrooms, 1 bath
- 16' x 7' and 9' x 7' overhead doors
- Sunny breakfast room positioned between the kitchen and the living area for convenience
- Complete list of materials

APARTMENT GARAGES

Second Floor

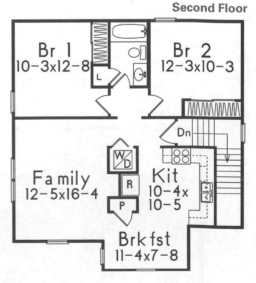

Br 1
10-3x12-8

Br 2
12-3x10-3

Dn

Family
12-5x16-4

Kit
10-4x
10-5

W/D

R

P

Brk fst
11-4x7-8

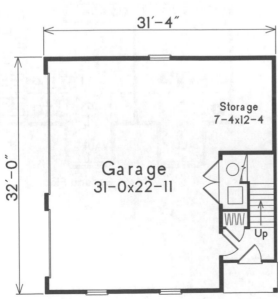

31'-4"

32'-0"

Storage
7-4x12-4

Garage
31-0x22-11

Up

First Floor

HOLZHAUER INC.

2-Car Garage Apartment
Total Living Area: 633

- Building height - 24'-0"
- Roof pitch - 9/12
- Ceiling height - 8'-0"
- 1 bedroom, 1 bath
- Two 8' x 7' overhead doors
- Lots of storage throughout including built-in shelves and a desk in the living area
- Complete list of materials

◄ **28'** ►

First Floor

▲
26'
▼

Second Floor

2-Car Garage Apartment

Total Living Area: 1,240

- Building height - 27'-0"
- Roof pitch - 9/12, 12/12, 6/12
- Ceiling heights -
  First Floor - 9'-0"   Second Floor - 8'-0"
- Kitchen/breakfast area includes island ideal for food preparation or dining
- Spacious bath directly accesses the bedroom as well as the sitting area
- Complete list of materials

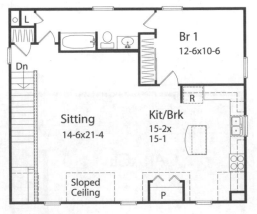

Second Floor

Br 1
12-6x10-6

Dn

Sitting
14-6x21-4

Kit/Brk
15-2x
15-1

Sloped
Ceiling

P

R

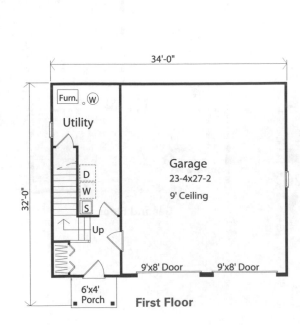

34'-0"

Furn.   W

Utility

Garage
23-4x27-2
9' Ceiling

32'-0"

D
W
S

Up

9'x8' Door   9'x8' Door

6'x4'
Porch   **First Floor**

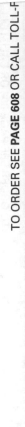

APARTMENT GARAGES

3-Car Garage Apartment - Cape Cod

Total Living Area: 813

- Building height - 22'-0"
- Roof pitch - 12/12, 4.25/12
- Ceiling height - 8'-0"
- Three 9' x 7' overhead doors
- Studio, 1 bath
- Spacious studio apartment with kitchen and bath
- Perfect for recreation, in-law or home office
- Complete list of materials

Second Floor

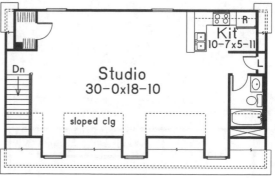

Kit
10-7x5-11

Dn

Studio
30-0x18-10

sloped clg

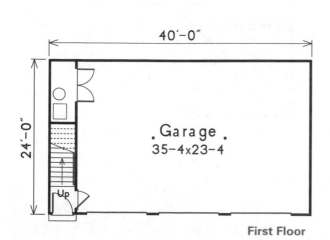

40'-0"

24'-0"

.Garage.
35-4x23-4

Up

First Floor

APARTMENT GARAGES

3-Car Garage Apartment

Total Living Area: 949

- Building height - 24'-10"
- Roof pitch - 6/12
- Ceiling heights -
  First Floor - 9'-0"   Second Floor - 8'-0"
- 1 bedroom, 1 bath
- Three 9' x 7' overhead doors
- Sitting area includes an attractive window seat which becomes focal point
- Complete list of materials

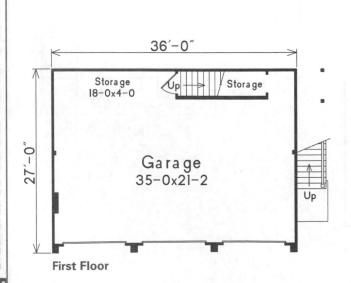

36'-0"

Storage
18-0x4-0

Storage

Up

27'-0"

Garage
35-0x21-2

Up

First Floor

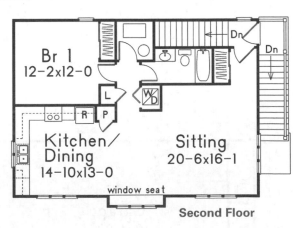

Dn

Dn

Br 1
12-2x12-0

L

W
D

R

P

Kitchen/
Dining
14-10x13-0

Sitting
20-6x16-1

window seat

Second Floor

2-Car Garage Apartment

Total Living Area: 568

- Building height - 26'-0"
- Roof pitch - 12/12
- Ceiling heights -
  First Floor - 9'-0"   Second Floor - 8'-0"
- 1 bedroom/sleeping area, 1 bath
- Beautiful dormers brighten interior
- Complete list of materials

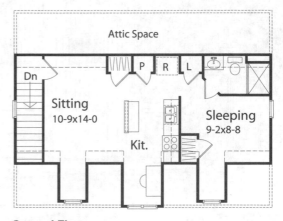

Second Floor

Attic Space

Dn

Sitting
10-9x14-0

Kit.

Sleeping
9-2x8-8

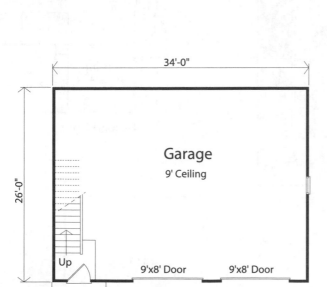

34'-0"

26'-0"

Garage
9' Ceiling

Up

9'x8' Door   9'x8' Door

7'x4' Covered
Porch

First Floor

APARTMENT GARAGES

Plan# 577-15015

Price Code P9

Second Floor

2-Car Garage Apartment - Tudor Style
Total Living Area: 784

- Building height - 24'-6"
- Roof pitch - 6/12
- Ceiling height - 8'-0"
- Two 9' x 7' overhead doors
- 1 bedroom, 1 bath
- Outdoor covered stairs are sheltered from the elements
- Complete list of materials
- Step-by-step instructions

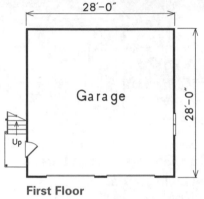

First Floor

Plan# 577-15020

Price Code P9

Second Floor

APARTMENT GARAGES

2-Car Garage Apartment - Western Style
Total Living Area: 784

- Building height - 24'-6"
- Roof pitch - 6/12
- Ceiling height - 8'-0"
- Two 9' x 7' overhead doors
- 1 bedroom, 1 bath
- Complete list of materials
- Step-by-step instructions

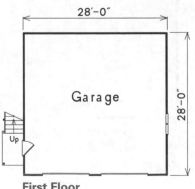

First Floor

546

2-Car Garage Apartment

Total Living Area: 588

- Building height - 23'-0"
- Roof pitch - 12/12 and 4/12
- Ceiling heights -
  First floor - 8'-0"   Second floor - 8'-0"
- Charming dormers add character to exterior
- 1 bedroom, 1 bath
- Complete list of materials

Second Floor

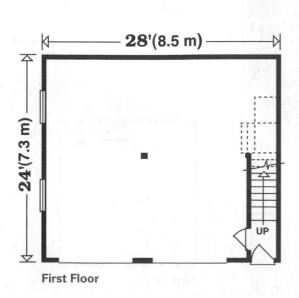

First Floor

APARTMENT GARAGES

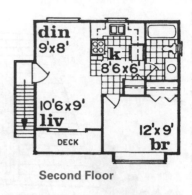

Second Floor

Width: 24'-0"
Depth: 22'-0"

two-car garage

First Floor

2-Car Garage Apartment

Total Living Area: 484

■ Building height - 25'-0"
■ Ceiling heights - 8'-0"
■ Roof pitch - 7/12
■ 1 bedroom, 1 bath
■ Complete list of materials

Plan# **577-15029** **Price Code P9**

Studio
14-11x22-3

Second Floor

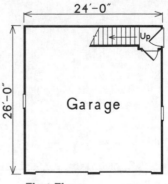

Garage

24'-0"

26'-0"

First Floor

2-Car Garage Apartment - Gambrel Roof

Total Living Area: 438

■ Building height - 21'-3"
■ Roof pitch - 6/12, 12/6
■ Ceiling heights-
  First Floor - 8'-0"   Second Floor - 7'-9"
■ Two 9' x 7' overhead doors
■ Complete list of materials
■ Step-by-step instructions

TO ORDER SEE **PAGE 608** OR CALL TOLL-FREE 1-800-DREAM HOME (373-2646)

2-Car Garage Apartment

Total Living Area: 840

- Building height - 25'-8"
- Roof pitch - 7/12
- Ceiling heights -
  Firot Floor - 9'-0"   Second Floor - 8'-0"
- 1 bedroom, 1 bath
- Two 9' x 7' overhead doors
- Cozy covered entry
- Complete list of materials

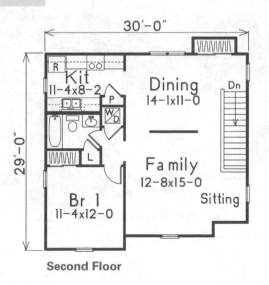

30'-0"

R

Kit
11-4x8-2

P

W/D

Dining
14-1x11-0

Dn

29'-0"

L

Family
12-8x15-0

Sitting

Br 1
11-4x12-0

Second Floor

Stor

Garage
25-8x24-4

Up

First Floor

APARTMENT GARAGES

549

TO ORDER SEE **PAGE 608** OR CALL TOLL-FREE **1-800-DREAM HOME** (373-2646)

Second Floor

First Floor

2-Car Apartment Garage With Atrium

Total Living Area: 902

- Building height - 27'-4"
- Roof pitch - 9/12
- Ceiling heights -
  First Floor - 9'-0"   Second Floor - 8'-0"
- Two 9' x 8' overhead doors
- 1 bedroom, 1 bath
- Complete list of materials

Plan# **577-15011**

Price Code P9

APARTMENT GARAGES

Second Floor

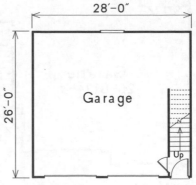

First Floor

2-Car Garage Apartment

Total Living Area: 746

- Building height - 22'-0"
- Roof pitch - 4/12
- Ceiling height - 8'-0"
- Two 9' x 7' overhead doors
- 1 bedroom, 1 bath
- Complete list of materials
- Step-by-step instructions

Plan# 577-15518

2-Car Garage Apartment

Total Living Area: 1,240

- Building height - 27'-0"
- Roof pitch - 9/12, 12/12, 6/12
- Ceiling heights -
  First Floor - 9'-0"   Second Floor - 8'-0"
- 2 bedrooms, 1 bath
- Kitchen/breakfast combine for added spaciousness
- Sloped ceiling adds appeal in sitting area
- Complete list of materials

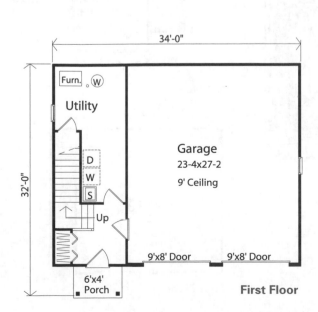

First Floor

34'-0"

32'-0"

Furn. W

Utility

D
W
S

Up

Garage
23-4x27-2

9' Ceiling

9'x8' Door   9'x8' Door

6'x4'
Porch

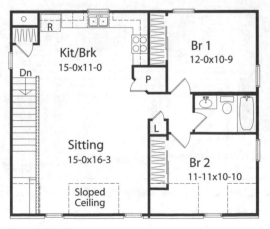

Second Floor

Kit/Brk
15-0x11-0

R

Dn

Br 1
12-0x10-9

P

L

Sitting
15-0x16-3

Br 2
11-11x10-10

Sloped
Ceiling

APARTMENT GARAGES

Plan# 577-15027

Price Code P9

Kit 9-0x9-4

Studio
23-4x14-0

Second Floor

2-Car Garage Apartment - Studio

Total Living Area: 576

- Building height - 21'-6"
- Roof pitch - 4/12
- Ceiling height - 8'-0"
- Two 9' x 7' overhead doors
- Contemporary style with private outside entrance
- Complete list of materials
- Step-by-step instructions

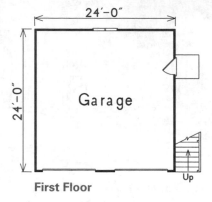

24'-0"

24'-0"

Garage

Up

First Floor

Plan# 577-15026

Price Code P10

Kitchen   Dining   Dn

Studio
17-4x14-7

Second Floor

2-Car Garage Apartment - Gambrel Roof

Total Living Area: 604

- Building height - 21'-4"
- Roof pitch - 4/12, 12/4.75
- Ceiling height - 8'-0"
- Two 9' x 7' overhead doors
- Complete list of materials
- Step-by-step instructions

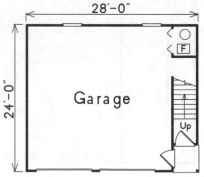

28'-0"

24'-0"

Garage

Up

First Floor

Vaulted Ceilings Add Spaciousness

Total Living Area: 2,318

- Great room area complemented with fireplace and patio access
- Breakfast bar has corner sink which overlooks great room
- Plant shelf graces vaulted entry
- Master suite provides walk in closet and private bath
- Each unit has 3 bedrooms, 2 baths, 1-car garage
- Basement foundation
- Duplex has 1,159 square feet of living space per unit

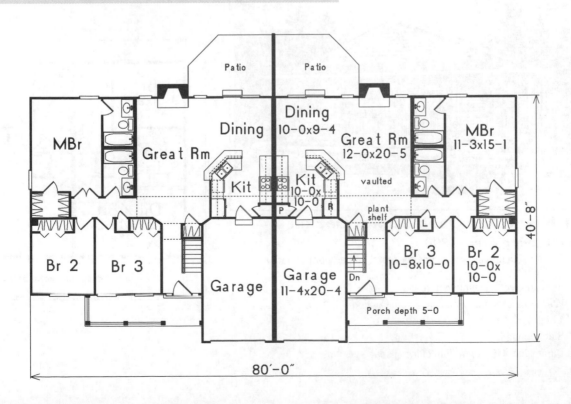

MULTI-FAMILY

553

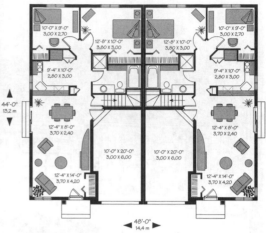

44'-0"
13,2 m

48'-0"
14,4 m

Cozy Country Duplex

Total Living Area: 1,668

- Easy access from garage into home
- Bath includes a tub as well as a separate shower
- Large living area combines with dining room making a nice area for entertaining
- Each unit has 2 bedrooms, 1 bath, 1-car garage
- Basement foundation
- Duplex has 834 square feet of living space per unit

Plan # **577-0764**

Price Code A

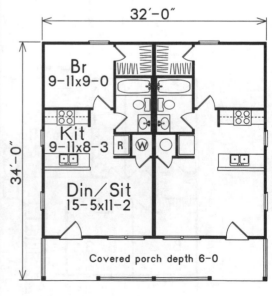

32'-0"

34'-0"

Br
9-11x9-0

Kit
9-11x8-3

Din/Sit
15-5x11-2

Covered porch depth 6-0

Efficient And Open Duplex Design

Total Living Area: 896

- Small cabin duplex well-suited for rental property or permanent residence
- Compact, yet convenient floor plan
- Well-organized for economical construction
- 1 bedroom, 1 bath
- Slab foundation
- Duplex has 448 square feet of living space per unit

Country Charm In A Double Feature
Total Living Area: 2,986

- Vaulted great room, kitchen and two balconies define architectural drama
- First floor master suite boasts a lavish bath and double walk-in closets
- Impressive second floor features two large bedrooms, spacious closets, hall bath and balcony overlook
- Each unit has 3 bedrooms, 2 1/2 baths, 2-car garage
- Basement foundation
- Duplex has 1,493 square feet of living space per unit

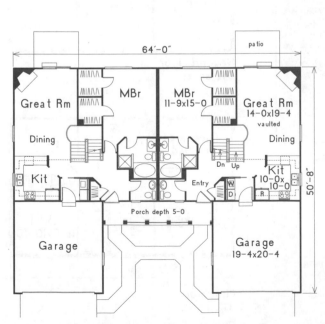

First Floor
960 sq. ft.
per unit

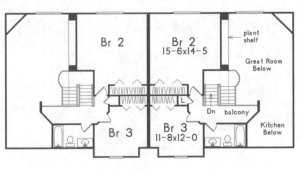

Second Floor
533 sq. ft.
per unit

TO ORDER SEE PAGE 608 OR CALL TOLL

MULTI-FAMILY

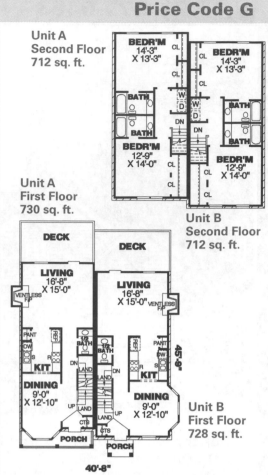

Unit A
Second Floor
712 sq. ft.

BEDR'M 14'-3" X 13'-3"

BEDR'M 14'-3" X 13'-3"

BATH / BATH

BEDR'M 12'-9" X 14'-0"

BEDR'M 12'-9" X 14'-0"

W/D

Unit A
First Floor
730 sq. ft.

Unit B
Second Floor
712 sq. ft.

DECK

DECK

LIVING 16'-8" X 15'-0"

LIVING 16'-8" X 15'-0"

VENTLESS F.P.

VENTLESS F.P.

PANT / REF / DW / KIT

1/2 BATH

1/2 BATH

REF / PANT / DW / KIT

DINING 9'-0" X 12'-10"

DINING 9'-0" X 12'-10"

PORCH

PORCH

Unit B
First Floor
728 sq. ft.

45'-9"

40'-8"

TO ORDER SEE PAGE 608 OR CALL T...

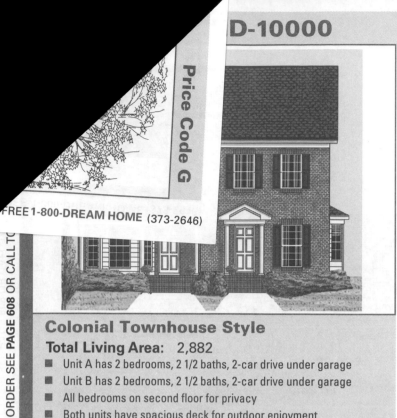

Colonial Townhouse Style

Total Living Area: 2,882

- Unit A has 2 bedrooms, 2 1/2 baths, 2-car drive under garage
- Unit B has 2 bedrooms, 2 1/2 baths, 2-car drive under garage
- All bedrooms on second floor for privacy
- Both units have spacious deck for outdoor enjoyment
- Basement foundation

Plan# 577-0473

Price Code D

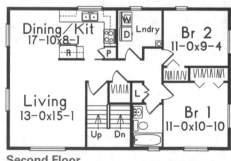

Dining/Kit 17-10x8-1

W/D Lndry

Br 2 11-0x9-4

Living 13-0x15-1

Up Dn

Br 1 11-0x10-10

Second Floor
912 sq. ft.

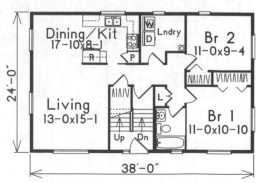

Dining/Kit 17-10x8-1

W/D Lndry

Br 2 11-0x9-4

Living 13-0x15-1

Up Dn

Br 1 11-0x10-10

24'-0"

38'-0"

First Floor
912 sq. ft.

Open Layout Creates Spacious Living

Total Living Area: 1,824

- Kitchen offers efficient layout with pantry and adjacent dining area
- Convenient linen and coat closet
- Centrally located laundry room
- Each unit has 2 bedrooms, 1 bath
- Shallow basement foundation
- Duplex has 912 square feet of living space per unit

MULTI-FAMILY

© Michael E. Nelson
NELSON DESIGN GROUP, LLC

Attractive Residential Styling

Total Living Area: 2,110

- Efficiently designed kitchen
- Formal dining room has an open feel with decorative columned wall
- Spacious living room with access to covered grilling porch
- Each unit has 2 bedrooms, 2 baths
- Crawl space or slab foundation, please specify when ordering
- Duplex has 1,055 square feet of living space per unit

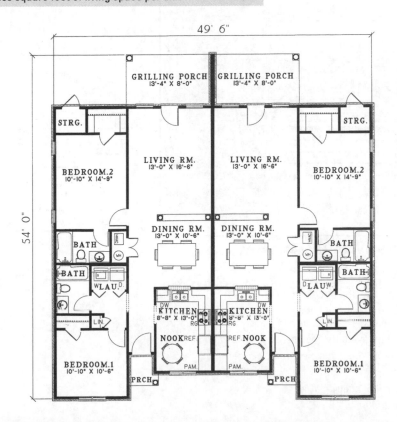

MULTI-FAMILY

Plan# 577-DR-2074

Traditional Duplex With Covered Porch

Total Living Area: 1,892

- Sliding door in kitchen for rear access
- Breakfast bar in kitchen overlooks dining and living areas
- Entry hall has closet for coats and extra storage
- Each unit has 2 bedrooms, 1 bath
- Basement foundation
- Duplex has 946 square feet of living space per unit

Plan# 577-0787

Double Cottage With Breezeway

Total Living Area: 844

- Unique design with maximum privacy for each unit featuring its own porch, breezeway entrance and large sundeck
- Living room offers separate entry with closet, fireplace, sliding doors to deck and opens to dining area with bay window
- The bedroom features a private bath, closet and views to porch
- Each unit has 1 bedroom, 1 bath and a shared 2-car garage
- Crawl space foundation
- Duplex has 422 square feet of living area

MULTI-FAMILY

Plan# 577-CHD-10001

Price Code H

TO ORDER SEE PAGE 608 OR CALL TOLL-FREE 1-800-DREAM HOME (373-2646)

Great Curb Appeal

Total Living Area: 5,516

- Units A and C both have 2 bedrooms, 2 1/2 baths, 1-car garage
- Unit B has 2 bedrooms, 2 baths, 1-car garage
- Unit D has 3 bedrooms, 2 1/2 baths, 1-car garage
- All master bedrooms have a private bath and walk-in closet
- Slab foundation

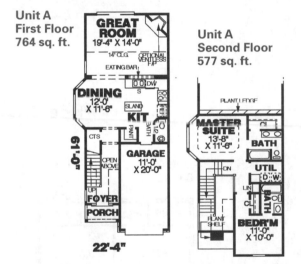

Unit A
First Floor
764 sq. ft.

Unit A
Second Floor
577 sq. ft.

Unit B
1,120 sq. ft.

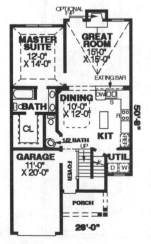

Unit C
First Floor
983 sq. ft.

Unit C
Second Floor
528 sq. ft.

Unit D
First Floor
788 sq. ft.

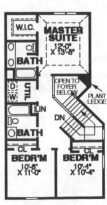

Unit D
Second Floor
756 sq. ft.

MULTI-FAMILY

Plan# 577-DR-3006

Price Code H

Fourplex With A Traditional Feel

Total Living Area: 3,648

- Kitchen is open to breakfast area
- Spacious bath includes laundry closet
- Sitting area is cozy and separate from other areas
- Each unit has 2 bedrooms, 1 bath
- Slab foundation
- Duplex has 912 square feet of living space per unit

Plan# 577-RJ-N17-1

Price Code D

MULTI-FAMILY

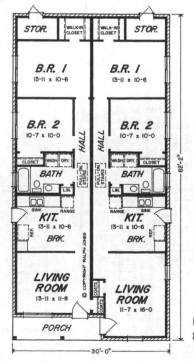

Unit A
833 sq. ft.

Unit B
880 sq. ft.

Cottage Appearance Has Cozy Feel

Total Living Area: 1,713

- Kitchen has access outdoors
- Handy washer and dryer closet located in the bath
- Bedrooms at the back of the home for privacy and quiet
- Each unit has 2 bedrooms, 1 bath
- Slab foundation

Atrium Duplex With Room To Grow

Total Living Area: 3,666

- Inviting porch and foyer leads to vaulted living room and dining balcony with atrium window wall
- Bedroom #2 doubles as a study with access to deck through sliding glass doors
- Atrium opens to large family room and third bedroom
- Each unit has 3 bedrooms, 2 baths, 2-car garage
- Walk-out basement foundation
- Duplex has 1,833 square feet of living space per unit

First Floor
1,073 sq. ft. per unit

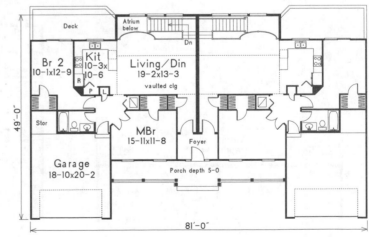

Deck

Atrium below

Dn

Br 2
10-1x12-9

Kit
10-3x
10-6

Living/Din
19-2x13-3
vaulted clg

Stor

MBr
15-11x11-8

Foyer

Garage
18-10x20-2

Porch depth 5-0

49'-0"

81'-0"

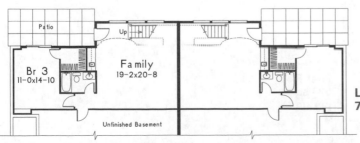

Patio

Up

Br 3
11-0x14-10

Family
19-2x20-8

Unfinished Basement

Lower Level
760 sq. ft. per unit

MULTI-FAMILY

TO ORDER SEE **PAGE 608** OR CALL TOLL-FREE 1-800-DREAM HOME (373-2646)

Residential Style Fits Any Neighborhood

Total Living Area: 2,796

- Two-story entry makes a big impression
- Laundry closet is located on the second floor near bedrooms for convenience
- Kitchen overlooks living and dining rooms and has island with eating bar
- 3 bedrooms, 2 1/2 baths, 2-car garage
- Crawl space foundation
- Duplex has 1,398 square feet of living space per unit

**Second Floor
775 sq. ft.
per unit**

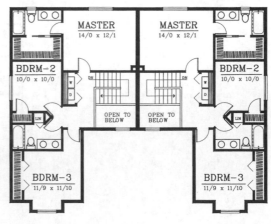

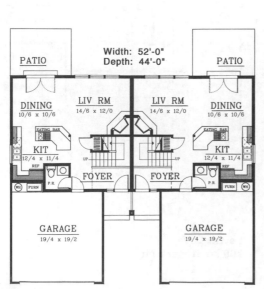

Width: 52'-0"
Depth: 44'-0"

**First Floor
623 sq. ft.
per unit**

Spacious Layout For Comfortable Living
Total Living Area: 3,360

- Bedrooms have ample closet space
- Laundry closet near both bedrooms
- Convenient U-shaped kitchen adjacent to dining room with access to deck on first floor and balcony on second floor
- Adjacent to living room is handy coat and linen closet
- Each unit has 2 bedrooms, 1 bath
- Crawl space foundation, drawings also include slab foundation
- Fourplex has 840 square feet of living space per unit

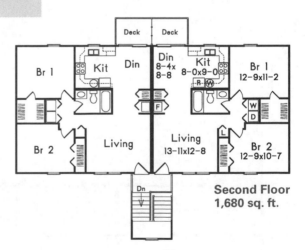

Second Floor
1,680 sq. ft.

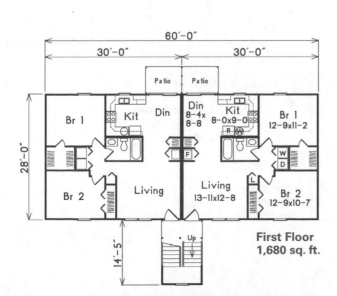

First Floor
1,680 sq. ft.

© Michael E. Nelson
NELSON DESIGN GROUP, LLC

Duplex Has Inviting Facade

Total Living Area: 2,502

- Decorative columns separate the dining area from the great room
- All bedrooms located on second floor for privacy
- Each unit has 3 bedrooms, 2 1/2 baths, 1-car garage
- Crawl space or slab foundation, please specify when ordering
- Duplex has 1,251 square feet of living space per unit

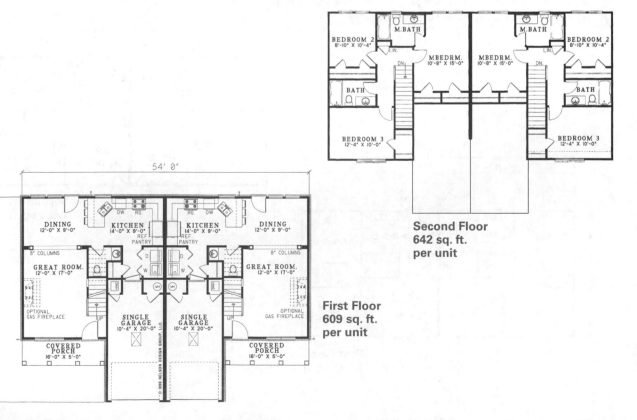

Second Floor
642 sq. ft.
per unit

First Floor
609 sq. ft.
per unit

TO ORDER SEE **PAGE 608** OR CALL TOLL-FREE 1-800-DREAM HOME (373-2646)

Stylish Living, Open Design

Total Living Area: 1,992

- Graciously designed ranch duplex with alluring openness
- Vaulted kitchen with accent on spaciousness features huge pantry, plenty of cabinets and convenient laundry room
- Master bedroom includes its own cozy bath and oversized walk-in closet
- Each unit has 2 bedrooms, 2 baths, 1-car garage
- Basement foundation
- Duplex has 996 square feet of living space per unit

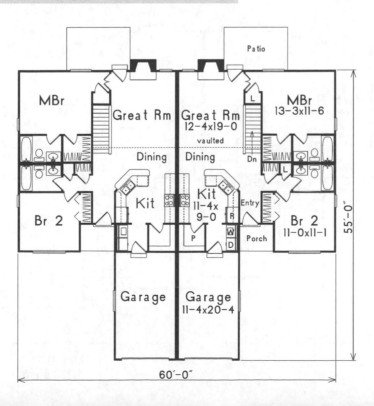

MULTI-FAMILY

Inviting Arched Entry

Total Living Area: 2,445

- 10' ceiling in great room along with transoms flanking fireplace creates a breathtaking atmosphere
- Kitchen includes convenient snack bar overlooking sunny breakfast room
- Master bedroom has box bay window, private bath and enormous walk-in closet
- Each unit has 2 bedrooms, 2 baths, 2-car garage
- Basement foundation

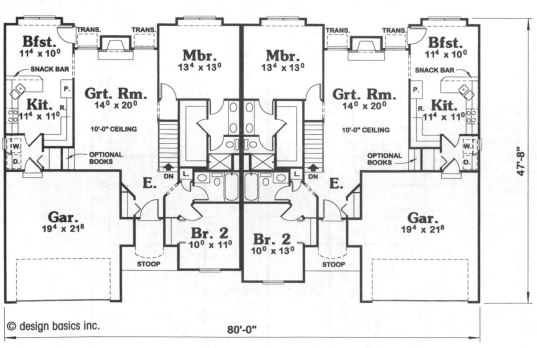

© design basics inc.

80'-0"

47'-8"

Unit A
1,212 sq. ft.

Unit B
1,233 sq. ft.

Plan# 577-CHD-10002

Price Code H

TO ORDER SEE **PAGE 608** OR CALL TOLL-FREE 1-800-DREAM HOME (373-2646)

Varied Front Facades Adds Interest

Total Living Area: 6,410

■ Unit A has 3 bedrooms, 2 1/2 baths, 2-car garage

■ Unit B has 2 bedrooms, 2 1/2 baths

■ Unit C has 2 bedrooms, 2 1/2 baths, 1-car garage

■ Unit D has 2 bedrooms, 2 baths, 1-car garage

■ All master bedrooms have private bath and walk-in closet

■ Slab foundation

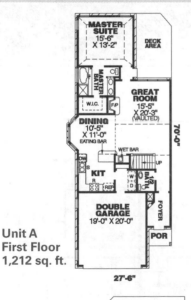

Unit A
First Floor
1,212 sq. ft.

Unit A
Second Floor
750 sq. ft.

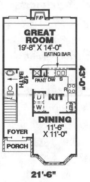

Unit B
First Floor
787 sq. ft.

Unit B
Second Floor
684 sq. ft.

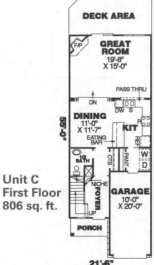

Unit C
First Floor
806 sq. ft.

Unit C
Second Floor
771 sq. ft.

Unit D
1,400 sq. ft.

MULTI-FAMILY

567

Elegant Exterior Accents Design

Total Living Area: 2,885

- Cozy study adjoins master suite
- Several windows brighten main living area
- Practical counter space in kitchen overlooks dining and living areas
- Convenient laundry closet on second floor
- Each unit has 3 bedrooms, 3 baths
- Slab foundation
- Unit A has 1,437 square feet of living space and unit B has 1,448 square feet of living space

MULTI-FAMILY

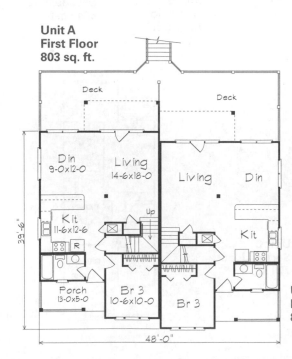

Unit A
First Floor
803 sq. ft.

Unit B
First Floor
803 sq. ft.

Unit A
Second Floor
634 sq. ft.

Unit B
Second Floor
645 sq. ft.

TO ORDER SEE PAGE 608 OR CALL TOLL-FREE 1-800-DREAM HOME (373-2646)

© COPYRIGHT 1986 RALPH JONES & ASSOC.

Appealing Double Gables

Total Living Area: 2,054

- Cozy living room has oversized window adding light
- Master suite has enormous walk-in closet and easy access to bath
- Convenient space in kitchen for washer and dryer
- Each unit has **3** bedrooms, 1 bath
- Slab foundation
- Duplex has 1,027 square feet of living space per unit

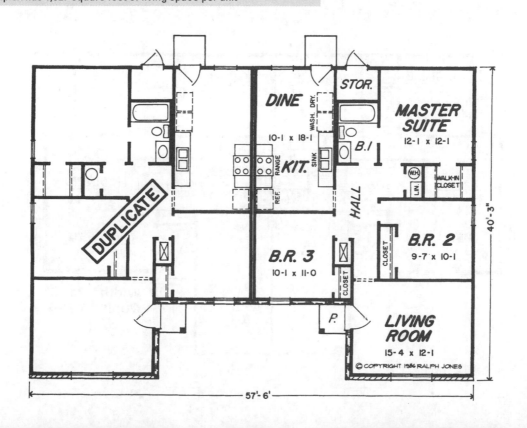

DUPLICATE

DINE
10-1 x 18-1

WASH. DRY.

STOR.

B.1

MASTER SUITE
12-1 x 12-1

KIT.

SINK

RANGE

REF.

W.H.

LIN.

WALK-IN CLOSET

HALL

B.R. 3
10-1 x 11-0

CLOSET

CLOSET

B.R. 2
9-7 x 10-1

P.

LIVING ROOM
15-4 x 12-1

© COPYRIGHT 1986 RALPH JONES

40'-3"

57'-6'

MULTI-FAMILY

Perfect Symmetry With This Duplex

Total Living Area: 2,068

- Open living area has cozy fireplace and views into dining area and kitchen
- Covered patio directly off dining area
- Both bedrooms have large walk-in closets for additional storage
- Each unit has 2 bedrooms, 1 bath, 1-car garage
- Slab foundation
- Duplex has 1,034 square feet of living space per unit

MULTI-FAMILY

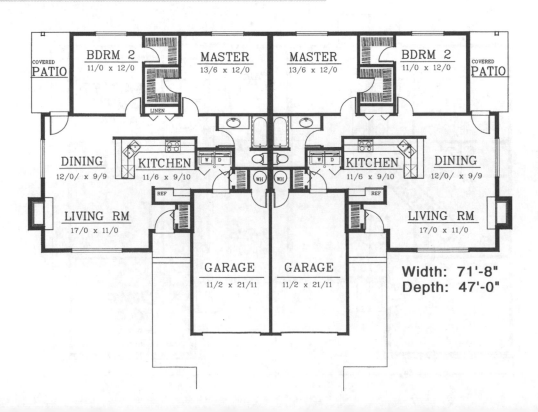

Width: 71'-8"
Depth: 47'-0"

A Fourplex With Distinction

Total Living Area: 3,492

- Beautiful stonework with planter boxes and large country porch provide a dazzling exterior
- First floor units have access to their own sundecks while lower level units each enjoy a private patio
- Each unit features a hookup for a stacked washer and dryer
- Units A and B have 2 bedrooms, 1 bath and units C and D have 1 bedroom, 1 bath
- Walk-out basement foundation with centrally located storage area
- Fourplex has 1,746 square feet per floor

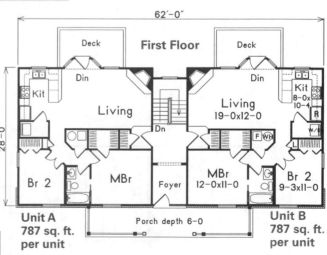

First Floor

62'-0"

28'-0"

Unit A
787 sq. ft.
per unit

Unit B
787 sq. ft.
per unit

Porch depth 6-0

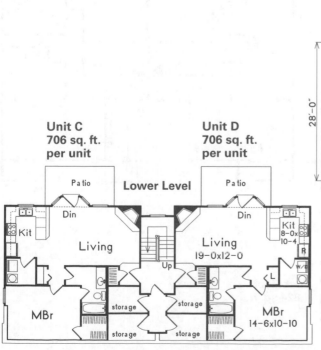

Unit C
706 sq. ft.
per unit

Unit D
706 sq. ft.
per unit

Lower Level

MULTI-FAMILY

Spacious Fourplex Has Large Living Area
Total Living Area: 3,648

- Large kitchen adjacent to living room
- Handy linen closet in hallway
- Spacious living area with easy access to patio or balcony
- Centrally located laundry closet for stackable washer and dryer
- Each unit has 2 bedrooms, 1 bath
- Crawl space/slab foundation
- Fourplex has 912 square feet of living space per unit

MULTI-FAMILY

Second Floor
1,824 sq. ft.

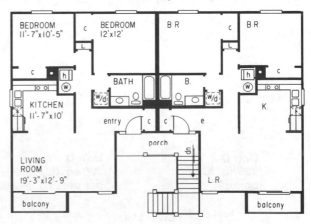

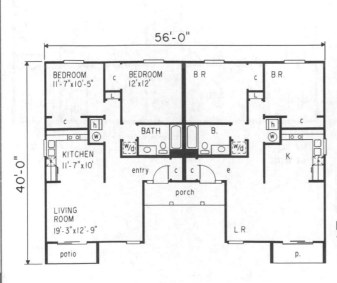

First Floor
1,824 sq. ft.

TO ORDER SEE **PAGE 608** OR CALL TOLL-FREE 1-800-DREAM HOME (373-2646)

© Michael E. Nelson
NELSON DESIGN GROUP, LLC

Lovely Design Has It All

Total Living Area: 2,910

- Sunny breakfast room is adjacent to kitchen and has access to outdoor covered grilling porch
- Master suite has intricate ceiling and a private luxurious bath with double closets
- Each unit has 3 bedrooms, 2 baths, 1-car garage
- Crawl space or slab foundation, please specify when ordering
- Duplex has 1,455 square feet of living space per unit

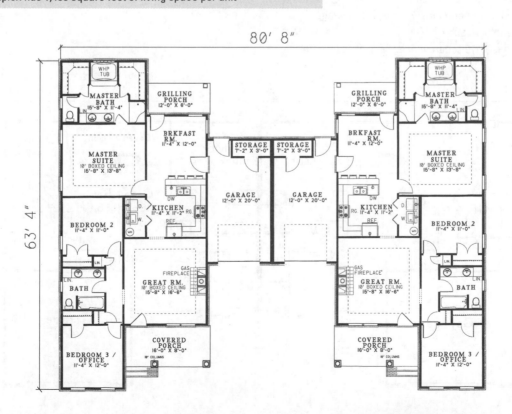

MULTI-FAMILY

Covered Porch Entrance To Duplex

Total Living Area: 2,830

- Great room, master bedroom and dining room access covered porch
- Master bedroom features double-door entry, walk-in closet and private bath with shower
- Great room has fireplace and wet bar
- U-shaped kitchen opens to dining room
- Laundry room with plenty of work space conveniently accesses the outdoors, garage and kitchen
- Each unit has 2 bedrooms, 2 baths, 2-car garage
- Basement foundation
- Duplex has 1,415 square feet of living space per unit

MULTI-FAMILY

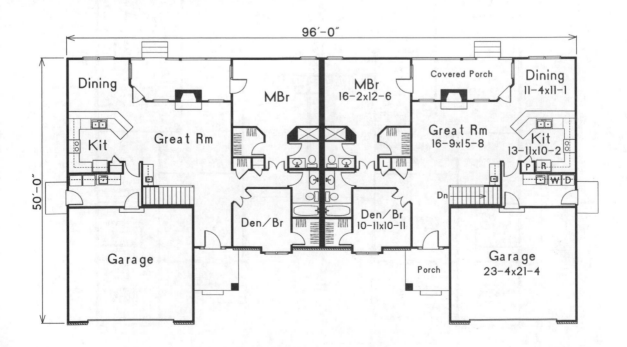

Living Room Perfect For Entertaining
Total Living Area: 2,046

- Large closet on the first floor houses stackable washer and dryer and utilities
- Convenient half bath located on first floor
- Spacious kitchen with access outdoors also includes room for dining area
- Each unit has 2 bedrooms, 1 1/2 baths
- Basement foundation, drawings also include crawl space/slab foundation
- Duplex has 1,023 total square feet of living space per unit

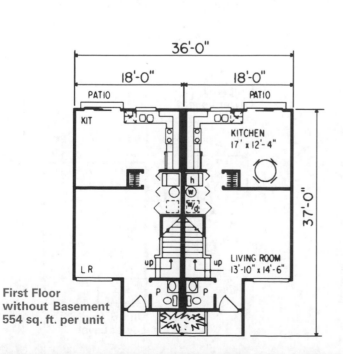

First Floor without Basement
554 sq. ft. per unit

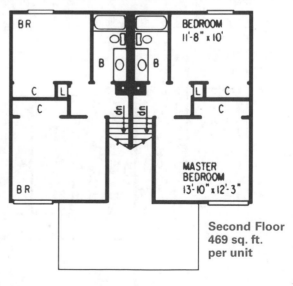

Second Floor
469 sq. ft. per unit

MULTI-FAMILY

575

TO ORDER SEE **PAGE 608** OR CALL TOLL-FREE 1-800-DREAM HOME (373-2646)

Fourplex With Multi-Gabled Facade

Total Living Area: 7,372

- Units A and D feature living/dining combination and master bedroom retreat with lower level family room and third bedroom

- Units A and D include 3 bedrooms, 3 baths, 2-car garage in a ranch plan with 1,707 square feet of living area with 1,149 on the first floor and 558 on the lower level

- Units B and C feature luxurious living area and second floor with spacious master suite featuring two walk-in closets and a lavish bath

- Units B and C include 3 bedrooms, 2 1/2 baths, 2-car garage in a two-story plan with 1,979 square feet of living area with 1,055 on the first floor and 924 on the second floor

- Basement foundation

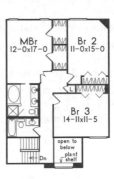

**Unit B, C
Second Floor**

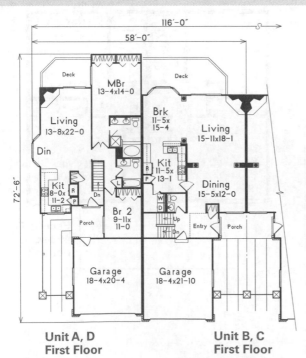

**Unit A, D
First Floor**

**Unit B, C
First Floor**

**Unit A, D
Lower Level**

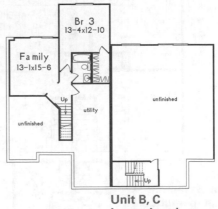

**Unit B, C
Lower Level**

MULTI-FAMILY

© COPYRIGHT 1987 RALPH JONES & ASSOC.

Gables Add Interesting Roofline

Total Living Area: 2,254

- Vaulted great room overlooks dining room which has easy access into kitchen
- Vaulted master suite has private bath and oversized walk-in closet
- Kitchen includes washer and dryer space for convenience
- Each unit has **3** bedrooms, **2** baths
- Slab foundation
- Duplex has 1,127 square feet of living space per unit

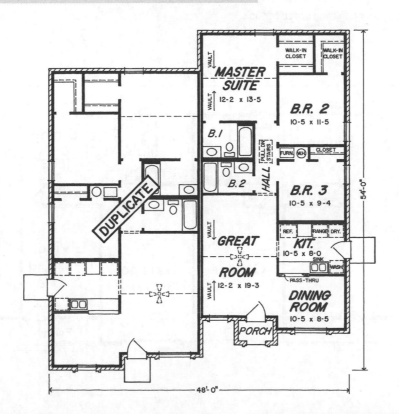

TO ORDER SEE PAGE 608 OR CALL TOLL-FREE 1-800-DREAM HOME (373-2646)

Duplex With Cozy Front Porch
Total Living Area: 1,904

- Convenient laundry area and dining room adjacent to kitchen
- Bedrooms feature ample closet space
- Garage has plenty of space for work/storage area
- Handy coat closets located near garage and living room
- Dining accesses outdoors
- Each unit has 2 bedrooms, 1 bath, 1-car garage
- Partial basement/crawl space foundation
- Duplex has 952 square feet of living space per unit

MULTI-FAMILY

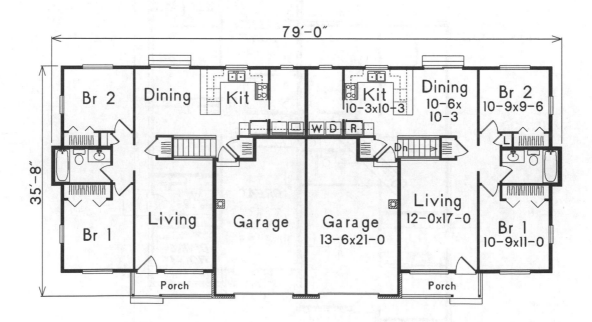

Private Entrances With Covered Porch

Total Living Area: 3,636

- Bayed breakfast room is centrally located between the great room and kitchen
- Two-story foyer adds dramatic feel with plant shelves above
- Great room has fireplace and wall of windows creating a cheerful atmosphere
- Each unit has 3 bedrooms, 2 1/2 baths, 2-car garage
- Basement foundation
- Duplex has 1,818 square feet of living space per unit

First Floor
829 sq. ft.
per unit

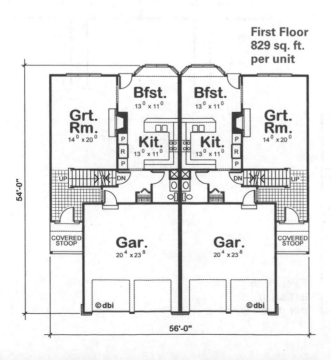

Second Floor
989 sq. ft.
per unit

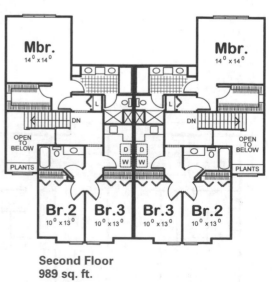

MULTI-FAMILY

© Michael E. Nelson
NELSON DESIGN GROUP, LLC

Unique Corner Fireplace Adds Drama

Total Living Area: 2,570

- U-shaped kitchen has all the conveniences
- First floor master bedroom is well-located for privacy
- Two second floor bedrooms share a bath
- Each unit has 3 bedrooms, 2 baths, 2-car garage
- Crawl space or slab foundation, please specify when ordering
- Duplex has 1,285 square feet of living space per unit

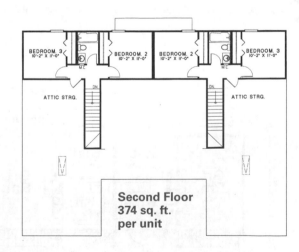

**Second Floor
374 sq. ft.
per unit**

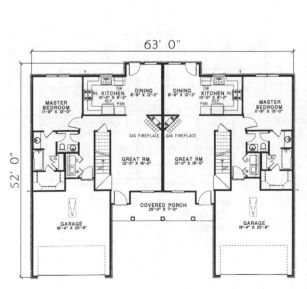

**First Floor
911 sq. ft.
per unit**

Gables And Arches Adds Drama

Total Living Area: 5,810

- Unit C has 2 bedrooms, 2 baths, 2-car garage
- Unit D has 3 bedrooms, 2 1/2 baths, 2-car garage
- Unit E has 3 bedrooms, 2 baths, 2-car garage
- All master baths have step-up tubs, separate showers, double vanities and walk-in closets
- Slab foundation

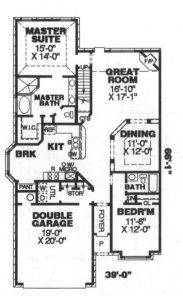

Unit C
1,780 sq. ft.

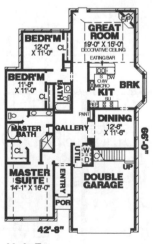

Unit E
1,939 sq. ft.

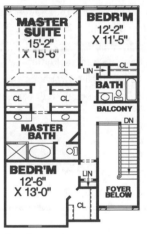

**Unit D
Second
Floor
1,127 sq. ft.**

**Unit D
First Floor
964 sq. ft.**

MULTI-FAMILY

581

Compact Home With Large Living Area
Total Living Area: 1,536

- Living room joins the kitchen/dining area for an open atmosphere
- L-shaped kitchen with outdoor access and convenient laundry area
- Linen and coat closet
- Welcoming front porch
- Each unit has 2 bedrooms, 1 bath
- Crawl space foundation, drawings also include slab foundation
- Duplex has 768 total square feet of living space per unit

MULTI-FAMILY

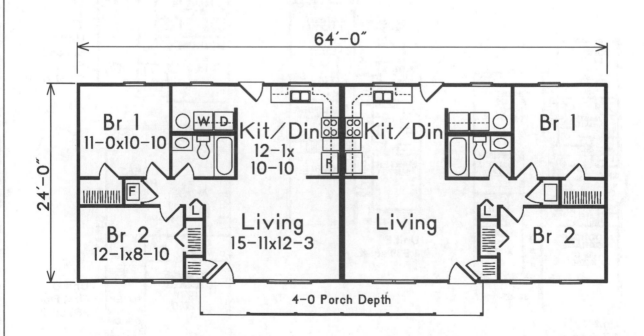

64'-0"

24'-0"

Br 1
11-0x10-10

W D

Kit/Din
12-1x
10-10

R

Kit/Din

Br 1

F

Br 2
12-1x8-10

L

Living
15-11x12-3

Living

L

Br 2

4-0 Porch Depth

Unique Angled Entry Welcomes Guests

Total Living Area: 3,536

- Spacious utility area has plenty of extra counterspace, a handy sink, a storage closet and a powder room for convenience
- Master suite has lots of luxury including a sunny bay window with seat, an oversized master bath with spa tub and enormous walk-in closet
- Dining area in the front of this home can easily be converted to a private study
- Each unit has 2 bedrooms, 1 1/2 baths, 2-car garage
- Basement foundation
- Duplex has 1,768 square feet of living space per unit

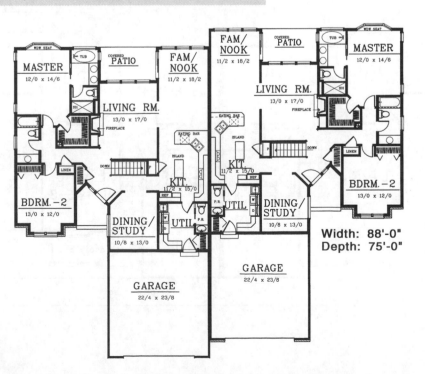

Width: 88'-0"
Depth: 75'-0"

MULTI-FAMILY

Duplex With Plenty Of Style

Total Living Area: 1,704

- Smartly designed layout with emphasis on efficiency
- Functional kitchen embraces the sun with its bay window, glass sliding doors and pass-through to living room
- Five generously designed closets offer an abundance of storage
- Each unit has 2 bedrooms, 1 bath, 1-car garage
- Basement foundation
- Duplex has 852 square feet of living space per unit

MULTI-FAMILY

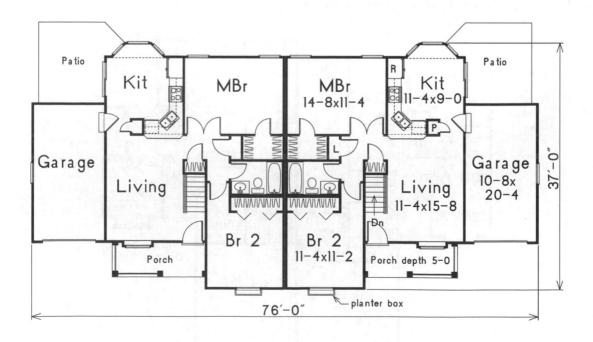

TO ORDER SEE **PAGE 608** OR CALL TOLL-FREE 1-800-DREAM HOME (373-2646)

Multi-Family With Residential Look

Total Living Area: 3,728

- This fiveplex home features an extra large porch and roof dormers that make it fit graciously into any residential neighborhood
- Three first floor units have access to their own balcony while the two lower level units each enjoy private patios
- Each unit has 1 bedroom, 1 bath
- Walk-out basement foundation with centrally located storage and laundry room
- Fiveplex has 1,868 square feet of living area on the first floor and 1,860 square feet of living area on the lower level

First Floor

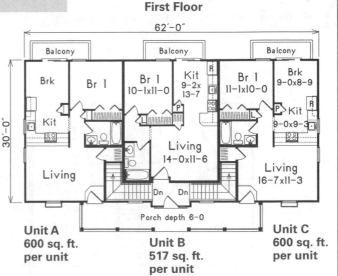

Unit A
600 sq. ft.
per unit

Unit B
517 sq. ft.
per unit

Unit C
600 sq. ft.
per unit

Lower Level

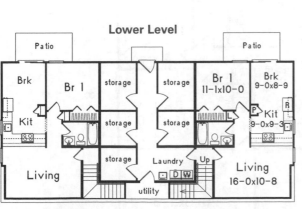

Unit D
592 sq. ft.
per unit

Unit E
592 sq. ft.
per unit

MULTI-FAMILY

585

TO ORDER SEE **PAGE 608** OR CALL TOLL-FREE 1-800-DREAM HOME (373-2646)

Duplex Has Garage And Entry Porch
Total Living Area: 1,700

- Front facade fits splendidly with residential surroundings
- Well-planned kitchen includes an abundance of cabinets
- Spacious bedroom with double closets
- Plant shelf, open stairway and vaulted ceilings highlight living space
- Convenient entrance from garage into main living area
- Dining room accesses deck
- Each unit has 2 bedrooms, 1 bath, 1-car side entry garage
- Basement foundation
- Duplex has 850 square feet of living space per unit

MULTI-FAMILY

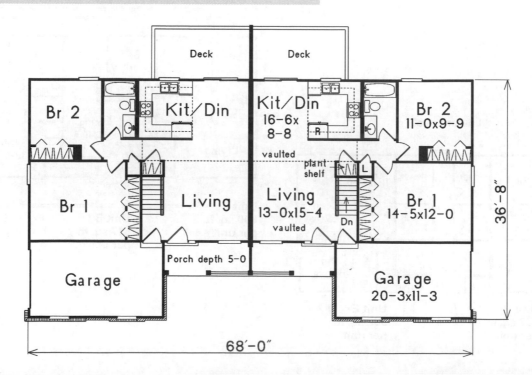

Deck   Deck

Br 2   Kit/Din   Kit/Din
16-6x
8-8   Br 2
11-0x9-9

vaulted

plant
shelf   L

Br 1   Living   Living
13-0x15-4   Br 1
14-5x12-0

vaulted

Dn

Garage   Porch depth 5-0   Garage
20-3x11-3

36'-8"

68'-0"

© COPYRIGHT RALPH JONES

Duplex Has Dormers And Gables

Total Living Area: 2,490

- Extra storage located at the rear of the design
- Living and dining rooms are open and airy
- Second floor has two bedrooms and a full bath
- Each unit has 3 bedrooms, 2 baths
- Slab foundation
- Duplex has 1,245 square feet of living space per unit

**First Floor
740 sq. ft.
per unit**

© COPYRIGHT RALPH JONES

STOR.   P.

LIVING
19-3 x 17-0

DINING

EATING BAR

RANGE KIT.

REF.   SINK   D.W.

DRY.   COATS

WASH.

B.1   WALK-IN CLOSET

HALL

DUPLICATE

UP   ENT.

B.R. 1
12-0 x 11-0

PORCH

46'-5"

40'-0"

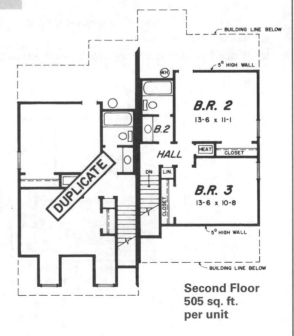

**Second Floor
505 sq. ft.
per unit**

BUILDING LINE BELOW

5° HIGH WALL

B.R. 2
13-6 x 11-1

HEAT   CLOSET

HALL

DUPLICATE

DN   LIN.

B.2

CLOSET

B.R. 3
13-6 x 10-8

5° HIGH WALL

BUILDING LINE BELOW

Expansive, Open Living Areas

Total Living Area: 2,800

- Large master suite has walk-in closet and private bath with linen area
- Covered entrance opens into entry with coat closet
- Work area in garage
- Convenient laundry room
- Half wall defines kitchen that opens into large living room with sliders to deck
- Each unit has 2 bedrooms, 2 baths, 2-car garage
- Basement foundation
- Duplex has 1,400 square feet of living space per unit

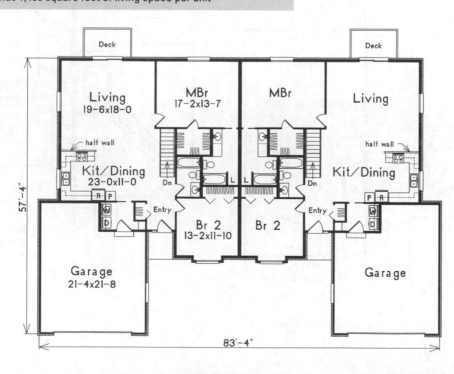

Deck

Deck

Living
19-6x18-0

MBr
17-2x13-7

MBr

Living

half wall

half wall

Kit/Dining
23-0x11-0

Dn

Dn

Kit/Dining

Entry

Entry

Garage
21-4x21-8

Br 2
13-2x11-10

Br 2

Garage

57'-4"

83'-4"

Compact And Efficient Design

Total Living Area: 2,436

- Master bedroom has private bath with double vanities and large walk-in closet
- Kitchen with snack bar overlooks breakfast room
- Great room has cheerful wall of windows brightening the interior
- Each unit has 2 bedrooms, 2 baths, 2 car garage
- Basement foundation
- Duplex has 1,218 square feet of living space per unit

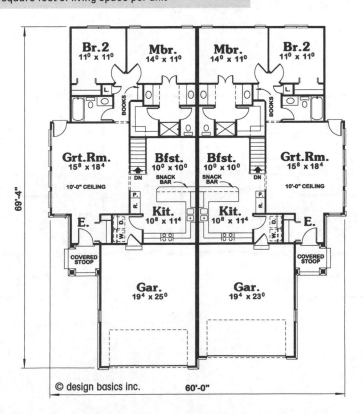

© design basics inc.   60'-0"

MULTI-FAMILY

Inviting Entry With Built-In Planter

Total Living Area: 1,966

- Entry opens into main living area or dining/kitchen
- Ample closet/storage space throughout duplex
- Large L-shaped dining/kitchen has garage access
- Several windows brighten living room
- Each unit has 2 bedrooms, 1 bath, 1-car garage
- Basement foundation
- Duplex has 983 square feet of living space per unit

MULTI-FAMILY

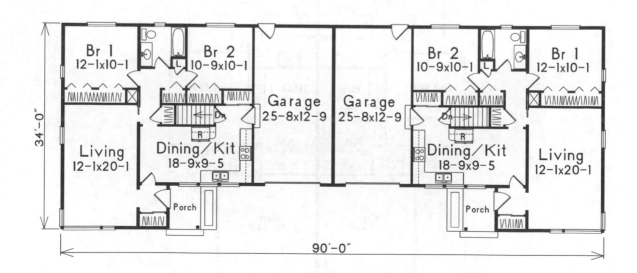

TO ORDER SEE **PAGE 608** OR CALL TOLL-FREE 1-800-DREAM HOME (373-2646)

Charming Victorian-Style Duplex

Total Living Area: 2,172

- Bay windows on both floors brighten living spaces
- Open living on first floor is a terrific layout for entertaining
- Unit A has 3 bedrooms, 1 1/2 baths
- Unit B has 2 bedrooms, 1 1/2 baths
- Basement foundation
- Duplex has 1,086 square feet of living space per unit

Second Floor
543 sq. ft.
per unit

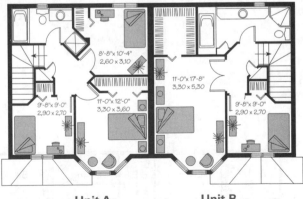

Unit A   Unit B

Unit A   Unit B

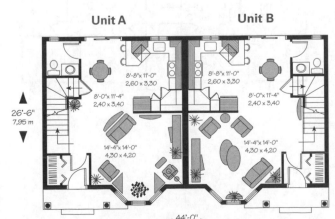

26'-6"
7,95 m

First Floor
543 sq. ft.
per unit

44'-0"
13,2 m

MULTI-FAMILY

591

All The Amenities In This Twelve-Plex

Total Living Area: 10,704

- Compact L-shaped kitchen joins dining area
- Spacious living room with convenient coat closet
- Bedrooms have plenty of closet space
- Large living room windows allow plenty of sunlight
- Each unit has 2 bedrooms, 1 bath
- Shallow basement foundation
- Twelve-plex has 768 square feet of living space per unit, 3,568 square feet per floor

MULTI-FAMILY

592

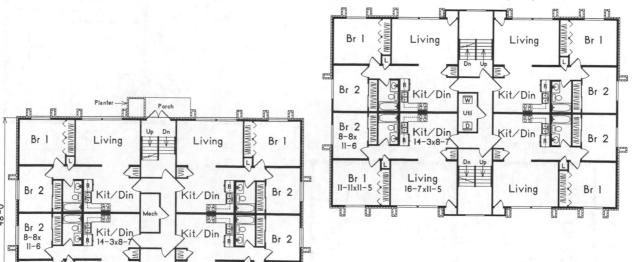

Second Floor and Third Floor
3,072 sq. ft. per floor

First Floor
3,072 sq. ft.

Gables Add Appeal To The Front Facade

Total Living Area: 4,131

- Unit A has 3 bedrooms, 2 baths, 2-car garage
- Unit B has 3 bedrooms, 2 1/2 baths, 2-car garage
- Unit A has luxurious master bedroom with double walk-in closets, private bath with step up tub, separate shower and double vanity
- Unit B features master suite on first floor and all bedrooms have walk-in closets
- Slab foundation

Unit B
Second Floor
642 sq. ft.

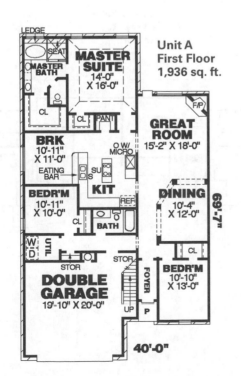

Unit A
First Floor
1,936 sq. ft.

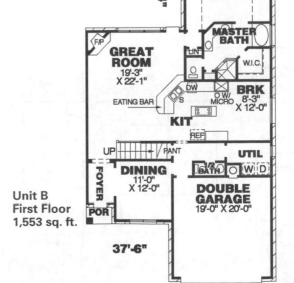

Unit B
First Floor
1,553 sq. ft.

MULTI-FAMILY

© Michael E. Nelson
NELSON DESIGN GROUP, LLC

Handsome Arched Entry

Total Living Area: 3,366

- 9' ceilings throughout the first floor
- Impressive kitchen with center island/snack bar has lots of counterspace and cabinetry
- Master suite has private bath and is conveniently located on the first floor
- Bonus room has an additional 265 square feet of living area per unit
- Each unit has 3 bedrooms, 2 1/2 baths, 1-car garage
- Crawl space or slab foundation, please specify when ordering
- Duplex has 1,683 square feet of living space per unit

Second Floor
529 sq. ft.
per unit

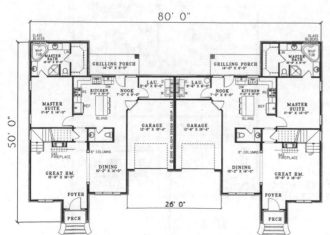

First Floor
1,154 sq. ft
per unit

TO ORDER SEE **PAGE 608** OR CALL TOLL-FREE **1-800-DREAM HOME (373-2646)**

Open Living Areas

Total Living Area: 2,622

- Charming covered porch
- Kitchen features snack bar whick overlooks great room as well as an island making food preparation easier
- Sunny dining room
- Each unit has 3 bedrooms, 2 baths, 2-car garage
- Basement foundation
- Duplex has 1,311 square feet of living space per unit

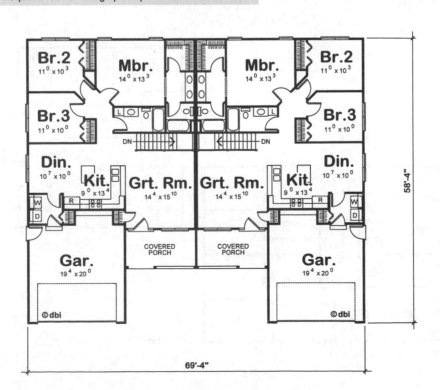

MULTI-FAMILY

TO ORDER SEE PAGE 608 OR CALL TOLL-FREE 1-800-DREAM HOME (373-2646)

Eight-Plex Has Corridor Laundry Room

Total Living Area: 7,848

- Bedrooms have ample closet space
- Kitchen and dining area combine for open space
- Living room boasts twin windows for plenty of sunlight
- Convenient closet by entry
- Each unit has 2 bedrooms, 1 bath
- Shallow basement foundation
- Eight-plex has 858 square feet of living space per unit, 3,924 square feet per floor

MULTI-FAMILY

Second Floor

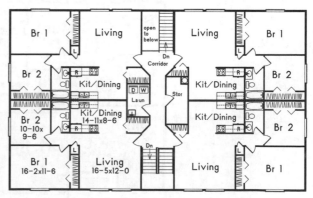

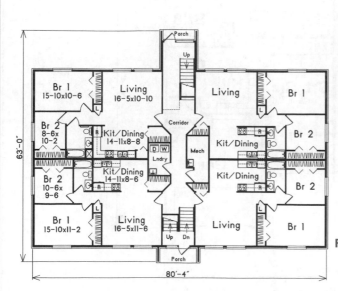

First Floor

TO ORDER SEE **PAGE 608** OR CALL TOLL-FREE 1-800-DREAM HOME (373-2646)

Neat Floor Plan Creates Open Living

Total Living Area: 1,796

- Large kitchen is perfect for entertaining
- Plenty of storage space in these units
- Each unit has 2 bedrooms, 1 bath
- Basement foundation, drawings also include crawl space/slab foundation
- Duplex has 898 square feet of living space per unit

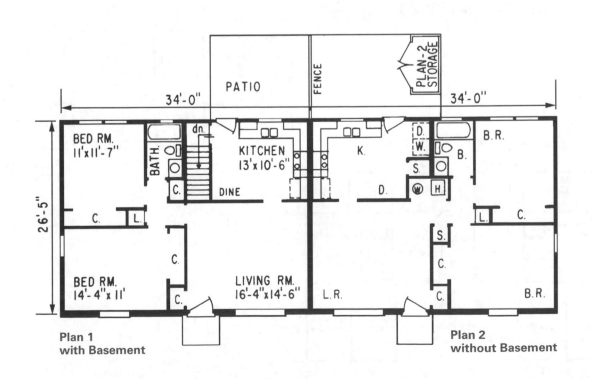

Plan 1
with Basement

Plan 2
without Basement

MULTI-FAMILY

TO ORDER SEE **PAGE 608** OR CALL TOLL-FREE 1-800-DREAM HOME (373-2646)

Welcoming And Distinctive

Total Living Area: 4,240

- Kitchen, brightened by a large bay window, accesses patio on first floor units and deck on second floor units
- Corner fireplace provides warmth and charm
- Bedrooms separated from living areas for privacy
- Laundry located off hall for accessibility
- Each unit has 3 bedrooms, 2 baths, 1-car garage
- Basement foundation
- Fourplex has 1,060 square feet of living space per unit

Second Floor
2,120 sq. ft.

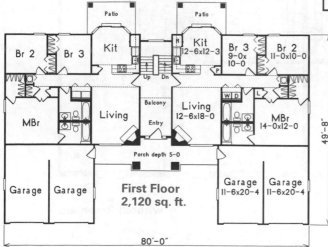

First Floor
2,120 sq. ft.

MULTI-FAMILY

TO ORDER SEE **PAGE 608** OR CALL TOLL-FREE 1-800-DREAM HOME (373-2646)

Convenient Well-Designed Duplex

Total Living Area: 2,042

- Both bedrooms have large walk-in closets
- Living and dining areas combine to become one large living area creating an open atmosphere
- Utility closet near kitchen for convenience
- Each unit has 2 bedrooms, 1 bath, 1-car garage
- Slab foundation
- Duplex has 1,021 square feet of living space per unit

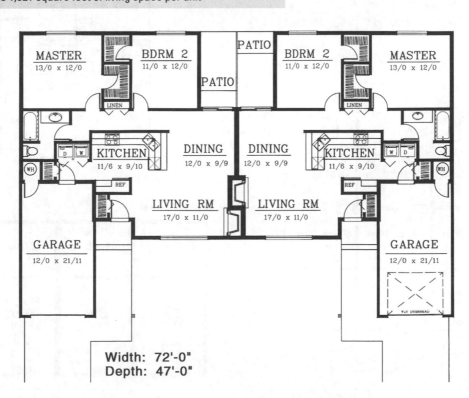

MASTER 13/0 x 12/0   BDRM 2 11/0 x 12/0   PATIO   PATIO   BDRM 2 11/0 x 12/0   MASTER 13/0 x 12/0

LINEN   LINEN

KITCHEN 11/6 x 9/10   DINING 12/0 x 9/9   DINING 12/0 x 9/9   KITCHEN 11/6 x 9/10

LIVING RM 17/0 x 11/0   LIVING RM 17/0 x 11/0

GARAGE 12/0 x 21/11   GARAGE 12/0 x 21/11

Width: 72'-0"
Depth: 47'-0"

MULTI-FAMILY

Bedrooms Separate From Living Areas

Total Living Area: 4,023

- Family room has fireplace for coziness and access outdoors on a covered porch
- Laundry closet is located on the second floor near bedrooms for convenience
- Master bedroom has private bath with double vanities, large walk-in closet and a sunny sitting area
- Each unit has 2 bedrooms, 2 1/2 baths, 1-car drive under garage
- Basement foundation
- Triplex has 1,341 square feet of living space per unit

Second Floor
657 sq. ft.
per unit

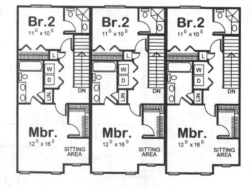

First Floor
684 sq. ft.
per unit

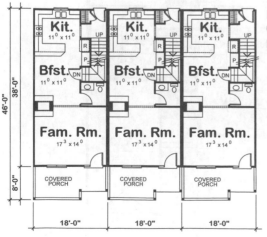

Lower Level

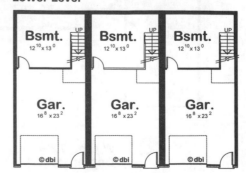

MULTI-FAMILY

Fourplex With Southern Charm

Total Living Area: 2,840

- Living room graced with bay window and fireplace
- Kitchen offers efficient layout and overlooks dining area
- Bedroom includes spacious walk-in closet
- Convenient laundry closet located off hall
- First floor units have patios and second floor units have decks located off the dining area
- Each unit has 1 bedroom, 1 bath
- Basement foundation
- Fourplex has 710 square feet of living space per unit

First Floor
1,420 sq. ft.

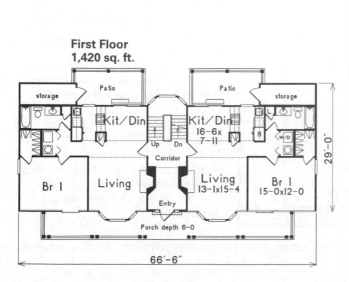

Second Floor
1,420 sq. ft.

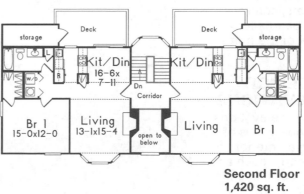

Our Blueprint Packages Offer...

Quality plans for building your future, with extras that provide unsurpassed value, ensure good construction and long-term enjoyment.

A quality home - one that looks good, functions well, and provides years of enjoyment - is a product of many things - design, materials, craftsmanship. But it's also the result of outstanding blueprints - the actual plans and specifications that tell the builder exactly how to build your home.

And with our BLUEPRINT PACKAGES you get the absolute best. A complete set of blueprints is available for every design in this book. These "working drawings," are highly detailed, resulting in two key benefits:

■ *Better understanding by the contractor of how to build your home, and...*

■ *More accurate construction estimates.*

When you purchase one of our designs, you'll receive all of the BLUEPRINT components shown here - elevations, foundation plan, floor plans, sections and details. Other helpful building aids are also available to help make your dream home a reality.

COVER SHEET
This sheet is the artist's rendering of the exterior of the home. It will give you an idea of how your home will look when completed and landscaped.

FOUNDATION PLAN
The foundation plan shows the layout of the basement, walk-out basement, crawl space, slab or pier foundation. All necessary notations and dimensions are included. See plan page for the foundation types included. If the home plan you choose does not have your desired foundation type, our Customer Service Representatives can advise you on how to customize your foundation to suit your specific needs or site conditions.

FLOOR PLANS
These plans show the placement of walls, doors, closets, plumbing fixtures, electrical outlets, columns, and beams for each level of the home.

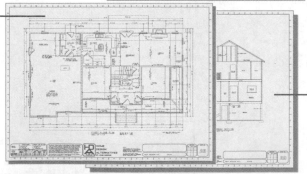

SECTIONS
Sections show detail views of the home or portions of the home as if it were sliced from the roof to the foundation. This sheet shows important areas such as load-bearing walls, stairs, joists, trusses and other structural elements, which are critical for proper construction.

INTERIOR ELEVATIONS
Interior elevations provide views of special interior elements such as fireplaces, kitchen cabinets, built-in units and other special features of the home.

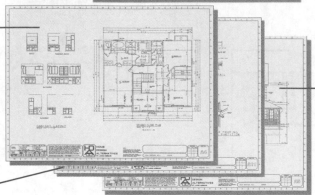

EXTERIOR ELEVATIONS
These drawings illustrate the front, rear and both sides of the house, with all details of exterior materials and the required dimensions.

DETAILS
Details show how to construct certain components of your home, such as the roof system, stairs, deck, etc.

Plan #	Price Code	Page	Material List / Price	Right Reading Reverse / Price	Use Canada Shipping
577-0101	AA	453	•/$55.00		
577-0102	A	274	•/$60.00		
577-0103	A	194	•/$60.00		
577-0104	A	238	•/$60.00		
577-0105	A	264	•/$60.00		
577-0106	A	242	•/$60.00		
577-0109	B	198	•/$60.00		
577-0110	B	136	•/$60.00		
577-0112	C	11	•/$65.00		
577-0113	C	336	•/$65.00		
577-0118	C	459	•/$65.00		
577-0120	D	167	•/$65.00		
577-0133	D	376	•/$65.00		
577-0134	D	360	•/$65.00		
577-0135	E	179	•/$70.00		
577-0138	E	51	•/$70.00		
577-0141	E	314	•/$70.00		
577-0143	E	311	•/$70.00		
577-0151	E	25	•/$70.00		
577-0152	E	320	•/$70.00		
577-0159	F	394	•/$70.00		
577-0161	B	89	•/$60.00		
577-0162	D	28	•/$65.00		
577-0163	C	101	•/$65.00		
577-0171	C	52	•/$65.00		
577-0173	A	17	•/$60.00		
577-0174	B	64	•/$60.00		
577-0176	A	239	•/$60.00		
577-0177	D	362	•/$60.00		
577-0180	B	280	•/$60.00		
577-0181	A	282	•/$60.00		
577-0183	E	312	•/$70.00		
577-0184	D	396	•/$65.00		
577-0185	D	423	•/$65.00		
577-0186	A	140	•/$60.00		
577-0187	E	387	•/$70.00		
577-0190	C	14	•/$65.00		
577-0191	D	160	•/$65.00		
577-0192	A	76	•/$60.00		
577-0195	AA	245	•/$55.00		
577-0201	D	328	•/$65.00		
577-0203	B	12	•/$60.00		
577-0206	C	214	•/$65.00		
577-0207	B	263	•/$65.00		
577-0209	B	302	•/$60.00		
577-0213	C	322	•/$65.00		
577-0216	B	521	•/$60.00		
577-0217	A	8	•/$60.00		
577-0218	D	180	•/$65.00		
577-0219	F	61	•/$70.00		
577-0220	F	390	•/$70.00		
577-0221	B	15	•/$60.00		
577-0222	D	390	•/$65.00		
577-0223	D	398	•/$65.00		
577-0224	D	57	•/$65.00		
577-0225	A	78	•/$60.00		
577-0226	A	98	•/$60.00		
577-0227	B	364	•/$60.00		
577-0228	C	185	•/$65.00		
577-0229	B	58	•/$60.00		
577-0230	D	34	•/$65.00		
577-0231	E	316	•/$70.00		
577-0232	F	45	•/$70.00		
577-0234	C	356	•/$65.00		
577-0236	F	424	•/$70.00		
577-0239	A	295	•/$60.00		
577-0241	AAA	240	•/$50.00		
577-0242	AAA	464	•/$50.00		
577-0243	AAA	460	•/$50.00		
577-0244	D	154	•/$65.00		
577-0249	B	41	•/$60.00		
577-0252	A	241	•/$60.00		
577-0253	A	269	•/$60.00		
577-0265	A	156	•/$60.00		
577-0267	A	142	•/$60.00		
577-0270	A	490	•/$60.00		
577-0271	A	300	•/$60.00		
577-0272	A	102	•/$60.00		
577-0273	AA	254	•/$55.00		
577-0275	A	261	•/$60.00		
577-0276	AA	505	•/$55.00		
577-0277	AA	292	•/$55.00		
577-0283	D	50	•/$65.00		
577-0284	C	156	•/$65.00		
577-0287	E	409	•/$70.00		
577-0288	E	438	•/$70.00		
577-0291	B	192	•/$60.00		
577-0292	A	512	•/$60.00		
577-0293	B	360	•/$60.00		
577-0294	B	318	•/$60.00		
577-0296	A	260	•/$60.00		
577-0297	A	298	•/$60.00		
577-0298	F	46	•/$70.00		
577-0299	E	315	•/$70.00		
577-0302	D	452	•/$65.00		
577-0306	D	173	•/$65.00		
577-0307	E	223	•/$70.00		
577-0310	D	308	•/$65.00		
577-0312	D	182	•/$65.00		
577-0316	C	491	•/$65.00		
577-0319	F	422	•/$70.00		
577-0321	E	388	•/$65.00		
577-0322	D	63	•/$65.00		
577-0335	D	235	•/$65.00		
577-0338	E	418	•/$70.00		
577-0339	E	18	•/$70.00		
577-0342	C	430	•/$65.00		
577-0344	F	411	•/$70.00		
577-0351	F	422	•/$70.00		
577-0352	E	62	•/$70.00		
577-0354	E	209	•/$70.00		
577-0355	G	16	•/$75.00		
577-0356	E	203	•/$70.00		
577-0357	B	117	•/$60.00		
577-0362	C	175	•/$65.00		
577-0364	D	59	•/$65.00		
577-0365	D	40	•/$65.00		
577-0366	E	26	•/$70.00		
577-0367	D	442	•/$65.00		
577-0368	D	49	•/$65.00		
577-0370	C	5	•/$65.00		
577-0372	D	171	•/$65.00		
577-0377	E	224	•/$70.00		
577-0382	C	81	•/$65.00		
577-0384	D	200	•/$65.00		
577-0386	C	217	•/$65.00		
577-0391	E	396	•/$70.00		
577-0393	B	162	•/$60.00		
577-0396	C	374	•/$65.00		
577-0400	C	78	•/$65.00		
577-0405	F	424	•/$70.00		
577-0407	D	107	•/$65.00		
577-0411	E	201	•/$70.00		
577-0413	D	324	•/$65.00		
577-0415	A	296	•/$60.00		
577-0416	C	297	•/$65.00		
577-0417	F	43	•/$70.00		
577-0418	F	441	•/$70.00		
577-0419	C	44	•/$65.00		
577-0425	C	73	•/$65.00		
577-0426	D	169	•/$65.00		
577-0429	E	436	•/$70.00		
577-0430	E	187	•/$70.00		
577-0434	D	22	•/$65.00		
577-0438	D	77	•/$65.00		
577-0439	E	210	•/$70.00		
577-0441	B	275	•/$60.00		
577-0444	D	222	•/$65.00		
577-0445	F	450	•/$70.00		
577-0447	B	278	•/$60.00		
577-0448	C	38	•/$65.00		
577-0449	D	23	•/$65.00		
577-0450	B	37	•/$60.00		
577-0451	D	586	•/$65.00		
577-0452	F	553	•/$70.00		
577-0453	G	601	•/$75.00		
577-0454	H	598	•/$80.00		
577-0455	H	576	•/$80.00		
577-0459	G	568	•/$75.00		
577-0461	AAA	456	•/$50.00		
577-0462	AA	484	•/$55.00		
577-0463	G	555	•/$75.00		
577-0464	E	565	•/$70.00		
577-0465	D	584	•/$65.00		
577-0466	G	574	•/$75.00		
577-0467	E	578	•/$70.00		
577-0468	G	588	•/$75.00		
577-0469	H	596	•/$80.00		
577-0470	H	592	•/$80.00		
577-0472	E	590	•/$70.00		
577-0473	D	556	•/$65.00		
577-0475	B	454	•/$60.00		
577-0476	AAA	524	•/$50.00		
577-0477	AA	32	•/$55.00		
577-0478	AA	55	•/$55.00		
577-0479	A	294	•/$60.00		
577-0484	A	270	•/$60.00		
577-0485	AA	242	•/$55.00		
577-0486	A	202	•/$60.00		
577-0487	AA	250	•/$55.00		
577-0488	C	376	•/$65.00		
577-0491	C	181	•/$65.00		
577-0492	C	332	•/$65.00		
577-0495	AA	262	•/$55.00		
577-0497	AA	281	•/$55.00		
577-0498	AA	303	•/$55.00		
577-0502	AAA	227	•/$50.00		
577-0503	AA	251	•/$55.00		

Plan #	Price Code	Page	Material List / Price	Right Reading Reverse / Price	Use Canada Shipping
577-HDG-97006	AA	230			
577-HDG-99004	A	254			
577-HDS-1558-2	C	70			
577-HDS-1670	B	256			
577-HDS-1758-2	B	113			
577-HDS-1768	B	87			
577-HDS-1806	C	104			
577-HDS-1963	C	358			
577-HDS-1993	C	94			
577-HDS-2140	C	157			
577-HDS-2802-2	E	351			
577-HDS-3098	F	431			
577-HDS-3818-2	G	395			
577-HDS-7002	H	445			
577-HDS-15712	B	232			
577-HP-C316	C	305	•/$125.00		
577-HP-C460	A	232	•/$125.00		
577-HP-C619	B	371	•/$125.00		
577-HP-C659	AA	262	•/$125.00		
577-HP-C662	C	131	•/$125.00		
577-HP-C675	B	326	•/$125.00		
577-HP-C681	B	334	•/$125.00		
577-HP-C689	A	74	•/$125.00		
577-JA-51394	B	72			
577-JA-52194	C	91			
577-JA-53594	B	151			
577-JA-59195	B	110			
577-JA-61495	B	118	•/$125.00		
577-JA-64396	C	141	•/$125.00		
577-JA-65396	B	226			
577-JA-77798	A	154			
577-JA-83899	A	172			
577-JA-92199	F	379			
577-JFD-10-1436-1	A	67			
577-JFD-10-1456-2	A	247			
577-JFD-15-14931	A	236	•/$125.00		
577-JFD-20-1873-1	C	188	•/$125.00		
577-JFD-20-2018-1	C	225			
577-JFD-20-2211-1	D	219			
577-JV-1268-A	A	234	•/$125.00		
577-JV-1325-B	A	76			
577-JV-1379	A	134			
577-JV-1675-A	B	99			
577-JV-1683-B	B	174			
577-JV-1735A	B	354	•/$125.00		
577-JV-1769-B	B	155	•/$125.00		
577-JV-1772-A-SJ	B	164			
577-JV-1869-A	A	139			
577-JV-1870-A	C	328			
577-LBD-10-1B	AA	485			
577-LBD-12-2A	A	74			
577-LBD-13-1A	A	238			
577-LBD-17-14A	B	382			
577-LBD-18-11A	C	93			
577-LBD-19-23A	C	143			
577-LBD-25-22A	D	429			
577-LBD-26-23A	E	401			
577-MG-01158	H	204			
577-MG-01240	G	172			
577-MG-02120	H	75			
577-MG-02125	G	487			
577-MG-02236	G	104			
577-MG-02245	E	277			
577-MG-9305	B	125			
577-MG-9510	D	196			
577-MG-96183	E	406			
577-MG-97099	AA	290			
577-N005	AA	517	•/$125.00		
577-N006	A	500	•/$125.00		
577-N010	AAA	496	•/$125.00		
577-N015	A	462	•/$125.00		
577-N020	C	518	•/$125.00		
577-N026	AA	502	•/$125.00		
577-N027	A	513	•/$125.00		
577-N042	A	492	•/$125.00		
577-N048	A	515	•/$125.00		
577-N049	A	514	•/$125.00		
577-N057	A	504	•/$125.00		
577-N061	A	509	•/$125.00		
577-N063	A	471	•/$125.00		
577-N064	AA	494	•/$125.00		
577-N065	B	474	•/$125.00		
577-N084	E	476	•/$125.00		
577-N085	A	478	•/$125.00		
577-N087	AAA	500	•/$125.00		
577-N089	AA	492	•/$125.00		
577-N107	B	457	•/$125.00		
577-N109	C	519	•/$125.00		
577-N113	A	506	•/$125.00		
577-N114	AAA	486	•/$125.00		
577-N118	AAA	488	•/$125.00		
577-N119	A	502	•/$125.00		
577-N124	B	523	•/$125.00		
577-N127	A	498	•/$125.00		

Plan #	Price Code	Page	Material List / Price	Right Reading Reverse / Price	Use Canada Shipping
577-N130	B	514	•/$125.00		
577-N131	AAA	516	•/$125.00		
577-N142	A	525	•/$125.00		
577-N145	AAA	522	•/$125.00		
577-N147	AAA	467	•/$125.00		
577-N149	A	520			
577-NDG-102	A	69	•/$125.00	•/$150.00	
577-NDG-106	AA	236	•/$125.00	•/$150.00	
577-NDG-113-1	B	123	•/$125.00	•/$150.00	
577-NDG-134	F	375	•/$125.00	•/$150.00	
577-NDG-148	B	293	•/$125.00	•/$150.00	
577-NDG-190	C	115	•/$125.00	•/$150.00	
577-NDG-204	D	437	•/$125.00	•/$150.00	
577-NDG-307	E	355	•/$125.00	•/$150.00	
577-NDG-393	E	557	•/$125.00	•/$150.00	
577-NDG-394	F	580	•/$125.00	•/$150.00	
577-NDG-407-1	H	594	•/$125.00	•/$150.00	
577-NDG-408-1	G	573	•/$125.00	•/$150.00	
577-NDG-413	F	564	•/$125.00	•/$150.00	
577-NDG-675	A	270	•/$125.00	•/$150.00	
577-NDG-698	E	421	•/$125.00	•/$150.00	
577-RDD-1374-9	A	292			
577-RDD-1429-9	A	133			
577-RDD-1753-9	B	325			
577-RDD-1791-9	B	79			
577-RDD-1815-8	C	332			
577-RJ-A10-50	AA	304			
577-RJ-A19-36	C	71			
577-RJ-A26-15	E	408			
577-RJ-A921	AA	512			
577-RJ-1053	E	569			
577-RJ-A1079	AA	288			
577-RJ-A1175	AA	153			
577-RJ-A1369A	A	507			
577-RJ-A1485	A	158			
577-RJ-A1491	A	121			
577-RJ-B123	A	298			
577-RJ-B1416	A	374			
577-RJ-N11-2	F	577			
577-RJ-N17-1	D	560			
577-RJ-T12-2	F	587			
577-SH-SEA-001	B	454	•/$125.00		•
577-SH-SEA-002	A	466	•/$125.00		•
577-SH-SEA-008	AA	494	•/$125.00	•/$150.00	•
577-SH-SEA-009	A	462			•
577-SH-SEA-013	A	527	•/$125.00	•/$150.00	•
577-SH-SEA-023	A	268	•/$125.00		•
577-SH-SEA-058	C	350	•/$125.00		•
577-SH-SEA-091	B	95	•/$125.00	•/$150.00	•
577-SH-SEA-100	D	342	•/$125.00		•
577-SH-SEA-212	E	393	•/$125.00		•
577-SH-SEA-225	A	480	•/$125.00	•/$150.00	•
577-SH-SEA-226	B	296	•/$125.00		•
577-SH-SEA-232	A	479	•/$125.00	•/$150.00	•
577-SH-SEA-242	A	119	•/$125.00	•/$150.00	•
577-SH-SEA-285	B	506	•/$125.00		•
577-SH-SEA-302	A	289	•/$125.00	•/$150.00	•
577-SH-SEA-400	B	174	•/$125.00	•/$150.00	•
577-SRD-106	C	200			
577-SRD-123	B	96			
577-SRD-142	C	189			
577-SRD-147	D	403			
577-SRD-150	B	291			
577-SRD-214	C	198			
577-SRD-241	A	300			
577-SRD-269	G	399			
577-SRD-279	B	83			
577-SRD-352	B	306			
577-UD-C142	B	160	•/$125.00	•/$150.00	
577-UD-C161	C	346	•/$125.00	•/$150.00	
577-UD-D162	C	220	•/$125.00	•/$150.00	
577-UD-D164	D	211		•/$150.00	
577-UD-D167	D	341	•/$125.00	•/$150.00	
577-UD-E120	E	435		•/$150.00	
577-UD-E141	F	415	•/$125.00	•/$150.00	
577-UD-E167	D	323	•/$125.00	•/$150.00	
577-UDG-92007	B	80			
577-UDG-97001	D	205			
577-UDG-97010	E	193			
577-UDG-99003	A	148			
577-UDG-99011	E	410			
577-VL947	AA	267	•/$125.00		
577-VL-1243	A	142	•/$125.00		
577-VL1267	A	100	•/$125.00		
577-VL1409	A	313	•/$125.00		
577-VL-1458	A	372	•/$125.00		
577-VL-1594	B	338	•/$125.00		
577-VL-1926	C	349	•/$125.00		
577-VL2069	C	135	•/$125.00		
577-VL3011	E	178	•/$125.00		
577-VL-3038	E	361	•/$125.00		
577-VL-3383	F	397	•/$125.00		

What Kind Of Plan Package Do You Need?

Once you find the home plan you've been looking for, here are some suggestions on how to make your Dream Home a reality. To get started, order the type of plans that fit your particular situation.

Your Choices:

The One-set package - We offer a 1-set plan package so you can study your home in detail. This one set is considered a study set and is marked "not for construction". It is a copyright violation to reproduce blueprints.

The Minimum 5-set package - If you're ready to start the construction process, this 5-set package is the minimum number of blueprint sets you will need. It will require keeping close track of each set so they can be used by multiple subcontractors and tradespeople.

The Standard 8-set package - For best results in terms of cost, schedule and quality of construction, we recommend you order eight (or more) sets of blueprints. Besides one set for yourself, additional sets of blueprints will be required by your mortgage lender, local building department, general contractor and all subcontractors working on foundation, electrical, plumbing, heating/air conditioning, carpentry work, etc.

Reproducible Masters - If you wish to make some minor design changes, you'll want to order reproducible masters. These drawings contain the same information as the blueprints but are printed on erasable and reproducible paper which clearly indicates your right to copy or reproduce. This will allow your builder or a local design professional to make the necessary drawing changes without the major expense of redrawing the plans. This package also allows you to print copies of the modified plans as needed. The right of building only one structure from these plans is licensed exclusively to the buyer. You may not use this design to build a second or multiple dwelling(s) without purchasing another blueprint. Each violation of the Copyright Law is punishable in a fine.

Mirror Reverse Sets - Plans can be printed in mirror reverse. These plans are useful when the house would fit your site better if all the rooms were on the opposite side than shown. They are simply a mirror image of the original drawings causing the lettering and dimensions to read backwards. Therefore, when ordering mirror reverse drawings, you must purchase at least one set of right reading plans.

Other Helpful Building Aids...

Your Blueprint Package will contain the necessary construction information to build your home. We also offer the following products and services to save you time and money in the building process.

Express Delivery - Most orders are processed within 24 hours of receipt. Please allow 7-10 business days for delivery. If you need to place a rush order, please call us by 11:00 a.m. CST and ask for express service (allow 1-2 business days).

Technical Assistance - If you have questions, call our technical support line at 1-314-770-2228 between 8:00 a.m. and 5:00 p.m. CST. Whether it involves design modifications or field assistance, our designers are extremely familiar with all of our designs and will be happy to help you. We want your home to be everything you expect it to be.

Material List - Material lists are available for many of our plans. Each list gives you the quantity, dimensions and description of the building materials necessary to construct your home. You'll get faster and more accurate bids from your contractor and material suppliers, and you'll save money by paying for only the materials you need. Refer to the Home Plan Index for availability.

Other Great Products To Help You Build Your Dream Home

BUILDING A HOME?

It sounds like lots of fun and just might be the biggest purchase you will ever make. But the process of building a home can be a tricky one. This program walks you through the process step-by-step. Compiled by consumers who have built new homes and learned the hard way. This is not a "how-to" video, but a visual checklist to open your eyes to issues you would never think about until you have lived in your home for years. *Available in VHS or DVD.*

$19.97 VHS   **$26.97** DVD

The Legal Kit - Avoid many legal pitfalls and build your home with confidence using the forms and contracts featured in this kit. Included are request for proposal documents, various fixed price and cost plus contracts, instructions on how and when to use each form, warranty statements and more. Save time and money before you break ground on your new home or start a remodeling project. All forms are reproducible. The kit is ideal for homebuilders and contractors. **Cost: $35.00**

Detail Plan Packages - Three separate packages offer homebuilders details for constructing various foundations; numerous floor, wall and roof framing techniques; simple to complex residential wiring; sump and water softener hookups; plumbing connection methods; installation of septic systems, and more. Each package includes three-dimensional illustrations and a glossary of terms. Purchase one or all three. Note: These drawings do not pertain to a specific home plan. **Cost: $20⁰⁰ each or all three for $40⁰⁰**

How To Order

For fastest service, Call Toll-Free 1-800-DREAM HOME (1-800-373-2646) day or night

Three Easy Ways To Order

1. CALL toll free 1-800-373-2646 for credit card orders. MasterCard, Visa, Discover and American Express are accepted.
2. FAX your order to 1-314-770-2226.
3. MAIL the Order Form to: **HDA, Inc.**
   4390 Green Ash Drive
   St. Louis, MO 63045

Order Form

Please send me -

PLAN NUMBER 577- _____

PRICE CODE _____ (see Plan Index)

Specify Foundation Type (see plan page for availability) $ _____
- ☐ Slab ☐ Crawl space ☐ Pier
- ☐ Basement ☐ Walk-out basement
- ☐ Reproducible Masters $ _____
- ☐ Eight-Set Plan Package $ _____
- ☐ Five-Set Plan Package $ _____
- ☐ One-Set Study Package (no mirror reverse) $ _____

Additional Plan Sets
- ☐ ____ (Qty.) at $20.00 each (Price Codes P9-P12)
- ☐ ____ (Qty.) at $45.00 each (Price Codes AAA-H) $ _____

Mirror Reverse
- ☐ Right-reading $150 one time charge
  (see index for availability) $ _____
- ☐ Print in Mirror Reverse (where right reading is not available)
  _____ (Qty.) at $15.00 each $ _____
- ☐ Material List (see index) $ _____
- ☐ Legal Kit (see page 607) $ _____

Detail Plan Packages: (see page 607)
- ☐ Framing ☐ Electrical ☐ Plumbing $ _____

Building Smart: (see page 607)
- ☐ VHS $19.97 #FP00001 ☐ DVD $26.97 #FP00002 $ _____

SUBTOTAL $ _____

SALES TAX (MO residents add 6%) $ _____

☐ Shipping / Handling (see chart at right) $ _____

TOTAL (US funds only - *sorry no CODs*) $ _____

I hereby authorize HDA, Inc. to charge this purchase to my credit card account (check one):

☐ MasterCard   ☐ VISA   ☐ DISCOVER NOVUS   ☐ AMERICAN EXPRESS Cards

Credit Card number _____

Expiration date _____

Signature _____

Name _____
(Please print or type)

Street Address _____
(Please **do not** use PO Box)

City _____

State _____

Zip _____

Daytime phone number (_____) - _____

e-mail address _____

I'm a ☐ Builder/Contractor ☐ Homeowner ☐ Renter

I ☐ have ☐ have not selected my general contractor

Thank you for your order!

Important Information To Know Before You Order

- **Exchange Policies -** Since blueprints are printed in response to your order, we cannot honor requests for refunds. However, if for some reason you find that the plan you have purchased does not meet your requirements, you may exchange that plan for another plan in our collection. At the time of the exchange, you will be charged a processing fee of 25% of your original plan package price, plus the difference in price between the plan packages (if applicable) and the cost to ship the new plans to you.

  Please note: Reproducible drawings can only be exchanged if the package is unopened, and exchanges are allowed only within 90 days of purchase.

- **Building Codes & Requirements -** At the time the construction drawings were prepared, every effort was made to ensure that these plans and specifications meet nationally recognized codes. Our plans conform to most national building codes. Because building codes vary from area to area, some drawing modifications and/or the assistance of a professional designer or architect may be necessary to comply with your local codes or to accommodate specific building site conditions. We advise you to consult with your local building official for information regarding codes governing your area.

Questions? Call Our Customer Service Number
314-770-2228

Blueprint Price Schedule BEST VALUE

		SAVE $110	SAVE $200	
Price Code	**1-Set**	**5-Sets**	**8-Sets**	**Reproducible Masters**
P9	$125	n/a	n/a	$200
P10	$150	n/a	n/a	$225
P11	$175	n/a	n/a	$250
P12	$200	n/a	n/a	$275
AAA	$225	$295	$340	$440
AA	$275	$345	$390	$490
A	$325	$395	$440	$540
B	$375	$445	$490	$590
C	$425	$495	$540	$640
D	$475	$545	$590	$690
E	$525	$595	$640	$740
F	$575	$645	$690	$790
G	$650	$720	$765	$865
H	$755	$825	$870	$970

Plan prices guaranteed through December 31, 2004.
Please note that plans are not refundable.

- **Additional Sets* -** Additional sets of the plan ordered are available for an additional cost (see order form at left). Five-set, eight-set, and reproducible packages offer considerable savings.

- **Mirror Reverse Plans* -** Available for an additional $5.00 per set, these plans are simply a mirror image of the original drawings causing the dimensions & lettering to read backwards. Therefore, when ordering mirror reverse plans, you must purchase at least one set of right reading plans.

- **One-Set Study Package -** We offer a one-set plan package so you can study your home in detail. This one set is considered a study set and is marked "not for construction". It is a copyright violation to reproduce blueprints.

*Available only within 90 days after purchase of plan package or reproducible masters of same plan.

Shipping & Handling Charges

U.S. SHIPPING	1-4 Sets	5-7 Sets	8 Sets or Reproducibles
Regular (allow 7-10 business days)	$15.00	$17.50	$25.00
Priority (allow 3-5 business days)	$25.00	$30.00	$35.00
Express* (allow 1-2 business days)	$35.00	$40.00	$45.00
CANADA SHIPPING (to/from) - *Plans with suffix DR & SH - see index*			
Standard (allow 8-12 business days)	$25.00	$30.00	$35.00
Express* (allow 3-5 business days)	$40.00	$40.00	$45.00

Overseas Shipping/International - Call, fax, or e-mail (plans@hdainc.com) for shipping costs.

* For express delivery please call us by 11:00 a.m. CST